"Nolo's home page is worth bookmarking."
—WALL STREET JOURNAL

W9-BXM-662

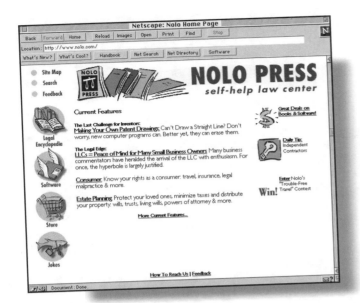

LEGAL INFORMATION ONLINE

www.nolo.com

24 HOURS A DAY

AT THE NOLO PRESS SELF-HELP LAW CENTER ON THE WEB, YOU'LL FIND:

- ◯ Nolo's comprehensive Legal Encyclopedia, with links to other online resources

- ◯ Downloadable demos of Nolo software and sample chapters of many Nolo books

- ◯ An online law store with a secure online ordering system

- ◯ Our ever-popular lawyer jokes

- ◯ Discounts and other good deals,
  our hilarious SHARK TALK game

THE NOLO NEWS

Stay on top of important legal changes with Nolo's quarterly magazine, *The Nolo News*. Start your free one-year subscription by filling out and mailing the response card in the back of this book. With each issue, you'll get legal news about topics that affect you every day, reviews of legal books by other publishers, the latest Nolo catalog, scintillating advice from Auntie Nolo and a fresh batch of our famous lawyer jokes.

3RD EDITION

Chapter 13 Bankruptcy

Repay Your Debts

BY ATTORNEY ROBIN LEONARD

NOLO PRESS BERKELEY

Your Responsibility When Using a Self-Help Law Book

We've done our best to give you useful and accurate information in this book. But laws and procedures change frequently and are subject to differing interpretations. If you want legal advice backed by a guarantee, see a lawyer. If you use this book, it's your responsibility to make sure that the facts and general advice contained in it are applicable to your situation.

Keeping Up to Date

To keep its books up to date, Nolo Press issues new printings and new editions periodically. New printings reflect minor legal changes and technical corrections. New editions contain major legal changes, major text additions or major reorganizations. To find out if a later printing or edition of any Nolo book is available, call Nolo Press at 510-549-1976 or check the catalog in the *Nolo News*, our quarterly newspaper. You can also contact us on the Internet at www.nolo.com.

To stay current, follow the "Update" service in the *Nolo News*. You can get a free one-year subscription by sending us the registration card in the back of the book. In another effort to help you use Nolo's latest materials, we offer a 25% discount off the purchase of the new edition your Nolo book when you turn in the cover of an earlier edition. (See the "Special Upgrade Offer" in the back of the book.)

This book was last revised in: **May 1998**

Third Edition	JANUARY 1998
Second Printing	MAY 1998
Editor	MARY RANDOLPH
Illustrations	MARI STEIN
Book Design	TERRI HEARSH
Production	NANCY ERB
Cover Design	TONI IHARA
Proofreading	ROBERT WELLS
Index	SAYRE VAN YOUNG
Printing	VERSA PRESS, INC.

Leonard, Robin.
    Chapter 13 bankruptcy : repay your debts / by Robin Leonard. --
3rd ed.
        p.   cm.
    Includes index.
    ISBN 0-87337-450-9
    1. Bankruptcy--United States--Popular works.   I. Title.
KF1524.6.L46   1997
346.7307'8--dc21   97-35580
                                            CIP

Copyright © 1995, 1996 and 1998 by Nolo Press.
ALL RIGHTS RESERVED. Printed in the USA

No part of this publication may be reproduced, stored in a retrieval system, or transmitted in any form or by any means, electronic, mechanical, photocopying, recording or otherwise without the prior written permission of the publisher and the author. Reproduction prohibitions do not apply to the forms contained in this product when reproduced for personal use.

Quantity sales: For information on bulk purchases or corporate premium sales, please contact the Special Sales department. For academic sales or textbook adoptions, ask for Academic Sales. 800-955-4775, Nolo Press, Inc., 950 Parker St., Berkeley, CA, 94710.

Acknowledgments

The author gratefully acknowledges the following people.

Barbara McEntyre, a bankruptcy attorney in San Rafael, California. Barbara is a smart, competent and extraordinarily ethical lawyer. Barbara was incredibly generous and gracious in sharing her time and knowledge with me, including meticulously reading the manuscript and sending me detailed comments. I am honored to be able to call her a friend.

Joan and Bob Leonard. Mom and Dad let me live in their house for nearly a month, 3,000 miles from my own home, away from telephone calls, meetings and the stress of day-to-day work life so I could actually write this book.

Mary Randolph, Senior Legal Editor at Nolo Press. Mary is the perfect editor. Her ability to take a good, but disorganized submission and turn it into a great and easy-to-use guide made writing the second, third and fourth drafts pleasurable.

Steve Elias, Associate Publisher at Nolo Press. Steve's knowledge of bankruptcy and skill in questioning everything he reads made the book even that much better.

Terri Hearsh, whose beautiful and user-friendly design makes the book a delight to read.

R.J. Harrison

Table of Contents

Introduction

A. The Basics of Chapter 13 Bankruptcy I/1

B. Do You Need a Lawyer? I/2

1 Should You File for Chapter 13 Bankruptcy?

A. Are You Eligible for Chapter 13 Bankruptcy? 1/1

    1. Businesses Can't File for Chapter 13 Bankruptcy 1/1

    2. You Must Have Stable and Regular Income 1/1

    3. You Must Have Disposable Income 1/1

    4. Your Debts Must Not Be Too High 1/2

B. When Chapter 13 Bankruptcy Is Better Than Chapter 7 .... 1/2

    1. The Basics of Chapter 7 Bankruptcy 1/2

    2. Determining Which Is Better for You 1/2

    3. If You Owe Back Taxes to the IRS 1/4

C. Other Alternatives 1/4

    1. Do Nothing 1/4

    2. Negotiate With Your Creditors 1/5

    3. Get Outside Help to Design a Repayment Plan 1/5

    4. File for Chapter 11 Bankruptcy 1/5

    5. File for Chapter 12 Bankruptcy 1/6

D. Converting From Chapter 7 Bankruptcy to Chapter 13 Bankruptcy 1/6

2 An Overview of Chapter 13 Bankruptcy

A. The Chapter 13 Process 2/1

B. Your Monthly Payments 2/2

C. How Much You'll Have to Repay Through the Plan 2/2

D. How Much You'll Still Owe When Your Case Is Over 2/3

    1. Child Support and Alimony 2/3

    2. Student Loans 2/4

	3.	Intoxicated Driving Debts	2/4
	4.	Restitution or Criminal Fine	2/4
E.		Filing With Your Spouse	2/4
F.		The Chapter 13 Trustee	2/5
	1.	Working With the Chapter 13 Trustee	2/5
	2.	Paying the Chapter 13 Trustee	2/5
G.		Going To Court	2/5

3 Adding Up Your Secured and Unsecured Debts

A.		Secured Debts	3/1
	1.	Liens You Agree To: Security Interests	3/1
	2.	Liens Created Without Your Consent: Nonconsensual Liens	3/4
	3.	Total Up Your Secured Debts	3/6
	4.	Turning Secured Debts Into Unsecured Ones: Lien Avoidance	3/6
B.		Unsecured Debts	3/7
	1.	Adding Up Your Unsecured Debts	3/8
	2.	Turning Unsecured Debts Into Secured Ones	3/8

4 Calculating Your Disposable Income

A.		What You Earn	4/1
	1.	Total Up Your Income	4/1
	2.	What Income Will Fund the Plan	4/2
B.		What You Spend	4/5
C.		What's Left—Your Disposable Income	4/9

5 Calculating the Value of Your Nonexempt Property

A.		Identifying Your Property	5/1
	1.	Property You Own and Possess	5/1
	2.	Property You Own but Don't Possess	5/2
	3.	Property You Are Entitled to Receive	5/2
	4.	Property You've Recently Given Away	5/2
	5.	Property You Own With Your Spouse (If You Are Filing Alone)	5/3
B.		Listing Your Exempt and Nonexempt Property	5/3
C.		Determining the Value of Your Nonexempt Property	5/11
	1.	Value of Your Property (Column 2)	5/11
	2.	Your Ownership Share (Column 3)	5/12
	3.	Amount of Liens (Column 4)	5/12
	4.	Amount of Your Equity (Column 5)	5/12
	5.	Is the Property Exempt? (Column 6)	5/13
	6.	The Minimum Amount You Must Pay in Chapter 13 Bankruptcy	5/15

6 Completing the Bankruptcy Forms

A. Finding the Right Bankruptcy Court 6/1

B. Before You Begin: Get Some Information From the Court 6/1

    1. Fees 6/2

    2. Forms 6/2

    3. Local Court Rules 6/2

    4. Number of Copies 6/3

C. What Forms to File 6/3

D. Tips for Filling In the Forms 6/4

E. Form 1—Voluntary Petition 6/5

F. Form 6—Schedules 6/9

    1. Schedule A—Real Property 6/9

    2. Schedule B—Personal Property 6/12

    3. Schedule C—Property Claimed as Exempt 6/17

    4. Schedule D—Creditors Holding Secured Claims 6/20

    5. Schedule E—Creditors Holding Unsecured Priority Claims 6/23

    6. Schedule F—Creditors Holding Unsecured Nonpriority Claims 6/26

    7. Schedule G—Executory Contracts and Unexpired Leases 6/30

    8. Schedule H—Codebtors 6/32

    9. Schedule I—Current Income of Individual Debtor(s) 6/32

    10. Schedule J—Current Expenditures of Individual Debtor(s) 6/34

    11. Summary of Schedules 6/36

    12. Declaration Concerning Debtor's Schedules 6/36

G. Form 7—Statement of Financial Affairs 6/40

H. Mailing Matrix 6/52

I. Income Deduction Order 6/52

7 Writing Your Chapter 13 Bankruptcy Plan

A. Chapter 13 Plan Forms 7/1

B. How Long Your Plan Will Last 7/2

    1. Fewer Than Three Years 7/2

    2. Longer Than Three Years 7/2

C. Your Payment Schedule 7/3

D. The Order in Which Creditors Will Be Paid 7/3

E. Reducing the Trustee's Fee 7/3

F. The Order in Which Priority Debts Will Be Paid 7/4

G. Paying Back Taxes 7/4

    1. Categorizing Your Federal Income Tax Debt 7/4

    2. Interest 7/4

    3. Penalties 7/4

    4. Other Tax Debts 7/4

H. Paying Mortgage Arrears 7/5
    1. Give the House Back 7/5
    2. Make Up Missed Payments and Reinstate the Loan 7/6
    3. Reduce the Note to the Current Value of the House 7/7
    4. Eliminate or Reduce Liens on the Property 7/8
I. Paying Other Secured Debts 7/8
    1. Give the Property Back 7/8
    2. Pay the Amount of the Debt or the Current Value of the Property 7/9
    3. Make Up Missed Payments and Reinstate the Loan 7/10
    4. Eliminate or Reduce Liens on the Property 7/11
    5. Sell the Property 7/11
    6. File a Chapter 7 Bankruptcy Before You File a Chapter 13 Bankruptcy 7/11
J. Paying Your Unsecured Creditors 7/12
    1. How Unsecured Creditors Will Be Paid 7/12
    2. Classifying Unsecured Creditors 7/13
    3. Compensation on Payments 7/14
K. Dealing With Contracts and Leases 7/15
L. Making Payments Directly to Creditors 7/15
M. Sample Plans 7/15

8 Filing Your Bankruptcy Papers

A. Basic Filing Procedures 8/1
B. Paying in Installments 8/2
C. Emergency Filing 8/2

9 After You File Your Case

A. The Automatic Stay 9/1
B. Dealing With the Trustee 9/3
    1. Reporting Expenditures or Acquisitions to the Trustee 9/3
    2. Providing the Trustee With Proof of Insurance 9/4
C. Make Your First Payment 9/4
D. Keep Your Business Going 9/4
E. The Meeting of Creditors 9/4
    1. Preparing for the Meeting of the Creditors 9/5
    2. Getting to the Meeting of the Creditors 9/6
    3. What Happens at the Meeting of the Creditors 9/6
F. Modifying Your Plan Before the Confirmation Hearing 9/7
G. Creditors' Objections to a Plan 9/7
    1. The Plan Is Not Submitted in Good Faith 9/9
    2. The Plan Is Not Feasible 9/10
    3. The Plan Fails the Best Interest of the Creditors Test 9/10
    4. The Plan Unfairly Discriminates 9/10

H. The Confirmation Hearing 9/10

    1. Preparing for the Confirmation Hearing 9/11

    2. Getting to the Confirmation Hearing 9/11

    3. What Happens at the Confirmation Hearing 9/11

    4. Issuing an Income Deduction Order 9/11

    5. The Judge's Order Confirming Your Plan 9/12

I. Modifying Your Plan After the Confirmation Hearing 9/12

J. Creditors' Claims 9/15

    1. Filing a Proof of Claim 9/15

    2. Objecting to a Creditor's Claim 9/15

K. Asking the Court to Eliminate Liens 9/15

    1. Avoiding a Lien 9/17

    2. Challenging a Tax Lien 9/21

L. Amending Your Bankruptcy Forms 9/25

    1. Common Amendments 9/25

    2. How to File an Amendment 9/26

M. Filing a Change of Address 9/26

N. Dealing With Creditors' Motions 9/26

    1. Objections to Your Eligibility for Chapter 13 .... 9/27

    2. Motion for "Adequate Protection" 9/27

    3. Motion for Relief From the Automatic Stay 9/27

    4. Motion for Relief From the Codebtor Stay 9/28

10 After Your Plan Is Approved

A. Making Plan Payments 10/1

    1. Including Extra Money in Your Payments 10/1

    2. If Your Income Increases 10/2

B. Selling Property 10/2

C. Modifying Your Plan When Problems Come Up 10/2

    1. You Miss a Payment 10/2

    2. Your Disposable Income Goes Down 10/3

    3. You Need to Replace Your Car 10/3

    4. You Incur New Debt 10/4

D. Attempts to Revoke Your Confirmation 10/4

E. If You Cannot Complete Your Plan 10/4

    1. Dismiss Your Case 10/5

    2. Convert Your Case to Chapter 7 Bankruptcy 10/5

    3. Seek a Hardship Discharge 10/6

F. When You Complete Your Plan 10/7

    1. Debts Covered by the Discharge 10/7

    2. The Discharge Hearing 10/7

    3. Ending the Income Deduction Order 10/7

    4. Debtor Rehabilitation Program 10/7

11 Life After Bankruptcy

A. Rebuilding Your Credit 11/1
   1. Create a Budget 11/1
   2. Keep Your Credit File Accurate 11/2
   3. Negotiate With Current Creditors 11/5
   4. Get a Secured Credit Card 11/5
   5. Borrow From a Bank 11/5
   6. Work With a Local Merchant 11/6
B. Attempts to Collect Clearly Discharged Debts 11/6
C. Post-Bankruptcy Discrimination 11/7
   1. Government Discrimination 11/7
   2. Non-Government Discrimination 11/7
D. Attempts to Revoke Your Discharge 11/7

12 Help Beyond the Book

A. Bankruptcy Lawyers 12/1
   1. How to Find a Bankruptcy Lawyer 12/1
   2. What to Look For in a Lawyer 12/2
   3. What Bankruptcy Attorneys Charge 12/2
B. Bankruptcy Petition Preparers 12/3
C. The Law Library 12/3
   1. Find a Law Library 12/4
   2. Use a Good Legal Research Resource 12/4
   3. Use *Collier on Bankruptcy* 12/4
   4. Use Other Background Resources 12/4
   5. Find and Read Relevant Statutes 12/5
   6. Read Procedural Rules 12/6
   7. Find and Read Relevant Cases 12/6
   8. Online Legal Resources 12/7

Appendices

A1 Appendix 1: State and Federal Exemptions Tables

A2 Appendix 2: Addresses of Bankruptcy Courts

A3 Appendix 3: Tear-Out Forms

Introduction

Americans learn almost from birth that it's good to buy all sorts of products and services. A highly paid army of persuaders surrounds us with thousands of seductive messages each day, all urging us to buy, buy, buy. Readily available credit makes living beyond our means easy and resisting the siren sounds of the advertisers difficult. But we're also told that if we fail to pay for it all right on time, we're miserable deadbeats. In short, much of American economic life is built on a contradiction.

If for some reason, such as illness, loss of work or just plain bad planning, our ability to pay for goods or services is interrupted, fear and guilt are often our first feelings. We may even feel we've fundamentally failed as human beings.

Nonsense. There's lots more to life than an A+ credit rating. The importance we have for our families, friends and neighbors should never be forgotten. Nor should we forget that the American economy is based on consumer debt. The guilt we may feel about the debts we've run up must be put in perspective; after all, we live in an age of $500-billion bailouts for poorly managed financial institutions. Large creditors view defaults and bankruptcies as a fact of life and treat them as a cost of doing business. The reason so many banks push their credit cards is that it is a very profitable business, even with so many bankruptcies.

Fortunately, for at least two dozen centuries it's been recognized that debts can get the better of even the most conscientious among us. From Biblical times to the present, sane societies have discouraged debtors from falling on their swords and provided sensible ways for debt-oppressed people to start new economic lives. In the United States, this process is called bankruptcy.

Bankruptcy is a truly worthy part of our legal system, based as it is on forgiveness rather than retribution. Certainly it helps keep families together, reduces suicide and keeps the ranks of the homeless from growing even larger.

A. The Basics of Chapter 13 Bankruptcy

Most people think of bankruptcy as a process in which you go to court and get your debts erased. But in fact, there are two types of bankruptcies: the more familiar liquidation bankruptcy, where your debts are wiped out completely (Chapter 7 bankruptcy) and reorganization bankruptcy, where you partially or fully repay your debts. The reorganization bankruptcy for individuals is called Chapter 13 bankruptcy. There are two other kinds of reorganization bankruptcy: Chapter 11, for businesses and for individuals with debts over $1 million, and Chapter 12, for family farmers. The names come from the chapters of the federal Bankruptcy Code.

Chapter 13 bankruptcy lets you rearrange your financial affairs, repay a portion of your debts and put yourself back on your financial feet. You repay your debts through a Chapter 13 plan. Under a typical plan, you make monthly payments to someone called a bankruptcy trustee, who is appointed by the bankruptcy court to oversee your case, for three to five years. The bankruptcy trustee distributes the money to your creditors.

Chapter 13 bankruptcy isn't for everyone. If your total debt burden is too high or your income is too low or irregular, you may not be eligible. You may be better off handling your debt problems in another way—such as filing for Chapter 7 bankruptcy, seeking help from a nonprofit debt counseling group or negotiating with your creditors on your own. (These options are explored in Ch. 1, *Should You File for Chapter 13 Bankruptcy?*)

Here are some important features of Chapter 13 bankruptcy:

- **Chapter 13 bankruptcy is very powerful.** You can use it to stop a house foreclosure, make up the missed mortgage payments and keep the house. You can also pay off back taxes through your Chapter 13 plan and stop interest from accruing on your tax debt.

- **Filing your papers with the bankruptcy court stops creditors in their tracks.** When you file for Chapter 13 bankruptcy or any other kind of bankruptcy, something called the automatic stay goes into effect. It immediately stops your creditors from trying to collect what you owe them. At least temporarily, creditors cannot legally grab (garnish) your wages, empty your bank account, go after your car, house or other property, or cut off your utility service or welfare benefits.

- **You can use Chapter 13 bankruptcy to buy time.** Some people use Chapter 13 bankruptcy to buy time. For example, if you are behind on mortgage payments and about to be foreclosed on, you can file Chapter 13 bankruptcy papers to stop collection efforts, and then attempt to sell the house before the foreclosure.

- **Chapter 13 bankruptcy requires discipline.** For the entire length of your case, three to five years, you will have to live under a strict budget; the bankruptcy court will not allow you to spend money on anything it deems nonessential.

- **The majority of debtors never complete their Chapter 13 repayment plans.** Although most people file for Chapter 13 bankruptcy assuming they'll complete their plan, only about 35% of all Chapter 13 debtors do. Many drop out very early in the process, without ever submitting a feasible repayment plan to the court. If you can come up with a realistic budget and stick to it, however, you should have no trouble completing your Chapter 13 plan.

- **Payments may be deducted from your wages during your case.** If you have a regular job with regular income, the bankruptcy court will probably order that the monthly payments under your Chapter 13 plan be automatically deducted from your wages and sent to the bankruptcy court.

- **Bankruptcy rules vary from court to court.** Bankruptcy law comes from the federal Congress and is meant to be uniform across the country. But when disputes arise about the bankruptcy laws, bankruptcy courts make the decisions—and they don't all decide the issues in the same way. The result is that bankruptcy law and practice vary significantly from court to court and from region to region. This book highlights the different ways courts have ruled on major issues in Chapter 13 bankruptcy. But this book can't possibly address every variation. If you research a question yourself or hire a bankruptcy lawyer, you'll need to be sure the information you get applies in your bankruptcy court.

- **Chapter 13 bankruptcy can stay in your credit file for up to ten years.** Most credit bureaus, however, under pressure from banks to encourage debtors to choose Chapter 13 over Chapter 7, report Chapter 13 bankruptcy for only seven years. No matter how long reported, after your case is over, you can take steps to improve your credit. In fact, some Chapter 13 bankruptcy courts have established programs to help you do just that. In such a program, if you have paid off around 75% or more of your debts, you may attend money management seminars and apply for credit from certain local creditors. These programs are discussed in Ch. 10, *After Your Plan Is Approved,* Section F.4.

B. Do You Need a Lawyer?

By using this book, you can file your own Chapter 13 bankruptcy case without a lawyer. Most of the papers you'll need to file are fill-in-the-blank forms. This book includes all the forms you'll need, and complete instruction for filling them out.

But becoming knowledgeable about Chapter 13 bankruptcy will require a lot of work on your part—Chapter 13 bankruptcy is fairly complex and has no short cuts. You will need to read every chapter of this book; within each chapter, we'll let you know what material you can skip because it isn't relevant in your case.

You may want to use this book to understand Chapter 13 bankruptcy, but hire a lawyer to actually handle your case. The majority of people who file for Chapter 13 bankruptcy use an attorney, for several reasons:

- The lawyer's fee (several hundreds or thousands of dollars) can be paid through the Chapter 13 plan. This means that you do not have to come up with a chunk of money in order to file for bankruptcy.
- Chapter 13 bankruptcy often requires a lot of negotiating with your creditors and with the bankruptcy trustee. If you'd rather have someone deal with creditors on your behalf, you can hire a lawyer to do it.
- Chapter 13 bankruptcy requires several court hearings or appearances, and you may feel more comfortable having a lawyer speak for you in court. Also, some of those court appearances may involving making legal arguments before the bankruptcy judge. You may not have the time to do the necessary research to prepare, or have the confidence that you can handle your own contested matter.
- Unlike Chapter 7 bankruptcy, which is fairly routine and quite predictable, every Chapter 13 bankruptcy case has many variables. An experienced lawyer can help you understand the specifics of your case, including the types of debts you have and the amount or percentage you must repay on each. The more complex your case is, the more likely you will need the help of an attorney.

The book flags situations in which you should consult a lawyer. If you file your own Chapter 13 bankruptcy case and have questions, get the professional help you need. Help may be as simple as hiring a non-lawyer bankruptcy petition preparer to help you prepare and file your forms. It may involve going to a bankruptcy attorney for advice or representation. Or it may involve hitting the law library and figuring things out for yourself. Ch. 12, *Help Beyond the Book,* discusses how to find the kind of help you need.

ICONS USED IN THIS BOOK

Look for these icons, which alert you to certain kinds of information.

 The "fast track" arrow alerts you that you can skip some material that isn't relevant to your case.

 This icon highlights information for married couples only.

 The caution icon warns you of potential problems.

 The briefcase icon lets you know when you need the advice of an attorney.

 This icon refers you to helpful books or other resources.

⚠ BANKRUPTCY LAWS MAY CHANGE

On October 20, 1997, the National Bankruptcy Review Commission (NBRC) submitted a 1,300-page report to Congress suggesting 172 changes to the U.S. Bankruptcy Code. The NBRC worked for two years reviewing every provision of the Code, hearing testimony and receiving input from thousands of people and organizations who have something to say about the U.S. bankruptcy system.

The NBRC's work and report have not been without controversy. The commission itself was deeply divided on its consumer recommendations. Many creditors believe the suggestions don't do enough to stem the current tide of consumer filings, which have been over one million for the second consecutive year. The main response to the NBRC's report has been a swift introduction of bills into the Congress. These bills cover a wide range of issues, but essentially would make it more difficult for a consumer to file for bankruptcy.

To find out if any of these bills have become law, please visit Nolo's Web site at www.nolo.com. ∎

Should You File for Chapter 13 Bankruptcy?

If you're considering filing for Chapter 13 bankruptcy, you need to know whether or not you are eligible, what Chapter 13 bankruptcy can do for you and what the alternatives are. The main alternative to Chapter 13 bankruptcy is Chapter 7 (liquidation) bankruptcy, discussed in Section B, below.

A. Are You Eligible for Chapter 13 Bankruptcy?

Chapter 13 bankruptcy has several important restrictions. Your first step is to see whether or not you are legally allowed to use the Chapter 13 process.

1. Businesses Can't File for Chapter 13 Bankruptcy

A business, even a sole proprietorship, cannot file for Chapter 13 bankruptcy in the name of that business. Businesses are steered toward Chapter 11 bankruptcy when they need help reorganizing their debts.

If you own a business, however, you can file for Chapter 13 bankruptcy as an individual. You can include in your Chapter 13 bankruptcy case business-related debts you are personally liable for.

There is one exception: Stockbrokers and commodity brokers cannot file a Chapter 13 bankruptcy case, even if just to include personal (nonbusiness) debts. (11 U.S.C. § 109(e).)

2. You Must Have Stable and Regular Income

You must have "stable and regular" income to be eligible for Chapter 13 bankruptcy. That doesn't mean you must earn the same amount every month. But the income must be steady—that is, likely to continue and it must be periodic—weekly, monthly, quarterly, semi-annual, seasonal or even annual. You can use the following income to fund a Chapter 13 plan:

- regular wages or salary
- income from self-employment
- wages from seasonal work
- commissions from sales or other work
- pension payments

- Social Security benefits (although one court has ruled that Social Security payments do not constitute regular income to fund a Chapter 13 plan)
- disability or workers' compensation benefits
- unemployment benefits, strike benefits and the like
- public benefits (welfare payments)
- child support or alimony you receive
- royalties and rents
- gifts of money from relatives or friends, and
- proceeds from selling property, especially if selling property is your primary business.

IF YOU ARE MARRIED

Your income does not necessarily have to be "yours." A nonworking spouse can file alone and use money from working spouse as a source of income. And an unemployed spouse can file jointly with a working spouse. (See Ch. 4, *Calculating Your Disposable Income*, for more details.)

3. You Must Have Disposable Income

For you to qualify for Chapter 13 bankruptcy, your income must be high enough so that after you pay for your basic human needs, you are likely to have money left over to make periodic (usually monthly) payments to the bankruptcy court for three to five years. The total amount you must pay will depend on how much you owe, the type of debts you have (certain debts have to be paid in full; others don't) and your court's attitude. A few courts allow you to repay nothing on debts, that legally, don't have to be repaid in full, as long as you repay 100% of the others. Some courts push you to repay as close to 100% of those debts as possible. Most courts fall somewhere in between.

To determine if your disposable income is high enough to fund a Chapter 13 plan, you must create a reasonable monthly budget. Ch. 4, *Calculating Your Disposable Income*, explains how. If you are not proposing to repay 100% of your debts and the court, the trustee or a creditor thinks your budget is too generous—that is, it includes expenses other than necessities—your budget will be challenged.

4. Your Debts Must Not Be Too High

You do not qualify for Chapter 13 bankruptcy if your secured debts exceed $807,750. A debt is secured if you stand to lose specific property if you don't make your payments to the creditor. Home loans and car loans are the most common examples of secured debts. But a debt might also be secured if a creditor—such as the IRS—has filed a lien (notice of claim) against your property.

In addition, for you to be eligible for Chapter 13 bankruptcy, your unsecured debts cannot exceed $269,250. An unsecured debt is any debt for which you haven't pledged collateral. The debt is not related to any particular property you possess, and failure to repay the debt will not entitle the creditor to repossess property. Most debts are unsecured, including bank credit card debts, medical and legal bills, student loans, back utility bills and department store charges.

How to classify and total up your debts is explained in Ch. 3, *Adding Up Your Secured and Unsecured Debts.*

B. When Chapter 13 Bankruptcy Is Better Than Chapter 7

There are many reasons why people choose Chapter 13 bankruptcy—and in particular, choose Chapter 13 bankruptcy instead of Chapter 7 bankruptcy. Generally, you are probably a good candidate for Chapter 13 bankruptcy if you are in any of the following situations:

- You are behind on your mortgage or car loan, and want to make up the missed payments over time and reinstate the original agreement.
- You have a tax debt that cannot be eliminated (discharged) in Chapter 7 bankruptcy, but can be paid off over time in a Chapter 13 plan. (See Section 3, below.)
- You have a sincere desire to repay your debts, but you need the protection of the bankruptcy court to do so.
- You need help repaying your debts now, but need to leave open the option of filing for Chapter 7 bankruptcy in the future. This would be the case if for some reason you can't stop incurring new debt.
- You are a family farmer who wants to pay off your debts, but you do not qualify for a Chapter 12 family farming bankruptcy because you have a large debt unrelated to farming.

1. The Basics of Chapter 7 Bankruptcy

If you file for Chapter 7 bankruptcy, many of your debts will be canceled without any further repayment. In exchange, you might have to surrender some of your property. It costs $175 to file; and the whole process takes about three to six months and commonly requires only one trip to the courthouse. You can probably do it yourself, without a lawyer.

You must give up your "nonexempt" property, which can be sold to pay your creditors. Most people who file for Chapter 7 bankruptcy, however, have no nonexempt property to turn over to the trustee. Common kinds of nonexempt property are listed below.

At the end of the Chapter 7 bankruptcy case, the debts that qualify for discharge are wiped out by the court. You no longer legally owe your creditors. You can't file for Chapter 7 bankruptcy again for six years from the date of your filing.

EXEMPT PROPERTY AT A GLANCE

Items you can typically keep (exempt property)	Items you must typically give up (nonexempt property)
motor vehicles, to a certain value	nonresidential real estate
reasonably necessary clothing (no mink coats)	second or vacation home
reasonably necessary household furnishings and goods	recreational vehicles
household appliances	second car or truck
jewelry, to a certain value	expensive musical instruments (unless you're a professional musician)
personal effects	stamp, coin and other collections
life insurance (cash or loan value, or proceeds), to a certain value	family heirlooms
pensions	cash, bank accounts, stocks, bonds and other investments
part of the equity in a residence	
tools of a trade or profession, to a certain value	
portion of unpaid but earned wages	
public benefits (welfare, Social Security, unemployment compensation) accumulated in a bank account	

2. Determining Which Is Better for You

Here are how certain common situations are handled in Chapter 13 and Chapter 7 bankruptcy. Scan it to see how the differences affect you.

COMPARING CHAPTER 13 AND CHAPTER 7 BANKRUPTCY

What happens if...	Chapter 13	Chapter 7
You're behind on your mortgage or car loan.	You can repay the arrears through your plan, over three to five years, and keep the house or car.	You'll probably have to either give the collateral back to the creditor or arrange to pay for it in full during your bankruptcy case.
You owe back taxes to the IRS.	The result depends on your circumstances. See Section 3, below.	The result depends on your circumstances. See Section 3, below.
You have valuable nonexempt property. (See Section 1, above.)	You keep all of your property.	You must give it up, pay the trustee its fair market value or, if the trustee agrees, swap exempt property of equal value for it.
You have codebtors on personal (nonbusiness) loans.	The creditor may not seek payment from your codebtor for the duration of your case.	The creditor will go after your codebtor for payment.
You received a bankruptcy discharge within the previous six years.	No problem; you can file anytime.	You can't file for Chapter 7 unless the recent bankruptcy was a Chapter 13 case, and you repaid at least 70% of your debts.
You want to keep secured property by paying the creditor its value.	You can pay it (with interest) over time through your plan.	You usually must pay it in a lump sum or in two or three payments.
Your disposable income is sufficient to fund a Chapter 13 plan.		The bankruptcy court might throw out your case or pressure you to convert it to Chapter 13.
You owe debts for: • back or prospective child support or alimony • student loans that first became due fewer than seven years ago (plus the time you were in deferment or forbearance), unless repaying the debt would be a severe hardship • court-ordered restitution or criminal fines • dues or assessments you owe a condominium or cooperative association • taxes less than three years past due, or • debts for personal injuries arising from your intoxicated driving.	These debts can be included in your Chapter 13 repayment plan.	These debts cannot be erased in Chapter 7 bankruptcy.
As part of your divorce settlement or divorce decree, you must pay certain debts (such as credit card balances) or you owe money to your ex-spouse to even up the property settlement.	These debts are treated like any other unsecured debts. You include them in your plan; if you do not pay them in full during your case, the balance is wiped out at the end. (This is called Chapter 13 bankruptcy's "super discharge.")	If your ex-spouse objects, these debts are not discharged unless you prove to the court that: • you will be unable to pay these debts after your bankruptcy case, or • the benefit you will get by discharging the debts will outweigh any detriment to your ex-spouse.
You have debts: • incurred by fraud, larceny (theft), breach of trust or embezzlement • incurred just before filing, including debts of $1,000 or more to any one creditor for luxury goods or services purchased within 60 days before filing, and debts for cash advances in excess of $1,000 obtained within 60 days of filing for bankruptcy, or • from your willful or malicious injury to another or another's property, including assault, battery, false imprisonment, libel or slander.	These debts are treated like any other unsecured debts. You include them in your plan; if you do not pay them in full during your case, the balance is wiped out at the end under the super discharge.	These debts are not dischargeable if the creditor objects and proves your bad acts to the court.

HELP WITH CHAPTER 7 BANKRUPTCY

If you decide that Chapter 7 bankruptcy is the best way to handle your debts, or you just want to learn more about it, look at *How to File for Bankruptcy*, by Stephen Elias, Albin Renauer and Robin Leonard (Nolo Press). That book contains detailed information on dischargeable and nondischargeable debts, exempt and nonexempt property, strategies for dealing with secured debts, along with all the forms and instructions needed to file your own Chapter 7 bankruptcy case.

3. If You Owe Back Taxes to the IRS

If a large part of your debt consists of federal taxes, what happens to your tax debts may determine whether Chapter 7 bankruptcy or Chapter 13 bankruptcy is a better choice for you.

You can discharge (wipe out) debts for federal income taxes in Chapter 7 bankruptcy only if *all* of these five conditions are true:

1. The IRS has not recorded a tax lien against your property. (If all other conditions are met, the taxes may be discharged, but even after your bankruptcy, the lien remains against all property you own, effectively giving the IRS a way to collect.)
2. You didn't file a fraudulent return or try to evade paying taxes.
3. The liability is for a tax return (not a Substitute For Return) actually filed at least two years before you file for bankruptcy.
4. The tax return was due at least three years ago.
5. The taxes were assessed (you received a "notice of assessment of federal taxes" from the IRS) at least 240 days (eight months) before you file for bankruptcy. (11 U.S.C. §§ 523(a)(1) and (7).)

Certain actions extend these time limits:

- If you filed any bankruptcy in the past—even if the case was kicked out of court the next day—the time the case was pending plus six months is added to the time requirements in numbers 3, 4 and 5 above.
- If you made an Offer in Compromise to the IRS, the time your offer was pending plus 30 days are added to the 240-day requirement.
- If you requested a Taxpayer Assistance Order, the time your request was pending is added to the three time requirements above.

C. Other Alternatives

In some situations, filing for bankruptcy is the only sensible remedy for debt problems. In many others, however, another course of action makes better sense. This section outlines some alternatives.

1. Do Nothing

Surprisingly, the best approach for some people deeply in debt is to take no action at all. You can't be thrown in jail for not paying your debts. And if you're living simply, with little income and property, and look forward to a similar life in the future, you may be what's known as "judgment proof." This means that anyone who sues you and wins won't be able to collect, simply because you don't have anything they can legally take. A creditor can't take away such essentials as basic clothing, ordinary household furnishings, personal effects, food, Social Security, unemployment benefits, public assistance or 75% of your wages.

If your creditors know it's unlikely they could collect a judgment, they probably won't sue you. Instead, they'll simply write off your debt and treat it as a deductible business loss for income tax purposes. In several years (usually between six and ten) it will become legally uncollectible under the state law called the statute of limitations.

> ### STOPPING BILL COLLECTOR
> ### ABUSE AND HARASSMENT
>
> You don't need to file for bankruptcy just to get an-
> noying collection agencies off your back. Federal law
> forbids them from threatening you, lying about what
> they can do to you or invading your privacy. Under
> this law, you can also legally force collection agencies
> to stop phoning or writing you simply by demanding
> that they stop, even if you owe them a bundle and
> can't pay a cent. (The Fair Debt Collections Practices
> Act, 15 U.S.C. § 1692 and following.)

2. Negotiate With Your Creditors

If you have some income, or you have assets you're willing
to sell, you may be a lot better off negotiating with your
creditors than filing for bankruptcy. Negotiation may simply buy you some time to get back on your feet, or you and
your creditors may agree on a complete settlement of your
debts for less than you owe. In particular, if you are behind
on a mortgage issued by Fannie Mae or Freddie Mac, your
lender is encouraged to try to work out an arrangement to
avoid having to foreclose or your filing for bankruptcy.

DEALING WITH CREDITORS
How to negotiate with creditors and collection
agencies, and how to stop bill collector abuse, are covered
in detail in *Money Troubles: Legal Strategies to Cope With
Your Debts*, by Robin Leonard (Nolo Press). That book
covers how to deal with creditors when you owe money on
credit cards, student loans, mortgage loans, car loans, child
support and alimony, among other debts.

3. Get Outside Help to Design a Repayment Plan

Many people can't do a good job of negotiating with their
creditors. Inside, they feel that their creditors are right to
insist on full payment. Or their creditors are so hard-nosed
or just plain irrational that the process is too unpleasant to
stomach.

If you don't want to negotiate with your creditors, you
can seek help from a nonprofit credit counselor, such as
Consumer Credit Counseling Service (CCCS). CCCS is a
nonprofit organization that helps people set up debt repayment plans. CCCS may charge you a monthly fee of about
$20 for setting up a repayment plan, although usually the
service is free. CCCS also helps people make monthly bud-

gets, and may charge a one-time fee of about $20. If you
can't afford the fee, CCCS will waive it.

To use CCCS, you must have some money to pay creditors—either have income or the proceeds from selling some
of your property. A CCCS counselor contacts your creditors
to let them know that you've sought CCCS assistance and
need more time to pay. Based on your income and debts,
the counselor, with your creditors, decides on a payment
schedule. You then make one or two direct payments each
month to CCCS, which in turn pays your creditors. A
CCCS counselor can often get wage garnishments revoked
and interest and late charges dropped.

While paying your debts through CCCS is similar to filing for Chapter 13 bankruptcy, there are major differences.

- With CCCS, you are usually required to repay your
  debts in full. You usually make reduced payments in
  Chapter 13 bankruptcy.
- Paying through CCCS doesn't legally stop creditors
  from trying to collect, as bankruptcy does. If your
  creditor doesn't accept your CCCS payments, it can
  come after you for payment of the full debt owed.
- If you owe the IRS, filing for bankruptcy will stop the
  accrual of interest and penalties. Paying through CCCS
  does not.
- Your creditors don't have to agree to accept payments
  from CCCS, although most do. Once your Chapter 13
  plan is approved by the court, on the other hand, your
  creditors must abide by it.
- A Chapter 13 bankruptcy notation will stay on your
  credit report usually for seven, but as many as ten
  years. Few creditors, if any, report that you are repaying your debts through CCCS and so you may be able
  to minimize the damage to your credit rating by paying your debts through CCCS.

CCCS has over 1,000 offices throughout the country.
Look in the phone book to find the one nearest you or con-
tact the main office at 8611 2nd Ave., Suite 100, Silver
Spring, Maryland 20910; (800) 388-2227.

4. File for Chapter 11 Bankruptcy

Chapter 11 bankruptcy is the type of bankruptcy used by
financially struggling businesses—such as Macy's—to
reorganize their affairs. It is also available to individuals.
Individuals who consider Chapter 11 bankruptcy usually
have debts in excess of the Chapter 13 bankruptcy limits,
$269,250 of unsecured debts or $807,750 of secured debts,
or substantial nonexempt assets, such as several pieces of
real estate.

The initial filing fee is currently $800, compared to $175 for Chapter 7 or $160 for Chapter 13 bankruptcy. In addition, you must pay a quarterly fee that is a percentage of your debts (often several hundreds or thousands of dollars) until your reorganization plan is approved or dismissed, or your case is converted to Chapter 7 bankruptcy. Most attorneys require a minimum $7,500 retainer fee to handle a Chapter 11 bankruptcy case. Add to that the Chapter 11 bankruptcy court fees, which one year after you file could run you $10,000. If you want to read more on this kind of bankruptcy, see *A Feast for Lawyers*, by Sol Stein (Evans, M., & Co. Inc.).

HELP FROM A LAWYER

You'll need a lawyer to file for Chapter 11 bankruptcy. A Chapter 11 bankruptcy often turns into a long, expensive, lawyer-infested mess, and many Chapter 11 filings end up being converted to Chapter 7 bankruptcy.

A "fast-track" Chapter 11 bankruptcy, for small businesses with debts up to $2 million, was created in 1994. (11 U.S.C. § 1121(e).) You will still need an attorney to use the fast-track procedure.

5. File for Chapter 12 Bankruptcy

Chapter 12 bankruptcy is almost identical to Chapter 13 bankruptcy. To be eligible for Chapter 12 bankruptcy, however, at least 80% of your debts must arise from the operation of a family farm.

HELP FROM A LAWYER

See a lawyer if you want to file for Chapter 12 bankruptcy.

D. Converting from Chapter 7 Bankruptcy to Chapter 13 Bankruptcy

Even if you've already filed for Chapter 7 bankruptcy, you can switch to Chapter 13 bankruptcy if you decide it would be better. For example, you might discover that a tax debt you thought you could discharge in a Chapter 7 bankruptcy can't be discharged, but can be included in a Chapter 13 repayment plan.

You have the absolute right to convert a Chapter 7 bankruptcy case into a Chapter 13 bankruptcy case at any time, as long as you did not previously convert this case to Chapter 13 bankruptcy from Chapter 7 bankruptcy. You do have to file a written request (called a motion) with the bankruptcy court, send a copy of your motion to each of your creditors and obtain an order from the court.

RESOURCES FOR MOTION FORMS

To see what a motion to convert your case to Chapter 13 bankruptcy looks like, consult a bankruptcy forms book at a law library. Also, *Consumer Bankruptcy Law and Practice*, written and published by the National Center for Consumer Law, contains sample motion forms. Check your local law library for this book or call the publisher at 617-523-8010.

The major issue that will come up at the court hearing on your request is whether or not you are eligible to file for Chapter 13 bankruptcy. Your debts must meet the $750,000 secured debt and $250,000 unsecured debt limits, and you must have sufficient disposable income to fund a Chapter 13 plan.

Courts are split as to whether your eligibility for Chapter 13 bankruptcy is based on your financial circumstances at the time you filed your Chapter 7 bankruptcy or at the time you seek to convert. For most people, it doesn't matter. But it may matter to you. For example, if you had no regular income when you filed for Chapter 7 bankruptcy, you may not be allowed to convert to Chapter 13 bankruptcy if your court bases eligibility on circumstances at the time you filed your Chapter 7 bankruptcy case. In that situation, the court would probably require you to dismiss your Chapter 7 case and refile a Chapter 13 case. You would have to pay a $160 filing fee.

If the court does approve your motion to convert, you must file your Chapter 13 repayment plan within 15 days and start making payments under the plan within 30 days after you file it. ∎

An Overview of Chapter 13 Bankruptcy

If you've decided that Chapter 13 bankruptcy seems to be the best solution to your debt problems, you've probably got a lot of questions. How much will I have to pay every month? How long will I have to make payments? When I'm done with my Chapter 13 plan, will I still owe any of my creditors?

This chapter can give you some preliminary answers to these and other questions.

A. The Chapter 13 Process

Before you file for Chapter 13 bankruptcy, you must fill out a packet of forms listing what you own, earn, owe and spend. You file these papers with the bankruptcy court, along with an additional form called the Chapter 13 repayment plan. This form is the most important paper in your entire Chapter 13 bankruptcy case. It describes in detail how (and how much) you will repay on every one of your debts. There is no official form for the plan, but many courts have designed their own forms. It costs $160 to file for Chapter 13 bankruptcy.

You can file for Chapter 13 bankruptcy at any time, even if you just received a Chapter 7 bankruptcy discharge or just completed another Chapter 13 repayment plan. If you file soon after completing another Chapter 13 case, however, you'll be required to pay back a large percentage of your debts. And a court may reject a subsequent filing if it feels you are not filing for Chapter 13 bankruptcy in good faith. (Good faith is covered in Ch. 9, *After You File Your Case.*)

You must begin making payments under your Chapter 13 plan within 30 days after you file it with the bankruptcy court. Usually, you make payments directly to the bankruptcy trustee, the person appointed by the court to oversee your case, who in turn distributes the money to your creditors. If you have a regular job with regular income, however, the bankruptcy court may order that your monthly payments be automatically deducted from your wages and sent directly to the bankruptcy court. Your must also make the regular payments on your secured debts, such as a car loan or mortgage.

Typically, you will make the payments called for in your original agreement on your *secured* debts, and reduced payments on your *unsecured* debts. (Secured and unsecured debts are defined in Ch. 3, *Adding Up Your Secured and Unsecured Debts,* Section A.4.) Most repayment plans last three years. After that, any remaining unpaid balance on the unsecured debts is wiped out (discharged). In some cases, the court will approve a five-year repayment plan.

You can dismiss your case at any time—you may want to do this to refile your case if you incur a large debt after you file but before your plan is approved by the bankruptcy court. If you dismiss and refile, you can include the new debt in your plan. (You cannot refile, however, if within the previous 180 days, the court dismissed your bankruptcy case for failing to follow a court order or if you voluntarily dismissed your case after a creditor asked the court to remove the automatic stay.)

If for some reason you cannot finish a Chapter 13 repayment plan—for example, you lose your job six months into the plan and can't keep up the payments—the trustee may modify your plan. The trustee may give you a grace period (if the problem looks temporary), reduce your total monthly payments or extend the repayment period. If it's clear that there's no way you'll be able to complete the plan because of circumstances beyond your control, the court might let you discharge your debts on the basis of hardship. Examples of hardship would be a sudden plant closing in a one-factory town or a debilitating illness.

If the bankruptcy court won't let you modify your plan or give you a hardship discharge, you have the right to:
- convert to a Chapter 7 bankruptcy (unless you received a Chapter 7 bankruptcy discharge within the previous six years), or
- have the bankruptcy court dismiss your Chapter 13 bankruptcy case. You would still owe your debts, however, any payments you made during your plan would be deducted. On the flip side, your creditors will add on interest they did not charge while your Chapter 13 case was pending.

(Modification, hardship discharge, conversion to Chapter 7 bankruptcy and dismissal of your case are all covered in Ch. 10, *After Your Plan Is Approved.*)

CHAPTER 13 BANKRUPTCY CHECKLIST

In every Chapter 13 case, you will need to do the steps set out below: This book will guide you through the process from start to finish.

1. Evaluate your alternatives and decide whether or not Chapter 13 bankruptcy is right for you. (Ch. 1)
2. Add up your debts. (Ch. 3)
3. Calculate your income. (Ch. 4)
4. Calculate the value of your property. (Ch. 5)
5. Fill out the bankruptcy forms and map out a repayment plan. (Chs. 6 and 7)
6. File your forms and plan with the bankruptcy court. (Ch. 8)
7. Attend two court hearings. (Ch. 9)
8. Make the payments under your plan and go back to court if any problems arise during your case. (Ch. 10)
9. Obtain your bankruptcy discharge (congratulations!). (Ch. 11)

B. How Much You'll Have to Repay Through the Plan

The total amount you'll have to repay your creditors over the length of your Chapter 13 case depends on a number of factors, including the type of debts you owe and the philosophy of the bankruptcy judges in your area. You can get a rough idea by following these steps and filling out Worksheet 1, below.

1. Add up the total value of your "nonexempt" property. This calculation is explained in Ch. 5, *Calculating the Value of Your Nonexempt Property.* To get a rough idea, look at the exemption list for your state in Appendix 1. All property you own that is *not* on that list is considered nonexempt.)

   Your unsecured creditors must receive at least the value of your nonexempt property, so you will have to pay your unsecured creditors at least this amount. Keep in mind that this amount is the minimum, by law, that you must pay. The court will require you to pay more if:

   • Any of your unsecured debts are "priority debts"— such as back taxes or child support—which must be repaid in full.

   • The court requires debtors to pay back a high percentage of unsecured debts. If you have little

nonexempt property, the amount you calculated will be very low. Your creditors might object to your plan on the ground that you have not proposed it in good faith. There is huge regional variation on this issue, however. For example, courts in Northern California typically approve Chapter 13 plans in which unsecured creditors receive nothing. In Northern Alabama, by contrast, unsecured creditors courts rarely approve Chapter 13 plans unless unsecured creditors will receive 100% of what they are owed. Most courts—and Chapter 13 plans—fall somewhere in between. (See Ch. 7, *Writing Your Chapter 13 Bankruptcy Plan.*)

2. Add the amount of missed payments you owe to any secured creditors, such as mortgage or car lenders, whose property you want to keep. In Chapter 13 bankruptcy, you have to make up all the missed payments to keep the property. As an alternative, you can pay the creditor the value of the property on your secured debts, except if you owe mortgage arrears. Include interest unless the loan in arrears is a mortgage you obtained after October 22, 1994. There are several ways to figure out the rate you'll have to pay; for now, just use the rate in your original contract.

3. Some courts require that you add an amount equal to at least three year's worth of interest on the amount in Step 1. There are several ways to figure out the rate you might have to pay; for now, leave this blank or use 10%. This money may be required to compensate creditors for the fact that they're getting their money over a period of years instead of all at once.

4. Add the trustee's fee—3% to 10% of each payment you make.

5. Total all the figures you've listed.

C. Your Monthly Payments

Your disposable income is the amount left over when you deduct your necessary monthly living expenses from your total monthly income. (You'll calculate this amount precisely in Ch. 4.) Bankruptcy law requires that you pay all your "disposable income" into your Chapter 13 plan for a minimum of 36 months.

If making 36 monthly disposable income payments will not be enough to repay the minimum amount required by the court (see Section B, above), you will have to do one of the following:

• Ask the court to approve a plan that lasts more than 36 months. The court cannot authorize a plan that lasts more than 60 months (five years), however.

WORKSHEET 1: HOW MUCH WILL YOU HAVE TO REPAY?

1. Total value of your nonexempt property, plus any increase for priority debts or to pay back a higher percentage	$ 37,754
2. Amount overdue to mortgage lender; add interest unless the loan was obtained after October 20, 1994	$ 8,075
3. Amount overdue to other secured creditors, or the value of the collateral lender, plus interest	$ 966
4. Compensation on payments on unsecured debts	$ 0
5. Trustee's fee	$ 4,680
Minimum Amount You Will Pay Into Your Plan	$ 51,475

• Increase your monthly disposable income. When you submit your repayment plan to the bankruptcy court for approval, the court will look at the budget you used to come up with your disposable income. If there isn't enough to pay your creditors, you will have to decrease your expenses in order to increase the money available to pay into your plan.

D. How Much You'll Still Owe When Your Case Is Over

It is possible that you will still owe money to some of your creditors when your Chapter 13 bankruptcy case is over. Certain unsecured debts cannot be eliminated in bankruptcy—these are called nondischargeable debts. In Chapter 13 bankruptcy, you have two choices in how to handle nondischargeable debts:

• pay them in full through your plan (which may increase the amount you calculated in Section B, above), or
• pay only a portion of them during your case and owe a balance at the end; to keep your creditors from tacking on interest abated during your Chapter 13, you could file a second Chapter 13 case to pay off the balance.

The following are debts nondischargeable in Chapter 13 bankruptcy. Ch. 7, *Writing Your Chapter 13 Bankruptcy Plan*, Section J, explains how to go about paying nondischargeable debts in your Chapter 13 repayment plan.

1. Child Support and Alimony

Alimony and child support debts generally aren't dischargeable. They may be however, if:

• You owe the debt under a state's general support law.
• You're paying the debt under a voluntary agreement between unmarried people—unless, before the bankruptcy case is filed, the recipient sues you and obtains a court judgment.
• You owe the support to someone other than your spouse, ex-spouse or child, unless it's owed to the welfare department. Be aware, however, that bankruptcy courts are increasingly characterizing debts to people other than parents, but for the benefit of children—such as attorney's fees or hospital delivery costs—as nondischargeable child support. (See *In re Jones,* 9 F.3d 878 (10th Cir. 1993); *In re Seibert,* 914 F.2d 102 (7th Cir. 1990); *In re Poe,* 118 B.R. 809 (N.D. Okla. 1990).)

If a court issued an order setting the amount of alimony or child support, or the welfare department is trying to collect child support from you, the debt is clearly nondischargeable. Some other debts may also be considered nondischargeable child support or alimony. These are usually marital debts—debts a spouse was ordered to pay when the couple divorced—which are really in lieu of support. Obligations that are generally considered support and aren't dischargeable include debts that:

- are paid to a spouse who is maintaining the primary residence of the children while there is a serious imbalance of incomes
- terminate on the death or remarriage of the recipient spouse
- depend on the future income of either spouse, or
- are paid in installments over a substantial period of time. (*In re Goin,* 808 F.2d 1391 (10th Cir. 1987); *In re Calhoun,* 10 Bankr. Ct. Dec. 1402 (6th Cir. 1983).)

2. Student Loans

In general, student loans are nondischargeable, even if you just cosigned the loan or are a parent who took out a PLUS (Parental Loans for Students) loan. Bankruptcy courts have little sympathy for debtors who want to eliminate their student loans.

In only three situations might a judge let you discharge a student loan:

- The payments first became due more than seven years ago. If your repayment obligation was postponed (for example, you received a deferment or forbearance on paying, or were in a previous bankruptcy case) for any length of time during the seven years before you file

for bankruptcy, however, the seven-year period is extended for the length of time of the postponement. If you obtained a consolidation loan, and the first payment on your consolidated loan became due fewer than seven years ago, the bankruptcy court probably will not let you discharge *any* of it, even if some of the original loans became due more than seven years ago. (*In re Menendez,* 151 B.R. 972 (M.D. Fla. 1993); *U.S. v. McGrath,* 143 B.R. 820 (D. Md. 1992).)

- It would cause you undue hardship to repay. On rare occasions, courts allow student loans to be discharged in bankruptcy in advance of the seven-year waiting period if there is evidence that repaying the loan would cause undue hardship. The court will likely grant you a discharge if, based on your current income and expenses, you cannot maintain a minimal living standard and repay the loan; your current financial condition is likely to continue for a significant portion of the repayment period of the loan; and you've made a good faith effort to repay the debt.
- Your Health Education Assistance Loan (HEAL) payments first became due more than seven years ago and it would impose an unconscionable burden on your life to repay them. (42 U.S.C. § 249f(g).)

3. Intoxicated Driving Debts

You cannot discharge debts resulting from the death of, or personal injury to, someone because you drove while intoxicated by alcohol or drugs. Even if you are sued and the judge or jury finds you liable but doesn't specifically find that you were intoxicated, the bankruptcy court can nevertheless declare the judgment against you nondischargeable if the creditor convinces the court that you were in fact intoxicated. You can, however, discharge debts for property damage resulting from your intoxicated driving.

4. Restitution or Criminal Fine

A bankruptcy court will not let you discharge a criminal fine imposed upon you for violating a law, or a debt for restitution included in a sentence you received after being convicted of committing a crime. Restitution is the payment you are ordered to make to a victim.

E. Filing With Your Spouse

A married person can file for Chapter 13 alone or with a spouse. It rarely makes sense, however, for only one spouse to file. The filing spouse must list the income, expenses and property of both spouses, and the bankruptcy case will have an impact on both spouses.

Only if you are separated from your spouse, have divided your property, agreed to pay the jointly-incurred marital debts and have otherwise ended your financial entanglements (other than paying or receiving alimony or child support) should you consider filing for Chapter 13 bankruptcy alone.

F. The Chapter 13 Trustee

In every Chapter 13 bankruptcy case, the court appoints a person called the Chapter 13 trustee to oversee the case. In most bankruptcy court districts, the same person serves as the trustee in all Chapter 13 cases. In large districts, however, such as Los Angeles, the court has more than one Chapter 13 trustee. The trustee may be a local bankruptcy attorney, very knowledgeable about Chapter 13 bankruptcy generally and the local court's rules and procedures specifically. In some courts, trustees are not attorneys, but are business people with specialized knowledge of finances or personal bankruptcy.

1. Working With the Chapter 13 Trustee

Just a few days after you file your bankruptcy papers, you'll get a letter telling you the name, address and phone number of the trustee. The trustee will work very closely with you throughout your case.

If you have trouble making your payments, the trustee may suggest ways for you to modify your plan, give you a temporary reprieve or take other steps to help you get back on track. The trustee doesn't do this simply to be nice, although many trustees genuinely want to help debtors. The trustee is doing this because the trustee's fee is deducted from the money you send the trustee to pay your creditors.

2. Paying the Chapter 13 Trustee

The trustee's fee can range anywhere from 3% to 10% of the payments you make. In bankruptcy districts with a high number of Chapter 13 cases (this includes various districts in Alabama, Georgia, Louisiana, North Carolina, Tennessee and Texas, among others), the percentage is often less than 10% because a lot of money flows through the court. In jurisdictions with few Chapter 13 cases (most of the rest of the country), trustees usually charge the full 10%.

There are two ways the trustee can calculate the fee. Let's say, for example, that you will propose paying your creditors $100 each month and the trustee will take 10% as com-

pensation. If the fee is based on the amount the trustee pays to your creditors, then you'll have to pay $110 so that the trustee can keep 10% of $100. If, however, it's based on what you pay the trustee, you'll have to pay $111.11 so that the trustee can keep 10% of that payment ($11.11), which leaves $100 for your creditors. Whenever you calculate the amount you'll have to pay in your Chapter 13 plan, remember to include the trustee's fee!

G. Going To Court

A Chapter 13 bankruptcy case requires at least two court appearances. These court appearances aren't anything like full-blown trials; they're usually brief hearings where you appear before the trustee or judge for just a few minutes.

Here are the most common types of appearances; they are covered in more detail in Ch. 9, *After You File Your Case*, and Ch. 10, *After Your Plan Is Approved.*

- **The meeting of the creditors** is the first court appearance you (and your spouse, if you filed together) must make. It's fairly routine and usually something you can handle easily without an attorney. Despite its name, usually only a few creditors, if any, show up. The judge isn't present. The trustee and any creditors who come will ask you about information in the bankruptcy papers you filed. Sometimes, creditors will try to negotiate with you about any objections they have to your plan.
- **The confirmation hearing** is the hearing at which the court approves or rejects your proposed repayment plan. Your creditors may raise many objections—including that you've gotten further behind on your mortgage, car payment or other secured debts since filing your bankruptcy papers, or that your plan isn't feasible, wasn't proposed in good faith or discriminates against certain creditors. The judge will rule on these objections and may require you to change your repayment plan. Courts commonly hold the confirmation hearing immediately after the meeting of the creditors.
- **A valuation hearing** may be requested by a creditor (or you) to determine the value of an item of collateral. This frequently comes up when you claim that the collateral (such as a car) is worth less than you owe and you want to pay only its value. If you or a creditor request a valuation hearing, your confirmation hearing will be postponed or the court will hold the valuation hearing immediately before the confirmation hearing.

- **A relief from stay hearing** may be requested by a creditor who wants to pursue collection efforts against you. This could come up, for example, if you fall further behind on your mortgage or car payments after you file your bankruptcy papers.

- **The discharge hearing** takes place at the end of your case. Few courts require you to come to court for a discharge hearing. You'll probably just receive a letter from the court letting you know that your case is over and that any balance remaining on your dischargeable debts has been discharged. ∎

Adding Up Your Secured and Unsecured Debts

CONVERTING FROM CHAPTER 7 BANKRUPTCY
If you originally filed for Chapter 7 bankruptcy and are now converting your case to Chapter 13 bankruptcy, you need only to file a Chapter 13 plan. Skip ahead to Ch. 7, *Writing Your Chapter 13 Bankrupty Plan.*

I f you think you want to file for Chapter 13 bankruptcy, you need to add up your debts and classify them as "secured" or "unsecured." This is important because to qualify for Chapter 13 bankruptcy, your unsecured debts cannot exceed $269,250, and your secured debts cannot exceed $807,750. (If your debts are over the limit, you may still qualify for Chapter 13 bankruptcy with a little effort. See Sections 4.A and B.2, below.)

This chapter explains how to classify your debts (it's easier than it may sound) and contains worksheets to help you add them up.

IF YOU CLEARLY QUALIFY
If you are pretty certain that your secured debts don't come close to $807,750 and your unsecured debts are way below $269,250, you can skip ahead to Ch. 4, *Calculating Your Disposable Income.*

A. Secured Debts

A secured debt is linked to a specific item of property, called collateral, that guarantees payment of the debt. If you don't pay, the creditor is entitled to take the collateral. For example, mortgages and car loans are secured debts.

Use Worksheets 2 and 3, below, to add up your secured debts. Keep in mind that there are two kinds of secured debts: those you agree to, such as a mortgage, and those created without your consent, such as a lien recorded against your home by the IRS because you haven't paid your taxes.

TERMINOLOGY

Lien: A creditor's legal claim against collateral.
Security interest: A lien you agree to, such as a mortgage.
Nonconsensual lien: A lien created without your consent.

1. Liens You Agree To: Security Interests

If you voluntarily pledge property as collateral—that is, as a guarantee that you will pay a debt—the lien on your property is called a security interest. If you signed a security agreement, it may well have given the creditor the right to take the property (the collateral) if you miss a payment.

Here are some common examples of security interests:
- **Mortgages** (called deeds of trust in some states), which are loans to buy or refinance a house or other real estate. The real estate is collateral for the loan. If you fail to pay, the lender can foreclose.
- **Home equity loans** (second mortgages) from banks or finance companies, such as loans to do work on your house. The house is collateral for the loan. If you fail to pay, the lender can foreclose.
- **Loans for cars, boats, tractors, motorcycles or RVs.** Here, the vehicle is the collateral. If you fail to pay, the lender can repossess it.
- **Store charges with a security agreement.** Almost all store purchases on credit cards are unsecured. Some stores, however, notably Sears, print on the credit card slip or other receipt that "Sears retains a security interest in all hard goods (durable goods) purchased" or make customers sign security agreements when they use their store charge card. For example, if you buy a major appliance on credit, the store may require you to sign a security agreement in which you agree that the item purchased is collateral for your repayment. If you don't pay back the loan, the seller can take the property. (In Vermont, a bankruptcy court has ruled that Sears charge debts are unsecured, not secured, under Vermont state law. *In re Oszajca*, No. 95-1079 (6/28/96).)

- **Personal loans from banks, credit unions or finance companies**. Often you must pledge valuable personal property, such as a paid-off motor vehicle, as collateral.

To add up your voluntary security interests, fill in the first two columns of Worksheet 2. (The other columns are explained later.) A sample is shown below; a blank tear-out is in Appendix 3.

As you fill in the worksheets, keep in mind the following:

- **Disputed debts.** List all debts claimed by creditors, even if you don't think you owe them or disagree about the amount. If the exact amount of a debt hasn't yet been determined, use the amount the creditor claims you owe.
- **Joint debts.** List 100% of all debts you incurred with someone else—such as a spouse, nonmarital partner, parent or child.

Column 1: Description of debt/name of creditor. In the first column, enter your secured debts in the appropriate categories. If a debt does not fall into a category on the form, list it under Other. For instance, you may have given a lawyer a

security interest in any money you may recover in a lawsuit against a person who injured you.

Column 2: Total outstanding balance. Enter the total amount you owe on each debt. You can find out the total by calling the lender. If you are uncertain about the amount, put your best estimate and a question mark.

→ **DOING SOME WORK NOW WILL SAVE YOU TIME LATER**
Once you've filled out Columns 1 and 2, you can skip ahead to Section 2 to calculate the amount of your nonconsensual liens. But if you want to speed up the process of completing your bankruptcy forms, fill out Columns 3, 4 and 5 now.

Column 3: Amount of regular monthly payment. Enter the amount of your regular monthly payment for each debt.

Column 4: Total amount of arrears. Multiply the amount of your regular monthly payment by the number of months you are behind. Add to that any late fees, attorney fees and collection costs assessed by the lender. Enter the total in Column 4.

Column 5: Present value of collateral. In this column, enter the current value of the property that secures the debt.

WORKSHEET 2: SECURED DEBTS WITH VOLUNTARY SECURITY INTERESTS

1 Description of debt/ name of creditor	2 Total outstanding balance	3 Regular monthly payment	4 Total amount of arrears	5 Present value of collateral
Mortgages and home equity loans				
Home Bank Mortgage	177,516	1,236	12,360	210,000
West Bank Home Equity Loan	14,000	1,000	13,000	210,000
Motor vehicle loans				
GMAC	9,171	405	405	8,500
Personal loans				
Department store charges with security agreements				
Sears—new washer and dryer	850	30	300	600
Other				
Martha Kwok, attorney —interest in	unknown	—	—	210,000
outcome of lawsuit (lien on house)				

Total $ 201,537

For purposes of completing the worksheet, use your best estimates. When you're ready to fill out and file your bankruptcy papers, you may need to come up with more precise figures.

2. Liens Created Without Your Consent: Nonconsensual Liens

A creditor can, in some circumstances, get a lien on your property without your consent. These liens are termed nonconsensual liens. In theory, a nonconsensual lien gives the creditor a right to force the sale of the property in order to get paid. In practice, however, few creditors (the IRS is the major exception) force a sale of property, because so much time and expense are involved. Instead, they wait until you sell or refinance the property—when the lien must be paid off to give the new owner clear title to the property.

There are three major types of nonconsensual liens:

• **Judicial liens.** A judicial lien can be imposed on your property only after somebody sues you and wins a money judgment against you. In most states, the judgment creditor then must record (file) the judgment with the county or state; the recorded judgment creates the lien on your real estate in that county or state. In a few states, a judgment entered against you by a court automatically creates a lien on the real estate you own in that county—that is, the judgment creditor doesn't have to record the judgment to get the lien.

• **Statutory liens.** Some liens are created automatically by law. For example, in most states when you hire someone to work on your house, the worker or supplier of materials automatically gets a mechanic's lien (also called a materialman's lien) on the house if you don't pay. So does a homeowners' association, in some states, if you don't pay your dues or special assessments.

• **Tax liens.** Federal, state and local governments have the authority to impose liens on your property if you owe delinquent taxes. If you owe money to the IRS or other taxing authority, the debt is secured *only* if a lien has been recorded against your property. If there is no lien, your tax debt is unsecured and should be included on Worksheet 4.

Use Worksheet 3 to add up these debts. A sample is shown below; a blank tear-out copy is in Appendix 3.

Column 1: Description of debt/name of creditor. List your nonconsensual lienholders in the appropriate categories.

Column 2: Amount of debt. Enter the total amount of each debt. If you are uncertain, put your best estimate and a question mark.

Filling out the rest of Worksheet 3 will let you determine whether any of your debts are "undersecured." An undersecured debt is partially secured (and so goes on this worksheet) and partially unsecured (and so goes on Worksheet 4, too).

Column 3: Property affected by lien. Identify the property affected by each lien. If you are like most people, this is your house—but not always. Let's look at this by type of lien.

• **Judicial liens.** In every state except Alabama, Georgia, Massachusetts and Mississippi, a judicial lien affects only the real estate you own in the county in which the lien is recorded or the judgment entered. In those four states, a judicial lien affects both your real estate and your personal property in the county.

  But that's not the end of it. A judgment creditor can also file the judgment with the state motor vehicles department, imposing a lien on any car, truck, motorcycle or other motor vehicle you own. You may not know about this lien until the creditor files a claim with the bankruptcy court describing its interest as secured (this is covered in Ch. 9, *After You File Your Case*) or you check with the motor vehicles department.

• **Statutory liens.** Statutory liens affect your real estate.

• **Tax liens.** A lien recorded by a local government for unpaid property tax affects your real estate. Similarly, if your state taxing authority sends you a bill and you don't contest or pay it, the state can record a tax lien against your real estate in that state. And if you don't pay an IRS bill, the IRS can record a Notice of Federal Tax Lien at your county land records office or your Secretary of State's office. The lien affects only your real estate.

Column 4: Present value of property. In this column, enter the current value of the property listed in Column 3. For purposes of completing the worksheet, use your best estimates. When you're ready to fill out and file your bankruptcy papers, you may need to come up with more precise figures.

To determine whether any of the debts are undersecured, you must subtract the amount of the debt (Column 2) from the present value of the collateral (Column 4).

EXAMPLE: Your car is worth $7,500 but a creditor has filed a lien with the motor vehicle department for $10,000. The debt is undersecured by $2,500.

A debt may also be undersecured if you have many liens all secured by the same property (Column 3), and the total of those liens (some may be on Worksheet 2 and some may be on Worksheet 3) exceeds the present value of the prop-

WORKSHEET 3: SECURED DEBTS CREATED WITHOUT YOUR CONSENT

1 Description of debt/ name of creditor	2 Amount of debt	3 Property affected by lien	4 Present value of property
Judicial liens			
Columbia Community Hospital	26,000	House	210,000
Dr. Anton Gurnev	16,000	House	210,000
Statutory liens			
Tax liens			
IRS	17,990	House	210,000

Total $ 59,990

erty. In that situation, the creditors who filed their liens the latest are the ones whose debts are undersecured.

EXAMPLE: Your house is worth $210,000. You still owe $177,000 on your mortgage (which is listed in Worksheet 2). In the same year, you took out a $14,000 home equity loan (in March), the IRS recorded a Notice of Federal Tax Lien for nearly $18,000 (in June), and two judgment creditors recorded judgment liens for $42,000 against your house (in July). The home equity loan and IRS' lien are secured. The judgment creditor' liens, however, are undersecured.

If all or any portion of a debt on this worksheet is undersecured, erase the undersecured amount from Column 2 and enter it on Worksheet 4, Unsecured Debts.

3. Total Up Your Secured Debts

Add together the totals from Worksheet 2, Column 2 (Total outstanding balance) and Worksheet 3, Column 2 (Total amount of debt). The figure must be under $807,250 for you to qualify for Chapter 13 bankruptcy.

4. Turning Secured Debts Into Unsecured Ones: Lien Avoidance

In certain limited circumstances, you can ask the bankruptcy court to eliminate (avoid) liens on certain property. This procedure, called lien avoidance, turns the debt into an unsecured one. This can help you in two situations:
- Your secured debts are over the $807,250 limit.
- If in your Chapter 13 plan you will propose repaying less than 100% of your unsecured debts, you can bring

down the total amount you will pay through your plan.

Although it may sound complicated, lien avoidance is a routine procedure that involves just a little time. You request lien avoidance by typing and filing a document called a "motion" with the bankruptcy court. Complete instructions for preparing and filing a motion to avoid a lien are Ch. 9, *After You File Your Case*, Section K. Liens that can be avoided are described here.

a. Security Interests

A security interest (remember—that's a secured debt you agree to) can be avoided only if it meets the three criteria listed below. If you determine that a lien can be avoided, erase the debt from this worksheet and enter it on Worksheet 4, Unsecured Debts.

1. The lien must be a nonpossessory nonpurchase money security interest. A nonpurchase money security interest is one in which you pledge property you already own as collateral for a loan. It is nonpossessory if you—not the creditor—keep possession of the property. Common examples are where you take out a home equity loan, or borrow from a credit union and pledge your car as security for the loan.

2. You must be able to claim the collateral to which the lien is attached as "exempt." To see whether the property is exempt, look at the state-by-state lists of exempt property in Appendix 1. Note that in 13 states, you can claim as exempt property specified by the federal bankruptcy law instead of by your state law. At the beginning of your state chart it will state whether or not the federal bankruptcy exemptions are available to you. They appear in Appendix 1 after Wyoming. Ch. 5, *Calculating the Value of Your Nonexempt Property*, contains an extensive discussion of exempt and nonexempt property.

3. The collateral must be any of the following property:
   - household furnishings, household goods, clothing, appliances, books and musical instruments or jewelry that are primarily for your personal, family or household use
   - health aids professionally prescribed for you or a dependent
   - animals or crops held primarily for your personal, family or household use—but only the first $5,000 of the lien can be avoided (11 U.S.C. § 522(f)(3)), or
   - implements, professional books or tools used in a trade (yours or a dependent's)—but only the first

SPECIAL RULES FOR AVOIDING JUDICIAL LIENS

Bankruptcy rules place additional limits on avoiding judicial liens on real estate or which arose from a divorce.

Real estate. When you file for bankruptcy, something called your homestead exemption protects your equity in your residence. Your equity is the amount by which the value of the property exceeds the total of any mortgages and other consensual liens on the property.

EXAMPLE: Zoe and Bud own a $100,000 house with an $80,000 mortgage; their equity is $20,000. The homestead exemption in their state is $30,000. Although a creditor has recorded a $200,000 judgment (judicial) lien against Zoe and Bud's home, their equity is fully protected because it is less than the homestead exemption amount. This means that if the creditor forced a sale of the house, Zoe and Bud would be entitled to their homestead exemption before the creditor with the $200,000 judgment would be entitled to any money.

If no equity remains after the consensual liens and homestead exemption are deducted, you can entirely eliminate (avoid) the judicial liens on the property.

EXAMPLE: Zoe and Bud could eliminate the entire $200,000 lien because the consensual lien (the $80,00 mortgage) plus the homestead exemption ($30,000) together total more than the value of their property. After the lien is gone, the debt is unsecured and treated like all other unsecured, dischargeable debts in Chapter 13.

Divorce. Because the law places a high priority on protecting the interests of children and former spouses, bankruptcy law prohibits you from avoiding a judicial lien that secures a debt to your ex-spouse or children for alimony or child support. But in some divorces, it's not always clear if a lien is for support or is just to pay marital bills. In the latter case, the lien may be avoided.

Also, a Supreme Court case limits your right to avoid liens arising out of a division of property that takes place during a divorce. For example, if you get sole ownership of your marital home at the same time that your ex-spouse gets a security interest (such as a promissory note) in the home, the court may not let you avoid the lien. The determining issues are when you *alone* acquired title to the property and when your ex-spouse's lien affixed. Consult a bankruptcy lawyer to determine how this case—and subsequent cases—may affect you if you intend to avoid a lien arising from a divorce. (The main case is *Farrey v. Sanderfoot,* 500 U.S. 291 (1991).)

$5,000 of the lien can be avoided. (11 U.S.C. § 522(f)(3).)

The lien cannot be removed from real estate or from a motor vehicle unless the vehicle is a tool of your trade. Generally, a motor vehicle is not considered a tool of trade unless you use it as an integral part of your business—for example, if you do door-to-door sales or delivery work. It is not considered a tool of trade if you simply use it to get to and from your workplace, even if you have no other means of commuting.

The Bankruptcy Reform Act of 1994 limits lien avoidance on animals, crops and implements, professional books or tools used in a trade to the extent that their value exceeds $5,000. Although the statute is unclear, we interpret it to mean that only the first $5,000 of the lien can be avoided. It is possible, however, that a court will interpret this new section to mean that you cannot avoid a nonpossessory nonpurchase money security interest on any exempt animals, crops, or implements, professional books or tools used in a trade worth if they are worth more than $5,000.

b.   Nonconsensual Liens

A nonconsensual lien (remember—that's a secured debt you didn't agree to) can be avoided only if it meets the two criteria listed below. If you determine that a lien can be avoided, erase the debt from this worksheet and enter it on Worksheet 4, Unsecured Debts.

1. The lien must be a judicial lien, which can be removed from *any* exempt property, including real estate and cars.
2. You must be able to claim the property as exempt.

B.   Unsecured Debts

An unsecured debt is any debt for which you haven't pledged collateral and for which the creditor has not filed a lien against you. If the debt is unsecured, the creditor is not entitled to repossess or seize any of your property if you don't pay.

Most debts are unsecured. Some of the common ones are:

- credit and charge card (Visa, Mastercard, American Express, Discover and the like) purchases and cash advances
- department store credit card purchases, unless the store "retains a security interest" in the items you buy or requires you to sign a security agreement (see Section A.1, above)
- gasoline company credit card purchases

- back rent
- medical bills
- alimony and child support
- student loans
- utility bills
- loans from friends or relatives, unless you signed a promissory note secured by some property you own
- health club dues
- lawyer's and accountants' bills
- church or synagogue dues, and
- union dues.

1. Adding Up Your Unsecured Debts

Use Worksheet 4 to record your unsecured debts. A sample is shown below; a blank tear-out copy is in Appendix 3.

When you total up your debts to figure out if you qualify for Chapter 13 bankruptcy, you don't have to include debts for which you don't yet know the exact amount you owe. An example would be where you are sued by someone who suffered injuries in an auto accident where you were at fault, but the court has not yet decided how much you have to pay.

Nor do you have to include debts that depend upon the occurrence of a future event, which may never occur. An example would be where you cosigned a loan, won't be liable to pay it unless the principal debtor defaults, and the principal debtor is current on the payments. Another example would be where you are sued for breaching a contract; you'll incur a debt for breaching the contract only if you lose the lawsuit.

If your liability for a debt, or the amount of the debt, depends on the outcome of a lawsuit, file your Chapter 13 bankruptcy papers before the case ends (or even begins). If your liability isn't settled, it won't be counted toward the $269,250 unsecured debt limit. Once you file your Chapter 13 bankruptcy papers, the lawsuit is automatically stopped.

⚠️ **LIST ALL DEBTS ON THE BANKRUPTCY FORMS**
If you file for bankruptcy before your liability is determined, you might assume it's okay to leave the debt off you bankruptcy papers. Don't. If you don't list the debt, you won't be able to eliminate it in your bankruptcy case. So be sure to list it—even if the other party has only threatened to sue you—and note that the amount is "not yet determined."

Column 1: Description of debt/name of creditor. List your debts in the appropriate categories. If a debt does not fall into a category—such as a debt to your child care provider or a judicial lien that is undersecured—list it under Other.

Column 2: Total outstanding balance. Enter the total amount you owe on each debt. Find out the total by looking at your most recent bill or calling the lender. If you are uncertain, put your best estimate and a question mark. When you've listed all debts, enter the total for Column 2.

➡️ **DOING SOME WORK NOW WILL SAVE YOU TIME LATER**
Once you figure out the total amount of your unsecured debts, you can skip ahead to Ch. 4. If you want to speed up the process of completing your bankruptcy papers, you can fill out Columns 3 and 4.

Column 3: Regular monthly payment. Enter the amount of your regular monthly payment for each debt or the monthly minimum for your credit and charge (including department store and gasoline company) cards. If there is no monthly minimum payment, leave this column blank.

Column 4: Total amount of arrears. Multiply the amount of your regular or minimum monthly payment by the number of months you are behind. If you are not required to make monthly payments, use the amount from Column 2, the total outstanding balance. Add any late fees, attorney fees and collection costs assessed by the lender. If the lender has declared you to be in default, enter the entire amount. Enter the total in Column 4.

2. Turning Unsecured Debts Into Secured Ones

If your debts are over the unsecured limit, but you're not at the secured limit, you can move some debts from the secured category to the unsecured category. All you have to do is voluntarily give a creditor a security interest in an unsecured debt. You can do this by pledging an item of your property, such as your house or car, as collateral to guarantee repayment of the debt. By making the debt secured, however, you will have to repay it in full in your Chapter 13 case.

WORKSHEET 4: UNSECURED DEBTS

1 Description of debt/ name of creditor	2 Total outstanding balance	3 Regular monthly payment	4 Total amount of arrears
Student loans			
Department of Education	18,140	600	18,140
Unsecured consolidation loans			
Unsecured personal loans			
Swamp Bank	4,000	275	1,110
Medical (doctors', dentists' and hospital) bills			
Lawyers' and accountants' bills			
Credit and charge cards			
American Express	6,841	6,841	6,841
Swamp Bank	9,111	30	180
Discover	4,400	35	210
Department store and gasoline credit cards			
Macy's	3,204	30	180
Chevron	289	—	289
J.C. Penney's	1,517	15	90

WORKSHEET 4: UNSECURED DEBTS (CONTINUED)

1 Description of debt/ name of creditor	2 Total outstanding balance	3 Regular monthly payment	4 Total amount of arrears
Alimony or child support arrears			
Back rent			
Unpaid utility bills (gas, electric, water, phone, cable, garbage)			
Bell Phone Company	737	—	737
Tax debts (no lien recorded or undersecured portion)			
Other			

Total $ __48,239__

If your unsecured debts add up to
more than $250,000, you cannot
file for Chapter 13 bankruptcy.

Calculating Your Disposable Income

When you submit your Chapter 13 repayment plan to the bankruptcy court, you must show that you are going to dedicate all of your "disposable income" to paying your creditors for at least three years. (11 U.S.C. § 1325(b).) For purposes of Chapter 13 bankruptcy, your disposable income is everything you earn, less reasonably necessary expenses for:

- supporting yourself and your dependents, and
- continuing, preserving and operating any business you run.

This chapter shows you how to calculate your monthly income and what the bankruptcy court will consider reasonably necessary expenses. When you file your court papers, your creditors, the bankruptcy trustee and the bankruptcy court will look to see that you are maximizing your income and minimizing your expenses in order to get your disposable income as high as possible. If you are not, your unsecured creditors may object to your Chapter 13 plan, on the ground that you are not making your best effort to repay your debts. (See Ch. 9, *After You File Your Case.*)

A. What You Earn

You bankruptcy papers must include the total amount of your income, and must identify one or more regular sources of income which you will use to pay your debts.

1. Total Up Your Income

The first step in determining your disposable income is to total up your income from all sources. You can use Worksheet 5: Your Total Monthly Income; a tear-out copy is in Appendix 3.

If you're married and filing for bankruptcy jointly, include information for both spouses. If you are married but filing alone, enter information for only you.

Column 1: Source of income. In Part A, list the jobs for which you receive a salary or wages. In Part B, list all self-employment for which you receive income, including farm income and sales commissions. In Part C, list any other sources of income. Here are some examples of other kinds of income.

- **Bonus pay.** List all regular bonuses you receive, such as an annual $500 end-of-year bonus.
- **Dividends and interest.** List all sources of dividends or interest—for example, bank accounts, security deposits or stocks.
- **Alimony or child support.** Enter the type of support you receive for yourself (alimony, spousal support or maintenance) or on behalf of your children (child support).
- **Pension or retirement income.** List the source of any pension, annuity, IRA, Keogh or other retirement payments you receive.
- **Other public assistance.** Enter the types of any public benefits, such as SSI, public assistance, disability payments, veterans' benefits, unemployment compensation, worker's compensation or any other government benefit, which you receive.
- **Other.** Identify any other sources of income, such as a tax refund you received within the past year or anticipate receiving within the next year, or payments you receive from friends or relatives. If, within the past 12 months, you received any one-time lump sum payment (such as the proceeds from an insurance policy or from the sale of a valuable asset), don't list it as income. (You should, however, include it in your bankruptcy papers as an asset.)

Column 2: Amount of each payment. For each source of income you listed in Parts A and B of Column 1, enter the amount you receive each pay period. If you don't receive the same amount each period, average the last 12. Then enter your mandatory deductions for each pay period. Again, enter an average of the last 12 months if these amounts vary. For the income you listed in Part A, you probably need to get out a pay stub to see how much is deducted from your paycheck. Subtract the deductions and enter your net income in the Subtotal blank in Column 2.

In Part C, enter the amount of each payment for each source of income.

Column 3: Period covered by each payment. For each source of income, enter the period covered by each payment—such as weekly, twice monthly (24 times a year), every other week (26 times a year), monthly, quarterly (common for royalties), or annually (common for farm income).

Column 4: Amount per month. Multiply or divide the subtotals (or amounts in Part C) in Column 2 to determine the monthly amount. For example, if you are paid twice a month, multiply the Column 2 amount by two. If you are paid every other week, multiply the amount by 26 (for the annual amount) and divide by 12. (The shortcut is to multiply by 2.167.)

When you are done, total up Column 4. This is your total monthly income.

2. What Income Will Fund the Plan

Although you must include all sources of income when figuring out your monthly disposable income, be aware that you may not be able to use all of these sources of income to fund your Chapter 13 plan. You will probably have no problem if you plan to use salary or wage income to fund your plan. Other types of income, however, may cause a problem if the court thinks they are not reliable enough. And there are special problems using government benefits and some pension payments.

a. Irregular or Fluctuating Income

Here is how a judge may rule if you propose to fund your plan with irregular or fluctuating income:

- **Receipts from a business.** You may have to provide the bankruptcy court with documents showing a history of regular draws that resemble income—such as $750 per week for a year. The court may not let you use receipts from a business to fund your plan if it appears that you simply draw money for personal purposes whenever necessary. Also, because you will need to show that your income is stable, the bankruptcy court may not approve a plan that relies on income from a recently started business.
- **Income from irregular or seasonal work.** If you receive a fairly steady amount of money over the course of a year—even if your work is irregular or seasonal and your pay is not the same from one month to the next —the court will probably approve your Chapter 13 plan. If your primary source of income is completely unpredictable—for example, you work through a temp agency—you may have problems getting your plan approved by the bankruptcy court.
- **Sales and other commissions.** As long as you can show the bankruptcy court that you receive commissions

fairly regularly, you should not have any problem using those commissions to fund your Chapter 13 plan.

- **Rent, lease or license receipts, royalties and note or trust income.** As long as the payments are regular and likely to continue, you should not have any trouble using this income to fund your plan. If you get royalties for a product where sales have been steadily decreasing, the court probably won't approve your plan. Note or trust income, in particular, is often used to fund Chapter 13 plans because it is regular, predictable and likely to continue.
- **Alimony or child support.** Alone, these may not be enough to fund your plan, but they can be a component. If your support is apt to go down any time in the next 36 months—for example, your son is 17 and child support will end when he turns 18—the court will probably not let you use the support to fund your plan or will require that you identify another source of income to make up the difference.
- **Payments from relatives or friends.** Many people are supported by grown children who help out or live at home and pay rent, or receive payments from a non-marital partner or a generous relative. Because there is rarely any legal obligation to make these payments, the difficulty in using this money to fund a Chapter 13 plan is convincing the bankruptcy court that the payments will continue. If you file for bankruptcy without your

WORKSHEET 5: YOUR TOTAL MONTHLY INCOME

1 Source of Income		2 Amount of each payment	3 Period covered by each payment	4 Amount per month
A. Wages or Salary				
Job 1:	Gross pay, including overtime:	$ 1,250	semi-monthly	
Medical Technician	Subtract:			
	Federal taxes	141		
	State taxes	40		
	Social Security (FICA)	96		
	Union dues	60		
	Insurance payments			
	Child support wage withholding			
	Other mandatory deductions (specify):			
	city tax	13		
	Subtotal	$ 900		1,800
Job 2:	Gross pay, including overtime:	$ 2,001	monthly	
P/T Teacher	Subtract:			
	Federal taxes	153		
	State taxes	296		
	Social Security (FICA)	89		
	Union dues			
	Insurance payments			
	Child support wage withholding			
	Other mandatory deductions (specify):			
	city tax	20		
	Subtotal	$ 1,443		1,443
Job 3:	Gross pay, including overtime:	$		
	Subtract:			
	Federal taxes			
	State taxes			
	Social Security (FICA)			
	Union dues			
	Insurance payments			
	Child support wage withholding			
	Other mandatory deductions (specify):			
	Subtotal	$		

WORSHEET 5: YOUR TOTAL MONTHLY INCOME (CONTINUED)

1 Source of Income		2 Amount of each payment	3 Period covered by each payment	4 Amount per month
B. Self-Employment Income				
Job 1:	Pay	$ _____	_____	
_____	Subtract:			
	Federal taxes	_____		
	State taxes	_____		
	Self-employment taxes	_____		
	Other mandatory deductions (specify):			
	_____	_____		
	Subtotal	$ _____		_____
Job 2:	Pay	$ _____	_____	
_____	Subtract:			
	Federal taxes	_____		
	State taxes	_____		
	Self-employment taxes	_____		
	Other mandatory deductions (specify):			
	_____	_____		
	Subtotal	$ _____		_____
C. Other Sources				
Bonuses _Christmas_		600	yearly	50
Dividends and interest _money market_		12	monthly	12
Rent, lease or license income _____		_____	_____	_____
Royalties _____		_____	_____	_____
Note or trust income _____		_____	_____	_____
Alimony or child support you receive _cs_		360	monthly	360
Pension or retirement income _____		_____	_____	_____
Social Security _____		_____	_____	_____
Other public assistance _____		_____	_____	_____
Other (specify): _____		_____	_____	_____
	Total monthly income			$ 3,665

spouse, but your spouse supports you, the bankruptcy court will probably not let you apply the support toward your plan payments.

- **Proceeds from selling property.** Like many people, you may want to fund your Chapter 13 plan by selling property. But if you propose to fund your plan wholly by selling assets, virtually every court will deny confirmation of your plan, although the court will probably let you supplement payments under the plan with the sales proceeds. A rare court will let you fund your plan with the proceeds of the sale of property, but only if you demonstrate the likelihood of the sale (such as a house being aggressively marketed, having an offer on it or the sale is already in escrow), and that it will be for enough money to fund the plan (such as the sale of a house with substantial equity in it). The court may also require you to outline your fallback plan in case a sale does not materialize.
- **Bonuses.** Bonuses will rarely be enough to fund an entire Chapter 13 plan, but the bankruptcy court may require that you make supplemental payments into your plan during the months in which you receive bonuses or vacation pay. Or, you may be able to use this money to make up missed payments on a secured debt ("cure a default") and use your other income to make the regular payments under your plan.
- **Dividends and interest.** This may be another good source of income to cure a default, but will rarely be enough to fund a plan.

b. Pension or Retirement Income

There are two potential limitations on using pension income to fund a Chapter 13 plan. First, bankruptcy courts sometimes order whoever pays you money—your employer, for example—to deduct a certain amount from your check and send it to the bankruptcy trustee. (This is called an income deduction order.) Many pension plans, however, prohibit the administrator from paying proceeds to anyone other than the beneficiary. The bankruptcy court might not let you use your pension payments to fund the plan if the pension plan administrator won't obey an income deduction order.

Second, one court has held that payments from a pension plan that meets the requirements of the federal Employee Retirement Income Security Act (ERISA) cannot be used to fund a Chapter 13 plan, because you have only limited access to the money. (*McLean v. Central States, Southeast & Southwest Areas Pension Fund*, 762 F.2d 1204 (4th Cir. 1985).)

c. Government Benefits

Social Security could present a problem if it's the only source of income for your Chapter 13 plan. The Social Security Act prohibits the Social Security Administration from paying benefits to anyone other than the designated recipient. Therefore, the Social Security Administration will not comply if the bankruptcy court orders it to pay your benefits directly to the court. One court has taken this to mean that Social Security payments do not constitute regular income to fund a Chapter 13 plan. (*In re Buren*, 725 F.2d 1080 (6th Cir. 1984).)

Other government entities that pay you benefits may also refuse to comply with an income deduction order. In addition, if you'll be using disability or workers' compensation benefits, the bankruptcy court will be concerned with the duration of the benefits, especially if you won't be able to go back to work when they end. Similarly, unemployment benefits last only 26 weeks, and you'll have to prove another source of income after they end. You could probably use strike funds to initially fund your plan because once the strike is over, you are likely to go back to work.

B. What You Spend

Your disposable income is your income minus your reasonably necessary expenses. These expenses include what it costs you to:

- support yourself and your dependents, and
- continue, preserve and operate any business you run.

When you file your bankruptcy papers, you will include a list of all your monthly expenses. Your creditors, the bankruptcy trustee and the judge will scrutinize the list. The most common objection raised by creditors is that a debtor's expenses are not reasonably necessary. The court will not be looking to reject your expenses just for the sake of a rejection, but a judge who sees inflated or unreasonable expenses will reject your repayment plan. Rejection of your plan isn't the end of your case. You can submit a modified plan or agree to a modification of your plan during the confirmation hearing (the court hearing at which the judge approves or rejects your plan).

Record your monthly expenditures on Worksheet 6: Your Total Monthly Expenses; a tear-out copy is in Appendix 3. You will use this information when you fill out your bankruptcy forms.

WHAT'S REASONABLE?

When it comes to expenses, what is considered reasonable varies from debtor to debtor, court to court, and even region to region. In general, expenses for luxury items or services (such as a gardener) will not be allowed. If an expense seems particularly high, the court will look to see if you can achieve the same goal by spending less—the court will let you live adequately, not high on the hog. For example, if you are making $550 per month payments on a Cadillac, the court will probably allow $300 per month toward a Chevrolet or other less expensive car, freeing another $250 per month of disposable income.

But some courts *will* allow a seemingly extravagant expense if all other expenses are reasonable. And some might allow an expense that isn't, strictly speaking, necessary, if it furthers a valid goal—such as sending your children to private school or making religious contributions. Probably most judges will let you buy the daily newspaper (courts like the public to be informed) but won't let you keep a ballet or opera subscription. (Don't worry, you can go to an occasional movie.)

HELPFUL RESOURCES

Cost of Living Schedules. The federal government publishes these schedules, which you can find at the public library, for different regions of the country. The schedules can help you figure out if your food and shelter costs are above average for where you live. The trustee will have these schedules; you will have to provide justification if your expenses are way out of line.

Chapter 13 Bankruptcy, by Keith M. Lundin (Wiley Law Publications). This clearly-written book contains several examples of what courts have ruled as reasonable and unreasonable expenses. Chapter 5, Sections 33 through 41, discusses disposable income; Section 36 specifically looks at expenses reasonably necessary for support. This book is written for attorneys, and you will probably have to go to a law library to find it. (Ch. 12, *Help Beyond the Book,* explains how to find a law library you can use.)

Here are some guidelines for completing Worksheet 6.

A. Your residence. If your rent or mortgage payment is unusually high for your area, the court might suggest that you move in order to bring this expense down, if alternate housing is easily available. If you will make your mortgage payment through your Chapter 13 repayment plan because you are behind a few months, don't list your payments here.

If your estimates of maintenance and upkeep are high, you may have to provide the court with documentation for past years' expenses. Obviously, the court will want you to maintain your home's condition, but will want you to do so as inexpensively as is reasonable.

B. Utilities. List your monthly utility expenses. Be sure to take an monthly average of gas, heating fuel and electricity if your bills vary month to month. Some courts might refuse high phone bills—for example, if you call a parent or child in a distant city every day. A court might also reject the expense of cable TV, so this may be a service you'll have to drop. Or the court might let you keep basic cable, but not allow expenses for premium channels.

C. Food. To determine whether or not your figure is reasonable, the court will most likely compare it to the federal cost of living figure for your area. (See "What's Reasonable?," above.) If your expenses are higher than average, be ready to explain them—for example, because a family member needs a special diet. The court is not going to allow much—if anything—for eating out beyond an occasional family dinner at McDonald's.

D. Personal effects. Certainly, the court will let you buy toiletries and drug store items and will even permit a monthly haircut. But the court will probably reject an expense of $75 per month to get your hair done, knowing that many discount places charge about $10.

E. Clothing. You are not expected to go naked or wear only hand-me-downs. You can buy clothes and even pay to have the clothing cleaned. But extravagant or frequent purchases won't be allowed. A court might reject a high amount or suggest that you buy used clothing for your still-growing children. To get an idea of how much you spend now, total up the clothing purchases you have receipts or credit card statements for, or are in your check register.

F. Medical. The court will want you to maintain your medical insurance coverage, so it will allow the expense of medical insurance for you and your dependents. Don't list payments for bills from medical providers and hospitals for

WORKSHEET 6: YOUR TOTAL MONTHLY EXPENSES

1 Expenses	2 Amount per month
A. Your residence	
Rent or mortgage	950
Second mortgage or home equity loan	150
Homeowners' association fee	
Property taxes	50
Homeowners' or renters' insurance	
Maintenance and upkeep	100
B. Utilities	
Telephone	70
Gas, heating fuel, electricity	35
Water and sewer	35
Garbage	40
Cable	20
C. Food	
At home	400
Restaurants	80
D. Personal effects	
Toiletries	50
Drug store items	30
Personal grooming (haircuts)	30
Other	
E. Clothing	
Purchases	40
Laundry/dry cleaning	15
F. Medical	
Medical or health insurance	
Dental insurance	15
Deductibles and copayments	60
Doctor	
Dentist	
Eye doctor	
Medicines/prescriptions	
Hospital	
Therapist	
G. Transportation	
Car payment	208
Gasoline	30
Tolls and parking	30
Auto insurance	100

1 Expenses	2 Amount per month
Maintenance	75
Registration	15
H. Dependents	
Child care	250
Allowances	
Clothes	
Tuition	
School books	
I. Your or your spouse's education	
(Do not include student loan payment)	
Tuition	
Books and fees	
J. Miscellaneous personal expenses	
Entertainment	20
Recreation/hobbies	
Newspapers and magazines	12
Books	
Gifts	10
Memberships	10
Pet supplies/veterinarian	10
K. Charitable contributions	25
L. Insurance	
(Do not include health, home or motor vehicle insurance)	
Disability	
Life	35
Other	
M. Support payments	
Alimony, maintenance or spousal support	
Child support	
Support of other dependents not living at home	
N. Regular business expenses	
O. Other	
(Do not include back income taxes or unsecured	
installment debts, such as student loan,	
personal loan or credit card accounts.	
These debts will be paid through your plan.)	
Total monthly expenses	$ 3,000

services you've already received. The court will probably want you to pay those through your Chapter 13 plan—that is, out of your disposable income. The court might let you include 100% of the bill as part of your monthly expenses if you need ongoing medical care and the provider won't provide it unless you pay your bill in full—if this is your situation, you can include the expense on this worksheet. The court may also reject expenses for mental health therapy and instead suggest that you visit a free or low-cost county mental health facility.

G. Transportation. The court will let you pay a reasonable amount to get to and from work. But if a less expensive alternative exists—for example, taking the bus instead of driving—the court may allow only enough to pay the lesser expense. As a practical matter, such a decision would mean that you wouldn't be allowed to deduct car expenses from your monthly income in determining your disposable income. It does not mean that the court would seize your car keys or prohibit you from driving your car to work. If the court objects completely to you having a car, the court might disallow monthly lease or purchase payments. This is highly unlikely, although if your payments are very high, the court might allow only a portion and suggest that you trade the car in for a less expensive model. The court will also allow expenses for vehicle insurance, maintenance and registration, if the court thinks it's necessary for you to have a car.

H. Dependents. You are permitted to claim expenses for the support of your dependents, including your children. These expenses include child care, clothes, books, an occasional movie and the like. The court may reject allowances for your children unless they're just some pocket change. Also, courts are reluctant to let you send your children to private school if it means your creditors won't be paid. You may be able to convince the court of the need for private school, however, if the public schools in your area are quite bad or dangerous, you want your children to receive religious education or your child has special educational needs. If your child is in college, a court may not let you deduct tuition at an expensive private university, but may let you make the payments for a state college.

I. Your or your spouse's education. If either you or your spouse is currently in school, list your expenses here. The court may reject a portion of these expenses if you or your spouse could be working and increasing the family's income.

J. Miscellaneous personal expenses. Often, these are the expenses that your creditors, the trustee and the court scrutinize the most. Some courts do not think you should be allowed any expenses for entertainment, to participate in

any hobbies that cost money or to buy gifts for friends or relatives. As with all expenses, the key to getting these expenses approved is their reasonableness. You can't include in your budget money to see Broadway shows, maintain a sailing hobby, keep a subscription to an expensive journal or renew your country club membership. You can probably budget to go out to or rent an occasional movie or go bowling, get your local newspaper, keep your membership at the local Y and take care of your pet.

K. Charitable contributions. This is another area of great controversy. Most courts reject all or most donations for nonreligious charities. A court will usually let you maintain your spiritual life, but only if it doesn't cost too much. Most courts, for example, will reject a request to tithe 10% of your income to a religious institution. A court might allow tithing, however, if the court believes it will sustain you and is necessary for you to make the payments under your Chapter 13 plan.

L. Insurance. The court generally will let you maintain your disability or life insurance, especially if your health is compromised and you may need the disability insurance, or if you have young children or other dependents who would need the life insurance money if you died. If you have a whole life insurance policy, you may be told to convert into a term policy, which has much lower premiums.

M. Support payments. You must continue making court-ordered child support and alimony payments during your Chapter 13 bankruptcy case; the court will not reject these payments. If you voluntarily support others, however, the court will not allow any unreasonable expenses for people you are not obligated to support. The court may allow expenses to support an elderly parent, but probably won't let you deduct expenses for a roommate, nonmarital partner, nonmarital partner's child or stepchild.

N. Regular business expenses. If you own or run a business, include your monthly necessary business expenses. You will have to prepare a separate statement of income and expenses for the operation of your business and attach it to your bankruptcy papers when you file them. This book doesn't tell you how to do that; however, anyone with a financial background, such as a banker, accountant, bookkeeper or tax preparer, can help you draft one.

O. Other. List any additional expenses here, other than payments you are making on back income taxes and on unsecured installment debts such as student loans, credit card accounts and personal loans. Don't include back taxes and unsecured installment debts because these debts are paid out of your disposable income through your Chapter 13 plan. Be ready to justify to the court the reasonableness of any expenses you do list.

WORKSHEET 7: YOUR DISPOSABLE INCOME

1. **Total Monthly Income** (from Worksheet 5) $ _____3,665_____

2. subtract **Total Monthly Expenses** (from Worksheet 6)   − _____3,000_____

3. **Total Monthly Disposable Income** $ _____665_____

Total Amount Proposed to Pay Unsecured Creditors

typical Chapter 13 repayment plan   x   36 months   = $ _____23,940_____

extended Chapter 13 repayment plan   x   60 months   = $ _____39,900_____

C. What's Left—Your Disposable Income

To repeat: your disposable income is the money you pay into your Chapter 13 plan.

To calculate your disposable income, use Worksheet 7, above. Begin with the Total Monthly Income figure at the bottom of Worksheet 5. Subtract from it the Total Monthly Expenses figure in the bottom of Worksheet 6. The difference is your total monthly disposable income—the amount you have to fund your Chapter 13 plan.

Next, multiply your total monthly disposable income by 36, the number of months in a typical Chapter 13 plan. This will give you the total amount you will propose to pay your creditors. This amount must equal or exceed the amount you calculated in Worksheet 1 in Ch. 2, *An Overview of Chapter 13 Bankruptcy*, Section B. If it doesn't, the bankruptcy court will not approve your plan. You may have to ask the court to extend your plan up to 60 months (the maximum allowed) or cut back your expenses in order to increase your disposable income. ■

CHAPTER

5   Calculating the Value of Your Nonexempt Property

➡ CONVERTING FROM CHAPTER 7 BANKRUPTCY

If you originally filed for Chapter 7 bankruptcy and are now converting your case to Chapter 13 bankruptcy, you need only to file a Chapter 13 repayment plan. Skip ahead to Ch. 7, *Writing Your Chapter 13 Bankruptcy Plan.*

In bankruptcy, the property you own falls into one of two categories: exempt or nonexempt. If you were to file for Chapter 7 bankruptcy, exempt property is what you would get to keep—under no circumstances could the bankruptcy trustee take it away from you. Nonexempt property, on the other hand, would be what the bankruptcy trustee could take and sell to pay off your unsecured creditors.

When you file for Chapter 13 bankruptcy, you do not give up any property to the bankruptcy trustee. But the difference between exempt and nonexempt property is still important, for two reasons:

1. When you file for Chapter 13 bankruptcy, you must list all your property and specify precisely which property you claim as exempt.

2. In Chapter 13 bankruptcy, you must pay your unsecured creditors at least as much as they would have gotten if you had filed for Chapter 7 bankruptcy. This means that you must figure out the current value of your nonexempt property, and make sure that your repayment plan provides that your unsecured creditors will receive at least that amount. (11 U.S.C. § 1325(a)(4).)

Using Worksheet 8 in this chapter, you can create an inventory of your property and total up the nonexempt portion.

A. Identifying Your Property

The property you own on the day you file for bankruptcy is called your "bankruptcy estate." With a very few exceptions (discussed below), property you acquire after you file for bankruptcy isn't included in your bankruptcy estate.

⚠ IT'S NOT ALWAYS OBVIOUS WHAT YOU OWN

When you file for bankruptcy, special rules determine what is considered yours and what you must report to the bankruptcy court. For example, property you've recently given away may still be considered yours. And not everything you might think you own is part of your bankruptcy estate—for example, a pension you are entitled to receive at retirement, but over which you have no or limited control now, is not part of your bankruptcy estate.

Before you start filling in Worksheet 8: Your Exempt and Nonexempt Property, read this section to make sure you understand what's yours, legally. A checklist of common types of property preceeds the worksheet; it may help you.

1. Property You Own and Possess

When you sit down to write out a list of everything you own, probably what comes to mind first is what you have in your possession—for example, a car, real estate, clothing, books, TV, stereo system, furniture, tools, boat, artworks or stock certificates. All these things are included in your bankruptcy estate.

Property you have control of but which belongs to someone else is not part of your bankruptcy estate, because you don't have the right to sell it or give it away.

EXAMPLE 1: A parent establishes a trust for her child and names you as trustee to manage the money in the trust until the child's 18th birthday. You possess and control the money, but it's solely for the child's benefit and cannot be used for your own purposes. It isn't part of your bankruptcy estate.

EXAMPLE 2: Your sister has gone to Zimbabwe for an indefinite period and has loaned you her TV while she's gone. Although you might have use of the set for years to come, you don't own it. It isn't part of your bankruptcy estate.

2. Property You Own but Don't Possess

You can own something even if you don't have physical possession of it. For instance, you may own a share of a vacation cabin in the mountains, but never go there yourself. Or you may own furniture or a car that someone else is using. Other examples include a deposit held by a stockbroker, a security deposit held by your landlord or a utility company, or a distant business you've invested money in.

3. Property You Are Entitled to Receive

Property that you have a legal right to receive but haven't yet received when you file for bankruptcy is included in your bankruptcy estate. The most common examples are:

- wages you have earned but have not yet been paid, and
- a tax refund that is legally due you but which you haven't yet received.

Here are some other examples:

- Vacation or termination pay you earned before filing for bankruptcy.
- Property you've inherited, but not yet received, from someone who has died. (If you're a beneficiary in the will or revocable trust of someone who is still alive, you're not yet entitled to receive the property, because the will or trust document could be changed.)
- Proceeds of an insurance policy, if the death, injury or other event that gives rise to payment has occurred. For example, if you were the beneficiary of your father's life insurance policy, and your father has died but you haven't received your money yet, the amount you're entitled to is part of your bankruptcy estate.
- Compensation you're legally entitled to receive for an injury, even if the amount hasn't yet been determined. If you have a valid claim against someone who injured you, you have a legal right to be compensated, even though the amount you're entitled to hasn't been determined in a lawsuit or agreement. Don't try to put an amount in your worksheet or bankruptcy papers; instead, just list your claim. The trustee may pursue the case on your behalf if the trustee thinks it will result in money for your creditors.
- Money owed you for goods or services you've provided (accounts receivable). Even if you're pretty certain you won't be paid, that money is considered part of your bankruptcy estate, and you must list the amount you are owed.
- Income generated by property in your bankruptcy estate before you filed for bankruptcy, but which you haven't received. This includes, for example, rent from commercial or residential real estate, royalties from copyrights or patents, and dividends earned on stocks.

ERISA-QUALIFIED PENSIONS

If you own a pension that is covered by the federal law ERISA (Employee Retirement Income Security Act), it is not considered part of your bankruptcy estate. The reason is somewhat complex, involving both ERISA law and bankruptcy law. (*Patterson v. Shumate*, 112 S.Ct. 2242 (1992).) Essentially, the pension is not considered property of the estate because you have limited access to the money. To find out whether or not your pension is covered by ERISA, call the benefits coordinator on your job or the pension plan administrator.

4. Property You've Recently Given Away

Property given away or repossessed shortly before you file for bankruptcy may still be considered part of your bankruptcy estate, and the trustee has legal authority to take it back.

On this worksheet, list the following:

- property you gave away during the year before you will file for bankruptcy
- property you gave away and didn't receive a reasonable amount for—giving something away or selling it for less than it's worth is the same thing for bankruptcy purposes
- property you sold and the result left you insolvent or greatly pushed you towards insolvency
- payments or transfers of property worth more than $600 to a creditor made within 90 days before you will file for bankruptcy, and

• payments or transfers of property worth more than $600 to a creditor made within the year before you will file for bankruptcy if the creditor was close to you—for example, a friend, relative, corporation owned by you or business partner.

⚠️ **DON'T UNLOAD PROPERTY**
Because you must pay your creditors at least the value of your nonexempt property, you may be tempted to give away some of that property to friends or relatives before you file, and then not list the items in your bankruptcy papers. This is both dishonest and foolhardy. If the bankruptcy court finds out, it will dismiss your case and probably bar you from filing for several years.

5. Property You Own With Your Spouse (If You Are Filing Alone)

If you're married but filing alone, your state's law determines which property is part of your bankruptcy estate and which isn't.

a. Community Property States

These nine states use a "community property" system of marital property ownership:

Arizona	Louisiana	Texas
California	Nevada	Washington
Idaho	New Mexico	Wisconsin

In community property states, as a general rule, all property either spouse earns during the marriage is community property, owned jointly by both spouses. Gifts and inheritances received specifically by one spouse, and property owned by one spouse before the marriage or acquired after permanent separation, are not community property.

If you're married and file for bankruptcy, all the community property you and your spouse own is considered part of *your* bankruptcy estate, even if your spouse doesn't file. (11 U.S.C. § 541(a)(2).) The only exception is that, in a few states, community property businesses that are solely managed by the non-filing spouse are not included in the filing spouse's bankruptcy estate.

EXAMPLE: Paul and Sonya live in Arizona, a community property state. They own a house and a savings account as community property. Under Arizona law, both Paul and Sonya have equal management responsibilities over their community property. If Paul files for bankruptcy, both the bank account and house are in Paul's bankruptcy estate, even though Sonya hasn't filed.

If you file alone, your separate property is also part of your bankruptcy estate. Your spouse's separate property isn't.

EXAMPLE: Paul owns an airplane as his separate property (he owned it before he married Sonya), and Sonya came to the marriage owning a grand piano. Because only Paul is filing for bankruptcy, Paul's airplane is part of his bankruptcy estate, but Sonya's piano isn't.

If you are not sure what is community property and what isn't, you may need to do some research into your state's property laws. (See Ch. 12, *Help Beyond the Book*, for tips on doing legal research.)

b. Noncommunity Property States

When only one spouse files for bankruptcy in a non-community property state (all states other than the nine listed in Subsection a, above), the bankruptcy estate includes:
• that spouse's separate property, and
• half of the couple's jointly owned property.
The general rules of property ownership in these states are as follows:
• Property that has only one spouse's name on a title certificate (car, house, stocks), even if bought with joint funds, belongs to that spouse separately.
• Property that was purchased, received as a gift or inherited jointly for the use of both spouses is jointly owned, unless a title slip has only one spouse's name on it (which means it belongs to that spouse separately, even if both spouses use it).
• Property that one spouse buys with separate funds or receives as a gift or inheritance for that spouse's separate use is that spouse's separate property (again, unless a title certificate shows differently).

B. Listing Your Exempt and Nonexempt Property

When you've completed Column 1 of Worksheet 8, you will have a complete inventory of your exempt and nonexempt property. (Ignore the other columns for now. Instructions for completing them are in Section C, below.)

List everything you own worth $50 or more. Lump together low valued items, such as kitchen utensils. The checklist preceeding the sample worksheet should help you think of items. A blank tear-out copy of the worksheet is in Appendix 3.

Worksheet 8 Checklist

Column 1: Your Property

1. Real Estate
- ☐ Residence
- ☐ Condominium or co-op apartment
- ☐ Mobile home
- ☐ Mobile home park space
- ☐ Rental property
- ☐ Vacation home or cabin
- ☐ Business property
- ☐ Undeveloped land
- ☐ Farmland
- ☐ Boat/marina dock space
- ☐ Burial site
- ☐ Airplane hangar

2. Cash on hand
- ☐ In your home
- ☐ In your wallet
- ☐ Under your mattress

3. Deposits of money
- ☐ Bank account
- ☐ Brokerage account (with stockbroker)
- ☐ Certificates of deposit (CDs)
- ☐ Credit union deposit
- ☐ Escrow account
- ☐ Money market account
- ☐ Money in a safe deposit box
- ☐ Savings and loan deposit

4. Security deposits
- ☐ Electric
- ☐ Gas
- ☐ Heating oil
- ☐ Prepaid rent
- ☐ Security deposit on rental unit
- ☐ Rented furniture or equipment
- ☐ Telephone
- ☐ Water

5. Household goods, supplies and furnishings
- ☐ Antiques
- ☐ Appliances
- ☐ Carpentry tools
- ☐ China and crystal
- ☐ Clocks
- ☐ Dishes
- ☐ Food (total value)
- ☐ Furniture
- ☐ Gardening tools
- ☐ Home computer (for personal use)
- ☐ Lamps
- ☐ Lawn mower or tractor
- ☐ Microwave oven
- ☐ Radios
- ☐ Rugs
- ☐ Sewing machine
- ☐ Silverware and utensils
- ☐ Small appliances
- ☐ Snow blower
- ☐ Stereo system
- ☐ Telephones and answering machines
- ☐ Televisions
- ☐ Vacuum cleaner
- ☐ Video equipment (VCR, Camcorder)

6. Books, pictures and other art objects, stamp, coin and other collections
- ☐ Art prints
- ☐ Bibles
- ☐ Books
- ☐ Coins
- ☐ Collectibles (such as political buttons, baseball cards)
- ☐ Compact disks, records and tapes
- ☐ Family portraits
- ☐ Figurines
- ☐ Original art works
- ☐ Photographs
- ☐ Stamps
- ☐ Videotapes

7. Apparel
- ☐ Clothing
- ☐ Furs

8. Jewelry
- ☐ Engagement and wedding ring
- ☐ Gems
- ☐ Precious metals
- ☐ Watches

9. Firearms, sports equipment and other hobby equipment
- ☐ Board games
- ☐ Bicycles
- ☐ Camera equipment
- ☐ Electronic musical equipment
- ☐ Exercise machine
- ☐ Fishing gear
- ☐ Guns (rifles, pistols, shotguns, muskets)
- ☐ Model or remote cars or planes
- ☐ Musical instruments
- ☐ Scuba diving equipment
- ☐ Ski equipment
- ☐ Other sports equipment
- ☐ Other weapons (swords and knives)

10. Interests in insurance policies
- ☐ Credit insurance
- ☐ Disability insurance
- ☐ Health insurance
- ☐ Homeowner's or renter's insurance
- ☐ Term life insurance
- ☐ Whole or universal life insurance

11. Annuities

12. Pension or profit-sharing plans
- ☐ IRA
- ☐ Keogh
- ☐ Pension or retirement plan
- ☐ 401(k) account

13. Stocks and interests in incorporated and unincorporated companies

14. Interests in partnerships
- ☐ Limited partnership interest
- ☐ General partnership interest

15. Government and corporate bonds and other investment instruments
- ☐ Corporate bonds
- ☐ Deeds of trust
- ☐ Mortgages you own
- ☐ Municipal bonds
- ☐ Promissory notes
- ☐ U.S. savings bonds

16. Accounts receivable
- ☐ Accounts receivable from business
- ☐ Commissions already earned

17. Family support
- ☐ Alimony (spousal support, maintenance) due under court order
- ☐ Child support payments due under court order
- ☐ Payments due under divorce property settlement

18. Other debts owed you where the amount owed is known and definite
- ☐ Disability benefits due
- ☐ Disability insurance due
- ☐ Judgments obtained against third parties you haven't yet collected
- ☐ Sick pay
- ☐ Social Security benefits due
- ☐ Tax refund due under returns already filed
- ☐ Vacation pay earned
- ☐ Wages due
- ☐ Worker's compensation due

19. Powers exercisable for your benefit other than those listed under real estate
- ☐ Right to receive, at some future time, cash, stock or other personal property placed in an irrevocable trust
- ☐ Current payments of interest or principal from a trust
- ☐ General power of appointment over personal property

20. Interests due to another person's death
- ☐ Property you are entitled to receive as a beneficiary of a living trust, if the trustor has died
- ☐ Expected proceeds from a life insurance policy if the insured has died
- ☐ Inheritance from an existing estate in probate (the owner has died and the court is overseeing the distribution of the property) even if the final amount is not yet known

- ☐ Inheritance under a will that is contingent upon one or more events occurring, but only if the will writer has died

21. All other contingent claims and claims where the amount owed you is not known, including tax refunds, counterclaims and rights to setoff claims (claims you think you have against a person, government or corporation, but haven't yet sued on—remember, you do not need to list the amount of your claim now; just list the claim itself)
- ☐ Claims against a corporation, government entity or individual
- ☐ Potential tax refund, if return not yet filed

22. Patents, copyrights and other intellectual property
- ☐ Copyrights
- ☐ Patents
- ☐ Trade secrets
- ☐ Trademarks
- ☐ Tradenames

23. Licenses, franchises and other general intangibles
- ☐ Building permits
- ☐ Cooperative association holdings
- ☐ Exclusive licenses
- ☐ Liquor licenses
- ☐ Nonexclusive licenses
- ☐ Patent licenses
- ☐ Professional licenses

24. Automobiles and other vehicles
- ☐ Car
- ☐ Mini-bike or motor scooter
- ☐ Mobile or motor home if on wheels
- ☐ Motorcycle
- ☐ Recreational vehicle (RV)
- ☐ Trailer
- ☐ Truck
- ☐ Van

25. Boats, motors and accessories
- ☐ Boat (canoe, kayak, rowboat, shell, sailboat, pontoon boat, yacht, etc.)

- ☐ Boat radar, radio or telephone
- ☐ Outboard motor

26. Aircraft and accessories
- ☐ Aircraft radar, radio or other accessories
- ☐ Aircraft

27. Office equipment, furnishings and supplies
- ☐ Art work in your office
- ☐ Computers, software, modems, printers (for business use)
- ☐ Copier
- ☐ Fax machine
- ☐ Furniture
- ☐ Rugs
- ☐ Supplies
- ☐ Telephones
- ☐ Typewriters

28. Machinery, fixtures, equipment and supplies used in business
- ☐ Military uniforms and accouterments
- ☐ Tools of your trade

29. Business inventory

30. Livestock, poultry and other animals
- ☐ Birds
- ☐ Cats
- ☐ Dogs
- ☐ Fish and aquarium equipment
- ☐ Horses
- ☐ Other pets
- ☐ Livestock and poultry

31. Crops—growing or harvested

32. Farming equipment and implements

33. Farm supplies, chemicals and feed

34. Other personal property of any kind
- ☐ Church pew
- ☐ Health aids (for example, wheelchair, crutches)
- ☐ Portable spa or hot tub
- ☐ Season tickets
- ☐ Country club or golf club membership

WORKSHEET 8: YOUR EXEMPT AND NONEXEMPT PROPERTY

1 Your property	2 Value of property (actual dollar or garage sale value)	3 Your ownership share (%, $)	4 Amount of liens	5 Amount of your equity	6 Exempt? If not, enter non- exempt amount
1. Real estate					
House	390,000	100%, 390,000	475,000	0	0
2. Cash on hand					
(state source, such as wages, public benefits, etc.)					
Wages	120	100%, 120	0	120	120
3. Deposits of money					
(state source, such as wages, public benefits, etc.)					
Checking account—wages	3,000	100%, 3,000	0	3,000	3,000
4. Security deposits					
Phone company	75	100%, 75	0	75	75
5. Household goods, supplies and furnishings					
Major appliances	2,500	100%, 2,500	0	2,500	0
Furniture	1,000	100%, 1,000	0	1,000	800
Kitchen goods, bedding	500	100%, 500	0	500	500
6. Books, pictures, art objects; stamp, coin and other collections					
Books	2,250	100%, 2,250	0	2,250	750
Photos	20	100%, 20	0	20	0

WORSHEET 8: YOUR EXEMPT AND NONEXEMPT PROPERTY (CONTINUED)

1 Your property	2 Value of property (actual dollar or garage sale value)	3 Your ownership share (%, $)		4 Amount of liens	5 Amount of your equity	6 Exempt? If not, enter non- exempt amount
7. Apparel						
Clothing	1,500	100%,	1,500	0	1,500	0
8. Jewelry						
Diamond brooch (antique)	3,000	100%,	3,000	0	3,000	3,000
Wedding/engagement rings	1,000	100%,	1,000	0	1,000	0
9. Firearms, sports equipment and other hobby equipment						
Skis	1,500	100%,	1,500	0	1,500	1,500
10. Interests in insurance policies						
Life insurance (cash value)	4,331	100%,	4,331	4,000	331	331
11. Annuities						
Annuity contract	8,007	100%,	8,007	0	8,007	0
12. Pension or profit-sharing plans (do not include ERISA-qualified pensions; see Chapter 5, Section A.3)						
13. Stocks and interests in incorporated and unincorporated companies						

WORKSHEET 8: YOUR EXEMPT AND NONEXEMPT PROPERTY (CONTINUED)

1 Your property	2 Value of property (actual dollar or garage sale value)	3 Your ownership share (%, $)	4 Amount of liens	5 Amount of your equity	6 Exempt? If not, enter non-exempt amount
14. Interests in partnerships					
15. Government and corporate bonds and other investment instruments					
Seattle city bond	500	100%, 500	0	500	500
16. Accounts receivable					
17. Family support					
18. Other debts owed you where the amount owed is known and definite					
Judgment against former landlord for security deposit	600	100%, 600	0	600	600
19. Powers exercisable for your benefit other than those listed under real estate					
20. Interests due to another person's death					

WORKSHEET 8: YOUR EXEMPT AND NONEXEMPT PROPERTY (CONTINUED)

1 Your property	2 Value of property (actual dollar or garage sale value)	3 Your ownership share (%, $)	4 Amount of liens	5 Amount of your equity	6 Exempt? If not, enter non- exempt amount
21. All other contingent claims and claims where the amount owed you is not known					
22. Patents, copyrights and other intellectual property					
23. Licenses, franchises and other general intangibles					
24. Automobiles and other vehicles					
1996 Saturn	11,700	100%, 11,700	9,500	2,200	0
1965 Mustang	20,000	25%, 5,000	0	1,000	4,700
25. Boats, motors and accessories					
26. Aircraft and accessories					
27. Office equipment, furnishings and supplies					
28. Machinery, fixtures, equipment and supplies used in business					

WORKSHEET 8: YOUR EXEMPT AND NONEXEMPT PROPERTY (CONTINUED)

1 Your property	2 Value of property (actual dollar or garage sale value)	3 Your ownership share (%, $)	4 Amount of liens	5 Amount of your equity	6 Exempt? If not, enter non- exempt amount
29. Business inventory					
30. Livestock, poultry and other animals					
Dog	300	100%, 300	0	300	300
31. Crops					
32. Farming equipment and implements					
33. Farm supplies, chemicals and feed					
34. Other personal property					
Mariners Season Tickets	1,800	50%, 900	0	900	900

Subtotal	17,076
Wild Card Exemption	– 1,000
Total Value of Nonexempt Property	16,076

This is the minimum amount you will have to pay your
unsecured creditors through your Chapter 13 plan.

![married icon] **IF YOU'RE MARRIED AND FILING JOINTLY**
Enter all property owned by you or your spouse, and indicate (in parentheses next ot the listed item) whether the property is owned by husband (H), wife (W) or jointly (J). If you are married and filing alone, read Section A.5, above, to figure out which property to include on the worksheet.

For cash on hand and deposits of money, state the source of each, such as wages or salary, public benefits, insurance policy proceeds or the proceeds from the sale of an item of property. You may be able to exempt a portion of that money if you can show it came from an exempt source, such as public benefits.

C. Determining the Value of Your Nonexempt Property

Remember that when you file for Chapter 13 bankruptcy, you must pay your unsecured creditors at least as much as they would have gotten if you had filed for Chapter 7 bankruptcy—that is, the amount your nonexempt property is worth. This means that before you can propose a repayment plan, you must figure out the current value of your nonexempt property. Completing Columns 2-6 of Worksheet 8 will help you make that determination.

1. Value of Your Property (Column 2)

In Column 2, enter a value for each item of property listed in Column 1. Estimate if you don't know the exact amount. As long as your estimates are reasonable, no one—not the bankruptcy judge, the bankruptcy trustee or your

creditors—is likely to object. Trustees have years of experience and a pretty good sense of what things are worth. On your bankruptcy papers, you can briefly explain any uncertainties.

If you own an item jointly with someone who is not filing for bankruptcy with you (such as a nonmarital partner, parent, child, sibling or nonfiling spouse), put the value of the entire asset, not just your share, here. In Column 3 you will enter your share. Also, if you still owe money on an item of property, put the entire value here. In Column 4 you'll list how much you still owe.

FLUCTUATING VALUES

The court will want to know the value of your property as of the date you file your bankruptcy papers. But the value of some property changes over time. Depending on the economy and the type of property, the value can fluctuate a lot, even in a short period of time. If you plan to file your papers within a few weeks, don't worry about changes in value. If you don't file your papers for several months, however, you probably should review your figures for any changes.

Here are some suggestions for valuing specific items:
- **Real estate.** For purposes of the worksheet, use your best estimate. When it comes time to transfer this information to your bankruptcy papers, you may have to do some work to determine a more precise figure. With a house, for example, you will need an estimate of its market value from a local real estate agent or appraiser. If you own another type of real estate—such as land used to grow crops—you will have to put the amount it would bring in at a forced sale. As a general rule, your estimate must be close to real market conditions to stand up in court.
- **Cars.** Start with the low *Kelly Blue Book* price. (You can find this book at the public library or online at www.kbb.com.) If the car needs substantial repairs, reduce the value by the amount they would cost. If the car's worth is below the *Blue Book* value, be prepared to show why. (A letter from a mechanic should be enough.)
- **Older goods.** Estimate their market value—that is, what you could sell the items for at a garage sale or through a classified ad. Want ads in a local flea market or penny-saver newspaper are a good place to look for

prices. If the item isn't listed, begin with the price you paid and then deduct about 20% for each year you've owned the item. For example, if you bought a camera for $400 three years ago, subtract $80 for the first year (down to $320), $64 for the second year (down to $256) and $51 for the third year (down to $205).

- **Insurance.** For unmatured whole and universal life insurance policies, put the accrued loan value; call your insurance agent for this figure. Don't put the amount of benefits the policy will pay, unless you're the beneficiary of an insurance policy and the insured person has died. Other kinds of insurance—term life, disability, renter's, homeowner's, etc.—have a loan value of zero.
- **Stocks and bonds.** If you have a mutual fund or brokerage account, use the value from your latest statement. You can look up a specific stock's current value in a newspaper business section. If you can't find the listing, call your broker and ask. If the stock isn't traded publicly, you will have to ask an officer of the corporation for the value assigned at the most recent shareholder meeting.
- **Jewelry, antiques and other collectibles.** Any valuable jewelry or collection should be appraised before you file your bankruptcy papers. For now, if you think you can give a fairly accurate estimate, put it down.

2. Your Ownership Share (Column 3)

In Column 3, enter two amounts:
- the percentage of your ownership interest in the property listed in Column 1, and
- the dollar value of your ownership interest in the property listed in Column 1.

EXAMPLE: You and your brother jointly bought a music synthesizer worth $10,000. Your ownership share is one-half, worth $5,000. List both the percentage (50%) and the dollar amount ($5,000) in Column 3.

IF YOU'RE FILING JOINTLY WITH YOUR SPOUSE If you're filing jointly with your spouse or if you're filing alone and live in a community property state, put your combined share here. If you live in a non-community property state and are filing alone, enter only your share here.

3. Amount of Liens (Column 4)

In Column 4, put the total amount of all legal claims (liens) against the property. Even if you own only part of the property, enter the full amount of the liens.

EXAMPLE: You own a house. You owe $63,000 on your first mortgage, the IRS has recorded a lien for a $17,000 tax debt, and a hospital sued you, got a judgment and recorded a lien for an $11,000 bill you owe. The total amount of all liens on your house is $91,000.

The amount of the liens may exceed the property's value. That means that there is no nonexempt value to include in the calculation of how much you must pay your unsecured creditors.

A complete list of liens—and information on matching a lien to the property it secures—is in Worksheets 2 and 3 in Ch. 3, *Adding Up Your Secured and Unsecured Debts*, Section A.

4. Amount of Your Equity (Column 5)

Your equity is the amount you would get to keep if you sold the property.

If you own the property alone (or if you and your spouse own it and are filing jointly), calculate your equity by subtracting the amount in Column 4 from the property's total value (Column 2). Put this amount in Column 5. If you get a negative number, enter "0."

EXAMPLE: The liens on your house total $91,000. Your house is worth $105,000. The amount of your equity is $14,000.

If you co-own the property with someone other than your spouse with whom you're filing for bankruptcy, calculating your equity is a little more complex. Only your property—not a co-owner's—is used to calculate how much you must pay your unsecured creditors in bankruptcy.

1. **All liens on the property are from jointly-incurred debts.** Subtract the amount of the liens from the total value of the property, and multiply the result by your ownership share.
2. **All liens on the property are from debts you incurred alone.** Subtract the amount of the liens from the total value of the property.
3. **The property has liens from both jointly- and solely-incurred debts.** Subtract the amount of the jointly-incurred liens from the total value of the property, and multiply the result by your ownership share. Then subtract the amount of the solely-incurred liens.

EXAMPLE: You co-own your $220,000 house with your nonmarital partner. You and your partner owe your mortgage lender $160,000. In addition, the IRS has filed a Notice of Federal Tax Lien against your house for a tax bill of $25,000 owed by you alone. You figure the amount of your equity as follows:

- Subtract the $160,000 joint mortgage lien from the $220,000 value, leaving $60,000. Multiply by your ownership share, 50%. The result is $30,000.
- Subtract the $25,000 IRS lien owed solely by you from the $30,000. Your equity in the house is $5,000, which is what you list in Column 5.

5.   Is the Property Exempt? (Column 6)

In Chapter 13 bankruptcy, you don't have to turn over any property to the bankruptcy trustee, but you need to tell the court what property you think is legally exempt. That's because the payments you make in Chapter 13 bankruptcy must, at a minimum, be equal to the value of your nonexempt property.

a.   An Overview of Exemptions

Each state has its own list of what items of property are exempt in bankruptcy. Many states exempt, for instance, all health aids, ordinary household furniture and clothing.

Other kinds of property are exempt up to a limit. For instance, cars are often exempt up to a certain amount—usually between $1,200 and $2,500. An exemption limit means that any equity above the limit is considered nonexempt. So if your car is worth $3,500 and your state's motor vehicle exemption is $1,200, you can claim only $1,200 of the equity as exempt. The other $2,300 is part of the nonexempt total—the minimum amount your unsecured creditors must receive in your Chapter 13 case.

b.   Determining Which of Your Property Is Exempt

To determine which of your property is exempt, carefully follow the steps below.

Keep in mind that the more property that is exempt, the less you will have to pay your creditors. As you go through the lists of exempt property, give yourself the benefit of the doubt. If it appears that a particular exemption covers all or part of a property item, claim it. If the trustee challenges you and asks the court to rule on the matter, you can decide then whether or not to fight.

DOUBLE YOUR EXEMPTIONS IF YOU'RE MARRIED AND STATE LAW ALLOWS IT

If you are married and filing jointly, you can double the amount of all exemptions unless your state expressly prohibits it. Look in your state's listing in Appendix 1; if it doesn't say doubling is prohibited, go ahead and double.

Step 1:   Choose an exemption system.

If you live in one of the states listed below, you must choose between two sets of exemptions. If your state isn't listed, skip to Step 2.

Arkansas	Michigan	Rhode Island
California	Minnesota	South Carolina
Connecticut	New Hampshire	Texas
District of Columbia	New Jersey	Vermont
Hawaii	New Mexico	Washington
Massachusetts	Pennsylvania	Wisconsin

In all of these states (except California), you must choose between your state's exemptions and a list of federal bankruptcy exemptions. You can't mix and match, however—if you pick your state's exemption system, you may use only its exemptions, and the same goes if you pick the federal bankruptcy system. If you and your spouse jointly file for bankruptcy, both of you must select the same system.

SPECIAL RULES FOR CALIFORNIANS

Californians must choose between two different systems enacted by the state, not a state system and the federal system. As you read the discussion below, substitute "California System 1" for "your state exemptions" and "California System 2" for "the federal exemptions."

Look in Appendix 1 for:
- your state's exemptions plus the federal *non-bankruptcy* exemptions—these are mostly federal pension benefits which all debtors who use state exemptions are entitled to select from (they are at the very end of Appendix 1), and
- the federal bankruptcy exemptions list (it appears after all the state lists but before the federal *non-bankruptcy* exemptions).

Compare the federal bankruptcy exemptions list to your state's list plus the federal *non-bankruptcy* exemptions to see how each treats valuable items, such as your home and car.

A FEDERAL SYSTEM ADVANTAGE

Keep in mind that unlike some state exemption systems, the federal bankruptcy exemptions can be doubled by a married couple filing together.

- **Your home.** If the equity in your home is your major asset, your choice may be dictated by the "homestead" exemption alone. Compare your state's homestead exemption to the $16,150 federal exemption. In several states (Arkansas, California System 1, Connecticut, Hawaii, Massachusetts, Minnesota, New Mexico, Texas, Vermont, Washington and Wisconsin), the homestead exemption is $20,000 or more, so choosing your state exemptions will keep more of your property exempt. In California System 2, the District of Columbia, Michigan, New Jersey, Pennsylvania, Rhode Island and South Carolina, the state homestead exemption is $16,150 or less, and you may be able to designate more of your property exempt by selecting the federal (or California System 1) exemptions.

EXAMPLE: Yolanda and Roland are married and live in California. Their home is worth $265,000. Their first mortgage is $155,000 and the IRS has recorded a Notice of Federal Tax Lien for $42,000. Their equity is $68,000 ($265,000 - $155,000 - $42,000). If they select California System 1, they could fully exempt the equity in their home, because the homestead exemption for a married person is $75,000. If they chose California System 2, however, they'd be able to exempt only $15,000 of their $68,000 equity. This means they'd have to pay a lot more to their unsecured creditors through their Chapter 13 plan.

- **Other valuable property.** If the equity in your home isn't a factor in your decision, identify the most valuable items you own. Look at the federal bankruptcy exemptions and your state and the federal *non-bankruptcy* exemptions. Which list helps you bring down the value of your nonexempt property?

EXAMPLE: Andy lives in South Carolina, which exempts several categories of items, including books, clothing, appliances, household goods and furnishings to a total of $2,500. Andy's rare book collection is worth $3,000, his clothing $500 and his household goods and furnishings another $1,500, for a total value of $5,000. If Andy uses his state exemptions, he will not be able to exempt all of these items. Instead, Andy uses the federal exemptions, which let him exempt books, clothing, appliances, household goods and furnishings to $400 per item, $8,000 total. All of his property is now exempt.

- **Your pension.** If your pension is covered by the federal law called ERISA, remember that it isn't considered part of your bankruptcy estate and has no effect on the value of your nonexempt property.

  If your pension is not covered by ERISA, it is exempt only if you use your state's exemptions and the pension is covered by either your state exemption list or the federal *non-bankruptcy* exemption list.

Step 2:   Decide which items you listed on Worksheet 8 are exempt under the exemption system you're using.
In evaluating whether or not your cash on hand and deposits of money are exempt, look to the source of the money, such as welfare benefits, insurance proceeds or wages.

Efficiency Suggestion: While you're determining which of your property is exempt, write down in Column 6 the laws that authorize each exemption. (These are listed in Appendix 1.) You will need this information when you fill out Schedule C of your bankruptcy papers.

Steps 3:   If you are using your state exemptions, decide which items you listed on Worksheet 8 are exempt under the federal *non-bankruptcy* exemptions.

If you use your state exemptions (this includes all Californians), you may also select from a list of federal *non-bankruptcy* exemptions. These are mostly military and other federal benefits, as well as 75% of wages you have earned but have not yet been paid. You cannot, however, combine your exemptions if the federal *non-bankruptcy* exemptions duplicate your state's exemptions.

EXAMPLE: You're using your state's exemptions. Both your state and the federal *non-bankruptcy* exemptions let you exempt 75% of unpaid wages owed you. You cannot combine the exemptions to claim 100% of your wages; 75% is all you can exempt.

Step 4:   Determine the value of all nonexempt items.
Look at each nonexempt property value. If an item (or group of items) is completely exempt, put "0" in Column 6.

If an item (or group of items) is exempt to a certain amount (for example, household goods to $4,000), total up the value of all items that fall into the category, using the values in Column 5. Subtract from the total the amount of the exemption. What is left is the nonexempt value. Enter that in Column 6.

EXAMPLE: Desmond's state exempts several categories of items, including books, clothing, appliances, household goods and furnishings to a total of $2,500. His rare book collection is worth $4,000 and his clothing $500 and his household goods and furnishings another $1,500, for a total value of $6,000. He can exempt only $2,500 worth of his books, clothing, appliances, household goods and furnishings. He enters the nonexempt amount—$3,500—in Column 6.

If an item (or group of items) is not exempt at all, copy the amount from Column 5 to Column 6.

6. The Minimum Amount You Must Pay in Chapter 13 Bankruptcy

Once you've filled in Steps Columns 1-6, total up Column 6. This is the value of your nonexempt property. If the exemption system you're using has a wild card exemption, subtract that amount from the total. The total amount goes on Worksheet 1 from Ch. 2, on which you calculate the minimum amount you must pay your unsecured creditors.

■

Completing the Bankruptcy Forms

Now that you've added up your secured and unsecured debts, calculated your disposable income and calculated the value of your nonexempt property, you are ready to fill out your bankruptcy papers.

This chapter shows you how to fill out all of the forms for a Chapter 13 bankruptcy case, except your Chapter 13 repayment plan. (How to write your plan is covered in Ch. 7, *Writing Your Chapter 13 Bankruptcy Plan.*) For the most part, filling out the forms in this chapter is simple—it's just a matter of putting the right information in the right blanks. If you completed the worksheets in the earlier chapters, you've already done much of the work.

➡ EMERGENCY FILING

Most people file all their bankruptcy forms at once, but you don't have to. If you need to stop a foreclosure or have another emergency, you can file the two-page Voluntary Petition, together with a list of the name, address and zip code of each of your creditors. The automatic stay, which stops collection efforts against you—including a foreclosure—will then go into effect. You will have 15 days to file the rest of the forms, including your Chapter 13 plan. (Bankruptcy Rules 1007(c), 3015(b).) See Ch. 8, *Filing Your Bankruptcy Papers*, Section C, for instructions.

A. Finding the Right Bankruptcy Court

Because bankruptcy is a creature of federal, not state, law, you must file for bankruptcy in a special federal bankruptcy court. There are federal bankruptcy courts all over the country. You need to find the right one to file in.

The federal court system divides the country into judicial districts. Every state has at least one judicial district; most states have more. Normally, you file in the bankruptcy court for the federal judicial district where you've lived during the greater part of the previous 180 days—probably in the nearest sizable city.

EXAMPLE: For the past two months, you've lived in San Luis Obispo, which is in California's central judicial district. Before that you lived in Santa Rosa, in California's northern judicial district. Because during the past six months you lived longer in the northern district than the central, you should file in the bankruptcy court in the northern district. If it's too inconvenient to file there, you could wait another month, when you would qualify to file in the central district court.

If you own or run a business and are including in your bankruptcy papers business debts for which you are personally liable, you have another option. You can file in the district where your principal place of business has been located during the previous 180 days, or where the business's principal assets were located during that period.

Appendix 2 lists the addresses and phone numbers of all federal bankruptcy courts. The easiest way to find the right court is to call the closest one and ask whether you live in its district. (Bankruptcy courts sometimes move. If an address or phone number in Appendix 2 is out-of-date, look in the federal government listings in your phone book's white pages or call directory assistance.)

If you live in a large urban area, there's a chance that your district is broken down into divisions—and that you'll have to find the correct division of your district in which to file. Section B, below, includes a sample letter you can send the bankruptcy court for information before you file. The letter asks whether or not your bankruptcy court district is further divided into divisions.

B. Before You Begin: Get Some Information From the Court

Although bankruptcy courts operate similarly throughout the country, every bankruptcy court has its own requirements for filing bankruptcy papers. If your papers don't meet these local requirements, the court clerk may reject them. So before you begin preparing your papers, write to or visit your bankruptcy court to find out its requirements.

You'll save yourself a lot of trouble—and probably impress the court clerk with your conscientiousness.

The sample letter below outlines what your need to find out from the court. A tear-out copy is in Appendix 3. When you send it, include a large, self-addressed envelope. Call the court and ask whether you need to affix return postage; many, but not all, courts mail without charge. Especially in urban areas, you may get no response to a letter. If you don't hear back within a reasonable time, visit the court and get the information in person.

1. Fees

Currently, the court charges a $130 filing fee and a $30 administrative fee for filing a Chapter 13 bankruptcy case. Fees change, however, so verify the amounts with the court.

You must pay the fees regardless of your income. You must pay the $30 administrative fee when you file your papers. You can, however, ask the court for permission to pay the $130 filing fee in installments. (Instructions for making this request are in Ch. 8, *Filing Your Bankruptcy Papers*, Section B.) You can pay in up to four installments over four months. You can't pay an attorney or typing service until you've fully paid your fees—the court is entitled to its money first.

2. Forms

This book contains all the official, fill-in-the-blanks bankruptcy forms. In addition to the official forms, which must be filed in every bankruptcy court, your local bankruptcy court may require you to file one or two forms that it has developed. Often, these forms ask for a summary of information you provide on the official forms.

There is no official fill-in-the-blank form for the Chapter 13 repayment plan. (Ch. 7, *Writing Your Chapter 13 Bankruptcy Plan*, provides detailed instructions on how to write a plan.) Several bankruptcy courts, however, have developed their own form, which they require debtors to use.

You must get all local forms from your local bankruptcy court. We can't, of course, include all local forms in this book, or tell you how to complete them. Most, however, are self-explanatory.

3. Local Court Rules

Bankruptcy courts must adhere to the local rules established for their federal judicial district, as described in Section A, above. In addition, most bankruptcy courts publish local rules that govern the court's procedures. To add

---

LETTER TO BANKRUPTCY COURT

Sandra Smith
432 Oak Street
Cincinnati, Ohio 45219

(123) 456-7890

July 2, 19XX

United States Bankruptcy Court
U.S. Courthouse
100 E. 5th Street, Room 735
Cincinnati, OH 45202

TO THE COURT CLERK:

Please send me the following materials or information:

- A copy of all local forms published by this court for filing a Chapter 13 bankruptcy, such as:
  - ☐ Chapter 13 bankruptcy cover sheet
  - ☐ Chapter 13 plan
  - ☐ worksheet showing the Chapter 13 plan calculation
  - ☐ summary of the Chapter 13 plan
  - ☐ separate creditor mailing list (matrix)
  - ☐ income deduction order and information on when to submit it
  - ☐ business report for debtor engaged in business
  - ☐ proof of claim (in case I must file claim on behalf of a creditor).
- Copies of all local rules applicable in a Chapter 13 case—rules for the judicial district, this bankruptcy court and any applicable division.
- A copy of the court's calendar.
- The number of copies or sets of all forms I must file.
- The order in which forms should be submitted.

I have additional questions:

1. Is the filing fee still $130? Is the administrative fee still $30?
2. Can I make my plan payments with a personal check? If not, can I use cash or am I limited to cashier's checks and money orders?
3. Is there more than one division for this bankruptcy court? If so, in which division should I file?
4. Must I submit a mailing matrix?
5. Must I submit an income deduction order?
6. Should I two-hole punch my papers or is that done by the court?

I've enclosed a self-addressed envelope for your reply. Thank you.

Sincerely,

Sandra Smith

Sandra Smith

further bureaucracy, in courts with multiple divisions, each division may develop its own set of local rules.

In general, local rules—whether set by your judicial district, bankruptcy court or local division—seldom apply to Chapter 13 bankruptcy cases; instead, they primarily concern Chapter 11 business bankruptcies and contested matters that rarely come up in Chapter 13 cases. But occasionally, a rule does affect a Chapter 13 bankruptcy. For example, in New Mexico, if you are married but filing alone, you must file a statement listing your spouse's name, address and Social Security number. You must also certify that your papers include your non-filing spouse's community income, expenses, debts and assets.

You can get your local rules from the bankruptcy court—but be prepared to comb through reams of material to find the one or two rules that might apply in your case. Having the rules on hand will help you, however, if the court clerk, trustee or bankruptcy judge refers you to a certain rule to follow when filing a form or making a request to the court.

One local practice set by your court is the dates and times the court schedules hearings. You can find out this information by requesting a copy of the court's calendar.

4. Number of Copies

Before filing your papers, be sure you know how many copies your court requires. Many courts require that you

file the original and as many as four additional copies of each form.

C. What Forms to File

You must file the forms listed below. Despite the length of this list, completing your bankruptcy forms will not be as hard as it looks. This is especially true if you completed the Worksheets in Chs. 2, 3, 4 and 5; most of the information you need for these forms you can transfer directly from the worksheets.

BANKRUPTCY FORMS CHECKLIST

- ☐ Form 1—Voluntary Petition
- ☐ Form 6, which consists of:
  - ☐ Schedule A—Real Property
  - ☐ Schedule B—Personal Property
  - ☐ Schedule C—Property Claimed as Exempt
  - ☐ Schedule D—Creditors Holding Secured Claims
  - ☐ Schedule E—Creditors Holding Unsecured Priority Claims
  - ☐ Schedule F—Creditors Holding Unsecured Nonpriority Claims
  - ☐ Schedule G—Executory Contracts and Unexpired Leases
  - ☐ Schedule H—Codebtors
  - ☐ Schedule I—Current Income
  - ☐ Schedule J—Current Expenditures
  - ☐ Summary of Schedules A through J
  - ☐ Declaration Concerning Debtor's Schedules (in which you declare under penalty of perjury that the information you put in the schedules is true and correct)
- ☐ Form 7—Statement of Financial Affairs (in which you provide information about your economic affairs during the past several years)
- ☐ Mailing Matrix (on which you list your creditors and their addresses)
- ☐ Required local forms

Note: Forms 2, 4 and 5 aren't on the list because they aren't used in Chapter 13 voluntary bankruptcy filings; Form 3 is an application to pay the filing fee in installments.

The content and numbering of the official bankruptcy forms are set by the Bankruptcy Rules, a set of rules issued by the United States Supreme Court. Private publishers are free to modify the format of official forms, as long as each form asks the same questions in the same order. (Bankruptcy Rule 9009 states: "The Official Forms prescribed by the Judicial Conference of the United States shall be observed and used with alterations as may be appropriate. Forms may be combined and their contents rearranged to permit economies in their us...")

Courts are required by law to accept all forms that:
- contain the questions and answers prescribed by the official forms
- are printed on one side only
- have adequate top margins, and
- have two pre-punched holes in the top margin. (Bankruptcy Rules 5005 and 9029.)

The forms in this book meet all official Bankruptcy Rule requirements, except that they don't have holes punched in the top—you'll have to do that yourself. If the court clerk tries to reject any of these forms—perhaps because the clerk is used to seeing forms published by a different company, with its own unique format—politely remind the clerk of the Rule.

D. Tips for Filling In the Forms

Here are some tips to make filling in your forms easier and the whole bankruptcy process smoother.

Use your worksheets. If you completed the worksheets in Chs. 2, 3, 4 and 5, you've already done a lot of the work. It will save you lots of time if you refer to them. If you skipped those chapters, refer to Worksheet 7 (Ch. 5) for help in identifying what property you should list in your bankruptcy forms.

Use the samples. A sample completed form accompanies each form's instructions. Refer to it while you fill in your bankruptcy papers. Bear in mind, though, that these are examples only. Even if you live in, Arizona, the same state as our fictional bankruptcy filers, your completed forms will look very different.

Photocopy the forms before you start. You can't tear out and file the forms in Appendix 3 because they are slightly smaller than regulation size, due to book-binding requirements. Good photocopies of the forms on 8H" by 11" paper will work fine, however. Make at least two photocopies of all the forms in the Appendix. Keep the originals (from Appendix 3) so you can make additional copies if you need them.

Start with drafts. First, fill in the forms in pencil, so you can make corrections along the way. Prepare final forms to file with the court only after you've double-checked your drafts.

Type your final forms. Although you are not required to type your forms, many courts prefer that they be typed, and the court clerk is likely to be friendlier if you show up with neatly typed forms. If you don't have a typewriter, many libraries have typewriters available to the public free or for a small rental fee. Or you can hire a bankruptcy petition preparer to type your forms with the information you provide. (See Ch. 12, *Help Beyond the Book*.)

Be ridiculously thorough. Always err on the side of giving too much information rather than too little. If you leave information off the forms, the bankruptcy trustee or court may become suspicious of your motives, and you may be in for rough sledding. If you leave creditors off the forms, these creditors won't be bound by your plan and can come after you for payment—hardly the result you want. And if you don't accurately describe your recent property transactions, the court may refuse to approve your Chapter 13 repayment plan.

Answer every question. Most questions have a box to check if your answer is "none." If a question doesn't have a "none" box and the question doesn't apply to you, type in "N/A" for "not applicable." This will let the trustee know that you didn't overlook it. If the question has a number of blanks, put "N/A" in only the first blank if it is obvious that it applies to the other blanks as well. If it's not clear, put "N/A" in every blank.

Don't worry about repetition. Sometimes different forms, or different questions on the same form, ask for the same or overlapping information. Don't worry about providing the same information multiple times—too much information is never a sin in bankruptcy court.

Explain uncertainties. If you can't figure out which category on a form to use for a debt or item of property, list the debt or item in what you think is the appropriate place and briefly note next to your entry that you're uncertain. The important thing is to disclose the information somewhere. The bankruptcy trustee will sort it out, if necessary.

Be scrupulously honest. You must swear, under penalty of perjury, that you've been truthful on your bankruptcy forms. If you are not scrupulously honest, the court will probably dismiss your bankruptcy case—and you could even be prosecuted for perjury if it's evident that you deliberately lied.

If you run out of room, use continuation pages. The space for entering information is sometimes skimpy, especially if you're filing jointly. Most of the forms come with pre-formatted continuation pages if you need more room. But if there is no continuation form, you can easily prepare one yourself, using a piece of regular white 8H" by 11" paper. (A sample is shown below.) On the official form, put "see continuation page" next to the question you're working on and then enter the additional information on the continuation page. Label the continuation pages with your name, the form name and "Continuation Page 1," "Continuation Page 2" and so on. Be sure to attach all continuation pages to the appropriate forms when you file your bankruptcy papers.

Get help if you need it. If your situation is very complicated, you're unsure about how to complete a form or you run into trouble when you go to file your papers, consult a bankruptcy attorney or bankruptcy petition preparer, or do some legal research before proceeding. (See Ch. 12, *Help Beyond the Book.*)

GETTING HELP FROM THE TRUSTEE BEFORE YOU FILE

In some small districts, where there is only one trustee, the Chapter 13 bankruptcy trustee may be willing to help you complete your bankruptcy forms or answer some basic questions. To contact the trustee before you file, call the bankruptcy court clerk. Explain that you are planning to file a Chapter 13 bankruptcy case and that you have a question for the trustee. The clerk should give you the trustee's name and phone number.

E. Form 1—Voluntary Petition

Filing your voluntary petition gets your bankruptcy started and puts the automatic stay into effect, stopping creditors from trying to collect from you. A sample Voluntary Petition and line-by-line instructions follow.

SAMPLE CONTINUATION PAGE

In re: Joshua and Alice Milton, Debtors.

Form 7, Statement of Financial Affairs

Continuation Page 1

11. Closed Financial Accounts: Bank of Iowa, 150 Broadway, Cedar Rapids, IA 52407; Savings Account No. 1-23-567-890, final balance of $3,446.18; closed September 11, 19XX.

First Page

Court Name. At the top of the first page, fill in the first two blanks with the name of the judicial district you're filing in, such as the "Central District of California." If your state has only one district, type XXXXXX in the first blank. If your state divides its districts into divisions, type the division after the state name, such as "Northern District of Ohio, Eastern Division." (Sections A and B, above, explain how to find out what district and division to file in.)

Name of Debtor. Enter your full name, last name first. Use the form of your name that you use on your checks, driver's license and other formal documents.

Name of Joint Debtor (Spouse). If you are married and filing jointly with your spouse, put your spouse's name, last name first, in the "joint debtor" box. Again, use the name that appears on formal documents. If you're filing alone, type "N/A" anywhere in the box.

All Other Names. If you have been known by any other name in the last six years, list it here. If you've operated a business as an individual proprietor during the previous six years, include your trade name (fictitious or assumed business name preceded by "dba" for doing business as). You don't need to include minor variations in spelling or form. For instance, if your name is John Lewis Odegard, don't put down that you're sometimes known as J.L. But if you've used the pseudonym J.L. Smith, list it. If you're uncertain, list the name if you think you may have used it with a creditor. It can't hurt. The purpose of this box is to make sure that when your creditors receive notice of your bankruptcy filing, they'll know who you are. Do the same for your spouse (in the box to the right) if you are filing jointly. If you're filing alone, type "N/A" anywhere in the box to the right.

Soc. Sec./Tax I.D. No. Enter your Social Security number. If you have a taxpayer I.D. number, enter it as well. Do the same for your spouse (in the box to the right) if you are filing jointly. If you're filing alone, type "N/A" anywhere in the box to the right.

Street Address of Debtor. Enter your current street address. Even if you get all of your mail at a post office box, list the address of your personal residence. Do the same for your spouse—in the box to the right—if you are filing jointly, even if it is the same.

County of Residence. Enter the county of your residence. Do the same for your spouse—in the box to the right—if you are filing jointly.

Mailing Address of Debtor. Enter your mailing address if it is different from your street address. If it isn't, put "N/A." Do the same for your spouse—in the box to the right—if you are filing jointly, even if it is the same.

Location of Principal Assets of Business Debtor. If you—or your spouse if you are filing jointly—have been self-employed or operated a business as a sole proprietor within the last two years, you'll be considered a "business debtor." This means you will have to provide additional information on Form 7 (Section G, below). If your business has assets—such as machines or inventory—list their primary location here. If they are all located at your home or mailing address, enter that address. If you haven't operated a business in the last two years, type "N/A."

Venue. Check the first box. This is where you explain why you're filing in this particular bankruptcy court. (See Section A, above.)

Type of Debtor. Check the first box, "Individual(s)," even if you have been self-employed or operated a sole proprietorship during the previous two years. The other boxes are for people filing different kinds of bankruptcy cases.

Nature of Debt(s). Check "Consumer/Non-Business" if you aren't in business and haven't been for the previous two years, or if most of your debts are owed personally, not by your business. If, however, the bulk of your indebtedness arises from your business, check "Business." If you are in doubt, check "Business."

Chapter 11 Small Business. Type "N/A" anywhere in the box.

Chapter or Section of Bankruptcy Code Under Which the Petition Is Filed. Check "Chapter 13."

Filing Fee. If you will attach the entire $160 fee, check the first box. If you plan to ask the court for permission to pay in installments, check the second box. (Instructions are in Ch. 8, *Filing Your Bankruptcy Papers*, Section B.)

Statistical/Administrative Information. Here you estimate information about your debts and assets. If you completed the worksheets in Chs. 2, 3, 4 and 5, you may be able to fill in these sections now. If you didn't complete those worksheets, wait until you've completed the other forms before providing this information. But remember to come back and check the appropriate boxes before filing.

If you plan to make an emergency filing (Ch. 8, *Filing Your Bankruptcy Papers*, Section C) use the worksheets to arrive at your best estimates.

FORM 1. VOLUNTARY PETITION

UNITED STATES BANKRUPTCY COURT XXXXXX DISTRICT OF Arizona, Tucson Division	**Voluntary Petition**

Name of Debtor (if individual, enter Last, First, Middle): Herchoo, Martin P.	Name of Joint Debtor (Spouse) (Last, First, Middle): Herchoo, Ellen G.
All Other Names used by the Debtor in the last 6 years (include married, maiden, and trade names): N/A	All Other Names used by the Joint Debtor in the last 6 years (include married, maiden, and trade names): Gomacho, Ellen A.
Soc. Sec./Tax I.D. No. (if more than one, state all): 123-456-7890	Soc. Sec./Tax I.D. No. (if more than one, state all): 987-654-3210
Street Address of Debtor (No. & Street, City, State & Zip Code): 19068 Cactus Drive Tucson, AZ 85700	Street Address of Joint Debtor (No. & Street, City, State & Zip Code): 19068 Cactus Drive Tucson, AZ 85700
County of Residence or of the Pima Principal Place of Business:	County of Residence or of the Pima Principal Place of Business:
Mailing Address of Debtor (if different from street address): N/A	Mailing Address of Joint Debtor (if different from street address): N/A

Location of Principal Assets of Business Debtor (if different from street address above): N/A

Information Regarding the Debtor (Check the Applicable Boxes)

Venue (Check any applicable box)

☒ Debtor has been domiciled or has had a residence, principal place of business, or principal assets in this District for 180 days immediately preceding the date of this petition or for a longer part of such 180 days than in any other District.

☐ There is a bankruptcy case concerning debtor's affiliate, general partner, or partnership pending in this District.

Type of Debtor (Check all boxes that apply)	**Chapter or Section of Bankruptcy Code Under Which the Petition is Filed** (Check one box)
☒ Individual(s) ☐ Railroad ☐ Corporation ☐ Stockbroker ☐ Partnership ☐ Commodity Broker ☐ Other _____	☐ Chapter 7 ☐ Chapter 11 ☒ Chapter 13 ☐ Chapter 9 ☐ Chapter 12 ☐ Sec. 304 – Case ancillary to foreign proceeding

Nature of Debts (Check one box)	**Filing Fee** (Check one box)
☒ Consumer/Non-Business ☐ Business	☒ Full Filing Fee attached

Chapter 11 Small Business (Check all boxes that apply)   N/A
☐ Debtor is a small business as defined in 11 U.S.C. § 101
☐ Debtor is and elects to be considered a small business under
    11 U.S.C. §1121(e) (Optional)
	☐ Filing Fee to be paid in installments. (Applicable to individuals only.)
	   Must attach signed application for the court's consideration certifying
	   that the debtor is unable to pay fee except in installments. Rule
	   1006(b). See Official Form No. 3.

Statistical/Administrative Information (Estimates only)	THIS SPACE FOR COURT USE ONLY
☒ Debtor estimates that funds will be available for distribution to unsecured creditors. ☐ Debtor estimates that, after any exempt property is excluded and administrative expenses paid, there will be no funds available for distribution to unsecured creditors.	

Estimated Number of Creditors

1-15	16-49	50-99	100-199	200-999	1000-over
☒	☐	☐	☐	☐	☐

Estimated Assets

$0 to $50,000	$50,001 to $100,000	$100,001 to $500,000	$500,001 to $1 million	$1,000,001 to $10 million	$10,000,001 to $50 million	$50,000,001 $100 million	More than $100 million
☐	☐	☒	☐	☐	☐	☐	☐

Estimated Debts

$0 to $50,000	$50,001 to $100,000	$100,001 to $500,000	$500,001 to $1 million	$1,000,001 to $10 million	$10,000,001 to $50 million	$50,000,001 $100 million	More than $100 million
☐	☐	☒	☐	☐	☐	☐	☐

Voluntary Petition
(This page must be completed and filed in every case.)

Name of Debtor(s):
Herchoo, Martin & Ellen

Form 1, Page 2

Prior Bankruptcy Case Filed Within Last 6 Years (If more than one, attach additional sheet)

Location Where Filed: **N/A**

Case Number:

Date Filed:

Pending Bankruptcy Case Filed by any Spouse, Partner or Affiliate of this Debtor (If more than one, attach additional sheet)

Name of Debtor: **N/A**

Case Number:

Date Filed:

District:

Relationship:

Judge:

Signatures

Signature(s) of Debtor(s) (Individual/Joint)

I declare under penalty of perjury that the information provided in this petition is true and correct.

[If petitioner is an individual whose debts are primarily consumer debts and has chosen to file under chapter 7] I am aware that I may proceed under chapter 7, 11, 12 or 13 of title 11, United States Code, understand the relief available under each such chapter, and choose to proceed under chapter 7.

I request relief in accordance with the chapter of title 11, United States Code, specified in this petition.

X *Martin Herchoo*
Signature of Debtor

X *Ellen Herchoo*
Signature of Joint Debtor

(520) 555-9394
Telephone Number (If not represented by attorney)

2/25/XX
Date

Signature of Debtor (Corporation/Partnership)

I declare under penalty of perjury that the information provided in this petition is true and correct and that I have been authorized to file this petition on behalf of the debtor.

The debtor requests relief in accordance with the chapter of title 11, United States Code, specified in this petition.

X **N/A**
Signature of Authorized Individual

Printed Name of Authorized Individual

Title of Authorized Individual

Date

Signature of Attorney

X **N/A**
Signature of Attorney for Debtor(s)

Printed Name of Attorney for Debtor(s)

Firm Name

Address

Telephone Number

Date

Signature of Non-Attorney Petition Preparer

I certify that I am a bankruptcy petition preparer as defined in 11 U.S.C. § 110, that I prepared this document for compensation, and that I have provided the debtor with a copy of this document.

N/A
Printed Name of Bankruptcy Petition Preparer

Social Security Number

Address

Names and Social Security numbers of all other individuals who prepared or assisted in preparing this document:

If more than one person prepared this document, attach additional sheets conforming to the appropriate official form for each person.

Exhibit A   N/A

(To be completed if debtor is required to file periodic reports (e.g., forms 10K and 10Q) with the Securities and Exchange Commission pursuant to Section 13 or 15(d) of the Securities Exchange Act of 1934 and is requesting relief under chapter 11.)

☐ Exhibit A is attached and made a part of this petition.

Exhibit B   N/A

(To be completed if debtor is an individual whose debts are primarily consumer debts.)

I, the attorney for the petitioner named in the foregoing petition, declare that I have informed the petitioner that [he or she] may proceed under chapter 7, 11, 12, or 13 of title 11, United States Code, and have explained the relief available under each such chapter.

X _____
Signature of Attorney for Debtor(s)   Date

X _____
Signature of Bankruptcy Petition Preparer

Date

A bankruptcy petition preparer's failure to comply with the provisions of title 11 and the Federal Rules of Bankruptcy Procedure may result in fines or imprisonment or both. 11 U.S.C. § 110; 18 U.S.C. § 156.

Second Page

Name of Debtor(s). Enter your name and your spouse's, if you are filing jointly.

Prior Bankruptcy Case Filed Within Last 6 Years. If you haven't filed a bankruptcy case within the previous six years, type "N/A" in the boxes. If you—or your spouse, if you're filing jointly—have filed recently, enter the requested information. You can still file for Chapter 13 bankruptcy unless within the previous 180 days, the court dismissed your bankruptcy case for failing to follow a court order or if you voluntarily dismissed your case after a creditor asked the court to remove the automatic stay.

Pending Bankruptcy Case Filed by Any Spouse, Partner or Affiliate of This Debtor. If your spouse has a bankruptcy case pending anywhere in the country, enter the requested information. The term affiliate refers to a related business under a corporate structure, and partner refers to a business partnership. Neither entity is eligible to file for Chapter 13 bankruptcy. If this doesn't apply, type "N/A" in the boxes.

Signatures of Debtors (Individual/Joint). You—and your spouse, if you are filing jointly—must sign where indicated. If you are filing singly, type "N/A" on the joint debtor signature line. Include your telephone number and date.

Signature of Debtor (Corporation/Partnership). Type "N/A" on the first line.

Signature of Attorney. Type "N/A" on the first line.

Exhibit B. Type "N/A" on the first line.

Signature of Non-Attorney Petition Preparer. If a BPP typed your forms, have that person complete this section. Otherwise, type "N/A" anywhere on the first line.

F. Form 6—Schedules

"Form 6" refers to a whole series of forms, called schedules, that provide the trustee and court with a picture of your current financial situation. Most of the information needed for these schedules was asked for in the worksheets which—we hope—you completed earlier. Completed sample forms and instructions are shown below.

1. Schedule A—Real Property

Here you list all the real property (real estate) you own as of the date you'll file the petition. Even if you don't own any real estate, you still must complete the top of this form.

If you filled in Worksheet 8: Your Exempt and Nonexempt Property, in Ch. 5, get it out. Much of the information you listed in the first section goes on Schedule A. If you didn't fill out the worksheet, go back to Ch. 5 for help on what to include here.

Note on Leases and Timeshares. All leases should be listed on Schedule G, not Schedule A. So if you hold a timeshare lease in a vacation cabin or property, lease a boat dock or underground portions of real estate for mineral or oil exploration, or otherwise lease or rent real estate of any description, don't list it on Schedule A. (See Section 7, below.) There is one exception: if you have an interest in a timeshare that is secured (you'll have to look at your timeshare agreement), list that interest here, not on Schedule G. You are really buying a part of that timeshare, not merely leasing it.

A completed sample of Schedule A and line-by-line instructions follow.

In re. Type your name and, if you're filing jointly, the name of your spouse.

Case No. If you made an emergency filing, fill in the case number assigned by the court. Otherwise, leave this blank.

Description and Location of Property. List the type of property—for example, house, farm or unimproved lot—and street address of every piece of real property you own. You don't need to include the legal description (the description on the deed) of the property.

IF YOU DON'T OWN REAL ESTATE
Type "N/A" anywhere in the first column and move on to Schedule B.

Nature of Debtor's Interest in Property. In this column, you need to give the legal term for the nature of the interest you, your spouse or you and your spouse together have in the real estate. The vast majority of people own property in "fee simple"—an ancient legal term that means simply that you own the property outright. Even if the property has a mortgage or other liens on it, as long as you have the right to sell the house, leave it to your heirs and make alterations to it, your ownership is fee simple. A fee simple interest may be owned by one person or by several people jointly. Normally, if you are listed on the deed as a owner—even if you own the property with someone else as joint tenants, tenants in common or tenants by the entirety—the ownership interest is fee simple.

Other kinds of ownership are much rarer, and much more complicated—and often involve property you don't even think of yourself as owning. But that property, too, must be listed. Several of these kinds of ownership are listed below. If this material makes your head spin, don't worry about it. Identify all property you own, think you own or might own in Column 1 and leave Column 2 blank. After you file for bankruptcy, the trustee can help you sort it out.

- **Life estate.** This is your right to possess and use property only during your lifetime. You can't sell the property, give it away or leave it to someone when you die. Instead, when you die, the property passes to whomever was named in the document (trust, deed or will) that created your life estate. This type of ownership is usually created when the owner of a piece of real estate wants his surviving spouse to live on the property for her life, but then have the property pass to his children. The surviving spouse has a life estate. Surviving spouses who are beneficiaries of A-B or marital bypass trusts have life estates.

- **Future interest.** This is your right to own property sometime in the future. A common future interest is owned by a person who—under the terms of a deed, will or trust—will own the property at some point in the future. But until the person who signed the will or living trust dies, you have no future ownership interest in the property because the person making the will or living trust can easily amend the document to cut you out.

- **Lienholder.** If you are the holder of a mortgage, deed of trust, judgment lien or mechanic's lien on real estate, you have an ownership interest in the real estate. Put "lienholder" in Column 2.

- **Easement holder.** If you are the holder of a right to travel on or otherwise use property owned by someone else, you have an easement.

- **Power of appointment.** If you have a legal right, given to you in a will or transfer of property, to sell a specified piece of someone's property, put "power of appointment" in Column 2.

- **Beneficial ownership under a real estate contract.** If you have signed a binding real estate contract, but don't yet own the property, you have a "beneficial interest"—that is, the right to own the property once the formalities are completed.

Husband, Wife, Joint or Community. If you're not married, put "N/A." If you are married—whether or not you are filing with your spouse—indicate whether the real estate is owned:

- by the husband (H)
- by the wife (W)
- jointly by husband and wife in a non-community law property state (J) or
- jointly by husband and wife as community property (C)—a form of joint ownership that applies to property acquired by couples living in Arizona, California, Idaho, Louisiana, Nevada, New Mexico, Texas, Wash-

ington or Wisconsin. California also includes in this category any real property acquired by a couple in another state that they own when they move to California.

Current Market Value of Debtor's Interest in Property Without Deducting Any Secured Claim or Exemption. Enter the current fair market value of your real estate ownership interest. With a house, you will need an estimate of its market value from a local real estate agent or appraiser. If you own another type of real estate—such as land used to grow crops—you will have to put the amount it would bring in at a forced sale. Don't figure in homestead exemptions or any mortgages or other liens on the property.

If you own the property with someone else who is not filing for bankruptcy, put only your ownership share in this column. For example, if you and your brother own a home as joint tenants (you each own 50%), split the current market value in half.

If your interest is intangible—for example, you are a beneficiary of real estate held in trust that won't be distributed for many years—provide an estimate, explaining why you can't be more precise.

Total. Add the amounts in the fourth column and enter the total in the box at the bottom of the column.

Amount of Secured Claim. Here is where you list mortgages and other debts secured by the property. If there is no secured claim of any type on the real estate, enter "None." If there is, enter separately the amount of each outstanding mortgage, deed of trust, home equity loan or lien (judgment lien, mechanic's lien, materialmen's lien, tax lien or the like) that is claimed against the property.

If you don't know the balance on your mortgage, deed of trust or home equity loan, call the lender. To find out the values of liens, visit the land records office in your county and look up the parcel in the records; the clerk can show you how. Or you can order a title search through a real estate attorney or title insurance company. If you own several pieces of real estate and there is one lien on file against all the real estate, list the full amount of the lien for each separate property item. Don't worry if, taken together, the value of the liens on property is higher than the value of the property; it's quite common.

How you itemize liens in this schedule won't affect how your property or the liens will be treated in bankruptcy. The idea here is to notify the trustee of all possible liens that may affect your real estate.

If you can't find the amounts and you can't afford to pay for a title search, identify the lien and state "amount unknown."

In re ___Herchoo, Martin & Ellen___,   Case No._____
                Debtor   (If known)

SCHEDULE A—REAL PROPERTY

Except as directed below, list all real property in which the debtor has any legal, equitable, or future interest, including all property owned as a co-tenant, community property, or in which the debtor has a life estate. Include any property in which the debtor holds rights and powers exercisable for the debtor's own benefit. If the debtor is married, state whether husband, wife, or both own the property by placing an "H," "W," "J," or "C" in the column labeled "Husband, Wife, Joint, or Community." If the debtor holds no interest in real property, write "None" under "Description and Location of Property."

Do not include interests in executory contracts and unexpired leases on this schedule. List them in Schedule G—Executory Contracts and Unexpired Leases.

If an entity claims to have a lien or hold a secured interest in any property, state the amount of the secured claim. See Schedule D. If no entity claims to hold a secured interest in the property, write "None" in the column labeled "Amount of Secured Claim."

If the debtor is an individual or if a joint petition is filed, state the amount of any exception claimed in the property only in Schedule C—Property Claimed as Exempt.

DESCRIPTION AND LOCATION OF PROPERTY	NATURE OF DEBTOR'S INTEREST IN PROPERTY	HUSBAND, WIFE, JOINT, OR COMMUNITY	CURRENT MARKET VALUE OF DEBTOR'S INTEREST IN PROPERTY WITHOUT DEDUCTING ANY SECURED CLAIM OR EXEMPTION	AMOUNT OF SECURED CLAIM
Home located at 19068 Cactus Drive Tucson, AZ 85700	Fee Simple	C	$275,000	$239,715 mortgage $16,080 home equity loan $1,215 judgment lien

Total ➡ $ $275,000

(Report also on Summary of Schedules.)

2. Schedule B—Personal Property

Here you must list and value all of your personal property—that is, everything except real estate. Include property that is security for a debt and property that is exempt. If you didn't fill in Worksheet 8, turn to Ch. 5, *Calculating the Value of Your Nonexempt Property*, for explanations and suggestions about property for each of the schedule's categories.

⚠️ BE SCRUPULOUSLY HONEST AND RIDICULOUSLY THOROUGH

Don't make the common mistake of thinking that listing your property isn't important because you don't have to turn any property over to the trustee in Chapter 13 bankruptcy. The court reviews your papers to determine whether or not your unsecured creditors will be receiving at least the value of the nonexempt property. If you omit property—deliberately or accidentally—and the court discovers your omission, your Chapter 13 plan will not be confirmed. Worse, your case may be dismissed.

A completed sample and line-by-line instructions follow. If you need more room, attach a continuation sheet. (See Section D, above.)

In re and **Case No.** Follow the instructions for Schedule A.

Type of Property. The form lists general categories of personal property. You can leave this column as is.

None. If you don't own property that fits in a category listed in the first column, enter an "X" in this column next to the category.

Description and Location of Property. List specific items that fall in each general category. See the checklist preceding Worksheet 8 (Ch. 5, *Calculating the Value of Your Nonexempt Property*) for some prompts on property to list here. Separately list all items worth $50 or more. Combine small items into larger categories whenever reasonable. For example, you don't need to list every spatula, colander, garlic press and ice cream scoop; instead, put "kitchen utensils." If you list numerous items in one category (as is likely for household goods and furnishings), you may need to attach a continuation sheet.

Most of your personal property is probably at your residence. If so, write a sentence at the top of the form or column to that effect: "All property is located at my/our residence unless otherwise noted." Indicate specifically when the facts are different. If someone else holds property for you (for example, you loaned your aunt your color TV), put that person's name and address in this column.

A few categories ask you to "give particulars." This is what you should do:

Category 16: List all child support or alimony arrears—that is, money that should have been paid to you but hasn't been. Specify the dates the payments were due and missed, such as "$250 monthly child support payments for June, July, August and September 19XX."

Category 17: List all money owed to you and not yet paid other than child support and alimony. If you've obtained a judgment against someone but haven't been paid, list it here. State the defendant's name, the date of the judgment, the court that issued the judgment, the amount of the judgment and the kind of case (such as car accident).

Category 21: State what the patent, copyright, trademark or the like is for. Give the number assigned by the issuing agency and length of time the patent, copyright, trademark or the like will last.

Category 22: List all licenses and franchises, what they cover, the length of time remaining, who they are with and whether or not you can transfer them to someone else.

Category 30: For your crops, state whether or not they've been harvested, whether or not they've been sold, and if so to whom and for how much, the amount of any loan you've taken out against them and whether or not they are insured.

Husband, Wife, Joint, or Community. If you're not married, put "N/A" at the top of the column.

If you are married and own all or most of your personal property jointly with your spouse, put one of the following statements on the top or bottom of the form:

- **If you live in a common law property state:** "All property is owned jointly unless otherwise indicated." Then note when a particular item is owned by only H or W.
- **If you live in a community property state:** "All property is owned jointly as community property unless otherwise indicated." Then note when a particular item is owned by only H or W.

If you are married and own many items separately, for each item specify:
- husband (H)
- wife (W)
- jointly by husband and wife (J), or
- jointly by husband and wife in a community property state (C).

For more information on ownership of property by married couples, see Ch. 5, *Calculating the Value of Your Nonexempt Property*, Section A.5.

Current Market Value of Debtor's Interest in Property, Without Deducting Any Secured Claim or Exemption. You can take the information requested here from Worksheet 8. Put the current market value of the property, without regard to any

In re ___Herchoo, Martin & Ellen___,   Case No._____
                  Debtor   (If known)

SCHEDULE B—PERSONAL PROPERTY

Except as directed below, list all personal property of the debtor of whatever kind. If the debtor has no property in one or more of the categories, place an "X" in the appropriate position in the column labeled "None." If additional space is needed in any category, attach a separate sheet properly identified with the case name, case number, and the number of the category. If the debtor is married, state whether husband, wife, or both own the property by placing an "H," "W," "J," or "C" in the column labeled "Husband, Wife, Joint, or Community." If the debtor is an individual or a joint petition is filed, state the amount of any exemptions claimed only in Schedule C—Property Claimed as Exempt.

Do not include interests in executory contracts and unexpired leases on this schedule. List them in Schedule G—Executory Contracts and Unexpired Leases.

If the property is being held for the debtor by someone else, state that person's name and address under "Description and Location of Property."

TYPE OF PROPERTY	NONE	* All property is located at our residence unless otherwise noted. DESCRIPTION AND LOCATION OF PROPERTY	HUSBAND, WIFE, JOINT, OR COMMUNITY	CURRENT MARKET VALUE OF DEBTOR'S INTEREST IN PROPERTY, WITHOUT DEDUCTING ANY SECURED CLAIM OR EXEMPTION
1. Cash on hand.		Cash from wages	C	300
2. Checking, savings or other financial accounts, certificates of deposit, or shares in banks, savings and loan, thrift, building and loan, and homestead associations, or credit unions, brokerage houses, or cooperatives.		Account #743-011-6281193 (checking) Pima County Bank, 1700 Truman Blvd., Tucson, AZ 85700 (wages)	C	500
		Account #9918736249 (money market) Sputter Investment House, P.O. Box E, Hackensack, NJ 07000 (wages)	C	300
3. Security deposits with public utilities, telephone companies, landlords, and others.	X			
4. Household goods and furnishings, including audio, video, and computer equipment.		Refrigerator	C	300
		Stove	C	250
		Dishwasher	C	250
		Microwave	C	200
		Kitchen table/chairs	C	300
		Stereo system	C	600
		2 TVs & VCR	C	450
		Living room couch, 2 chairs, coffee table	C	475
		2 beds with bedding	C	300
		2 dressers	C	125
		2 desks (1 specially designed)	C	1,000
		10 bookcases	C	500
		Mac computer & printer	C	2,000
		Washer/Dryer	C	400
		Minor appliances	C	100
		Barbecue	C	50
		Children's toys	C	60
		Kitchen utensils, gadgets, etc.	C	50

In re ___Herchoo, Martin & Ellen_____ ,   Case No._____
                      Debtor   (If known)

SCHEDULE B—PERSONAL PROPERTY
(Continuation Sheet)

TYPE OF PROPERTY	NONE	DESCRIPTION AND LOCATION OF PROPERTY	HUSBAND, WIFE, JOINT, OR COMMUNITY	CURRENT MARKET VALUE OF DEBTOR'S INTEREST IN PROPERTY, WITHOUT DEDUCTING ANY SECURED CLAIM OR EXEMPTION
5. Books, pictures and other art objects, antiques, stamp, coin, record, tape, compact disc, and other collections or collectibles.		Books Lithographs Record/tape/CD Collection	C C C	250 150 300
6. Wearing apparel.		Clothing	C	500
7. Furs and jewelry.		Wedding & engagement rings Watches Earrings	C C C	1,000 200 100
8. Firearms and sports, photographic, and other hobby equipment.		Camera, lenses, tripod Ice skates	W C	600 150
9. Interests in insurance policies. Name insurance company of each policy and itemize surrender or refund value of each.		Life insurance policy, Lively Ins. Co., 120 Manhattan Street, NY, NY 10000 Policy #631171-41 Life insurance policy, Lifetime, Co., 52 Mitchell Ave., Hartford, CT 06400. Policy #71WY5919-1160	C C	4,000 2,000
10. Annuities. Itemize and name each issuer.	X			
11. Interests in IRA, ERISA, Keogh, or other pension or profit sharing plans. Itemize.		Teachers Fund, 1000 Wallace Way, Phoenix, AZ 85700. Policy #X145900-1730 IRA at Pima County Bank, 1700 Truman Blvd., Tucson, AZ 85700. Account #743-011-6287491	H/C W/C	18,900 8,633
12. Stock and interests in incorporated and unincorporated businesses. Itemize.	X			
13. Interests in partnerships or joint ventures. Itemize.	X			

In re ___Herchoo, Martin & Ellen_____ ,   Case No._____

Debtor   (If known)

SCHEDULE B—PERSONAL PROPERTY
(Continuation Sheet)

TYPE OF PROPERTY	NONE	DESCRIPTION AND LOCATION OF PROPERTY	HUSBAND, WIFE, JOINT, OR COMMUNITY	CURRENT MARKET VALUE OF DEBTOR'S INTEREST IN PROPERTY, WITHOUT DEDUCTING ANY SECURED CLAIM OR EXEMPTION
14. Government and corporate bonds and other negotiable and non-negotiable instruments.	X			
15. Accounts receivable.	X			
16. Alimony, maintenance, support, and property settlements to which the debtor is or may be entitled. Give particulars.	X			
17. Other liquidated debts owing debtor including tax refunds. Give particulars.		First quarter 19XX royalty payment due Martin	H/C	6,911
18. Equitable or future interest, life estates, and rights or powers exercisable for the benefit of the debtor other than those listed in Schedule of Real Property.	X			
19. Contingent and noncontingent interests in estate of a decedent, death benefit plan, life insurance policy, or trust.	X			
20. Other contingent and unliquidated claims of every nature, including tax refunds, counterclaims of the debtor, and rights to setoff claims. Give estimated value of each.	X			
21. Patents, copyrights, and other intellectual property. Give particulars.		Martin holds a copyright in several high school and junior college level math textbooks, some published before marriage, others during	H/C	unknown
22. Licenses, franchises, and other general intangibles. Give particulars.	X			

In re ___Herchoo, Martin & Ellen_____,   Case No._____
                     Debtor   (If known)

SCHEDULE B—PERSONAL PROPERTY
(Continuation Sheet)

TYPE OF PROPERTY	NONE	DESCRIPTION AND LOCATION OF PROPERTY	HUSBAND, WIFE, JOINT, OR COMMUNITY	CURRENT MARKET VALUE OF DEBTOR'S INTEREST IN PROPERTY, WITHOUT DEDUCTING ANY SECURED CLAIM OR EXEMPTION
23. Automobiles, trucks, trailers, and other vehicles and accessories.		19XX Nissan Maxima 19XX Ford Taurus	C W	7,400 1,000
24. Boats, motors, and accessories.	X			
25. Aircraft and accessories.	X			
26. Office equipment, furnishings, and supplies.	X			
27. Machinery, fixtures, equipment, and supplies used in business.	X			
28. Inventory.	X			
29. Animals.		2 Horses	C	1,000
30. Crops—growing or harvested. Give particulars.	X			
31. Farming equipment and implements.	X			
32. Farm supplies, chemicals, and feed.	X			
33. Other personal property of any kind not already listed, such as season tickets. Itemize.	X			

Total ➡ $ 61,604

_____0_____ continuation sheets attached

(Include amounts from any continuation sheets attached. Report total also on Summary of Schedules.)

secured interests or exemptions. For example, if you own a car worth $6,000, still owe $4,000 on the car note and your state's motor vehicle exemption is $1,200, put down $6,000 for the market value of the car.

Total. Add the amounts in this column and put the total in the box at the bottom of the last page. If you used any continuation pages in addition to the preprinted form, remember to attach those pages and include the amounts from them in the total.

3. Schedule C—Property Claimed as Exempt

When you work on this form, you'll need to refer frequently to several other documents. Have in front of you:

- Worksheet 8 (from Ch. 5)
- your drafts of Schedules A and B
- the list of state or federal bankruptcy exemptions you'll be using (from Appendix 1), and
- if you're using your state's exemptions, the additional *non-bankruptcy* federal exemptions (from Appendix 1).

Set out below are a sample completed Schedule C and line-by-line instructions.

In re and **Case No.** Follow the instructions for Schedule A.

Debtor elects the exemptions to which the debtor is entitled under. If you're using the federal exemptions, check the top box. If you're using your state exemptions (this includes all Californians), check the lower box.

The following instructions cover one column at a time. The easiest way to proceed is to list one exempt item and complete all columns for that item before moving on to the next exempt item.

Description of Property. In this column, you list the property, both real and personal, you claim is exempt under bankruptcy law. In completing this schedule, be sure to use the same descriptions you used Schedule A and Schedule B.

⚠ IF YOUR STATE HAS A WILD CARD EXEMPTION

In Ch. 5, when you completed Worksheet 8, you simply subtracted the amount of the wild card exemption from the total amount of your nonexempt property. Now you must identify property, up to the value of your wild card exemption, that you couldn't otherwise exempt. You can do this by adding the wild card exemption to an item of property only partially exempt, or by exempting an item which otherwise isn't exempt at all.

EXAMPLE: Kentucky doesn't exempt family heirlooms, but does provide a wild card exemption of $1,000 for any property. Loretta has three antiques, each worth $300,

that she wants to keep. She applies the $1,000 wild card exemption to these items, which makes them exempt. She can use the remaining $100 on any other property she chooses.

Specify Law Providing Each Exemption. For every item, you must list the specific law that allows you to claim the item as exempt. You can find citations to the specific laws that create exemptions in the state and federal exemption lists in Appendix 1.

You can simplify this process by typing, on the top of the form, the name of the statutes you are using. The name is noted at the top of the exemption list you use. For example, you might type "All law references are to the Florida Statutes Annotated unless otherwise noted."

For each item of property, enter the citation (number) of the specific law that creates the exemption, as set out on the exemption list. If you use any reference other than one found in your state statutes, such as federal *non-bankruptcy* exemptions or a court case, list the entire reference for the exempt item.

Value of Claimed Exemption. List the full exemption amount allowed, up to the value of the item. The amount allowed is listed in Appendix 1.

👫 BANKRUPTCY RULES ALLOW MARRIED COUPLES TO DOUBLE ALL EXEMPTIONS UNLESS STATE LAW EXPRESSLY PROHIBITS IT

That means that each of you can claim the entire amount of each exemption, if you are filing jointly. If your state's chart in Appendix 1 doesn't say that your state forbids doubling, go ahead and double. If you are married and doubling your exemptions, put a note to this effect on the form. (See sample Schedule C.)

If you are using part or all of a wild card exemption in addition to a regular exemption, list both amounts. For example, if the regular exemption for an item of furniture is $200, and you plan to exempt it to $500 using $300 from your state's wild card exemption, list $200 across from the citation for the regular exemption, and the $300 across from the citation for the wild card exemption (or across from the term "wild card").

Current Market Value of Property Without Deducting Exemption. Enter the fair market value of the item you are claiming as exempt. This information will already be listed on Schedule A or Schedule B.

In re ___Herchoo, Martin & Ellen_____,   Case No._____
                         Debtor   (If known)

SCHEDULE C—PROPERTY CLAIMED AS EXEMPT

Debtor elects the exemptions to which debtor is entitled under:

(Check one box)

☐ 11 U.S.C. § 522(b)(1):   Exemptions provided in 11 U.S.C. § 522(d). **Note: These exemptions are available only in certain states.**

☒ 11 U.S.C. § 522(b)(2):   Exemptions available under applicable nonbankruptcy federal laws, state or local law where the debtor's domicile has been located for the 180 days immediately preceding the filing of the petition, or for a longer portion of the 180-day period than in any other place, and the debtor's interest as a tenant by the entirety or joint tenant to the extent the interest is exempt from process under applicable nonbankruptcy law.

DESCRIPTION OF PROPERTY	SPECIFY LAW PROVIDING EACH EXEMPTION	VALUE OF CLAIMED EXEMPTION	CURRENT MARKET VALUE OF PROPERTY WITHOUT DEDUCTING EXEMPTIONS
Real Property Home located at 19068 Cactus Drive, Tucson, AZ 85700	33-1101	17,990	275,000
Financial accounts Account #743-011-6281193 (checking). Pima County Bank, 1700 Truman Blvd., Tucson, AZ 85700	33-1126(A)(7)	300	300
Household goods			
Refrigerator	33-1123	300	300
Stove	33-1123	250	250
Dishwasher	33-1123	250	250
Microwave	33-1123	200	200
Kitchen table/chairs	33-1123	300	300
Stereo System	33-1123	600	600
2 TVs & VCR	33-1123	450	450
Living room couch, 2 chairs, coffee table	33-1123	475	475
2 beds with bedding	33-1123	300	300
2 dressers	33-1123	125	125
2 desks (1 specially designed)	33-1123	1,000	1,000
10 bookcases	33-1123	500	500
Mac computer & printer	33-1123	2,000	2,000
Washer/dryer	33-1123	400	400
Minor appliances	33-1123	100	100
Barbecue	33-1123	50	50
Children's toys	33-1123	60	50
Kitchen utensils, gadgets, etc.	33-1123	50	50
Books, pictures, etc.			
Books	33-1125	250	250
Lithograph	33-1127	150	150

Because we are married, we each claim a full set of exemptions to the extent permitted by law. All references are to the Arizona Revised Statues unless otherwise noted.

In re <u>Herchoo, Martin & Ellen</u>

SCHEDULE C—PROPERTY CLAIMED AS EXEMPT
(Continuation Sheet)

DESCRIPTION OF PROPERTY	SPECIFY LAW PROVIDING EACH EXEMPTION	VALUE OF CLAIMED EXEMPTION	CURRENT MARKET VALUE OF PROPERTY WITHOUT DEDUCTING EXEMPTIONS
<u>Apparel</u>			
Clothing	33-1125	500	500
<u>Furs & jewelry</u>			
Wedding & engagement rings	33-1125	1,000	1,000
Watches	33-1125	200	200
<u>Insurance</u>			
Life insurance policy with Lively Insurance Co., 120 Manhattan St., NY, NY 10000 #631171-41	20-1131(D)	4,000	4,000
Life insurance policy with Lifetime Co., 52 Mitchell Ave., Hartford, CT 06400. #71 WY5919-1160	33-1126(A)(5)	2,000	2,000
<u>Pensions</u>			
Teacher's Fund, 1000 Wallace Way, Phoenix, AZ Policy #X145900-1730	38-762	18,900	18,900
IRA at Pima County Bank, 1700 Truman Blvd., Tucson, AZ 85700. #743-011-6287491	<u>In re Herrscher</u>, 121 B.R. 29 (D. Ariz. 1990)	8,633	8,633
<u>Automobiles</u>			
19XX Ford Taurus	33-1125	1,000	1,000
<u>Animals</u>			
2 Horses	33-1125	1,000	1,000

4. Schedule D—Creditors Holding Secured Claims

In this schedule, you list all creditors who hold claims secured by your property. This includes:

- lenders who hold a mortgage or deed of trust on your real estate
- creditors who have won lawsuits against you and recorded judgment liens against your property
- lawyers to whom you have granted a security interest in the outcome of a lawsuit, so that the collection of their fees would be postponed (the expected court judgment is the collateral)
- contractors who have filed mechanics' or materialmen's liens on your real estate
- taxing authorities, such as the IRS, that have obtained tax liens against your property
- creditors with either a purchase money or non-purchase money security agreement (for definitions, see Ch. 3, *Adding Up Your Secured and Unsecured Debts*, Section A), and
- all parties who are trying to collect a secured debt, such as collection agencies and attorneys.

CREDIT CARD DEBTS

Most credit card debts, whether the card is issued by a bank, gasoline company or department store, are unsecured and should be listed on Schedule F. Some department stores, however—notably, Sears—retain a security interest in all durable goods such as appliances and electronics bought using the store credit card. (A bankruptcy court in Vermont, however, has ruled that Sears charge debts are unsecured under state law. *In re Oszajca*, 199 B.R. 103 (D. Vt. 1996).) Also, if you were issued a bank or store credit card as part of a plan to restore your credit, you may have had to post property or cash as collateral for debts incurred on the card. If either of these exceptions applies to you, list the credit card debt on Schedule D.

Line-by-line instructions and a completed sample of Schedule D follow. Worksheets 1, 2 and 3 from Ch. 3, *Adding Up Your Secured and Unsecured Debts*, may be of help here.

In re and **Case No.** Follow the instructions for Schedule A.

☐ **Check this box if debtor has no creditors holding secured claims to report on this Schedule D.** Check the box at the bottom of Schedule D's instructions if you have no secured

creditors. If you have no secured creditors, you can go on to Schedule E.

Creditor's Name and Mailing Address. Here you list all secured creditors, preferably in alphabetical order. For each, fill in the account number, if you know it, the name and the complete mailing address, including zip code (call the creditor or the post office and get it if you don't have it).

If you have more than one secured creditor for a given debt, list the original creditor first and then immediately list the other creditors. For example, if you've been sued or hounded by a collection agency, list the information for the attorney or collection agency after the original creditor.

If, after typing up your final papers, you discover that you've missed a few creditors, don't retype the papers to preserve perfect alphabetical order. Simply add the creditors at the end. If your creditors don't all fit on the first page of Schedule D, make as many copies of the preprinted continuation page as you need to fit them all.

Codebtor. If someone else can be legally forced to pay your debt to a listed secured creditor, enter an "X" in this column and list the codebtor in the creditor column of this schedule. If there is no codebtor, leave it blank.

The most common codebtors are:

- cosigners
- guarantors (people who guarantee payment of a loan)
- ex-spouses with whom you jointly incurred debts before divorcing
- joint owners of real estate or other property, if a lien was filed against the property
- co-parties in a lawsuit, if a judgment lien has been recorded against both co-parties
- non-filing spouses in a community property state (most debts incurred by a non-filing spouse during marriage are considered community debts, which means both spouse are equally liable for them), and
- non-filing spouses in states other than community property states, for debts incurred by the filing spouse for necessities such as food, shelter, clothing and utilities.

Husband, Wife, Joint, or Community. Follow the instructions for Schedule A.

Date Claim Was Incurred, Nature of Lien, and Description and Market Value of Property Subject to Lien. This column calls for a lot of information about each secured debt. Let's take the elements one at a time.

Date Claim Was Incurred. Enter the date the secured claim was incurred. For most claims, this is the date you signed the security agreement or mortgage. If you didn't sign a security agreement with the creditor, the date is most likely the date a contractor, judgment creditor or

In re ___Herchoo, Martin & Ellen_____ ,   Case No._____
　　　　　　　Debtor　　　　　　　　　　　　　　　　　　　　　　　　(If known)

SCHEDULE D—CREDITORS HOLDING SECURED CLAIMS

　　State the name, mailing address, including zip code, and account number, if any, of all entities holding claims secured by property of the debtor as of the date of filing of the petition. List creditors holding all types of secured interest such as judgment liens, garnishments, statutory liens, mortgages, deeds of trust, and other security interests. List creditors in alphabetical order to the extent practicable. If all secured creditors will not fit on this page, use the continuation sheet provided.

　　If any entity other than a spouse in a joint case may be jointly liable on a claim, place an "X" in the column labeled "Codebtor," include the entity on the appropriate schedule of creditors, and complete Schedule H—Codebtors. If a joint petition is filed, state whether husband, wife, both of them, or the marital community may be liable on each claim by placing an "H," "W," "J," or "C" in the column labeled "Husband, Wife, Joint, or Community."

　　If the claim is contingent, place an "X" in the column labeled "Contingent." If the claim is unliquidated, place an "X" in the column labeled "Unliquidated." If the claim is disputed, place an "X" in the column labeled "Disputed." (You may need to place an "X" in more than one of these three columns.)

　　Report the total of all claims on this schedule in the box labeled "Total" on the last sheet of the completed schedule. Report this total also on the Summary of Schedules.

　　☐　Check this box if debtor has no creditors holding secured claims to report on this Schedule D.

CREDITOR'S NAME AND MAILING ADDRESS INCLUDING ZIP CODE	CODEBTOR	HUSBAND, WIFE, JOINT, OR COMMUNITY	DATE CLAIM WAS INCURRED, NATURE OF LIEN, AND DESCRIPTION AND MARKET VALUE OF PROPERTY SUBJECT TO LIEN	CONTINGENT	UNLIQUIDATED	DISPUTED	AMOUNT OF CLAIM WITHOUT DEDUCTING VALUE OF COLLATERAL	UNSECURED PORTION, IF ANY
ACCOUNT NO.　XX-1149-20811 Big Home Loan Bank 232 Desert Way Tucson, AZ 85700		C	11/XX; purchase money secured debt; mortgage on home VALUE $　275,000				239,715	0
ACCOUNT NO.　XX-1149-63114 Big Home Loan Bank 232 Desert Way Tucson, AZ 85700		C	3/XX; nonpurchase-money secured debt, home equity loan VALUE $　275,000				16,080	0
ACCOUNT NO.　VR00M396 Car Finance Co. P.O. Box 1183 San Ramon, CA 94000		C	6/XX; purchase-money secured debt, car loan (19XX Nissan Maxima) VALUE $　7,400				8,250	850
ACCOUNT NO.　SCC 157381 Ken Williams 17 North Rippington St. Tucson, AZ 85700		C	6/XX; judgment lien on real property in Pima county VALUE $　275,000				1,215	1,215 (We will file Motion to Avoid Lien)

____0____ continuation sheets attached

Subtotal ➡ (Total of this page)　$　265,260

Total ➡ (Use only on last page)　$　265,260

(Report total also on Summary of Schedules)

taxing authority recorded a lien against your property. If you listed two or more creditors on the same secured claim (such as the lender and a collection agency), put the same date for both.

Nature of Lien. Here are the possibilities:

- **Purchase-money security interest**—if the debt was incurred to purchase the property, as with a mortgage or car note.
- **Nonpossessory non-purchase-money security interest**—if the debt was incurred for a purpose other than buying the collateral, as with home equity loans or loans from finance companies.
- **Possessory non-purchase-money security interest**—if you own property that has been pledged to a pawnshop.
- **Judgment lien**—if the creditor sued you, obtained a court judgment and recorded a lien against your property.
- **Tax lien**—if a taxing authority placed a lien on your property.
- **Child support lien**—if you owe child support and your child's other parent has recorded a lien against your property.
- **Mechanic's or materialmen's liens**—if someone performed work on real property, a vehicle or other property, wasn't paid and recorded a lien.

If you don't know what kind of lien you are dealing with, put "Don't know nature of lien" after the date. The bankruptcy trustee will help you figure it out later.

See Ch. 3, *Adding Up Your Secured and Unsecured Debts*, Section A, for complete definitions of the different types of liens.

Description of Property. Describe each item of real estate and personal property that is collateral for the secured debt you owe the creditor listed in the first column. Use the same description you used on Schedule A for real estate, or Schedule B for personal property. If a creditor's lien covers several items of property, list all items affected by the lien.

Market Value. The amount you put here must be consistent with what you put on Schedule A or B. If you put only the total value of a group of items on Schedule B, you must now get more specific. For instance, if a department store has a secured claim against your washing machine, and you listed your "washer/dryer set" on Schedule B, now you must provide the washer's specific market value. This may be on Worksheet 8; if it isn't, see the instructions for the "Current Market Value" of Schedule B.

Contingent, Unliquidated, Disputed. Indicate whether the creditor's secured claim is contingent, unliquidated or disputed. Check all categories that apply. If you're uncertain of which to choose, check the one that seems closest. If none applies, leave them blank. Briefly, these terms mean:

Contingent. The claim depends on some event that hasn't yet occurred and may never occur. For example, if you cosigned a secured loan, you won't be liable unless the principal debtor defaults. Your liability as cosigner is contingent upon the default.

Unliquidated. This means that a debt apparently exists, but the exact amount hasn't been determined. For example, say you've sued someone for injuries you suffered in an auto accident, but the case isn't over. Your lawyer has taken the case under a contingency fee agreement—she'll get a third of the recovery if you win, and nothing if you lose—and has a security interest in the final recovery amount. The debt to the lawyer is unliquidated, because you don't know how much, if anything, you'll win.

Disputed. There's a dispute over the existence or amount of the debt. For instance, the IRS says you owe $10,000 and has put a lien on your property, and you say you owe $500.

Amount of Claim Without Deducting Value of Collateral. For each secured creditor, put the amount it would take to pay off the secured claim, regardless of what the property is worth. The lender can tell you the amount if you call and ask for the "payoff amount."

> **EXAMPLE:** Your original loan was for $13,000 plus $7,000 in interest (for $20,000 total). You've made enough payments so that $10,000 in principal will cancel the debt; you would put $10,000 in the column.

If you have more than one creditor for a given secured claim (for example, the lender and a collection agency), list the amount of the debt only for the lender and put ditto marks (") for each subsequent creditor.

Subtotal/Total. Total the amounts in the Amount of Claim column for each page. Do not include the amounts represented by the ditto marks if you listed multiple creditors for a single debt. On the final page of Schedule D (which may be the first page or a preprinted continuation page), enter the total of all secured claims.

Unsecured Portion, If Any. If the market value of the collateral is equal to or greater than the amount of the claim, enter "0," meaning that the creditor's claim is fully secured. If the market value of the collateral is less than the amount of the claim(s) listed, enter the difference here. If you will file a motion with the court to eliminate the lien, note that here.

EXAMPLE: The market value of your collateral is $5,000, but you still owe $6,000 on it and a judgment creditor filed a $2,000 lien against it. The claims against the property total $8,000. Therefore, put $3,000 ($8,000 – $5,000) in this column.

5. Schedule E—Creditors Holding Unsecured Priority Claims

Schedule E identifies certain "priority" creditors who are usually entitled to be paid first in your Chapter 13 plan.

Set out below are a sample completed Schedule E and line-by-line instructions.

In re and **Case No.** Follow the instructions for Schedule A.

☐ **Check this box if debtor has no creditors holding unsecured priority claims to report on this Schedule E.** The most common priority claims are unsecured income tax debts and past due alimony or child support. There are several other categories of priority debts, however. Before deciding whether or not you can check this box, examine each of the following categories.

☐ **Extensions of credit in an involuntary case.** Don't check this box. You are filing a voluntary, not an involuntary, Chapter 13 case.

☐ **Wages, salaries and commissions.** If you owe a current or former employee of your business wages, vacation pay or sick leave which was earned within 90 days before you file for bankruptcy or within 90 days of the date you ceased your business, check this box. If you owe money to an independent contractor who did work for you which was earned within 90 days before you file for bankruptcy or within 90 days of the date you ceased your business, check this box if in the 12 months before you file for bankruptcy, this independent contractor earned at least 75% of his or her total independent contractor receipts from you. In either case, only the first $4,300 you owe (per employee or independent contractor) is a priority debt.

☐ **Contributions to employee benefit plans.** Check this box only if you owe contributions to an employee benefit fund for services rendered by an employee of your business within 180 days before you file your petition or within 180 days of the date you ceased your business.

☐ **Certain farmers and fishermen.** Check this box only if you operated a grain storage facility and owe money to a grain producer, or if you operated a fish produce or storage facility and owe money to a U.S. fisherman for fish or fish products. In either case, only the first $4,300 you owe (per grain producer or fisherman) is a priority debt.

☐ **Deposits by individuals.** If you took deposit money from people who planned to purchase, lease or rent goods or services from you, which you never delivered, you may owe a priority debt. For the debt to qualify as a priority, the goods or services would have had to have been put to personal, family or household use. Only the first $1,950 owed (per person) is a priority debt.

☐ **Alimony, maintenance or support.** Check this box if you are behind on your payments to a spouse, former spouse, child, the court, your welfare department or anyone else for alimony or child support.

☐ **Taxes and certain other debts owed to governmental units.** Check this box if you owe unsecured back taxes or any other debts to the government, such as fines imposed for driving under the influence of drugs or alcohol. As explained in Ch. 7, Section G, *Writing Your Chapter 13 Bankruptcy Plan,* not all tax debts are unsecured priority claims. If the IRS has recorded a lien against your real property, and the equity in your property fully covers the amount of your tax debt, your debt is a secured debt. It should be on Schedule D, not on this schedule.

☐ **Commitments to Maintain the Capital of an Insured Depository Institution.** Don't check this box. It's for business bankruptcies.

If you checked none of the priority debt boxes, go back and check the first box on the form, showing you have no unsecured priority claims to report.

If you checked any of the priority debt boxes, make as many photocopies of the Schedule E continuation sheet as the number of priority debts you owe. You will need to complete a separate sheet for each debt. Here is how to complete a continuation page for each type of debt.

In re and **Case No.** Follow the instructions for Schedule A.

Type of Priority. Enter one of the types of priority you checked on page 1 of this schedule.

Creditor's Name and Mailing Address, Including Zip Code. List the name and complete mailing address (including zip code) of each priority creditor, as well as the account number if you know it. You may have more than one priority creditor for a given debt. For example, if you've been sued or hounded by a collection agency, list the attorney or collection agency in addition to the lender.

Codebtor. If someone else can be legally forced to pay your debt to a listed priority creditor, enter an "X" in this column and list the codebtor in the creditor column of this schedule. Common codebtors are listed in the instructions for Schedule D.

Husband, Wife, Joint or Community. Follow the instructions for Schedule A.

Date Claim Was Incurred and Consideration for Claim. State the date the debt was incurred—a specific date or a period

In re _____Herchoo, Martin & Ellen_____ ,   Case No._____
      Debtor   (If known)

SCHEDULE E—CREDITORS HOLDING UNSECURED PRIORITY CLAIMS

A complete list of claims entitled to priority, listed separately by type of priority, is to be set forth on the sheets provided. Only holders of unsecured claims entitled to priority should be listed in this schedule. In the boxes provided on the attached sheets, state the name and mailing address, including zip code, and account number, if any, of all entities holding priority claims against the debtor or the property of the debtor, as of the date of the filing of the petition.

If any entity other than a spouse in a joint case may be jointly liable on a claim, place an "X" in the column labeled "Codebtor," include the entity on the appropriate schedule of creditors, and complete Schedule H—Codebtors. If a joint petition is filed, state whether husband, wife, both of them, or the marital community may be liable on each claim by placing an "H," "W," "J," or "C" in the column labeled "Husband, Wife, Joint, or Community."

If the claim is contingent, place an "X" in the column labeled "Contingent." If the claim is unliquidated, place an "X" in the column labeled "Unliquidated." If the claim is disputed, place an "X" in the column labeled "Disputed." (You may need to place an "X" in more than one of these three columns.)

Report the total of all claims listed on each sheet in the box labeled "Subtotal" on each sheet. Report the total of all claims listed on this Schedule E in the box labeled "Total" on the last sheet of the completed schedule. Repeat this total also on the Summary of Schedules.

☐ **Check this box if debtor has no creditors holding unsecured priority claims to report on this Schedule E.**

TYPES OF PRIORITY CLAIMS (Check the appropriate box(es) below if claims in that category are listed on the attached sheets)

☐ **Extensions of credit in an involuntary case**

Claims arising in the ordinary course of the debtor's business or financial affairs after the commencement of the case but before the earlier of the appointment of a trustee or the order for relief. 11 U.S.C. § 507(a)(2).

☐ **Wages, salaries, and commissions**

Wages, salaries, and commissions, including vacation, severance, and sick leave pay owing to employees and commissions owing to qualifying independent sales representatives up to $4,300* per person, earned within 90 days immediately preceding the filing of the original petition, or the cessation of business, whichever occurred first, to the extent provided in 11 U.S.C. § 507(a)(3).

☐ **Contributions to employee benefit plans**

Money owed to employee benefit plans for services rendered within 180 days immediately preceding the filing of the original petition, or the cessation of business, whichever occurred first, to the extent provided in 11 U.S.C. § 507(a)(4).

☐ **Certain farmers and fishermen**

Claims of certain farmers and fishermen, up to a maximum of $4,300* per farmer or fisherman, against the debtor, as provided in 11 U.S.C. § 507(a)(5).

☐ **Deposits by individuals**

Claims of individuals up to a maximum of $1,950* for deposits for the purchase, lease, or rental of property or services for personal, family, or household use, that were not delivered or provided. 11 U.S.C. § 507(a)(6).

☐ **Alimony, Maintenance, or Support**

Claims of a spouse, former spouse, or child of the debtor for alimony, maintenance, or support, to the extent provided in 11 U.S.C. § 507(a)(7).

☒ **Taxes and Certain Other Debts Owed to Governmental Units**

Taxes, customs, duties, and penalties owing to federal, state, and local governmental units as set forth in 11 U.S.C. § 507(a)(8).

☐ **Commitments to Maintain the Capital of an Insured Depository Institution**

Claims based on commitments to the FDIC, RTC, Director of the Office of Thrift Supervision, Comptroller of the Currency, or Board of Governors of the Federal Reserve system, or their predecessors or successors, to maintain the capital of an insured depository institution. 11 U.S.C. § 507 (a)(9).

* Amounts are subject to adjustment on April 1, 1998, and every three years thereafter with respect to cases commenced on or after the date of adjustment.

       __1__ continuation sheets attached

In re <u>Herchoo, Martin & Ellen</u>,   Case No._____
           Debtor   (If known)

SCHEDULE E—CREDITORS HOLDING UNSECURED PRIORITY CLAIMS
(Continuation Sheet)

<u>   Taxes   </u>
TYPE OF PRIORITY

CREDITOR'S NAME AND MAILING ADDRESS INCLUDING ZIP CODE	CODEBTOR	HUSBAND, WIFE, JOINT, OR COMMUNITY	DATE CLAIM WAS INCURRED AND CONSIDERATION FOR CLAIM	CONTINGENT	UNLIQUIDATED	DISPUTED	TOTAL AMOUNT OF CLAIM	AMOUNT ENTITLED TO PRIORITY
ACCOUNT NO. 123-456-7890 IRS Fresno, CA 93776		C	April 15, 19XX, 19XY, 19XZ Tax Liability				33,762	33,762
ACCOUNT NO.								
ACCOUNT NO.								
ACCOUNT NO.								
ACCOUNT NO.								

Subtotal ➡ $ 33,762
(Total of this page)

Total ➡ $ 33,762
(Use only on last page)

Sheet no. <u>1</u> of <u>1</u> sheets attached to
Schedule of Creditors Holding Unsecured Priority Claims

(Report total also on Summary of Schedules)

of time—and brief details about why you owe (or might owe) the debt. With wages, salaries, commissions, contributions to employee benefit plans, money owed farmers and fisherman, deposits by individuals, and child support or alimony, put the approximate time over which you failed to make the payments unless you can identify one or two specific dates. With taxes and other debts to the government, note the most recent date you received notice that you owe money or the date any unfiled tax returns were due.

Contingent, Unliquidated, Disputed. Follow the instructions for Schedule D.

Total Amount of Claim. For the priority debt being addressed on this page, put the amount it would take to pay off the debt in full, even if it's more than the amount considered a priority. For taxes, if part of your tax debt is secured and included on Schedule D, list only the amount that is unsecured (and therefore a priority). If the amount isn't determined, write "not yet determined" in this column.

Subtotal/Total. Total the amounts in the Total Amount of Claim column on each page. If you use continuation pages for additional priority debts, enter the total of all priority debts on the final page. If the amount of any debt has not yet been determined, put the total of all the other debts. At the bottom of the first page, fill in the number of continuation pages you are attaching.

Amount Entitled to Priority. If the priority claim is larger than the maximum permitted (for example, you owe $5,000 in wages to a former employee), put the maximum ($4,300) here. If the claim is less than the maximum, put the amount you entered in the Total Amount of Claim column.

6. Schedule F—Creditors Holding Unsecured Nonpriority Claims

In this schedule, list all creditors you didn't list in Schedules D or E. For purposes of completing Schedule F, it doesn't matter that the debt might be nondischargeable (that is, it won't be wiped out at the end of your bankruptcy case), such as back child support or a student loan. It also doesn't matter if you believe that you don't owe the debt. It's essential that you list every creditor to whom you owe, or possibly owe, money. You might be able to copy most of this information from Worksheet 4, Unsecured Debts (Ch. 3), if you filled it out.

Below are a sample completed Schedule F and line-by-line instructions. Use as many preprinted continuation pages as you need.

In re and **Case No.** Follow the instructions for Schedule A.

☐ **Check this box if debtor has no creditors holding unsecured nonpriority claims to report on this Schedule F.** Check this box if you have no other unsecured debts beyond those you listed on Schedule E. For example, if you are filing for Chapter 13 bankruptcy to get current on your mortgage or to pay off your fully secured tax debt, and you have no other creditors, you would check this box. But read the instructions, and the sidebar on "Easy-to-Overlook Creditors," below, before checking this box.

Creditor's Name and Mailing Address, Including Zip Code. List, preferably in alphabetical order, the name and complete mailing address of each unsecured creditor currently owed or who is trying to collect the debt, as well as the account number if you know it. If you have more than one unsecured creditor for a given debt, list the original creditor first and then immediately list the other creditors. For example, if you've been sued or hounded by a collection agency, list the attorney or collection agency in addition to the original creditor. (But you don't have to list a collection agency that had the debt a while back and has ceased collection efforts.)

When you are typing your final papers, if you get to the end and discover that you left a creditor off, don't redo the whole list in search of perfect alphabetical order. Just add the creditors at the end.

In re ___Herchoo, Martin & Ellen___ ,   Case No._____
                        Debtor   (If known)

SCHEDULE F—CREDITORS HOLDING UNSECURED NONPRIORITY CLAIMS

State the name, mailing address, including zip code, and account number, if any, of all entities holding unsecured claims without priority against the debtor or the property of the debtor as of the date of filing of the petition. Do not include claims listed in Schedules D and E. If all creditors will not fit on this page, use the continuation sheet provided.

If any entity other than a spouse in a joint case may be jointly liable on a claim, place an "X" in the column labeled "Codebtor," include the entity on the appropriate schedule of creditors, and complete Schedule H—Codebtors. If a joint petition is filed, state whether husband, wife, both of them, or the marital community may be liable on each claim by placing an "H," "W," "J," or "C" in the column labeled "Husband, Wife, Joint, or Community."

If the claim is contingent, place an "X" in the column labeled "Contingent." If the claim is unliquidated, place an "X" in the column labeled "Unliquidated." If the claim is disputed, place an "X" in the column labeled "Disputed." (You may need to place an "X" in more than one of these three columns.)

Report the total of all claims listed on this schedule in the box labeled "Total" on the last sheet of the completed schedule. Report this total also on the Summary of Schedules.

☐ Check this box if debtor has no creditors holding unsecured nonpriority claims to report on this Schedule F.

CREDITOR'S NAME AND MAILING ADDRESS INCLUDING ZIP CODE	CODEBTOR	HUSBAND, WIFE, JOINT, OR COMMUNITY	DATE CLAIM WAS INCURRED AND CONSIDERATION FOR CLAIM. IF CLAIM IS SUBJECT TO SETOFF, SO STATE	CONTINGENT	UNLIQUIDATED	DISPUTED	AMOUNT OF CLAIM
ACCOUNT NO. 4931 802 1171A City Savings Visa P.O. Box 110110 Indianapolis, IN 46000		C	4/XX–12/XX, credit card charges				12,789
ACCOUNT NO. Miles Murayama, Esq. Jones, Jones, Jones & Murayama 19 Whitehall Ave. Tucson, AZ 85700		C	"				"
ACCOUNT NO. 6968371142 River Bank 11 River Road Sacramento, CA 95000	X	C	12/XX; personal consolidation loan				3,918
ACCOUNT NO.							

___1___ continuation sheets attached

Subtotal ➡ (Total of this page)	$	16,707
Total ➡ (Use only on last page)	$	N/A

(Report total also on Summary of Schedules)

In re Herchoo, Martin & Ellen_____,   Case No._____
                    Debtor   (If known)

SCHEDULE F—CREDITORS HOLDING UNSECURED NONPRIORITY CLAIMS
(Continuation Sheet)

CREDITOR'S NAME AND MAILING ADDRESS INCLUDING ZIP CODE	CODEBTOR	HUSBAND, WIFE, JOINT, OR COMMUNITY	DATE CLAIM WAS INCURRED AND CONSIDERATION FOR CLAIM. IF CLAIM IS SUBJECT TO SETOFF, SO STATE	CONTINGENT	UNLIQUIDATED	DISPUTED	AMOUNT OF CLAIM
ACCOUNT NO. 5564113211 Rural Bank MasterCard P.O. Box 2105 Chicago, IL 60600		C	6/XX–12/XX; credit card charges				6,452
ACCOUNT NO. Patricia Washington, Esq. Washington & Lincoln Legal Plaza, Suite 1 Chicago, IL 60600		C	"				"
ACCOUNT NO. 31-6294-81172 Sweeter's Bank 937 Main Street Tucson, AZ 85700	X	C	1/XX; personal loan to pay for dental work				1,411
ACCOUNT NO.							
ACCOUNT NO.							

Subtotal ➡ (Total of this page)	$	7,863
Total ➡ (Use only on last page)	$	24,570

Sheet no. __1__ of __1__ continuation sheets attached to
Schedule of Creditors Holding Unsecured Nonpriorty Claims

(Report total also on Summary of Schedules)

EASY-TO-OVERLOOK CREDITORS

One debt may involve several different creditors. Remember to include:

- your ex-spouse, if you are obligated under a divorce decree or settlement agreement to pay alimony or child support, to pay joint debts, to turn any property over to your ex or to make payments as a result of your property division
- anyone who cosigned a promissory note, loan application or the like for you
- any holder of a loan or promissory note that you cosigned for someone else
- anybody to whom the debt has been assigned or sold by the original creditor and any other person (such as a bill collector or attorney) trying to collect the debt, and
- anyone who may sue you because of a car accident, business dispute or the like.

Codebtor. If someone else can be legally forced to pay your debt to a listed unsecured creditor, enter an "X" in this column and list the codebtor in the creditor column of this schedule. Common codebtors are listed at Schedule D.

Husband, Wife, Joint or Community. Follow the instructions for Schedule A.

Date Claim Was Incurred and Consideration for Claim. If Claim is Subject to Setoff So State. Specify when the debt was incurred. It may be one date or a period of time. With credit card debts, put the approximate time over which you ran up the charges unless the unpaid charges were made on one or two specific dates. If there is more than one creditor for a single debt, list the same date for each creditor.

Then state what the debt was for. You can be general ("clothes" or "household furnishings") or specific ("refrigerator" or "teeth capping").

If you are entitled to a setoff against the debt—that is, the creditor owes you some money, too—give the amount and briefly state why you think you are entitled to a setoff.

Contingent, Unliquidated, Disputed. Follow the instructions for Schedule D.

Amount of Claim. List the amount of the debt claimed by the creditor, even if you dispute the amount. That way, it will all be wiped out if it's discharged at the end of your bankruptcy case. If there's more than one creditor for a single debt, put the debt amount across from the original creditor and put ditto marks (") across from each subsequent creditor you list.

Subtotal/Total. Total the amounts in the last column for this page. Do not include the amounts represented by the ditto marks if you listed multiple creditors for a single debt. On the final page (which may be the first page or a preprinted continuation page), enter the total of all unsecured claims. On the first page, in the bottom left corner, note the number of continuation pages you are attaching.

7. Schedule G—Executory Contracts and Unexpired Leases

In this form, you list every executory contract or unexpired lease that you're a party to. "Executory" means the contract is still in force—that is, both parties are still obligated to perform important acts under it. Similarly, "unexpired" means that the contract or lease period hasn't run out—that is, it is still in effect.

If you are delinquent in payments that were due under a contract or lease, list the delinquency as a debt on Schedule D, E or F, not here. The purpose of this schedule is to identify your existing obligations. As a part of your Chapter 13 plan, you will state whether you want to continue the lease or contract, or end your obligation.

Common examples of executory contracts and unexpired leases are:

- residential leases or rental agreements
- business leases or rental agreements
- service contracts
- business contracts
- time-share contracts or leases
- contracts of sale for real estate
- copyright or patent license agreements
- leases of real estate (surface and underground) for the purpose of harvesting timber, minerals or oil
- future homeowners' association fee requirements
- agreements for boat docking privileges, and
- insurance contract policies.

Below are a sample completed Schedule G and line-by-line instructions.

In re and **Case No.** Follow the instructions for Schedule A.

☐ **Check this box if debtor has no executory contracts or unexpired leases.** Check this box if it applies and go on to Schedule H; otherwise, complete the form.

Name and Mailing Address, Including Zip Code, of Other Parties to Lease or Contract. Provide the name and full address (including zip code) of each party—other than yourself—to each lease or contract. These parties are either people who signed agreements or the companies for whom these people work. If you're unsure about whom to list, include the person who signed an agreement, any company whose name appears on the agreement, and anybody who might have an interest in having the contract or lease enforced. If you still aren't sure, put "don't know."

Description of Contract or Lease and Nature of Debtor's Interest. State Whether Lease Is for Nonresidential Real Property. State Contract Number of any Government Contract. For each lease or contract, give:

- a description of the basic type (for instance, residential lease, commercial lease, car lease, business obligation, copyright license)
- the date the contract or lease was signed
- the date the contract is to expire (if any)
- a summary of each party's rights and obligations under the lease or contract, and
- the contract number, if the contract is with any government body.

In re ___Herchoo, Martin & Ellen___ ,
Debtor

Case No._____
(If known)

SCHEDULE G—EXECUTORY CONTRACTS AND UNEXPIRED LEASES

Describe all executory contracts of any nature and all unexpired leases of real personal property. Include any timeshare interests.

State nature of debtor's interest in contract, i.e., "Purchaser," "Agent," etc. State whether debtor is the lessor or lessee of a lease.

Provide the names and complete mailing addresses of all other parties to each lease or contract described.

NOTE: A party listed on this schedule will not receive notice of the filing of this case unless the party is also scheduled in the appropriate schedule of creditors.

☐ Check this box if debtor has no executory contracts or unexpired leases.

NAME AND MAILING ADDRESS, INCLUDING ZIP CODE, OF OTHER PARTIES TO LEASE OR CONTRACT	DESCRIPTION OF CONTRACT OR LEASE AND NATURE OF DEBTOR'S INTEREST. STATE WHETHER LEASE IS FOR NONRESIDENTIAL REAL PROPERTY. STATE CONTRACT NUMBER OF ANY GOVERNMENT CONTRACT
Summer Vacations Co. P.O. Box 1811 53 West Waterway Blvd. Cape Cod, MA 01000 Manager: Darcy Perkpoint	Leased Timeshare; agreement signed 7/XX; 25-year lease with 22 years remaining

8. Schedule H—Codebtors

In Schedules D, E and F, you identified those debts for which you have codebtors—usually, a cosigner, guarantor, ex-spouse, non-filing spouse or nonmarital partner. You must also list those codebtors here.

As long as your Chapter 13 case is pending, collection efforts against your codebtors must cease. The creditor can't go after the codebtor unless at the end of your Chapter 13 bankruptcy case, the court discharges (wipes out) a balance on the debt. Most Chapter 13 debtors avoid this by paying in full their debts with codebtors.

Below are a sample completed Schedule H and line-by-line instructions.

In re and **Case No.** Follow the instructions for Schedule A.

☐ **Check this box if debtor has no codebtors.** Check this box if it applies; otherwise, complete the form.

Name and Address of Codebtor. List the name and complete address (including zip code) of each codebtor. If the codebtor is a nonfiling spouse, put all names by which that person was known during the previous six years.

Name and Address of Creditor. List the name and address of each creditor (as listed on Schedule D, E or F) to which each codebtor is indebted.

> **EXAMPLE:** Tom Martin cosigned three different loans—with three different banks—for Mabel Green, who is now filing for Chapter 13 bankruptcy. In the first column, Mabel lists Tom Martin as a codebtor. In the second, Mabel lists each of the three banks.

IF YOU ARE MARRIED AND FILING ALONE
If you live in a community property state, your spouse may be a codebtor for most of the debts you listed in Schedules D, E and F. This is because in these states, most debts incurred by one spouse are owed by both spouses. In this event, just list your spouse as a codebtor; and in the second column, simply write "all creditors listed in Schedules D, E and F, except:" and then list any creditors whom you owe solely.

9. Schedule I—Current Income of Individual Debtor(s)

Worksheet 5 in Ch. 4, designed to calculate your income, contains all the information you need to complete Schedule I.

Below is a sample completed Schedule I, and line-by-line instructions. If you're married and filing jointly, you must fill in information for both spouses. If you are mar-

ried but filing alone, you must still fill in the information for both spouses unless you and your spouse are separated.

In re and **Case No.** Follow the instructions for Schedule A.

Debtor's Marital Status. Enter your marital status. Your choices are single, married, separated (you aren't living with your spouse and plan never to again), widowed or divorced. You are divorced only if you have received a final judgment of divorce from a court.

Dependents of Debtor and Spouse. List the names, ages and relationships of all persons who receive at least half of their support from you and your spouse. This may include your children, your spouse's children, your parents, other relatives and domestic partners. It does not include your spouse, unless you are filing alone.

Employment. Provide the requested employment information. If you have more than one employer, enter "See continuation sheet" just below the box containing the employment information and then complete a continuation sheet. If you are retired, unemployed or disabled, put when you last worked and what you did.

Income. Enter your estimated monthly gross income from regular employment, before any payroll deductions are taken. In the second blank, put your estimated monthly overtime pay. Add them together and enter the subtotal in the third blank.

If you are self-employed or an independent contractor, use the blank below labeled "Regular income from operation of business or profession or farm." Also, attach a sheet of paper. Call it "Attachment to Schedule I" and include your name (and spouse's name if you're filing jointly) and a separate statement of income and expenses for the operation of your business. Anyone with a financial background (such as a banker, accountant, bookkeeper or tax preparer) can help you draft one.

Payroll Deductions. In the four blanks, enter the deductions taken from your gross salary. The deductions listed are the most common ones, but you may have others to report. Other possible deductions are state disability taxes, wages withheld or garnished for child support, credit union loan payments or perhaps payments on a student loan or a car.

Subtotal of Payroll Deductions. Add your payroll deductions and enter the subtotal.

Total Net Monthly Take Home Pay. Subtract your payroll deductions subtotal from your income subtotal.

Regular income from operation of business or profession or farm. If you are self-employed or operate a sole proprietorship, enter your monthly income from that source here. If it's been fairly steady for at least one calendar year, divide the amount you entered on your most recent tax return

In re ___Herchoo, Martin & Ellen___ ,

Debtor

Case No._____

(If known)

SCHEDULE H—CODEBTORS

Provide the information requested concerning any person or entity, other than a spouse in a joint case, that is also liable on any debts listed by debtor in the schedules of creditors. Include all guarantors and co-signers. In community property states, a married debtor not filing a joint case should report the name and address of the nondebtor spouse on this schedule. Include all names used by the nondebtor spouse during the six years immediately preceding the commencement of this case.

☐ Check this box if debtor has no codebtors.

NAME AND ADDRESS OF CODEBTOR	NAME AND ADDRESS OF CREDITOR
Maria Montumba 63 "C" Street Sacramento, CA 95000	River Bank 11 River Road Sacramento, CA 95000 Sweeter's Bank 937 Main Street Tucson, AZ 85700

(IRS Form 1040 Schedule C) by 12 for a monthly amount. If your income hasn't been steady for at least one calendar year, enter the average net income from your business or profession for the past three months. In either case you must attach a statement of your income. Use your most recent filed IRS Schedule C.

Income from real property. Enter your monthly income from real estate rentals, leases or licenses (such as mineral exploration, oil and the like).

Interest and dividends. Enter the average estimated monthly interest you receive from bank or security deposits and other investments, such as stocks.

Alimony, maintenance or support payments payable to the debtor for the debtor's use or that of dependents listed above. Enter the average monthly amount you receive for your support (alimony, spousal support or maintenance) or that of your children (child support).

Social Security or other government assistance. Enter the total monthly amount you receive in Social Security, AFDC, SSI, public assistance, disability payments, veterans' benefits, unemployment compensation, worker's compensation or any other government benefit. If you receive food stamps, include their monthly value. Specify the source of the benefits.

Pension or retirement income. Enter the total monthly amount of all pension, annuity, IRA, Keogh or other retirement benefits you currently receive.

Other monthly income. Specify any other income (such as royalty payments or payments from a trust) you receive on a regular basis and enter the monthly amount here. You may have to divide by 3, 6 or 12 if you receive the payments quarterly, semi-annually or annually.

Total Monthly Income. Add all additional income to the Total Net Monthly Take Home Pay amount and enter the grand total in the box.

Total Combined Monthly Income. If you are filing jointly, add your total income to your spouse's total income and enter the result here.

Your Total Monthly Income (or Total Combined Monthly Income if you are filing jointly) should be the same figure as your Total Monthly Income on Worksheet 5.

Describe any increase or decrease of more than 10% in any of the above categories anticipated to occur within the year following the filing of this document. Identify any changes in your pay or other income—in excess of 10%—that you expect in the coming year. This information could be crucial in getting your Chapter 13 plan approved by the court. If your income is apt to go down, you'll need to show where you will make up the difference in order to make your Chapter 13 plan payments. If your income is likely to go up, the court will probably schedule an increase in your Chapter 13 plan payments.

10. Schedule J—Current Expenditures of Individual Debtor(s)

Worksheets 6 and 7 in Ch. 4, designed to calculate your expenses and disposable, contain all the information you need to complete Schedule J.

In re ___Herchoo, Martin & Ellen___ , Case No._____

Debtor (If known)

SCHEDULE I—CURRENT INCOME OF INDIVIDUAL DEBTOR(S)

The column labled "Spouse" must be completed in all cases filed by joint debtors and by a married debtor in a Chapter 12 or 13 case whether or not a joint petition is filed, unless the spouses are separated and a joint petition is not filed.

DEBTOR'S MARITAL STATUS:	DEPENDENTS OF DEBTOR AND SPOUSE		
	NAMES	AGE	RELATIONSHIP
Married	Randy Herchoo	12	son

Employment:	DEBTOR		SPOUSE
Occupation	Teacher/Writer		Lab Technician
Name of Employer	Tucson High School & Community College		Pima County Hospital
How long employed	16 years / 1 year		3 months
Address of Employer	37 Wichita Path Tucson, AZ 85700	190 Kline Road Tucson, AZ 85700	4000 Carpenter Drive Tucson, AZ 85700

INCOME: (Estimate of average monthly income)	DEBTOR	SPOUSE
Current monthly gross wages, salary, and commissions (pro rate if not paid monthly)	$ 4,000	$ 2,000
Estimated monthly overtime	$ 0	$ 0
SUBTOTAL	$ 4,000	$ 2,000
LESS PAYROLL DEDUCTIONS		
a. Payroll taxes and Social Security	$ 800	$ 400
b. Insurance	$ 250	$ 0
c. Union dues	$ 50	$ 0
d. Other (Specify: _____)	$ 0	$ 0
SUBTOTAL OF PAYROLL DEDUCTIONS	$ 1,100	$ 400
TOTAL NET MONTHLY TAKE HOME PAY	$ 2,900	$ 1,600
Regular income from operation of business or profession or farm (attach detailed statement)	$ 0	$ 0
Income from real property	$ 0	$ 0
Interest and dividends	$ 0	$ 0
Alimony, maintenance or support payments payable to the debtor for the debtor's use or that of dependents listed above	$ 0	$ 0
Social Security or other government assistance (Specify:_____)	$ 0	$ 0
Pension or retirement income	$ 0	$ 0
Other monthly income	$ 0	$ 0
(Specify: Royalties from math textbooks)	$ 1,600	$ 0
_____	$ 0	$ 0
TOTAL MONTHLY INCOME	$ 4,510	$ 1,600
TOTAL COMBINED MONTHLY INCOME $ 6,110	(Report also on Summary of Schedules)	

Describe any increase or decrease of more than 10% in any of the above categories anticipated to occur within the year following the filing of this document:

Ellen currently works 30 hours/week, and is in a probation period. At six months, her income should go up (we're not sure how much) and she hopes to go up to 40 hours some time in the coming year.

Below is a sample completed Schedule J, and line-by-line instructions. If you're married and filing jointly, you must fill in information for both spouses. If you are married but filing alone, only fill in the information for yourself.

In re and **Case No.** Follow the instructions for Schedule A.

☐ **Check this box if a joint petition is filed and debtor's spouse maintains a separate household. Complete a separate schedule of expenditures labeled "Spouse."** If you and your spouse are jointly filing for bankruptcy, but maintain separate households (for example, you've recently separated), check this box and make sure that you each fill out a separate Schedule J.

Expenditures. For each listed item, fill in your monthly expenses. If you make some payments biweekly, quarterly, semi-annually or annually, prorate them to show your monthly payment. Here are some pointers:

- Do not list payroll deductions that you listed on Schedule I.
- Include payments you make for your dependents' expenses, as long as those expenses are reasonable and necessary for their support.
- **Utilities—Other:** This includes garbage and cable TV service.
- **Installment payments—Other:** Write "credit card accounts" on one line and enter your total monthly payments for them. Put the average amount you actually pay, even if it's less than it should be. On the other line put "loans" (except auto loans) and enter your total payments.

Total Monthly Expenses. Total up all your expenses. Your Total Monthly Expenses should be the same figure as your Total Monthly Expenses on Worksheet 6.

For Chapter 12 and Chapter 13 Debtors Only. Enter your Total Monthly Income (or Total Combined Monthly Income if you are filing jointly) from Schedule I in blank A. Enter the Total Monthly Expenses from just above in blank B. Subtract the difference and enter it in blank C. (This should match your Total Monthly Disposable Income amount from Worksheet 7.)

Blank D asks for the amount you are proposing to pay your creditors during your Chapter 13 case. You probably won't be able to fill this in until you after you write your plan in Ch. 7. For now, you can put a checkmark on the form next to blank D as a reminder that you must return to this question after you write your plan.

Once your plan is written. If you proposed in your Chapter 13 repayment plan to pay your unsecured creditors less than 100% of what you owe, then enter the number you put in blank C—that is, your entire disposable income for the length of your plan. If you proposed to pay your unsecured creditors 100% of what you owe, then enter the amount you intend to pay each month to pay off your creditors over 36 months or however many months you want your plan to last.

11. Summary of Schedules

This form helps the bankruptcy trustee and judge get a quick look at your bankruptcy filing. Below is a completed Summary; line-by-line instructions follow it.

Court Name. Copy this information from Form 1— Voluntary Petition.

In re and **Case No.** Follow the instructions for Schedule A.

Name of Schedule. This column just lists the schedules you've filled out. Don't add anything.

Attached (Yes/No). You should have completed all of the schedules, so type "Yes" in this column for each schedule.

Number of Sheets. Enter the number of pages you completed for each schedule. Remember to count continuation pages. Enter the total at the bottom of the column.

Amounts Scheduled. For each column—Assets, Liabilities and Other—copy the totals from Schedules A, B, D, E, F, I and J and enter them where indicated. Add up the amounts in the Assets and Liabilities columns and enter their totals at the bottom.

Now, go back and fill in the statistical/administrative information on page 1 of Form 1—Voluntary Petition.

12. Declaration Concerning Debtor's Schedules

In this form, you are required to swear that everything you have said on your schedules is true and correct. Deliberate lying (perjury) is a major sin in bankruptcy. It could cost you your bankruptcy discharge, a fine of up to $500,000 and up to five years in prison.

Below is a completed Declaration and instructions.

In re and **Case No.** Follow the instructions for Schedule A.

Declaration Under Penalty of Perjury by Individual Debtor. Enter the total number of pages in your schedules (the number on the Summary plus one for the summary itself). Enter the date and sign the form. If you are filing jointly, be sure that your spouse signs and dates the form.

Certification and Signature of Non-Attorney Bankruptcy Petition Preparer. If a BPP typed your forms, have that person complete this section. Otherwise, type "N/A" anywhere in the box.

Declaration Under Penalty of Perjury on Behalf of Corporation or Partnership. Enter "N/A" anywhere in this blank.

In re ___Herchoo, Martin & Ellen___ ,   Case No._____
                     Debtor   (If known)

SCHEDULE J—CURRENT EXPENDITURES OF INDIVIDUAL DEBTOR(S)

Complete this schedule by estimating the average monthly expenses of the debtor and the debtor's family. Pro rate any payments made bi-weekly, quarterly, semi-annually, or annually to show monthly rate.

☐ Check this box if a joint petition is filed and debtor's spouse maintains a separate household. Complete a separate schedule of expenditures labeled "Spouse."

Rent or home mortgage payment (include lot rented for mobile home)	$ 2,160
Are real estate taxes included? Yes _X_ No _____	
Is property insurance included? Yes _X_ No _____	
Utilities: Electricity and heating fuel	$ 75
Water and sewer	$ 65
Telephone	$ 50
Other ___garbage, cable___	$ 40
Home maintenance (repairs and upkeep)	$ 150
Food	$ 600
Clothing	$ 50
Laundry and dry cleaning	$ 15
Medical and dental expenses	$ 50
Transportation (not including car payments)	$ 60
Recreation, clubs and entertainment, newspapers, magazines, etc.	$ 20
Charitable contributions	$ 20
Insurance (not deducted from wages or included in home mortgage payments)	
Homeowner's or renter's	$ 0
Life	$ 125
Health	$ 0
Auto	$ 60
Other ___Disability___	$ 80
Taxes (not deducted from wages or included in home mortgage payments)	
(Specify: _____)	$ _____
Installment payments: (In Chapter 12 and 13 cases, do not list payments to be included in the plan)	
Auto	$ 355
Other ___Home equity loan___	$ 335
Other _____	$ 0
Alimony, maintenance, and support paid to others	$ 0
Payments for support of additional dependents not living at your home	$ 0
Regular expenses from operation of business, profession, or farm (attach detailed statement)	$ 0
Other _____	$ 0
TOTAL MONTHLY EXPENSES (Report also on Summary of Schedules)	$ 4,310

[FOR CHAPTER 12 AND CHAPTER 13 DEBTORS ONLY]
Provide the information requested below, including whether plan payments are to be made bi-weekly, monthly, annually, or at some other regular interval.

A. Total projected monthly income	$ 6,110
B. Total projected monthly expenses	$ 4,310
C. Excess income (A minus B)	$ 1,800
D. Total amount to be paid into plan each ___month___	$ 1,800
(interval)	

United States Bankruptcy Court

_____XXXXX_____ District of __Arizona, Tucson Division__

In re __Herchoo, Martin P._____,   Case No._____
            Debtor   (If known)

SUMMARY OF SCHEDULES

Indicate as to each schedule whether that schedule is attached and state the number of pages in each. Report the totals from Schedules A, B, D, E, F, I and J in the boxes provided. Add the amounts from Schedules A and B to determine the total amount of the debtor's assets. Add the amounts from Schedules D, E and F to determine the total amount of the debtor's liabilities.

| NAME OF SCHEDULE | ATTACHED (YES/NO) | NUMBER OF SHEETS | AMOUNTS SCHEDULED | | |
			ASSETS	LIABILITIES	OTHER
A Real Property	Yes	1	$ 275,000		
B Personal Property	Yes	4	$ 61,604		
C Property Claimed as Exempt	Yes	2			
D Creditors Holding Secured Claims	Yes	1		$ 265,260	
E Creditors Holding Unsecured Priority Claims	Yes	2		$ 33,762	
F Creditors Holding Unsecured Nonpriority Claims	Yes	2		$ 24,570	
G Executory Contracts and Unexpired Leases	Yes	1			
H Codebtors	Yes	1			
I Current Income of Individual Debtor(s)	Yes	1			$ 6,110
J Current Expenditures of Individual Debtor(s)	Yes	1			$ 4,310

Total Number of Sheets of All Schedules ➡   16

Total Assets ➡ $ 336,604

Total Liabilities ➡ $ 323,592

In re ___Herchoo, Martin & Ellen___ ,   Case No._____
                    Debtor   (If known)

DECLARATION CONCERNING DEBTOR'S SCHEDULES

DECLARATION UNDER PENALTY OF PERJURY BY INDIVIDUAL DEBTOR

I declare under penalty of perjury that I have read the foregoing summary and schedules consisting of _____17_____
sheets, and that they are true and correct to the best of my knowledge, information, and belief.   (Total shown on summary page plus 1)

Date_____2/25/XX_____   Signature _____*Martin Herchoo*_____
                                                                    Debtor

Date_____2/25/XX_____   Signature _____*Ellen Herchoo*_____
                                                            (Joint Debtor, if any)

                                        [If joint case, both spouses must sign.]

CERTIFICATION AND SIGNATURE OF NON-ATTORNEY BANKRUPTCY PETITION PREPARER (See 11 U.S.C. § 110)

I certify that I am a bankruptcy petition preparer as defined in 11 U.S.C. § 110, that I prepared this document for compensation, and that I have provided the debtor with a copy of this document.

_____N/A_____   _____
Printed or Typed Name of Bankruptcy Petition Preparer   Social Security No.

_____

_____

Address

Names and Social Security numbers of all other individuals who prepared or assisted in preparing this document:

If more than one person prepared this document, attach additional signed sheets conforming to the appropriate Official Form for each person.

X_____   _____
Signature of Bankruptcy Petition Preparer   Date

A bankruptcy petition preparer's failure to comply with the provisions of Title 11 and the Federal Rules of Bankruptcy Procedure may result in fine or imprisonment or both.
11 U.S.C. § 110; 18 U.S.C. § 156.
                    N/A

DECLARATION UNDER PENALTY OF PERJURY ON BEHALF OF CORPORATION OR PARTNERSHIP

I, the _____ [the president or other officer or an authorized agent of the corporation or a member or an authorized agent of the partnership] of the _____ [corporation or partnership] named as debtor in this case, declare under penalty of perjury that I have read the foregoing summary and schedules, consisting of _____ sheets, and that they are true and correct to the best of my knowledge, information, and belief.
(Total shown on summary page plus 1)

Date_____   Signature _____

                                        _____
                                        [Print or type name of individual signing on behalf of debtor]

[An individual signing on behalf of a partnership or corporation must indicate position or relationship to debtor.]

Penalty for making a false statement or concealing property: Fine of up to $500,000, imprisonment for up to 5 years, or both. 18 U.S.C. §§ 152 and 3571.

G. Form 7—Statement of Financial Affairs

Congratulations—you're almost through. For most people, the Statement of Financial Affairs is the last form to fill in before writing the repayment plan (Ch. 7). This form gives information about your recent financial transactions, such as payments to creditors, sales or other transfers of property and gifts. The questions on the form are, for the most part, self-explanatory. Spouses filing jointly combine their answers and complete only one form.

If you have no information for a particular item, check the "None" box. If you fail to answer a question and don't check "None," you will have to amend your papers—that is, file a corrected form—after you file. Add continuation sheets if necessary. Be sure the information you put on this form matches the information you put on other forms asking the same questions.

A completed Statement of Financial Affairs and instructions for questions that are not self-explanatory follow.

Court name. Copy this information from Form 1—Voluntary Petition.

In re and **Case No.** Follow the instructions for Schedule A.

1. Income from employment or operation of business. Enter your gross income so far this calendar year and for the two prior calendar years. This means the total income before taxes and other payroll deductions or business expenses are removed.

2. Income other than from employment or operation of business. Include interest, dividends, royalties, worker's compensation, other government benefits and all other money you have received from sources other than your job or business during the last two years. Provide the source of each amount, the dates received and the reason you received the money so that the trustee can verify it.

3. Payments to creditors. Here you list payments you've recently made to creditors. There are two kinds of creditors—arm's-length and insiders. An insider—defined on the first page of the Statement of Financial Affairs—is essentially a relative or close business associate. All other creditors are arm's-length creditors.

a. List any payment over $600 made to an arm's-length creditor, if the payment was made:
  • to repay a loan, installment purchase or other debt
  • during the 90 days before you file your bankruptcy petition.

b. List any payment made to an insider creditor, if the payment was made within one year before you file your bankruptcy petition. Include alimony and child support payments.

The purpose of these questions is discover if you have "preferred" any creditor over others. The trustee can demand that the creditor turn over the amount of any payment listed here to the court, so the trustee can use the money to pay your other unsecured creditors. This rarely happens in Chapter 13 bankruptcy, however, unless you propose to pay your unsecured creditors very little (such as 10%) or nothing.

4. Suits, executions, garnishments and attachments.

a. Include all court actions that you are currently involved in or which you were involved in during one year before filing. Court actions include personal injury cases, small claims court lawsuits, contract disputes, divorces, paternity suits, support or custody modification actions, criminal prosecutions and the like. For each case, include:
Caption of the suit and case number. The caption is the case title (such as John Jones v. Ginny Jones). The case number is assigned by the court clerk and appears on the first page of any court-filed paper.
Nature of the proceeding. A phrase, or even a one-word description, is sufficient. For example, "suit by debtor for damage to debtor's car caused by accident" or "divorce."
Court and location. This information is on any court paper you received or prepared.
Status or disposition. State whether the case is awaiting trial, is pending a decision, is on appeal or has ended.

b. If, at any time during the year before you file for bankruptcy, your wages, real estate or personal property were taken from you under the authority of a court order to pay a debt, enter the requested information. If you don't know the exact date, put "on or about" the approximate date.

5. Repossessions, foreclosures and returns. If, at any time during the year before you file for bankruptcy, a creditor repossessed or foreclosed on property you had bought and were making payments on, or had pledged as collateral for a loan, give the requested information. For instance, if your car, boat or video equipment was repossessed because you defaulted on your payments, describe it here. Also, if you voluntarily returned property to a creditor because you couldn't keep up the payments, enter that here.

6. Assignments and receiverships.

a. If, at any time during the 120 days (four months) before you file for bankruptcy, you assigned (legally transferred) your right to receive benefits or property to a creditor to pay a debt, list it here. Examples include voluntarily assigning a percentage of your wages to a creditor for several months or assigning a portion of a personal injury award to an attorney. (Involuntarily turning your wages or property over to someone else is a garnishment or attachment—Item 4—not an assignment.) The assignee is the person to whom the assignment was made, such as the creditor or attorney. The terms of the assignment should be given briefly— for example, "wages assigned to Snorkle's Department Store to satisfy debt of $500."

b. Identify all of your property that has been in the hands of a court-appointed receiver, custodian or other official during the year before you file for bankruptcy. If you've made child support payments directly to a court, and the court in turn paid your child's other parent, list those payments here.

7. Gifts. Provide the requested information about gifts you've made in the past year. The bankruptcy court and trustee want this information to make sure you haven't improperly unloaded any property before filing for bankruptcy so you wouldn't have to pay much to your unsecured creditors. List all charitable donations over $100 and gifts to family members over $200.

You don't have to list gifts to family members that are "ordinary and usual," but there is no easy way to identify such gifts. The best test is whether someone outside of the family might think the gift was unusual under the circumstances. If so, list it. Forgiving a loan is also a gift, as is charging interest substantially below the market rate. Other gifts include giving a car or prepaid trip to a business associate.

8. Losses. Provide the requested information about recent financial losses.

9. Payments related to debt counseling or bankruptcy. If you paid an improperly high fee to an attorney, bankruptcy petition preparer, debt consultant or debt consolidator, the trustee may try to get some of it back if you are not proposing to pay much to your unsecured creditors. Be sure to list all payments made by someone else on your behalf (such as your mother helping you out by paying your attorney's bill) as well as payments you made directly.

10. Other transfers. List all real estate and personal property that you've sold or used as collateral for a secured debt during the last year. Some examples are selling or abandoning (junking) a car, pledging your house as security (collateral) for a loan, granting an easement on real estate or trading property.

Don't include any gifts you listed in Item 7. Also, don't list property you parted with as a regular part of your business or financial affairs. For example, if you operate a mail order book business, don't list the books you sold during the past year. Similarly, don't put down payments for regular goods and services, such as your phone bill, utilities or rent.

11. Closed financial accounts. Provide information for each account in your name or for your benefit that was closed during the past year or transferred to someone else.

12. Safe deposit boxes. Provide information for each safe deposit box you've had within the past year.

13. Setoffs. A setoff is when a creditor, often a bank, uses money in a customer's account to pay a debt owed to the creditor by that customer. Here, list any setoffs your creditors have made during the last 90 days.

14. Property held for another person. Describe all property you've borrowed, or are storing or holding in trust for someone. Examples are funds in an irrevocable trust controlled by you and property you're holding as executor or administrator of an estate.

➡ SHORTCUT FOR NONBUSINESS DEBTORS
Only business debtors must complete questions 16-21. A business debtor is anyone who operated a profession or business, or who was otherwise self-employed, anytime during the two years before filing for bankruptcy. If you are not a business debtor, put an X in the remaining "None" boxes, type "N/A" right before question 16 and go on to the signature lines at the end of this form.

16. Nature, location and name of business. Provide the information requested in question "a." If question "b" or "c" applies to you, you should not be using this book.

17. Books, records and financial statements.

a. Identify every person other than yourself who was involved in the accounting of your business during the previous six years. Usually this means a bookkeeper or accountant. If you were the only person involved in your business's accounting, check "None."

b. If your books weren't audited by a firm or individual during the past two years, check "None." Otherwise, fill in the requested information.

c. Usually, you, your bookkeeper, accountant, ex-business associate or possibly an ex-mate will have business records. If any are missing, explain; the more the loss of your records was beyond your control, the better off you'll be.

d. You may have prepared a financial statement if you applied to a bank for a loan or line of credit for your business or in your own name. If you're self-employed and applied for a personal loan to purchase a car or house, you probably submitted a financial statement as

FORM 7. STATEMENT OF FINANCIAL AFFAIRS

UNITED STATES BANKRUPTCY COURT

_____ XXXXX _____ DISTRICT OF __Arizona, Tucson Division__

In re: _____Herchoo, Martin & Ellen_____ ,   Case No. _____

          (Name)   (If known)

          Debtor

STATEMENT OF FINANCIAL AFFAIRS

This statement is to be completed by every debtor. Spouses filing a joint petition may file a single statement on which the information for both spouses is combined. If the case is filed under Chapter 12 or Chapter 13, a married debtor must furnish information for both spouses whether or not a joint petition is filed, unless the spouses are separated and a joint petition is not filed. An individual debtor engaged in business as a sole proprietor, partner, family farmer, or self-employed professional, should provide the information requested on this statement concerning all such activities as well as the individual's personal affairs.

Questions 1–15 are to be completed by all debtors. Debtors that are or have been in business, as defined below, also must complete Questions 16–21. **Each question must be answered. If the answer to any question is "None," or the question is not applicable, mark the box labeled "None."** If additional space is needed for the answer to any question, use and attach a separate sheet properly identified with the case name, case number (if known), and the number of the question.

DEFINITIONS

"In business." A debtor is "in business" for the purpose of this form if the debtor is a corporation or partnership. An individual debtor is "in business" for the purpose of this form if the debtor is or has been, within the two years immediately preceding the filing of this bankruptcy case, any of the following: an officer, director, managing executive, or person in control of a corporation; a partner, other than a limited partner, of a partnership; a sole proprietor or self-employed.

"Insider." The term "insider" includes but is not limited to: relatives of the debtor; general partners of the debtor and their relatives; corporations of which the debtor is an officer, director, or person in control; officers, directors, and any person in control of a corporate debtor and their relatives; affiliates of the debtor and insiders of such affiliates; any managing agent of the debtor. 11 U.S.C. § 101(30).

1. **Income from employment or operation of business**

None   State the gross amount of income the debtor has received from employment, trade, or profession, or from operation of the debtor's
☐   business from the beginning of this calendar year to the date this case was commenced. State also the gross amounts received during the **two years** immediately preceding this calendar year. (A debtor that maintains, or has maintained, financial records on the basis of a fiscal rather than a calendar year may report fiscal year income. Identify the beginning and ending dates of the debtor's fiscal year.) If a joint petition is filed, state income for each spouse separately. (Married debtors filing under Chapter 12 or Chapter 13 must state income of both spouses whether or not a joint petition is filed, unless the spouses are separated and a joint petition is not filed.)

AMOUNT	SOURCE (If more than one)
$6,000 (1/1/XX–2/15/XX)	Husband's job
$3,000 (1/1/XX–2/15/XX)	Wife's job
$41,000 (1/1/XY–12/31/XY)	Husband's job
$2,000 (12/1/XY–12/31/XY)	Wife's job
$36,000 (1/1/XZ–12/31/XZ)	Husband's job
$28,000 (1/1/XZ–12/31/XZ)	Wife's job

2. Income other than from employment or operation of business

None

☐

State the amount of income received by the debtor other than from employment, trade, profession, or operation of the debtor's business during the **two years** immediately preceding the commencement of this case. Give particulars. If a joint petition is filed, state income for each spouse separately. (Married debtors filing under Chapter 12 or Chapter 13 must state income for each spouse whether or not a joint petition is filed, unless the spouses are separated and a joint petition is not filed.)

AMOUNT	SOURCE
$19,200	19XX (husband's royalties)
$16,307	19XY (husband's royalties)
$ 120	19XX (joint money market account)
$ 175	19XY (joint money market account)

3. Payments to creditors

None   a.

☐

List all payments on loans, installment purchases of goods or services, and other debts, aggregating more than $600 to any creditor, made within **90 days** immediately preceding the commencement of this case. (Married debtors filing under Chapter 12 or Chapter 13 must include payments by either or both spouses whether or not a joint petition is filed, unless the spouses are separated and a joint petition is not filed.)

NAME AND ADDRESS OF CREDITOR	DATES OF PAYMENTS	AMOUNT PAID	AMOUNT STILL OWING
Big Home Loan Bank (home equity loan)	2/19/XX	$335	$16,080
232 Desert Way	1/19/XX	$335	
Tucson, AZ 85700	12/19/XY	$335	
Car Finance Co.	1/5/XX	$355	$7,400
P.O. Box 1183	12/5/XY	$355	
San Ramon, CA 94001			

None   b.

☒

List all payments made within **one year** immediately preceding the commencement of this case, to or for the benefit of, creditors who are or were insiders. (Married debtors filing under Chapter 12 or Chapter 13 must include payments by either or both spouses whether or not a joint petition is filed, unless the spouses are separated and a joint petition is not filed.)

NAME AND ADDRESS OF CREDITOR; RELATIONSHIP TO DEBTOR	DATES OF PAYMENTS	AMOUNT PAID	AMOUNT STILL OWING

4. Suits, executions, garnishments and attachments

None   a.

☐

List all suits to which the debtor is or was a party within **one year** immediately preceding the filing of this bankruptcy case. (Married debtors filing under Chapter 12 or Chapter 13 must include information concerning either or both spouses whether or not a joint petition is filed, unless the spouses are separated and a joint petition is not filed.)

CAPTION OF SUIT AND CASE NUMBER	NATURE OF PROCEEDING	COURT AND LOCATION	STATUS OR DISPOSITION
Williams v. Herchoo SCC157381	suit for property damage to car	Pima County Small Claims Court, Tucson, Arizona	Judgment for Williams, who recorded a lien against our house. He also has garnished Martin's wages

None
☐

b. Describe all property that has been attached, garnished or seized under any legal or equitable process within **one year** immediately preceding the commencement of this case. (Married debtors filing under Chapter 12 or Chapter 13 must include information concerning property of either or both spouses whether or not a joint petition is filed, unless the spouses are separated and a joint petition is not filed.)

NAME AND ADDRESS OF PERSON FOR WHOSE BENEFIT PROPERTY WAS SEIZED	DATE OF SEIZURE	DESCRIPTION AND VALUE OF PROPERTY
Ken Williams 17 North Rippington St. Tucson, AZ	2/15/XX 2/1/XX 1/15/XX 1/2/XX 12/15/XY	each pay period Mr. William's garnished $100 of Martin's wages

5. **Repossessions, foreclosures and returns**

None
X

List all property that has been repossessed by a creditor, sold at a foreclosure sale, transferred through a deed in lieu of foreclosure or returned to the seller within **one year** immediately preceding the commencement of this case. (Married debtors filing under Chapter 12 or Chapter 13 must include information concerning property of either or both spouses whether or not a joint petition is filed, unless the spouses are separated and a joint petition is not filed.)

NAME AND ADDRESS OF CREDITOR OR SELLER	DATE OF REPOSSESSION, FORECLOSURE SALE, TRANSFER OR RETURN	DESCRIPTION AND VALUE OF PROPERTY

6. **Assignments and receiverships**

None
X

a. Describe any assignment of property for the benefit of creditors made within **120 days** immediately preceding the commencement of this case. (Married debtors filing under Chapter 12 or Chapter 13 must include any assignment by either or both spouses whether or not a joint petition is filed, unless the spouses are separated and a joint petition is not filed.)

NAME AND ADDRESS OF ASSIGNEE	DATE OF ASSIGNMENT	TERMS OF ASSIGNMENT OR SETTLEMENT

None b.   List all property which has been in the hands of a custodian, receiver, or court-appointed official within **one year** immediately preceding
[X]   the commencement of this case. (Married debtors filing under Chapter 12 or Chapter 13 must include information concerning property
         of either or both spouses whether or not a joint petition is filed, unless the spouses are separated and a joint petition is not filed.)

NAME AND ADDRESS OF CUSTODIAN	NAME AND LOCATION OF COURT; CASE TITLE & NUMBER	DATE OF ORDER	DESCRIPTION AND VALUE OF PROPERTY

7.   Gifts

None   List all gifts or charitable contributions made within **one year** immediately preceding the commencement of this case except ordinary
[ ]   and usual gifts to family members aggregating less than $200 in value per individual family member and charitable contributions aggregating
         less than $100 per recipient. (Married debtors filing under Chapter 12 or Chapter 13 must include gifts or contributions by either or both
         spouses whether or not a joint petition is filed, unless the spouses are separated and a joint petition is not filed.)

NAME AND ADDRESS OF PERSON OR ORGANIZATION	RELATIONSHIP TO DEBTOR, IF ANY	DATE OF GIFT	DESCRIPTION AND VALUE OF GIFT
Arizona AIDS Association P.O. Box 11029 Phoenix, AZ 85000	N/A	3/15/XX	donation of $500 in memory of Ellen's nephew

8.   Losses

None   List all losses from fire, theft, other casualty or gambling within **one year** immediately preceding the commencement of this case **or since**
[ ]   **the commencement of this case.** (Married debtors filing under Chapter 12 or Chapter 13 must include losses by either or both spouses
         whether or not a joint petition is filed, unless the spouses are separated and a joint petition is not filed.)

DESCRIPTION AND VALUE OF PROPERTY	DESCRIPTION OF CIRCUMSTANCES AND, IF LOSS WAS COVERED IN WHOLE OR IN PART BY INSURANCE, GIVE PARTICULARS	DATE OF LOSS
Horse shed; $3,000	Brush fire on 8/5/XX destroyed the shed & contents; insurance covered complete cost to rebuild & restock	8/5/XX

9.   **Payments related to debt counseling or bankruptcy**

None   List all payments made or property transferred by or on behalf of the debtor to any person, including attorneys, for consultation
☐   concerning debt consolidation, relief under the bankruptcy law or preparation of a petition in bankruptcy within **one year** immediately
preceding the commencement of this case.

NAME AND ADDRESS OF PAYEE	DATE OF PAYMENT; NAME OF PAYOR IF OTHER THAN DEBTOR	AMOUNT OF MONEY OR DESCRIPTION AND VALUE OF PROPERTY
Fernando Gomez, Esq. LeHigh, Parker & Gomez 1100 MLK Tower Tucson, AZ 87500	1/6/XX	$500 consultation fee

10.   **Other transfers**

None   a.   List all other property, other than property transferred in the ordinary course of the business or financial affairs of the debtor, transferred
☒   either absolutely or as security within **one year** immediately preceding the commencement of this case. (Married debtors filing under
Chapter 12 or Chapter 13 must include transfers by either or both spouses whether or not a joint petition is filed, unless the spouses are
separated and a joint petition is not filed.)

NAME AND ADDRESS OF TRANSFEREE; RELATIONSHIP TO DEBTOR	DATE	DESCRIBE PROPERTY TRANSFERRED AND VALUE RECEIVED

11.   **Closed financial accounts**

None   List all financial accounts and instruments held in the name of the debtor or for the benefit of the debtor which were closed, sold, or
☐   otherwise transferred within **one year** immediately preceding the commencement of this case. Include checking, savings, or other financial
accounts, certificates of deposit, or other instruments; shares and share accounts held in banks, credit unions, pension funds, cooperatives,
associations, brokerage houses and other financial institutions. (Married debtors filing under Chapter 12 or Chapter 13 must include
information concerning accounts or instruments held by or for either or both spouses whether or not a joint petition is filed, unless the
spouses are separated and a joint petition is not filed.)

NAME AND ADDRESS OF INSTITUTION	TYPE AND NUMBER OF ACCOUNT AND AMOUNT OF FINAL BALANCE	AMOUNT AND DATE OF SALE OR CLOSING
Arizona State Credit Union 400 Monroe Place Tucson, AZ 87500	Checking account #1807143-218 $319.06	7/1/XX

12. Safe deposit boxes

None

[X]   List each safe deposit or other box or depository in which the debtor has or had securities, cash, or other valuables within **one year** immediately preceding the commencement of this case. (Married debtors filing under Chapter 12 or Chapter 13 must include boxes or depositories of either or both spouses whether or not a joint petition is filed, unless the spouses are separated and a joint petition is not filed.)

NAME AND ADDRESS OF BANK OR OTHER DEPOSITORY	NAMES AND ADDRESSES OF THOSE WITH ACCESS TO BOX OR DEPOSITORY	DESCRIPTION OF CONTENTS	DATE OF TRANSFER OR SURRENDER, IF ANY

13. Setoffs

None

[X]   List all setoffs made by any creditor, including a bank, against a debt or deposit of the debtor within **90 days** preceding the commencement of this case. (Married debtors filing under Chapter 12 or Chapter 13 must include information concerning either or both spouses whether or not a joint petition is filed, unless the spouses are separated and a joint petition is not filed.)

NAME AND ADDRESS OF CREDITOR	DATE OF SETOFF	AMOUNT OF SETOFF

14. Property held for another person

None

[ ]   List all property owned by another person that the debtor holds or controls.

NAME AND ADDRESS OF OWNER	DESCRIPTION AND VALUE OF PROPERTY	LOCATION OF PROPERTY
Eleanor Herchoo 17 Swingset Lane Albuquerque, NM 87100	Horse equipment; $1,000	our home

15. Prior address of debtor

None

[X]   If the debtor has moved within the **two years** immediately preceding the commencement of this case, list all premises which the debtor occupied during that period and vacated prior to the commencement of this case. If a joint petition is filed, report also any separate address of either spouse.

ADDRESS	NAME USED	DATES OF OCCUPANCY

The following questions are to be completed by every debtor that is a corporation or partnership and by any individual debtor who is or has been, within the **two years** immediately preceding the commencement of this case, any of the following: an officer, director, managing executive, or owner of more than 5 percent of the voting securities of a corporation; a partner, other than a limited partner, of a partnership; a sole proprietor or otherwise self-employed.

*(An individual or joint debtor should complete this portion of the statement **only** if the debtor is or has been in business, as defined above, within the two years immediately preceding the commencement of this case.)*   N/A

16. Nature, location and name of business

None a. If the debtor is an individual, list the names and addresses of all businesses in which the debtor was an officer, director, partner, or
☒   managing executive of a corporation, partnership, sole proprietorship, or was a self-employed professional within the **two years** immediately preceding the commencement of this case, or in which the debtor owned 5 percent or more of the voting or equity securities, within the **two years** immediately preceding the commencement of this case.

     b. If the debtor is a partnership, list the names and addresses of all businesses in which the debtor was a partner or owned 5 percent or more of the voting securities, within the **two years** immediately preceding the commencement of this case.

     c. If the debtor is a corporation, list the names and addresses of all businesses in which the debtor was a partner or owned 5 percent or more of the voting securities, within the **two years** immediately preceding the commencement of this case.

NAME	ADDRESS	NATURE OF BUSINESS	BEGINNING AND ENDING DATES OF OPERATION

17. Books, records and financial statements

None a. List all bookkeepers and accountants who within the **six years** immediately preceding the filing of this bankruptcy case kept or
☒   supervised the keeping of books of account and records of the debtor.

NAME AND ADDRESS	DATES SERVICES RENDERED

None b. List all firms or individuals who within the **two years** immediately preceding the filing of this bankruptcy case have audited the books of
☒   account and records, or prepared a financial statement of the debtor.

NAME AND ADDRESS	DATES SERVICES RENDERED

None
☒   c. List all firms or individuals who at the time of the commencement of this case were in possession of the books of account and records of the debtor. If any of the books of account and records are not available, explain.

NAME   ADDRESS

None
☒   d. List all financial institutions, creditors and other parties, including mercantile and trade agencies, to whom a financial statement was issued within the **two years** immediately preceding the commencement of this case by the debtor.

NAME AND ADDRESS   DATE ISSUED

18. Inventories

None
☒   a. List the dates of the last two inventories taken of your property, the name of the person who supervised the taking of each inventory, and the dollar amount and basis of each inventory.

DATE OF INVENTORY   INVENTORY SUPERVISOR   DOLLAR AMOUNT OF INVENTORY
                                                                             (Specify cost, market or other basis)

None
☒   b. List the name and address of the person having possession of the records of each of the two inventories reported in a., above.

                                                                      NAME AND ADDRESSES OF
DATE OF INVENTORY   CUSTODIAN OF INVENTORY RECORDS

19. Current partners, officers, directors and shareholders

None
☒   a. If the debtor is a partnership, list the nature and percentage of partnership interest of each member of the partnership.

NAME AND ADDRESS   NATURE OF INTEREST   PERCENTAGE OF INTEREST

None b.   If the debtor is a corporation, list all officers and directors of the corporation, and each stockholder who directly or indirectly owns,
 X   controls, or holds 5 percent or more of the voting securities of the corporation.

NAME AND ADDRESS	TITLE	NATURE AND PERCENTAGE OF STOCK OWNERSHIP

20. Former partners, officers, directors and shareholders

None a.   If the debtor is a partnership, list each member who withdrew from the partnership within **one year** immediately preceding the
 X   commencement of this case.

NAME	ADDRESS	DATE OF WITHDRAWAL

None b.   If the debtor is a corporation, list all officers or directors whose relationship with the corporation terminated within **one year**
 X   immediately preceding the commencement of this case.

NAME AND ADDRESS	TITLE	DATE OF TERMINATION

21. Withdrawals from a partnership or distributions by a corporation

None   If the debtor is a partnership or corporation, list all withdrawals or distributions credited or given to an insider, including compensation
 X   in any form, bonuses, loans, stock redemptions, options exercised and any other perquisite during **one year** immediately preceding the
      commencement of this case

NAME AND ADDRESS OF RECIPIENT; RELATIONSHIP TO DEBTOR	DATE AND PURPOSE OF WITHDRAWAL	AMOUNT OF MONEY OR DESCRIPTION AND VALUE OF PROPERTY

[If completed by an individual or individual and spouse]

I declare under penalty of perjury that I have read the answers contained in the foregoing statement of financial affairs and any attachments thereto and that they are true and correct.

Date _____ 2/25/XX _____   Signature of Debtor _____ *Martin Herchoo* _____

Date _____ 2/25/XX _____   Signature of Joint Debtor (if any) _____ *Ellen Herchoo* _____

CERTIFICATION AND SIGNATURE OF NON-ATTORNEY BANKRUPTCY PETITION PREPARER (See 11 U.S.C. § 110)

I certify that I am a bankruptcy petition preparer as defined in 11 U.S.C. § 110, that I prepared this document for compensation, and that I have provided the debtor with a copy of this document.

N/A

_____   _____
Printed or Typed Name of Bankruptcy Petition Preparer   Social Security No.

_____

_____
Address

Names and Social Security numbers of all other individuals who prepared or assisted in preparing this document:

If more than one person prepared this document, attach additional signed sheets conforming to the appropriate Official Form for each person.

X _____   _____
Signature of Bankruptcy Petition Preparer   Date

A bankruptcy petition preparer's failure to comply with the provisions of title 11 and the Federal Rules of Bankruptcy Procedure may result in fine or imprisonment or both. 11 U.S.C. § 110; 18 U.S.C. § 156.

N/A

[If completed by or on behalf of a partnership or corporation]

I declare under penalty of perjury that I have read the answers contained in the foregoing statement of financial affairs and any attachments thereto and that they are true and correct to the best of my knowledge, information and belief.

Date _____   Signature _____

_____
Print Name and Title

[An individual signing on behalf of a partnership or corporation must indicate position or relationship to debtor.]

0 _____ *continuation sheets attached*

Penalty for presenting fraudulent claim: Fine of up to $500,000 or imprisonment for up to 5 years, or both. 18 U.S.C. §§ 152 and 3571.

evidence of your ability to repay. Financial statements include:

- balance sheet (compares assets with liabilities)
- profit and loss statement (compares income with expenses)
- financial statement (provides an overall financial description of a business).

18. Inventories. If your business doesn't have an inventory because it's a service business, check "None." If your business does deal in products, but you were primarily the middle person or original manufacturer, put "no inventory required" or "materials purchased for each order as needed." If you have an inventory, fill in the information requested in items "a" and "b."

19. Current partners, officers, directors and shareholders. Check "None" for "a" and "b."

20. Former partners, officers, directors and shareholders. Check "None" for "a" and "b."

21. Withdrawals from a partnership or distributions by a corporation. Check "None."

If completed by an individual or individual and spouse. Sign and date this section. If you're filing jointly, be sure your spouse dates and signs it as well.

Certification and Signature of Non-Attorney Bankruptcy Petition Preparer. If a BPP typed your forms, have that person complete this section. Otherwise, type "N/A" anywhere in the box.

If completed on behalf of a partnership or corporation. Type "N/A."

Be sure to insert the number of continuation pages, if any, you attached.

H. Mailing Matrix

When you file your bankruptcy forms, you may need to include something called a "mailing matrix." The mailing matrix is a blank page divided into approximately 30 boxes. You type in the names and addresses of your creditors. The trustee photocopies the page to create mailing labels and mail notice of your bankruptcy filing to your creditors.

Some courts don't require a mailing matrix, while other courts have their own forms. (This is one of the questions you should ask the court clerk before you fill out your papers.) If you need to provide a matrix, but your court doesn't have its own, you can use the form in Appendix 3. Here's how to fill it out:

Step 1: On a separate piece of paper, make a list of all your creditors, in alphabetical order. You can copy them off of Schedules D, E, F and H. Be sure to include cosigners and joint debtors. If you and your spouse

jointly incurred a debt and are filing jointly, however, don't include your spouse. Also include collection agencies or attorneys, if you've been sued. And if you're seeking to discharge marital debts you assumed during a divorce, include both your ex-spouse and the creditors.

Step 2: Make several copies of the mailing matrix form.

Step 3: In the top left-hand box on the sheet you designate as the first page of your mailing matrix, enter your name and address. Then enter the names and addresses of each creditor, one per box and in alphabetical order (or in the order required by your local bankruptcy court). Use as many sheets as you need.

I. Income Deduction Order

Your bankruptcy court might require you to draft and submit an Income Deduction Order with the rest of your Chapter 13 bankruptcy papers. (You can ask the court clerk if you must prepare one when you send your letter requesting local forms and information.)

An Income Deduction Order is an order from the bankruptcy court sent to your employer. It requires the employer to automatically deduct from your wages your Chapter 13 monthly payment and send that money to the bankruptcy court.

Below is a sample Income Deduction Order. To complete your own, type up the sample—filling in the information requested in italics—using the paper in Appendix 3 with the numbers on the left side (called pleading paper). Some courts have their own forms; if yours does, use it. Leave blank any information you don't yet know.

1	*[Your Name*
	Your Street Address
2	*Your City, State, Zip*
	Your Phone Number]
3	In Propria Persona
4	
5	
6	
7	
8	UNITED STATES BANKRUPTCY COURT
9	_____ *[name of district]* _____ DISTRICT OF _____ *[your state]* _____
10	_____ *[name of division, if any]* ___ DIVISION
11	

12	In re:	)	
	[your name(s)]	)	Case No. ____ *[leave this blank]* ____
13		)	
		)	Chapter 13
14		)	
		)	Income Deduction Order
15		)	
	Debtor(s) _____	)	

TO: *[Name of Employer*
        Address
        City, State, Zip Code]
        Attention: Payroll Department

_____ *[Name of debtor employed by this employer]*___, (Debtor), whose Social Security number is *[your or your*

*spouse's Social Security number]*_, has filed a Petition under Chapter 13 of the Bankruptcy Code with this Court, and a proposed plan

for paying his/her debts.

[Name of trustee] has been appointed Standing Chapter 13 Trustee by the U.S. Trustee and has accepted the appointment.

Section 1325(b) of the Bankruptcy Code authorizes this Court to order an entity from whom Debtor receives income to pay all or any

part of that income to the Standing Trustee.

/ / /

/ / /

/ / /

1

2

3

4

5

        IT IS THEREFORE ORDERED that until you receive further order from this Court or from the Standing Trustee that you withhold from

the wages payable to the Debtor, the sum of $ _*[monthly plan amount]*_ each month, beginning with the date of this Order. You are

further Ordered to pay the money withheld to the Standing Trustee, at the address shown below, in convenient installments at least once a

month, the first payment to be paid within one month from the date below. Each successive monthly installment must be paid to the Standing

Trustee on or before the last day of each month thereafter.

6

7

Dated: _____   _____

                                             U.S. Bankruptcy Judge

8

9

10

Order prepared by:
[Your name
Your street address
Your city, state, zip
Your telephone number]

11

12

Copy mailed to:

[Trustee's name]
Standing Chapter 13 Trustee
[Trustee's street address
Trustee's city, state, zip
Trustee's telephone number]

13

14

15

16

[Name of Employer
Employer's street address
Employer's city, state, zip
Employer's telephone number]

17

18

19

20

21

22

23

24

25

26

27

28

Writing Your Chapter 13 Bankruptcy Plan

Your Chapter 13 bankruptcy plan is the key to your whole bankruptcy case. It's the document in which you tell the court exactly how you plan to repay your debts: the total amount you intend to pay to each creditor, how much you can pay each month and how many months you need to pay.

This chapter shows you how to put together your plan, using the information on the sample bankruptcy forms in Ch. 6.

Because your Chapter 13 plan is such an important part of your bankruptcy case, you may be anxious about writing one. To make matters worse, if you've seen any Chapter 13 plan forms, they may have put you off with their legal jargon and their requests for information you don't have or understand. *Don't worry.* Writing a Chapter 13 plan is not that difficult. The plan is usually only one or two pages. This chapter will tell you everything you must include in your plan, and it includes sample filled-in forms. Looking at them as you go along may make things clearer.

Do your best in writing your plan. If you don't know what information should go in a certain blank, leave it empty or venture a guess.

Before you file, you can ask the trustee to go over your plan and help you fill in the gaps (See Ch. 6, *Completing the Bankruptcy Forms*, Section D, for tips on working with the trustee before you file.) Or, you can hire a lawyer to review your plan—or to write it for you. (See Ch. 12, *Help Beyond the Book.*)

If you submit a plan with a number of mistakes, that's okay too. The trustee will help you sort it all out. You have an absolute right to file a modified plan with the bankruptcy court any time before your confirmation hearing; most Chapter 13 debtors submit at least one modified plan.

A. Chapter 13 Plan Forms

There is no official Chapter 13 plan form that all bankruptcy courts use. About a third of all courts, however, have developed their own forms. If your court has its own Chapter 13 plan form, use the information in this chapter to complete it. (You may already know if your court has its

own form; see Ch. 6, *Completing the Bankruptcy Forms*, Section B.)

If your court doesn't have its own plan form or you haven't been able to figure out if your court has its own plan form, you have three choices:

- **Visit the law library.** See if it has *Chapter 13 Practice Guide*, by Keith M. Lundin (Wiley Law Publications). This two-volume loose-leaf book contains the "required, preferred or sample" plan form for every bankruptcy court in the nation. It's organized first by state, then by district and even further by division.

- **Use other plans from your court as models.** In some bankruptcy districts where there is no court-generated form, many of the local attorneys submit similar-looking Chapter 13 plans. If you'd like to create a plan that might be familiar to your court, ask the court clerk for a court file that contains a completed and approved Chapter 13 plan. (Court files are a matter of public record.) If the clerk won't help you, ask for the Chapter 13 trustee's phone number. Call the trustee and make the same request.

- **Use one of the forms in this book.** Appendix 3 contains Chapter 13 plan forms from three different bankruptcy courts. You can photocopy and use any of these forms. If you do, the bankruptcy judge or trustee may be unfamiliar with the format or (pleasantly) surprised to see such a complete Chapter 13 plan from a do-it-yourselfer. If you are asked how you developed your Chapter 13 plan, just explain that you used forms from other courts (found in this Nolo Press publication) as models.

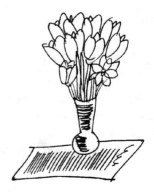

If you will create your own form from scratch, or need more room than is provided on one of the forms in Appendix 3, just use plain white paper, 8½" x 11". No matter what source you use to create your plan, be sure to type your final draft.

CHECKLIST OF CHAPTER 13 PLAN ELEMENTS

Your Chapter 13 plan must tell the court how you propose to pay:
- ☐ The trustee's fee
- ☐ Priority tax debts
- ☐ Other priority debts
- ☐ Mortgage arrears
- ☐ Other secured debts
- ☐ Nondischargeable unsecured debts
- ☐ General unsecured debts
- ☐ Post-confirmation debts (optional)

In addition, your plan must specify:
- ☐ How long your plan will last
- ☐ How often you'll make payments
- ☐ How you'll deal with your contracts and leases
- ☐ Whether you'll be making any direct payments to creditors—that is, outside of your plan
- ☐ The order in which creditors will be paid (optional)

B. How Long Your Plan Will Last

One of the first things you state in your plan is how long you want it to last. The bankruptcy code does not specify precisely how long a Chapter 13 plan must last. (11 U.S.C. § 1322(c).) Most debtors, however, propose three-year repayment plans. If you want a longer or shorter plan, you will need the permission of the bankruptcy court. (Additional information on the length of the plan is in Ch. 2, *An Overview of Chapter 13 Bankruptcy*, Section C, and Ch. 4, *Calculating Your Disposable Income*, Section C.)

1. Fewer Than Three Years

If you have enough income to pay off all of your unsecured debts (this includes your priority debts) in less than three years, you can propose a shorter plan. Otherwise, you'll have to make payments for at least three years. The bankruptcy code requires that you dedicate your disposable income to your plan for a minimum of three years unless you can pay off your debts sooner.

2. Longer Than Three Years

The bankruptcy court might approve a plan that lasts more than three years, but under no circumstances can the court approve a plan that lasts more than five years. Here are some situations in which you might want to request a longer-term plan:

- **To pay off a secured debt.** Section I, below explains how to handle secured debts (other than mortgages) in your plan. One way is to reduce your debt to the value of your collateral and pay it off through your plan. For example, if you owe $9,000 on your car but it's only worth $4,500, you could keep your car through Chapter 13 bankruptcy by paying $4,500 through your plan. If you can't afford to pay it off in three years, you can propose a longer plan.

- **To meet any payment percentage required by the court.** In some courts, the judge will not approve your plan unless you propose paying your unsecured creditors a significant portion of what you owe them, usually at least 70%. To meet that goal, these courts will readily approve a plan up to five years.

  In other courts, the judge will approve plans that propose paying unsecured creditors nothing at all or as little as 5% of what you owe. These courts usually won't approve a plan lasting more than three years if the sole reason is to pay unsecured creditors more. These courts reason that if you dedicate your disposable income for three years, that's all the bankruptcy law requires, even if your unsecured creditors receive very little.

- **To avoid objections from unsecured creditors who must wait to get paid.** When you start making plan payments, the trustee will pay your secured creditors and priority creditors before your general unsecured creditors. If the unsecured creditors think they'll have to wait a long time to be paid, they'll probably object to your plan unless you agree to extend it beyond three years. So a court may approve a plan that lasts more than three years to assuage the unsecured creditors, who would otherwise get paid very little (and would get it very late, no less). For example, if you have mortgage arrears (a secured debt) and a tax debt (a priority debt) that will take you 28 months to pay, your unsecured creditors would receive money for only the last eight months of a three-year plan. But if your plan lasted four years, these same creditors would be paid for 20 months.

- **To repay your nondischargeable debts.** If you have an unsecured nondischargeable debt, such as a student loan or child support delinquency, most bankruptcy courts will approve a plan that lasts more than three years so you can pay off the debt. If, however, you propose a plan that will pay 100% on such a debt, you may have to pay 100% on your other unsecured debts, too. (See Section J, below.)

C. Your Payment Schedule

Somewhere near the top of your plan, you'll need to say how often you want to make your plan payments to the trustee. Most Chapter 13 bankruptcy debtors make plan payments once a month. If you are paid more often or less often, however, you can pay the trustee on your schedule, such as:

- weekly
- every other week
- twice a month (such as on the 1st and 16th)
- quarterly (this might be convenient if you receive royalties, quarterly dividends or quarterly payments from a trust)
- semi-annually (some publishers and producers pay royalties only twice a year; farmers often sell crops only twice yearly)
- annually (usually in the case of farmer who is paid once a year for crops), or
- seasonally (if you're a construction worker, you may not be able to make payments in winter; a teacher may make small payments, or none at all, during the summer).

If you propose making quarterly, semi-annual or annual payments to the trustee, the payments will have to be large. You will also need to show the bankruptcy court, at the confirmation hearing, evidence of your past income (copies of your income tax returns for the past three to five years), which the court will use as an indication of your future income. The court might especially be inclined to approve your plan if you offer to make small monthly payments in between the larger quarterly, semi-annual or annual payments.

D. The Order in Which Creditors Will Be Paid

Most trustees pay creditors in the order in which they appear on the Chapter 13 repayment plan. You are not required to follow that order. But if you want your creditors paid in a different order, you'll have to specify how in your Chapter 13 plan.

Most plan forms direct the trustee to pay priority debts before paying secured debts. If you have mortgage arrears, however, your mortgage lender will probably object to your plan if it doesn't provide for payment of your mortgage arrears first. And you'll probably want to pay those debts early because you must pay interest on them.

Below is the order in which most debtors ask the trustee to pay their creditors. If this isn't the order on your plan form, or you want to change this order, specify the changes you want in the "Other Provisions" or "Special Provisions" section of your plan. (See Section M, below.)

1. **Administrative claims.** The bulk of your first few payments will go toward your filing fee if you ask the court for permission to pay it in installments. In addition, the trustee's fee will come off the top of all of your payments. The bankruptcy code states that the filing fee and trustee's fee must be paid before your debts are. (11 U.S.C. § 1326(b).)
2. **Support arrears.** These are priority debts, which you may not want paid until after your secured debt defaults are paid. But public policy dictates that child support and alimony arrears be paid as soon as possible in Chapter 13 bankruptcy.
3. **Mortgage defaults.** You'll probably want these claims paid early because you must pay interest on them (unless your loan was obtained after October 22, 1994.)
4. **Other secured debt defaults.** Again, these claims should be paid early because you must pay interest on them.
5. **Priority debts.** The IRS and other priority creditors are entitled to be paid before your unsecured creditors. (Paying priority creditors is covered in Sections F and G, below.)
6. **Unsecured creditors.** They are usually paid last. But you may have to specify how you want unsecured creditors paid. (See Section J, below.)

E. Reducing the Trustee's Fee

Remember—the trustee is entitled to keep 3% to 10% of every payment you make, and most trustees take the full 10%. So for every $100 you pay your creditors, you actually have to pay the trustee either $110 or $111.11. (Trustees use different formulas to calculate their fees; they are explained in Ch. 2, *An Overview of Chapter 13 Bankruptcy*, Section F.)

Here are some ways to reduce the trustee's fee:

- If you are current on your mortgage, propose making your mortgage payments directly to your lender—that is, "outside of the plan." (See Section L, below.) The trustee doesn't get a cut of the payments you make directly.

- If you are not current on your mortgage—that is, you will use your Chapter 13 plan to make up the missed payments and get back on track—you can ask the trustee at the creditors' meeting (explained in Ch. 9, *After You File Your Case*, Section E) to waive the portion of the fee that is based on your regular mortgage payment. The trustee might be willing, if making the monthly payments will be really tight for you.

- If you will propose selling a valuable asset to make certain payments, you should also propose disbursing the money yourself. Otherwise, up to 10% of the proceeds will go to the trustee, not your creditors.

F. The Order in Which Priority Debts Will Be Paid

Many plans ask you to identify "priority" creditors. You listed them on Schedule E—Creditors Holding Unsecured Priority Claims. Other plans simply state that the trustee will pay all priority creditors in full; presumably, the trustee will get the information from Schedule E.

The trustee will pay priority debts in the order listed below unless you request otherwise in your plan. The only reason you might change this order is if a creditor threatens to object to your plan unless you agree to pay that creditor earlier. You might as well go along with a creditor who decides to be a squeaky wheel this way. Because these creditors are paid in full (and without interest), the order in which they are paid doesn't really matter.

1. Administrative costs and fees paid to the bankruptcy court, including filing and administrative fees, and the trustee's fee.
2. Attorney's fees, if you hire an attorney for help with your Chapter 13 case.
3. Wages, salaries and commissions earned by people who worked for you within 90 days before you filed for bankruptcy, up to $4,300.
4. Contributions you owe to an employee benefit fund for services rendered by an employee of your business.
5. Deposits you took from individuals who intended to purchase, lease or rent goods or services which you never delivered, up to $1,950.
6. Claims of certain people who produce grain or run fisheries, up to $4,300.
7. Alimony and child support you owe to an ex-spouse and children from former relationships.
8. Tax debts. (Figuring out the priority portion of your tax debt is covered in Section G, below.)

G. Paying Back Taxes

In your plan, you must provide for payment of your back taxes, interest and penalties. Unlike your other debts, your tax debts may fall into one, two or even three different categories on your Chapter 13 plan. Pay close attention to the rules.

1. Categorizing Your Federal Income Tax Debt

If you have a federal income tax debt, how you handle it in your plan depends on what category it falls into: dischargeable, secured or priority. (See sidebar, "Classifying Your Tax Debts," below.)

2. Interest

The majority of bankruptcy courts have ruled that "interest follows the tax." This means that if your income tax debt is dischargeable, so is the interest on that debt. And if your tax debt is secured or a priority debt, so is the interest you owe on it.

3. Penalties

Penalties are treated a little differently than is interest.
A penalty is dischargeable if:

- the event giving rise to the penalty (such as your failure to file a return or to file it on time) occurred over three years before you file for bankruptcy, or
- the tax is dischargeable.

Income tax penalties are considered a priority only if you are fined because the IRS suffered a monetary loss. This is rarely, if ever, the case.

4. Other Tax Debts

State income tax debts are usually handled the same way federal income taxes are.

CLASSIFYING YOUR TAX DEBTS

If...	Your tax debt is...
All of the following are true: • the tax year for which you owe taxes ended more than three years before the date you plan to file your bankruptcy case • you properly filed your tax return (if the IRS filed a Substitute for Return for you, it doesn't count) for the year in question at least two years before filing for bankruptcy • the IRS has not assessed the taxes against you within 240 days before you plan to file your bankruptcy case, and • the IRS has not recorded a Notice of Federal Tax Lien with your county land records office.	**Dischargeable**, meaning you can completely eliminate your income tax debt, and the interest and penalties associated with it. If your bankruptcy court approves Chapter 13 plans in which unsecured creditors receive nothing or very little, you can eliminate your dischargeable tax debt without paying very much. You'll pay a small amount through your plan, and at the end of your case the balance will be wiped out. (See Section J, below.) If, however, your bankruptcy court requires you to pay a higher percentage of unsecured debts, you might be better off filing for Chapter 7 bankruptcy. (This is explained in Ch. 1, *Should Your File for Chapter 13 Bankruptcy?*)
All of the following are true: • the IRS has recorded a Notice of Federal Tax Lien • you own real estate, and • your equity in the real estate is enough to cover the tax debt. (Equity is the market value minus the debts against the property such as a mortgage.)	**Secured**; secured tax debts are covered in Section I, below.
Your tax debt is not dischargeable or secured.	**Priority**, which means that it must be paid in full in your Chapter 13 plan.
The IRS has recorded a federal tax lien, but you don't own real estate or equity in the real estate you own is less than what you owe the IRS.	**Undersecured** (if you own no real estate) or partially undersecured (if your equity is less than what you owe the IRS). The undersecured portion is dischargeable if the first three conditions listed above for dischargeable taxes are met; otherwise it is a priority debt. If you have any real estate with equity, the balance of your tax debt is secured.

HELP FROM A LAWYER

If you have a substantial state income tax debt, speak to a bankruptcy attorney before you file to find out if any special state rules apply.

All other tax debts—including payroll taxes, excise taxes and property taxes—are priority debts. (If your county has filed a lien against your property for your failure to pay your property taxes, however, the debt is secured, not a priority.)

H. Paying Mortgage Arrears

If you're like a lot of people, you're filing for Chapter 13 bankruptcy because you've gotten behind on your mortgage and are afraid of losing the house. In general, Chapter 13 bankruptcy lets you get back on track with a mortgage.

IF YOUR MORTGAGE IS CURRENT

If you are not behind on your mortgage, you can skip this section. The bankruptcy court will probably let you continue making your regular mortgage payments directly to your lender. (See Section L, below.)

If you are behind on your mortgage, you most likely have two choices: either give the house back to the lender or pay the overdue amount and the regular payments in your plan. In a small number of cases, you may have a third or fourth option: to reduce your obligation under the mortgage to the current value of your house or to eliminate some liens on the property. Each of these options is discussed below.

1. Give the House Back

If you just can't deal with your mortgage any longer, you can simply give your house back to the lender, who will then sell it at a foreclosure sale. The lender cannot refuse to take the house back.

If the sale nets the lender enough money to pay off your debt, you're home free—the debt is gone. If there is any excess (which is highly unlikely), you are entitled to it.

If, however, the market value of the house has fallen and the sale brings in less than what you owe, or there are additional liens on the house, the difference is called a deficiency balance. You treat it like any other dischargeable unsecured debt. (See Section J, below.) In the few states listed below, however, even if the sale brings in less than you owe, the sale wipes out your obligation completely—that is, there is no deficiency balance.

STATES THAT DON'T IMPOSE DEFICIENCY BALANCES ON HOME MORTGAGES

State	Code Section	When Deficiency Balance Prohibited
California	Cal. CCP 580d	If the house is returned to a lender from whom you borrowed the money to finance the purchase (or an institution that purchased the loan from your lender).
Minnesota	MSA 582.30	If the foreclosure has a redemption period (a time during which you can buy your house back from the person who bought it at the foreclosure sale) of at least six months. (Check your loan documents to see if you have a redemption period.)
Montana	MCA 71-1-232	If the house is returned to a lender from whom you borrowed the money to finance the purchase (or an institution that purchased the loan from your lender).
North Carolina	GSNC 45-21.38	If you used the mortgage to purchase the home. In contrast, there will be a deficiency if you give the house back to a lender who gave you a home equity loan.
Washington	RCW 61.24.100	If the property was purchased for family, personal or household (that is, noncommercial) use.

If you want to give your house back to the lender rather than get current on your mortgage, state that in your plan. In the section of your Chapter 13 plan labeled "Special Provisions" or "Other Provisions," write "I am behind on my house mortgage. I want to surrender the collateral rather than cure the default."

2. Make Up Missed Payments and Reinstate the Loan

If you want to keep your house, you must make up your missed payments, reinstate the loan and keep making the payments under the original contract. This is called, in Chapter 13 parlance, "curing the default."

In the section of your plan labeled "Home Mortgage" or something similar, you must provide information about your mortgage loan, including some or all of the following:

- the name of the mortgage company
- the total amount you are behind (called arrears), plus late fees, attorney fees and collection costs
- the rate of interest you propose to pay on the arrears (if the mortgage loan was signed before October 22, 1994; see subsection 2.b, below)
- the months you missed your payments

- how many months you propose to take to pay the arrears, and
- the amount of your regular monthly payment. (While you pay off the past due amount, you also make the regular payments called for under your original agreement.)

Bankruptcy rules require that your mortgage arrears be paid through your plan within a "reasonable time." Virtually every court has a rule (written or unwritten) limiting you to a specific number of months—anywhere from six to 60. Most courts want the mortgage made current within a year. For example, in your plan you might state that you want the trustee to apply all of your first seven months' payments to your mortgage arrears.

IF YOUR LENDER HAS STARTED FORECLOSURE PROCEEDINGS

If your lender has started to foreclose against you, your right to cure the default depends on how far along the foreclosure proceeding is. If the lender has accelerated the loan (declared the entire balance due), or has gone to court and obtained a foreclosure judgment, you usually can still cure the default. An increasing number of courts are allowing lenders to proceed with foreclosure if you don't immediately cure the default, however, reasoning that a plan proposal or its confirmation isn't a cure and that only the cure stops a foreclosure. Of course, your lender may be happy to stop the foreclosure when you file the plan.

If the foreclosure sale has already occurred, you cannot cure the default through Chapter 13 bankruptcy. This is true even if your state law gives you a "redemption right," which lets you buy back the house from the person who bought it at the foreclosure sale as long as a new deed hasn't yet been recorded. (11 U.S.C. § 1322(c)(1).)

HELP FROM A LAWYER
If your house has been sold at foreclosure, see a lawyer before filing for Chapter 13 bankruptcy.

a. Curing a Balloon Payment Default

Since October 1994, you can cure the default even if the final mortgage payment (in your original contract) is due before the final payment in your Chapter 13 plan. (11 U.S.C. §

1322(c)(2).) This change in the law was intended to help people cure a default on a balloon payment.

EXAMPLE: When Ed bought his house, he took out a 30-year first mortgage from a bank and borrowed the rest (in the form of a second mortgage) from the seller. The second mortgage required Ed to make monthly payments of $200 for 24 months and then pay a balance (balloon) of $12,000. Ed paid made the 24 monthly payments, but he defaulted on balloon. He can use Chapter 13 bankruptcy to pay it off over time.

This new law will also help people who are in arrears with only a few months or years left on their mortgage (very few people who file for Chapter 13 bankruptcy).

b. Paying Interest on Mortgage Arrears

If your mortgage loan was signed on or after October 22, 1994, you do not have to pay interest on the arrears. (11 U.S.C. § 1322(e).)

If, however, you propose to cure a default on a mortgage loan signed before that date, you must pay interest on the arrears. (*Rake v. Wade,* 113 S.Ct. 2187 (1993).) This is tantamount to paying interest on interest, because each mortgage payment already includes interest. (Presumably, that's why Congress eliminated the interest requirement in the 1994 legislation.)

No law prescribes the exact interest rate you must pay. Most bankruptcy judges require you to pay your mortgage rate; others allow you to pay the current market interest rate.

Most plan forms don't have a blank for mortgage arrears interest. If your court's form doesn't have a blank, your best bet is to leave the interest figure off. If the lender doesn't object, you won't have to pay it. If the lender does object, you can amend your plan and add it to the "Special Provisions" or "Other Provisions" section.

3. Reduce the Note to the Current Value of the House

Although the Bankruptcy Code generally prohibits debtors from modifying the terms of their mortgage in Chapter 13 bankruptcy, a growing number of courts allow debtors to get around this restriction. If your court allows it, you can reduce the secured portion of your debt to the value of the house and treat the difference as a general unsecured debt.

Modification is not a realistic option for most people, however, for two reasons:

- To get the court to approve a modification, you must show that at least a part of the loan is secured by some-

thing other than your residence and the land it is sitting on. (11 U.S.C. § 1322(b)(2).)
- If the court allows the modification, you will have to pay the present value of your house in full *during* your plan—just three to five years.

Modification could help you if you still have a lot to pay on your mortgage and your property has dropped substantially in value.

HELP FROM A LAWYER
Modifying your mortgage as a part of your Chapter 13 bankruptcy case is beyond the scope of this book. Consult a bankruptcy attorney.

To figure out whether you might qualify for a modification, look at your mortgage agreement to see if anything besides your residence is collateral for your mortgage loan. Here are some possibilities:

- **Multi-unit property.** If you live in one unit (your primary residence), but your loan was for the purchase of a multi-unit building, the court may allow modification because the mortgage is secured by units other than your residence.
- **An adjacent lot or other buildings on the premises.** The other property is especially likely to be considered not a part of your residence if it produces income—for example, farm land.
- **A mobile home you live in, but which is considered personal property.** If you have a mobile home on the property and it is part (or all) of the collateral for the mortgage loan, it isn't considered your residence if your state law defines mobile homes as personal property, not real estate. The court may reject this argument if the mobile home is permanently attached to the land.
- **Fixtures, rents, royalties, mineral rights, insurance proceeds, escrow accounts, equipment and appliances.** The court might reject your request if the other security interest (such as an empty escrow account) has no value.
- **Credit, life or other insurance.**
- **The residence and personal property.** Some creditors, such as consolidation lenders, take a security interest in appliances, furniture and other personal property. In this situation, the mortgage loan is not secured solely by the residence.
- **Two loans from the same lender for the residence and something else.** You might have a mortgage and car loan from the same lender, and clauses in both agreements declare house and car collateral for both loans. In this situation, the security for your mortgage is the house and the car, not just your house.

In addition, the court might permit modification if the value has dropped so significantly that your mortgage debt is total unsecured.

4. Eliminate or Reduce Liens on the Property

As explained in Ch. 3, *Adding Up Your Secured and Unsecured Debts*, Section A.4, you may be able to eliminate or reduce some liens on your real estate.

I. Paying Other Secured Debts

One of the most alluring features of Chapter 13 bankruptcy is that it offers many ways of dealing with secured debts. Secured debts, remember, are those for which you pledged a particular item of property as collateral (such as a car loan) or where the creditor has recorded a lien against you. (Mortgage arrears are handled differently from all other secured debts in Chapter 13 bankruptcy; see Section H, above.)

The options for dealing with non-mortgage secured debts are described below. In your plan, you must state what option you've chosen for every secured debt. Here are your choices:

- Give the property back.
- Pay, through your plan, the amount of the debt or the current value of the property, whichever is less.
- Make up the missed payments and reinstate the loan.
- Eliminate or reduce liens on the property.
- Sell the property.
- File a Chapter 7 bankruptcy before you file a chapter 13 bankruptcy.

1. Give the Property Back

You can always simply give the collateral back to the lender after you file for bankruptcy. The lender will sell the property at a repossession sale. The lender cannot refuse to take the collateral back.

If the sale nets the lender enough money to pay off your debt, you're home free—the debt is gone. If there is any excess (which is highly unlikely), you are entitled to it.

If, however, the sale brings in less than what you owe, the difference is called a deficiency balance. You treat it like any other dischargeable unsecured debt—pay off some or all of it through your plan, and have the rest wiped out at the end of your case. (See Section J, below.) In the states listed below, however, even if the sale brings in less than you owe, giving the property back wipes out your obligation completely—that is, there is no deficiency balance.

STATES THAT DON'T IMPOSE DEFICIENCY BALANCES ON PERSONAL PROPERTY

State	Code Section	When Deficiency Balance Prohibited
Alabama	AC 5-19-13	If you paid $1,000 or less for the collateral.
Arizona	ARS 44-5501	If you paid $1,000 or less for the collateral.
California	Cal. HS 18038.7	On a mobile home, manufactured home, commercial coach, truck camper or floating home.
Colorado	CRS 5-5-103	If you paid $2,100 or less for the collateral.
Connecticut	CGS 42-98	In all repossession (including voluntarily returning the property) sales except for cars sold for cash for more than $2,000.
District of Columbia	DCCA 28-3812	If you paid $2,000 or less for the collateral.
Florida	FSA 516.31	If you paid $2,000 or less for the collateral.
Idaho	IC 28-45-103	If you paid $1,000 or less for the collateral.
Indiana	ISA 24-4.5-5-103	If you paid $2,800 or less for the collateral.
Kansas	KSA 16a-5-103	If you paid $1,000 or less for the collateral.
Louisiana	LRS 13:4106	If the seller does not obtain an appraisal before the sale.
Maine	MRSA 9A-5-103	If you paid $2,800 or less for the collateral.
Massachusetts	MGLA Ch. 255 ¶ 13J	If you paid $1,000 or less for the collateral.
Minnesota	MSA 325G.22	If you paid $4,800 or less for the collateral.
Missouri	AMS 408.556	If you paid $500 or less for the collateral.
Oklahoma	OSA 14A-5-103	If you paid $2,500 or less for the collateral.
Oregon	ORS 83.830	If you paid $1,250 or less for the collateral.
South Carolina	SCCA 37-5-103	If you paid $1,500 or less for the collateral.
Utah	UCA 70C-7-101	If you paid $3,000 or less for the collateral.
West Virginia	WVC 46A-2-119	If you paid $1,000 or less for the collateral.
Wisconsin	WSA 425.209	If you paid $1,000 or less for the collateral.
Wyoming	WSA 40-14-503	If you paid $1,000 or less for the collateral.

Offering to give back the property is a good strategy in four situations:

- Under your state's law, you will not be liable for any deficiency balance.
- The creditor wants the property back because it is still worth a lot, and in exchange, will not require you to pay the deficiency balance, if any.
- You will propose, and the court is apt to approve, a plan under which your unsecured creditors get nothing or very little.
- The creditor doesn't want the property back because it has depreciated in value. If you propose to give the collateral back, the creditor may offer to let you keep it and pay back the loan at a low interest rate. (You must pay interest on secured debts in your Chapter 13 plan. Negotiating the interest rate is discussed in Section 2.b, below.)

If you want to give back the property, indicate it in the "Other Provisions" or "Special Provisions" section of your plan. You can simply put something like, "We want to return the washer and dryer set to Sears."

2. Pay the Amount of the Debt or the Current Value of the Property

If you want to keep an item of collateral, you can propose, in your plan, to pay either the amount you owe the creditor or the current value of the property, whichever is less. No matter which amount you propose to pay, you can pay it off over time—that is, through your Chapter 13 plan.

Most people choose to pay the creditor the value of the property. That's because if you've had the secured property for a while, it's probably gone down in value to the point that you owe more than it's worth. If you decide on this course, bear in mind the following:

- You must repay the entire amount during your plan. If you can't pay off the debt within 36 months, you can propose a plan to last up to 60 months.
- In the plan, you must agree that the creditor's security interest—the lien on the property—will remain until you have paid the debt off. Some plans include this language. If yours does not, you'll have to list the collateral in the "Secured Debts" section of your plan. If you don't, the creditor will object to your plan, and the court won't approve it.
- The creditor will probably insist that you sign a document in which you agree to maintain insurance on the property and otherwise take good care of it. This is called providing "adequate protection." You must do this in case you can't finish your Chapter 13 plan and later want to give the property back to the creditor.

- In the plan, where you list the amount of the secured claim, put down the current value of the property, not the amount you owe on the original debt. (You and the creditor must agree on this amount; see Section a, below.)
- In the plan, you must specify the interest rate you will pay. (Determining the interest rate is covered in Section b, below.)

a. Determining the Current Value of the Property

You and the creditor must agree on the current value. But first, you must agree on what is meant by "current." Most debtors and creditors agree to use the value of the property on the date of the hearing where the judge confirms or denies the plan. If the property needs to be appraised, you could use the date of the appraisal. A few debtors and creditors agree to use the value of the property as of the date the debtor filed the bankruptcy petition. For most property, it doesn't really matter.

Then comes the important part: agreeing on the value of the property, which is the amount you'll have to pay the creditor. In reality, debtors and creditors disagree not only on the value of the property, but also on the method to use to determine the value. Debtors, who obviously want the figure as low as possible, have tried to argue that the value should be the amount they would get if they were forced to sell the property after a repossession or at a yard sale. Creditors, who want the figure as high as possible, assert that the value should be the replacement value—that is, the amount it would cost a debtor to buy a comparable item. Until June of 1997, negotiations—or a court decision—often ended somewhere in the middle.

The method to be used to establish the value of the property became clear when the U.S. Supreme Court issued its decision in *Associates Commercial Corporation v. Rash*, __ S.Ct. __ (1997). There, the court held that the creditor is entitled to receive the replacement value, which generally means the amount it would cost a debtor to obtain property of like age and condition.

While this standard adds guidance, it by no means settles the issue. You and the creditor will now have to agree on the condition of your property. In addition, the creditor is not entitled to a windfall. So, for example, if you have a car in great condition and the replacement value would essentially be its retail value, that amount would have to be reduced by amounts that don't reflect the value of the car, such as warranties, inventory storage or reconditioning. You can further reduce the value by amounts that reflect modifications you made after buying the vehicle, such as an enhanced car stereo or a roof rack.

Negotiations regarding the value of the collateral usually take place informally. You can begin the process by calling the creditor before you file your plan to see if you can agree on an amount. If you can't, just include a value in your Chapter 13 plan; if the creditor disagrees, the creditor will have to take the next step.

If the creditor disagrees with your chosen value, the creditor will probably file a paper scheduling a "valuation hearing" before the bankruptcy judge. This hearing will probably be held just before your confirmation hearing. Asking for a valuation hearing will prevent the trustee from using your value if you and the creditor can't reach an agreement informally.

At the same time the creditor files the paper (you'll get a copy), the creditor will contact you (or your attorney) and try to reach an agreement. Sometimes negotiations take place over the telephone. Often, you actually negotiate the value at the meeting of the creditors, which takes place before the confirmation and valuation hearings.

If you can't reach an agreement, the judge will establish the value at the valuation hearing. If you have reached an agreement by then, the court will review the amount, if the creditor requested a valuation hearing. Only in rare instances would a court reject the value agreed to by you and the creditor and set the value on its own.

b. Determining the Interest Rate

A few bankruptcy courts set an interest rate to be paid secured claims other than mortgages in a Chapter 13 plan. The rate may be stated on the plan form itself; if it isn't, check your local rules or ask the Chapter 13 trustee. (See Ch. 6, *Completing the Bankruptcy Forms*, Section B, for information on getting local rules or Section D for information on contacting the trustee.)

If your court has not set an interest rate, you and the creditor will have to negotiate a rate or ask the court to decide. The process is similar to setting the value of the collateral. (See Section a, above.)

DETERMINING THE INTEREST RATE

The interest rate currently charged by commercial lenders in your region for a similar loan.	This may be the fairest rate.
The interest rate in your original contract.	This may be unfair to you if rates have dramatically decreased or unfair to the creditor if rates have increased since the date of your original contract.
The current interest rate for U.S. Treasury bills (T-bills).	You have several options here, including: the current rate on 52-week T-bills, the interest rate at maturity, the average rate over a three-month period and the current rate increased by a half point. These rates are listed in the business pages of most newspapers.
The current prime interest rate.	This rate, set by the Federal Reserve Board, is what banks charge their wealthiest borrowers. It is listed in the business pages of most newspapers. It is usually lower than most other rates, and creditors usually object. Courts that let debtors use the current prime rate feel that higher rates provide an inappropriate windfall for creditors.
The current T-bill rate or prime rate plus a risk factor of one to three percentage points.	Many courts are looking to the T-bill or prime rate and adding a few percentage points.
The average of several current interest rates.	Offer this compromise if you insist on one rate and the creditor insists on another.

3. Make Up Missed Payments and Reinstate the Loan

If you want to keep a particular item of secured property, you can make up your missed payments, reinstate the loan and make the payments under the original contract. This is called, in Chapter 13 parlance, "curing the default."

You can cure the default and reinstate the loan only if the final payment in your original contract is due after the final payment in your Chapter 13 plan will be made. For example, you could cure a default on a car loan if your car note has 40 monthly payments left on it and you are proposing a standard 36-month Chapter 13 plan.

This strategy makes sense in three situations:
- The property is worth as much as or more than you owe. If the property is worth less than the debt, you are better off paying only the value of the property. (See Section 2, above.)
- The property is worth less than you owe, but it would take you more than 60 months (the maximum length of a Chapter 13 plan) to pay it off.

EXAMPLE: You have eight years left on your boat loan; although the boat has decreased in value, it is worth only slightly less than what you still owe. In addition, your Chapter 13 plan payments are being used mostly to pay off a large tax bill. You cannot afford to also pay the value of your boat in only five years. You could afford to keep the boat if you paid off the rest of the loan in the remaining eight years.

• The interest rate in the original contract is much lower than the interest rate the lender will agree to now. If you reduced your debt to the current value of the property, but would end up paying more overall because you would have to pay a higher interest rate, you are better off curing the default.

EXAMPLE: Laurel bought professional photography equipment for $14,500, to be paid over two years at 6.25%. She still owes $12,000 and the equipment is now worth $10,500. She is tempted to pay that amount through her plan, but interest rates have jumped and she'll have to pay at least 10.75% on the balance. Laurel would need the full three years of her plan to pay the $10,500. At 10.75%, she'll pay more than if she cures the default and pays off the $12,000.

4. Eliminate or Reduce Liens on the Property

You can ask the court to eliminate or reduce ("avoid") liens on certain types of property. This procedure, which is called lien avoidance, applies only to certain property considered "exempt" under bankruptcy law. (11 U.S.C. § 522(f).) (You should have already listed your exempt property on Worksheet 8 in Ch. 5, *Calculating the Value of Your Nonexempt Property.*)

How much a lien is reduced depends on the value of the property and the limits, in any, on the amount of the exemption. Here are the rules:

• If the property is entirely exempt or worth less than the legal exemption limit, the court will eliminate the entire lien. You'll get to keep the property without paying anything.

• If the property is worth more than the exemption limit, the lien is not entirely eliminated. It is reduced to the difference between the exemption limit and either the property's value or the amount of the debt, whichever is less.

EXAMPLE: A creditor has a $500 lien on Harold's guitar, which is worth $300. In Harold's state, a guitar is exempt only to $200. He could get the lien reduced to $100. The other $400 of the lien is eliminated (avoided).

Lien avoidance costs nothing, involves only a moderate amount of paperwork, and allows you to keep property without paying anything. It is the best and most powerful tool for getting rid of liens. But it has several important restrictions, which are described in Ch. 3, *Adding Up Your Secured and Unsecured Debts*, Section A.

If you want to avoid a lien on your secured property, you must state that in your Chapter 13 plan. In the section of your plan labeled "Special Provisions" or "Other Provisions," write "I will file a motion to avoid the [*specify either judicial lien or nonpossessory nonpurchase money security interest*] from my [*identify the collateral.*]" The actual procedure for asking the court to avoid the lien is in Ch. 9, *After You File Your Case*, Section H.

5. Sell the Property

You can propose, in the "Special Provisions" or "Other Provisions" section of your plan, to sell secured property to get cash to pay the secured creditor. But this option isn't usually a good one. First, few bankruptcy courts will let you sell secured property. Second, you would want to do it only if the sale would bring in more than you owe the creditor— that is, the property has increased in value since you acquired it. But most secured property, such as cars, household goods and furniture, goes down in value over time, not up.

6. File a Chapter 7 Bankruptcy Before You File a Chapter 13 Bankruptcy

The last option is to put your Chapter 13 bankruptcy on hold for a while and file for Chapter 7 bankruptcy first. This is sometimes called a "Chapter 20" bankruptcy.

The reason to add this layer of complexity to your bankruptcy is that in Chapter 7 bankruptcy, you can eliminate your personal liability on a secured debt. Then, as soon as your Chapter 7 bankruptcy is over (the typical case lasts three to six months), you can immediately file a Chapter 13 bankruptcy to pay off the liens that remain on your property. In your Chapter 13 bankruptcy, you would use one of the options discussed just above.

This strategy makes good sense if you have little or no nonexempt property and a lot of dischargeable unsecured debts which you could wipe out in Chapter 7 bankruptcy. If your debts are mostly secured, priority or nondischargeable and would have to be paid in full, however, don't bother filing a Chapter 7 bankruptcy first because Chapter 7 bankruptcy won't eliminate enough of your debts to justify filing.

J. Paying Your Unsecured Creditors

In Chapter 13 bankruptcy, unsecured debts are handled less formally than are secured debts and priority debts. After all, most people file a Chapter 13 bankruptcy case to take care of secured debts and priority debts. Their unsecured creditors generally get only whatever money is left over.

The information that follows on unsecured debts is long. But you may not have to read all—or even any—of it. Before going on, look at the sections of your plan form which deal with unsecured creditors. If your plan simply asks you list the name of each creditor and the amount you owe, copy that information from Schedule F—Creditors Holding Unsecured Nonpriority Claims—which you completed in Ch. 6. Then go on to Section K. The trustee will pay your secured and priority debts first and give the leftovers to your unsecured creditors. The trustee will pay them equal amounts. If you have five unsecured creditors and pay $525 into your plan every month, each creditor will get $105 until the end of your case, no matter how much they are owed.

Keep reading this section, however, if:

- Your plan form requires more information—for example, you must label the type of plan you are submitting.
- You want to pay a greater percentage of some unsecured debts than others.
- Your plan form asks you to specify how much each secured creditor will receive every month.
- You want to include a provision in your plan for paying postpetition debts—that is, the bills you default on after your plan is confirmed.
- Your court requires you to add a certain percentage to payments you unsecured creditors receive.

1. How Unsecured Creditors Will Be Paid

Some Chapter 13 plan forms require that you label the plan as either a "pro tanto" or a "fixed percentage" plan. Other plans require you to specify how the trustee should pay your unsecured creditors, but don't require a label.

In a typical Chapter 13 bankruptcy case, your first several payments (perhaps even the first year of payments) or the bulk of each early payment is used to pay your priority and secured debts (your mortgage and tax arrears, for example). Later payments, or a small portion of the early ones, are divided among your unsecured creditors.

a. Pro Tanto Plans

In a pro tanto (Latin for "for so long") plan, you pay X dollars for Y months without specifying in your plan how much your unsecured creditors will receive. All you do is specify the order in which you want your priority and secured creditors paid. What's left goes to your unsecured creditors.

Pro tanto plans are easy to administer, so bankruptcy trustees like them. Unsecured creditors sometimes object to pro tanto plans at the confirmation hearing, however, because they simply receive what's left over, not a specified amount of money.

b. Fixed Percentage Plans

In a fixed percentage plan, you pay your unsecured creditors a set percentage of what you owe. (The three sample plans in Section M are fixed percentage plans.) Some fixed percentage plans provide for payment of 100% of unsecured debts, others less. A fixed percentage plan is completed when your unsecured creditors have received the percentage stated in the plan, not a specific number of months. For example, you might anticipate that it will take 43 months to pay your unsecured creditors 17% of what they are owed. If any creditor fails to file a claim with the trustee requesting to be paid (creditors must file claims to get paid), the trustee won't pay that creditor and you'll be done with your plan in fewer than 43 months.

There are four types of fixed percentage plans: base, greater than, pro rata and per capita. Bankruptcy trustees are least likely to object to base and greater than plans. Trustees favor them because they let the bankruptcy court confirm your plan before the deadline for filing creditor's claims has passed. Pro rata and per capital plans don't. (How this works is explained in Ch. 9, *After You File Your Case*.)

Another reason trustees like base and greater than plans is that they have found that debtors do a good job of estimating the amount owed on their unsecured debts and therefore propose realistic plans.

Here is how the four kinds of plans work.

- **Base plan.** In a base plan, you calculate the total amount you must pay on all claims—secured, priority and unsecured—over the life of your case. When you have paid the amount you initially calculated, your bankruptcy case is over. It is similar to a pro tanto plan, except that in a pro tanto plan, you specify how much you will pay each month for a set number of months. In a base plan, you pay a set amount of money no matter how long it takes—if you're short a few months, your plan will have to be extended to make up the difference. If you pay extra during some months, your plan will end sooner than you might have originally thought.

- **Greater than plan.** In a greater than plan, you first estimate the amount you owe your unsecured creditors. You then propose paying your unsecured creditors a set amount or a set percentage, whichever is greater.

  EXAMPLE: In your plan, you state that you will pay a "base of $5,700 or 75% of unsecured claims, whichever is greater." You believe that you owe $7,600 in unsecured debts. After your Chapter 13 plan is approved, an unsecured creditor you forgot about files a claim for $1,200. Your total unsecured debts are $8,800, not the $7,600 you originally believed. To satisfy your greater than plan, you must pay 75% of $8,800, or $6,600 not 75% of $7,600. The court can just extend the plan until you've paid a minimum.

- **Pro rata plan.** In a pro rata plan, creditors with small claims receive a smaller percentage of your monthly payment than to creditors with large claims. Each creditor is paid a percentage equal to the percentage its claim is compared to your total unsecured debts. In your plan, you state the actual dollar amount that each creditor will receive each month.

  EXAMPLE: You plan to pay the trustee $110 each month ($10 for the trustee's fee) with $100 of it to be divided among your three unsecured creditors. You owe these creditors $500, $1,000 and $1,500 respectively. Each month, the trustee will pay the first creditor $17/(1/6 of the $100), the second one $33 (1/3 of the $100) and the third one $50 (1/2 of the $100).

- **Per capita plan.** In a per capita plan, your creditors split the monthly payment equally. So in the above example, each creditor would receive $33 (actually, one would get $34 because trustees don't pay out change). This means that smaller claims are paid more quickly than the larger ones. Some trustees prefer this kind of plan because it's easy to administer. Many creditors, however, consider per capita plans unfair, and may object at the confirmation hearing. Their reason is that if you dismiss your case or convert it to Chapter 7 bankruptcy (which happens in the majority of Chapter 13 cases), the creditors with smaller debts will have unfairly benefited.

2.   Classifying Unsecured Creditors

Some plans require that you specify, in the section labeled "Unsecured Creditors," who gets paid in full and who gets less. The simplest way to handle it is to propose paying all your existing unsecured creditors the same percentage. This method is allowed even if some creditors have nondischargeable debts (which you must eventually pay back completely) and some have dischargeable debts (which you need pay only a portion of). But if you choose this option and pay less than 100%, you will owe a balance on your nondischargeable debts at the end of your case. (See Section b, below.)

Your other option is to create classes of unsecured creditors, specifying what percentage each class will receive. Some plan forms ask, in the section labeled "Separate Class of Unsecured Creditors" or "Special Classes" (or "Other Provisions" or "Special Provisions" if you plan has no specific section) for the following:

- a description of the class (these are described in Sections a and b, below)
- the total amount owed to the class of creditors
- the creditors who fall into the class.

The court must approve your classifications, and you cannot unfairly discriminate against any specific creditor. Any creditor who feels your classifications are unfair will object to your Chapter 13 plan. The rest of this section discusses how you may want to classify creditors.

a.   Dischargeable Debts

Even though you are not required to repay dischargeable debts in full in bankruptcy, you may want to pay back 100% of some or all of them. Not all courts permit separate classifications in order to pay these debts in full, however. Here is how the court is likely to rule if you create a separate class for one or more dischargeable debts.

- **Your codebtors.** Courts sometimes allow a separate classification of debts with codebtors so that you can repay the debt in full. A court is especially likely to permit it if you must maintain a working relationship with your codebtor (such as a business partner), or if your codebtor can't pay the debt because of illness or disability.
- **Creditors with whom you have an ongoing relationship.** The court may permit a separate class if you or a family member has an ongoing medical problem and needs continued treatment from the practitioner you want to pay. Your other creditors may object, however, and demand that you provide proof that the medical care cannot be provided by a different practitioner. Or,

if you want to make up past due rent and it would be difficult for you to find a new place to live, a court might allow your landlord to be put in a separate class.

- **Debts to business creditors.** The court will probably allow this separate class to be repaid in full if the creditor provides you with insurance coverage or materials essential to run your business.
- **Debts based on their amounts.** Many bankruptcy courts allow you to classify unsecured debts based on their amounts, especially if you have no nonexempt property. For instance, you could create two classes: one to pay 100% of debts of $1,000 and less and another to pay 10% of debts over $1,000. Unsecured creditors rarely object to this kind of classification, because at least they are getting something through your plan.
- **Postpetition debts.** You may want to create a class of "postpetition debts," or new debts you incur after your plan is approved. If you don't create such a class now, you'll have to pay any postpetition debts out of your income (what you're not paying into your plan). To pay them through your plan, state the following in the section labeled "Special Class of Unsecured Creditors" or something similar: "separate class of postpetition debts to be repaid at 100%, with interest." You can include the class now—when you write your plan—or you can file a written request (motion) with the bankruptcy court to modify your plan later on. (See Ch. 10, *After Your Plan Is Approved*, Section B.)

b. Nondischargeable Debts

A nondischargeable debt is an unsecured debt that must be repaid in full. If you don't pay it in full in your Chapter 13 bankruptcy case, you will owe a balance after your case is over. You may want to create a separate class of nondischargeable debts so you can pay them in full while paying a smaller percentage to other unsecured creditors.

This practice, however, is rarely permitted, because it means other unsecured creditors get less of the pie. Probably the best way to deal with most nondischargeable debts is to pay them with your general class of unsecured creditors. If the creditor insists that you acknowledge that you will owe a balance at the end of your Chapter 13 case, add a sentence to the "Other Provisions" or "Special Provisions" section stating as much. Here's an example:

> "I will pay my unsecured creditors, including the Department of Education, 38% through my plan. I agree that I will owe the balance to the Department of Education at the end of my case."

To keep the creditor from adding on the interest abated during your bankruptcy case when it's over, you can file a

second Chapter 13 case at the close of the first case to pay off the balance, Alternatively, you might propose paying all unsecured debts the same percentage for 36 months and then paying only the nondischargeable debts during months 37-60.

For detailed information on determining whether or not debts are dischargeable, see Ch. 2, *An Overview of Chapter 13 Bankruptcy*, Section D.

Here is how courts are likely to rule if you want to separately classify common kinds of nondischargeable debts.

Alimony or child support. Because courts favor payment of past due support, virtually all of them will allow you to separately classify this debt to repay it in full, even if it means you will pay less to your other unsecured creditors.

Student loans. Bankruptcy courts have little sympathy for debtors who want to eliminate a student loan at the expense of their other creditors. Only a few bankruptcy courts will let you create a separate class of student loans to repay them in full.

You have another option for dealing with a nondischargeable student loan. You can treat it like a long-term secured debt—that is, pay back the arrears through your plan (cure the default), and then make payments during and after your plan. (See Section I, above.)

Intoxicated driving debts. Bankruptcy courts have even less sympathy for debtors who want to eliminate a debt resulting from the death of, or personal injury to, someone because you drove while intoxicated by alcohol or drugs, while your other creditors get less. You probably will not be able to create a separate class.

Restitution or criminal fine. Don't look to the bankruptcy court for help in separately classifying a criminal fine or a debt for restitution included in a sentence you received while you pay your other creditors less. You probably will not be able to create a separate class.

3. Compensation on Payments

Because your unsecured creditors will be paid through your plan over several years, they will actually receive less than they're entitled to because the payments you make years from now will be made with inflated dollars, worth less than they are now.

To see that your unsecured creditors aren't short-changed, some bankruptcy courts require you to increase your overall payments by a percentage established by the court. It's based on the current interest rate in your area; you can find out by calling the trustee. Although this is in essence an interest charge, courts never call it that—the law says that in Chapter 13 bankruptcy, unsecured creditors aren't entitled to interest.

Few, if any, plan forms ask you to include this unofficial interest payment in your calculations. But if you don't calculate it in, your unsecured creditors may object. You can leave it off your plan to begin with; if the trustee or a creditor objects, you can add it to your plan before the confirmation hearing.

K. Dealing With Contracts and Leases

In the "Special Provisions" or "Other Provisions" section of your Chapter 13 bankruptcy plan, you must tell the court what you plan to do with any executory contracts and unexpired leases. (You listed these on Schedule G, in Ch. 6, *Completing the Bankruptcy Forms.*) Type in one of the following three choices:

- "I will reject the contract or lease." In this case, your obligation under the agreement ends.
- "I will assume the contract or lease." In this case, your obligation under the agreement continues.
- "I will assign the contract or lease." In this case, your obligation under the agreement is transferred to someone else.

Here are some issues to keep in mind as you make your choices:

- In most courts, if you do not specifically reject, assume or assign a nonresidential lease, the lease is considered rejected, and you must surrender the leased property. (11 U.S.C. § 365(d)(4).)
- If you have defaulted on a lease or contract—for example, you owe back rent—but you still have some rights under the agreement, you can continue it by paying the arrears through your plan (curing the default) and making payments through the plan. (See Section I, above.)
- If you have defaulted on a lease or contract in a nonmonetary way—for example, you breached a residential lease clause prohibiting pets—you can use the time Chapter 13 bankruptcy automatic stay gives you to get into compliance. So while the landlord is barred from proceeding with an eviction, you could find a home for the animal and continue payments on your lease.
- If you decide to continue (assume) a lease or contract, there may be consequences as well:
  - If, after your plan is confirmed, you change your mind and reject the agreement, you must compensate the creditor in full for any loss resulting from the rejection—such as the costs the landlord incurs in rerenting your apartment.
  - If your lease has a purchase option, and your right to exercise that option arises during your Chapter

13 case, you cannot postpone that option until after your bankruptcy case ends. Your only option is to proceed as specified in the agreement.

L. Making Payments Directly to Creditors

You can propose, in your Chapter 13 plan, to pay certain debts directly—that is, not through the bankruptcy court. The main reason to do that is to reduce the trustee's fee you must pay. (See Section E, above.)

Bankruptcy courts and trustees frown on direct payments for several reasons:

- **They reduce the trustee's fee.**
- **They may reduce your ability to make the payments under your plan.** The failure rate for Chapter 13 bankruptcy cases is much higher when debtors make direct payments than when they don't. This is because when funds are tight, debtors tend to make the direct payments before paying the trustee.
- **You may be creating an unfair classification.** Creditors paid through the plan may object that the creditors who are paid directly are being treated more favorably.

Many trustees, however, allow debtors to make limited payments outside the plan. The most common payments allowed are:

- **Regular mortgage payments if you are not in default.** If, however, you are in default and intend to pay the arrears through your plan, you must make your regular mortgage payments through the plan, too.
- **Regular car purchase or lease payments if you are not in default.**
- **Payments to a creditor with whom you have an ongoing relationship.** For example, you may want to pay a doctor outside the plan, so you or a family member can continue to receive treatment.

M. Sample Plans

Even if you've breezed through the instructions in this chapter, you may still feel a little intimidated when its time to sit down and write your own plan. Keep in mind that your plan doesn't have to be flawless when you first submit it. To help you, here are three sample Chapter 13 plans, using the forms in Appendix 3. Your plan, obviously, won't look like any of them—but it may make things easier if you see how some debtors fill in all the blanks.

The hypothetical debtors who completed these plan forms are Martin and Ellen Herchoo, the same debtors who completed the forms in Ch. 6. A summary of their debts appears below.

SUMMARY OF DEBTS:
MARTIN AND ELLEN HERCHOO

Debt	Amount	Type	Comments
Mortgage arrears	$10,800	Secured	They are in arrears five months at $2,160 per month.
Interest on arrears	1,080		They must pay 10% interest on arrears.
Car loan arrears	372	Secured	They are in arrears one month; figure includes interest. They will propose paying the balance of this loan directly—$355 per month.
IRS	33,762	Priority	
Bank personal loan	3,918	Unsecured	This loan has a cosigner; they propose paying it back in full.
Bank personal loan	1,411	Unsecured	This loan has a cosigner; they propose paying it back in full.
Leased timeshare	8,880	Unsecured	They will reject this lease, making the debt unsecured.
Visa	12,789	Unsecured	
MasterCard	6,452	Unsecured	
Court judgment	1,215	Unsecured	They will file motion to avoid judicial lien on house, making the debt unsecured.
Home equity loan	—	Secured	This debt is not in default; they will propose to pay it directly—$335 per month.

The Herchoos propose paying their disposable income—$1,800 a month—into their plan to pay these debts. Their secured and priority debts, which must be paid in full, plus the unsecured debts for which they have cosigners and want to pay back in full, total $51,343. Their trustee charges a fee of 10%; that amounts to $5,134, meaning they must pay at least $56,477. The Herchoos calculate that by paying $1,800 a month, it will take a little over 31 months to pay the $56,477.

To keep the trustee's fee down, the Herchoos decide to propose paying their regular monthly mortgage and car loan payments directly to the creditors instead of through their plan. They trustee may, however, require them to pay these debts through the plan.

Their other debts total $29,336. They don't know how much of these debts their court will require them to repay. So they calculate how many additional months it will take them to pay a small percentage (26%), about half and 100% of these debts.

Here are the results:

		36 months		40 months		49 months
Amount paid each month	x	1,800	x	1,800	x	1,800
Total amount paid	=	64,800	=	72,000	=	88,200
Amount paid on secured, priority and cosigned debts	−	$ 56,477	−	$ 56,477	−	$ 56,477
Total left for unsecured debts	=	8,323	=	15,523	=	31,723
Less 10% for trustee	−	832	−	1,552	−	3,172
Total paid to unsecured creditors	=	$ 7,491	=	$13,971	=	$28,551
Percentage repaid on unsecured debts		26%		48%		97%*

*To repay their unsecured debts in full, they'd make a smaller payment in the 50th month.

The plan forms, below, will give you an idea of what a plan looks like, but keep in mind that even if you have similar debts, your plan will look very different.

26% PLAN

(ATTORNEY NAME:) ___not applicable___

(ADDRESS:) _____

(CITY) _____ (STATE:) _____

(ZIP:) _____

(PHONE NUMBER:) (____) _____

(BAR NUMBER:) ___Debtors Pro Se___

DEBTORS: ___Martin and Ellen Herchoo___   CASE NO.: _____

DEBTORS PRELIMINARY CHAPTER 13 PLAN

DATE OF PLAN ___2/23/XX___   FIRST PAYMENT DUE TO TRUSTEE ___3/25/XX___

INCOME $ ___6,110___   TRUSTEE PAYMENTS $ ___1,800___ FOR ___36___ MONTHS   PLAN BASE AMOUNT $ _____

EXPENSES $ ___4,310___ $ _____ FOR ____ MONTHS   UNSECURED % ___26___

SURPLUS $ ___1,800___ $ _____ FOR ____ MONTHS

ADMINISTRATIVE   NOTICING FEES: # _____   + 3 X 3 X .79 = $ _____

ATTORNEY FEES: TOTAL _____ THRU PLAN _____

HOME MORTGAGE   Regular payments beginning ___3/1/XX___   to be paid direct. Arrearages to be paid by Trustee as follows:

	ARREARS	THRU	%	TERM	PAYMENT
1ST LIEN ___Big Home Loan Bank___	$ ___10,800___	_____	10	6 mos	$ ___1,800___
2ND LIEN _____	$ _____	_____	____	____	$ _____

SECURED CREDITORS	COLLATERAL	CLAIM	VALUE	%	TERM	PAYMENT
1. ___Car Finance Co.___	___19XX Nissan___	$ ___372___	$ ___7,400___	8	1 mo.	$ ___372___
2. _____	_____	$ _____	$ _____	____	____	$ _____
3. _____	_____	$ _____	$ _____	____	____	$ _____
4. _____	_____	$ _____	$ _____	____	____	$ _____
5. _____	_____	$ _____	$ _____	____	____	$ _____

ANY DEFICIENCY WILL AUTOMATICALLY BE "SPLIT" AND INCLUDED IN UNSECURED.

PRIORITY CREDITORS	TYPE	DISPUTED AMOUNT	CLAIM	TERM	PAYMENT
1. ___IRS___	tax	$ _____	$ ___33,762___	19 mos.	$ ___1,800___
2. _____	_____	$ _____	$ _____	_____	$ _____

SPECIAL CLASS	BASIS		AMOUNT	TERM	PAYMENT
1. ___River Bank___	codebtor	_____	$ ___3,918___	2+ mos.	$ ___1,800___
2. ___Sweeter's Bank___	codebtor	_____	$ ___1,411___	1 mo.	$ ___1,411___

UNSECURED CREDITORS	CLAIM	CREDITORS	CLAIM	CREDITORS	CLAIM
1. ___Summer Vacations Co.___	$ ___8,880___	6. _____	$ _____	11. _____	$ _____
2. ___Visa___	$ ___12,789___	7. _____	$ _____	12. _____	$ _____
3. ___MasterCard___	$ ___6,452___	8. _____	$ _____	13. _____	$ _____
4. ___Ken Williams___	$ ___1,215___	9. _____	$ _____	14. _____	$ _____
5. _____	$ _____	10. _____	$ _____	15. _____	$ _____

TOTAL UNSECURED AND DEFICIENCIES $ ___29,336___

___X___ CHECK HERE IF ADDITIONAL INFORMATION APPEARS ON REVERSE SIDE (EXECUTORY CONTRACTS? MISCELLANEOUS?)

CERTIFICATE OF SERVICE

I certify that a copy of the above and foregoing "Debtor's Preliminary Chapter 13 Plan" and an "Authorization for Pre-Confirmation Disbursement" was by me on this ___25th___ day ___February___ of 19 _XX_ served on the trustee and all creditors listed on the original matrix and any amended matrix filed in this case by United States First Class mail.

___Martin Herchoo___

Attorney for Debtor or Pro Se Debtor

SPECIAL PROVISIONS:

(Balloon, proceeds of sale;

recovery on lawsuit, etc.

1. We reject our leased time share with Summer Vacations Co.

2. We will file a Motion to avoid Ken William's judicial lien against our house.

3. We propose making our regular house and car payments, and our home equity loan payments ($335/month), outside the plan.

ADDITIONAL CREDITORS:

HOME MORTGAGE:

	ARREARS	THRU	%	TERM	PAYMENT
3RD LIEN	$				$
4TH LIEN	$				$

SECURED CREDITORS	COLLATERAL	CLAIM	VALUE	%	TERM	PAYMENT
6.		$	$			$
7.		$	$			$
8.		$	$			$
9.		$	$			$
10.		$	$			$

PRIORITY CREDITORS	DISPUTED AMOUNT	CLAIM	TERM	PAYMENT
3.	$	$		$
4.	$	$		$

SPECIAL CLASS	BASIS	AMOUNT	TERM	PAYMENT
3.		$		$
4.		$		$

UNSECURED CREDITORS	CLAIM	CREDITORS	CLAIM	CREDITORS	CLAIM
	$		$		$
	$		$		$
	$		$		$
	$		$		$
	$		$		$

48% PLAN

DEBTOR(S)   Martin and Ellen Herchoo   CASE NO. _____

CHAPTER 13 PLAN OR SUMMARY

I. The projected disposable income of the debtor(s) is submitted to the supervision and control of the Trustee and the Debtor(s) shall pay to the Trustee the sum of:

$ 1,800 _____   ☐ Weekly   ☐ Bi-weekly   ☐ Semi-monthly   ☒ Monthly

☒ Direct Payment   ☐ Payroll Deduction on Wages of: ☐ Debtor   ☐ Spouse

Length of plan is approximately ___40___ months, and total debt to be paid through plan is approximately $_____70,445_____ .

II. From the payments so received the Trustee shall make disbursements as follows:

A. PRIORITY payments described in 11 USC §507 in full in deferred cash payments.

B. The holder of each allowed SECURED claim shall retain the lien securing such claim until a discharge is granted and such claim shall be paid in full with interest at a rate of ___10___ % per annum in deferred cash payments as follows:

1. Mortgage Debts:

Name of Mortgage company	Home-stead Yes/No	Total amount of debt	Arrears to be paid by Trustee	Months included in arrearage amount	Post-petition –OR– payments to begin Month/Year* (Direct to creditor)	Amount of regular mortgage to be paid by Trustee
Big Home Loan Bank	yes	239,715	10,800	10/XX–2/XX	3/XX	

2. Other Secured Debts:

Name of creditor	Total amount of debt	Debtor's value	Description collateral	Interest factor (If Applicable**)	Debtor's Fixed Payments (If Applicable**)
Car Finance Co.	8,250		19XX Nissan		355

C. The Debtor(s) will make direct payments as follows:

Name of creditor	Total of debt	Description of collateral	Reason for direct payment
Car Finance Co.	8,250	19XX Nissan	only one month in arrears
Big Home Loan Bank	16,080	home	not in default (335/mo)

D. Special provisions. Explanation:

1. We reject our leased homeshare with Summer Vacations Co.

2. We will give a Motion to Avoid Ken William's judicial lien against our house

3. Please pay 100% on unsecured debts with codebtors: Personal loan from River Bank; Personal loan from Sweeter's Bank

☒ This is an original plan.

☐ This is an amended plan replacing plan dated _____ .

☒ This plan proposes to pay unsecured creditors ___48___ %.

☒ Insurance on vehicle: ☒ Proof of Insurance attached, OR:

                     ☐ Insurance through Trustee requested

Dated: _2/23/XX_____   *Martin Herchoo*
                                   Signature of Debtor

Dated: _2/23/XX_____   *Ellen Herchoo*
                                   Signature of Debtor

100% PLAN

CHAPTER 13 PLAN

In Re: Martin and Ellen Herchoo

Dated: ___2/23/XX___

Debtor
In a joint case,
debtor means debtors in this plan.

Case No. _____

1. PAYMENTS BY DEBTOR —

     a. As of this date of this plan, the debtor has paid the trustee $ ___0___ .

     b. After the date of this plan, the debtor will pay the trustee $ __1,800__ per __month__ for __49__ months, beginning within 30 days after the filing of this plan for a total of $ __88,200__ .

     c. The debtor will also pay the trustee ____$1,203 in the 50th month____

     d. The debtor will pay the trustee a total of $ __89,403__ [line 1(a) + line 1(b) + line 1(c)].

2. PAYMENTS BY TRUSTEE — The trustee will make payments only to creditors for which proofs of claim have been filed, make payments monthly as available, and collect the trustee's percentage fee of 10% for a total of $ __8,940__ [line 1 (d) x .10] or such lesser percentage as may be fixed by the Attorney General. For purposes of this plan, month one (1) is the month following the month in which the debtor makes the debtor's first payment. Unless ordered otherwise, the trustee will not make any payments until the plan is confirmed. Payments will accumulate and be paid following confirmation.

3. PRIORITY CLAIMS — The trustee shall pay in full all claims entitled to priority under § 507, including the following. The amounts listed are estimates only. The trustee will pay the amounts actually allowed.

Creditor	Estimated Claim	Monthly Payment	Beginning in Month #	Number of Payments	TOTAL PAYMENTS
a. Attorney Fees	$	$			$
b. Internal Revenue Service	$ 33,762	$ 1,800	7	19	$ 33,762
c. State Dept. of Revenue	$	$			$
d. _____	$	$			$
e. TOTAL					$ 33,762

4. LONG-TERM SECURED CLAIMS NOT IN DEFAULT — The following creditor have secured claims. Payments are current and the debtor will continue to make all payments which come due after the date the petition was filed directly to the creditors. The creditors will retain their liens.

     a. Home equity loan through Big Home Loan Bank ($335 a month)

     b. _____

5. HOME MORTGAGES IN DEFAULT [§ 1322 (b)(5)] — The trustee will cure defaults (plus interest at the rate of 8 per cent per annum) on claims secured only by a security interest in real property that is the debtor's principal residence as follows. The debtor will maintain the regular payments which come due after the date the petition was filed. The creditors will retain their liens. The amounts of default are estimates only. The trustee will pay the actual amounts of default.

Creditor	Amount of Default	Monthly Payment	Beginning in Month #	Number of Payments	TOTAL PAYMENTS
a. Big Home Loan Bank	$ 10,800	$ 2,160	$ 1	$ 6	$ 10,800
b. _____	$	$	$	$	$
c. _____	$	$	$	$	$
d. TOTAL					$ 10,800

Chapter 13 Plan Page 2

6. OTHER LONG-TERM SECURED CLAIMS IN DEFAULT [§ 1322 (b)(5)] — The trustee will cure defaults (plus interest at the rate of 8 per cent per annum) on other claims as follows and the debtor will maintain the regular payments which come due after the date the petition was filed. The creditors will retain their liens. The amounts of default are estimates only. The trustee will pay the actual amounts of default.

Creditor	Amount of Default	Monthly Payment	Beginning in Month #	Number of Payments	TOTAL PAYMENTS
a. Car Finance Co.	$ 372	$ 355	7	1	$ 372
b.	$	$			$
c.	$	$			$
d. TOTAL					$ 372

7. OTHER SECURED CLAIMS [§ 1325 (a)(5)] — The trustee will make payments to the following secured creditors having a value as of confirmation equal to the allowed amount of the creditor's secured claim using a discount rate of 8 percent. The creditor's allowed secured claim shall be the creditor's allowed claim or the value of the creditor's interest in the debtor's property, whichever is less. The creditors shall retain their liens. NOTE: NOTWITHSTANDING A CREDITOR'S PROOF OF CLAIM FILED BEFORE OR AFTER CONFIRMATION, THE AMOUNT LISTED IN THIS PARAGRAPH AS A CREDITOR'S SECURED CLAIM BINDS THE CREDITOR PURSUANT TO 11 U.S.C. § 1327 AND CONFIRMATION OF THE PLAN WILL BE CONSIDERED A DETERMINATION OF THE CREDITOR'S ALLOWED SECURED CLAIM UNDER 11 U.S.C. § 506 (a).

Creditor	Claim Amount	Secured Claim	Monthly Payment	Beginning in Month #	Number of Payments	TOTAL PAYMENTS
a.	$	$	$			$
b.	$	$	$			$
c.	$	$	$			$
d. TOTAL						$ 0

8. SEPARATE CLASS OF UNSECURED CREDITORS — In addition to the class of unsecured creditors specified in ¶ 9, there shall be a separate class of nonpriority unsecured creditors described as follows: ___debts with codebtors___
   a. The debtor estimates that the total claims in this class are $ 5,329 .
   b. The trustee will pay this class $ 5,329 .

9. TIMELY FILED UNSECURED CREDITORS — The trustee will pay holders of nonpriority unsecured claims for which proofs of claim were timely filed the balance of all payments received by the trustee and not paid under ¶ 2, 3, 5, 6, 7 and 8 their pro rata share of approximately $ 29,336 [line 1(d) minus lines 2, 3(e), 5(d), 6(d), 7(d) and 8 (b)].
   a. The debtor estimates that the total unsecured claims held by creditors listed in ¶ 7 are $ 0
   b. The debtor estimates that the debtor's total unsecured claims (excluding those in ¶ 7 and ¶ 8) are $ 29,336 .
   c. Total estimated unsecured claims are $ 29,336 [line 9(a) + line 9(b)].

10. TARDILY-FILED UNSECURED CREDITORS — All money paid by the debtor to the trustee under ¶ 1, but not distributed by the trustee under ¶ 2, 3, 5, 6, 7, 8 or 9 shall be paid to holders of nonpriority unsecured claims for which proofs of claim were tardily filed.

11. OTHER PROVISIONS —
   1. We reject our leased timeshare with Summer Vacations Co.
   2. We will file a motion to avoid Ken William's judicial lien against our house.
   3. We propose making our regular house and car payments outside the plan.

12. SUMMARY PAYMENTS —
Trustee's Fee [Line 2]	$ 8,940
Priority Claims [Line 3(e)]	$ 33,762
Home Mortgage Defaults [Line 5(d)]	$ 10,800 + 864 (interest)
Long-Term Debt Defaults [Line 6(d)]	$ 372
Other Secured Claims [Line 7(d)]	$ 0
Separate Class [Line 8(b)]	$ 5,329
Unsecured Creditors [Line 9(c)]	$ 29,336
TOTAL [must equal Line 1(d)]	$ 89,403

Signed: _Martin Herchoo_
DEBTOR

Signed: _Ellen Herchoo_
DEBTOR (if joint case)

Filing Your Bankruptcy Papers

Filing your papers with the bankruptcy court clerk should be simple. Most people file all their bankruptcy forms—the court forms and the plan—at the same time, but you don't have to. You can file the official forms in Ch. 6 first, and file your Chapter 13 plan a maximum of 15 days later.

→ EMERGENCY FILING

If you need to stop a foreclosure or have another emergency, you can file the two-page Voluntary Petition, together with a list of the name, address and zip code of each of your creditors. The automatic stay, which stops all other collection efforts against you—including a foreclosure—will then go into effect. You will have 15 days to file the rest of the forms, including your Chapter 13 plan. (Bankruptcy Rules 1007(c), 3015(b).) See Section C, below.

A. Basic Filing Procedures

You don't have to make a trip to the courthouse to file your bankruptcy papers. Most people prefer to file by mail. You can, however, take your papers to the bankruptcy court clerk. Going to the court will let you correct minor mistakes on the spot.

Filing your bankruptcy papers is an eight-step process.

Step 1: Make sure you have the following information:
  - the amount of the filing and administrative fees
  - the specific order in which documents should be presented, and
  - the number of copies of each document needed.
    If you don't know any of this, check with the bankruptcy court clerk. (See Ch. 6, *Completing the Bankruptcy Forms*, Section B.)

Step 2: Put all your bankruptcy forms in the order required by the bankruptcy court or, if your court doesn't specify the order, in the order they appear in this book. Put each continuation sheet directly after the form to which it applies. Don't staple any forms together.

BANKRUPTCY FORMS CHECKLIST

Unless your court specifies a different order, stack your forms as follows:
- ☐ Form 1—Voluntary Petition
- ☐ Schedule A—Real Property
- ☐ Schedule B—Personal Property
- ☐ Schedule C—Property Claimed as Exempt
- ☐ Schedule D—Creditors Holding Secured Claims
- ☐ Schedule E—Creditors Holding Unsecured Priority Claims
- ☐ Schedule F—Creditors Holding Unsecured Nonpriority Claims
- ☐ Schedule G—Executory Contracts and Unexpired Leases
- ☐ Schedule H—Codebtors
- ☐ Schedule I—Current Income
- ☐ Schedule J—Current Expenditures
- ☐ Summary of Schedules A through J
- ☐ Declaration Concerning Debtor's Schedules
- ☐ Form 7—Statement of Financial Affairs
- ☐ Mailing Matrix (if required)
- ☐ Income Deduction Order (if required)
- ☐ Chapter 13 repayment plan
- ☐ Required local forms

Step 3: Check that you, and your spouse if you're filing a joint petition, have signed each form where required.

Step 4: Make the number of copies required by the court (sometimes as many as four), plus two additional copies of all forms. One extra set is for the clerk to file-stamp and give or send back to you, and one is for your records just in case your papers are lost in the mail (if you file by mail).

Step 5: Unless the court clerk will two-hole punch your papers when you file them, use a standard two-hole punch (copy centers have them) to punch holes in the top of all your bankruptcy papers.

Step 6: If you plan to mail your documents to the court, address a 9" x 12" envelope to yourself. The court clerk will use it to mail back a file-stamped set of your papers. You don't need to affix postage.

Step 7: If you can pay the $130 filing fee and $30 administrative fee when you file, clip or staple a $160 money order or cashier's check (courts do not accept personal checks), payable to "U.S. Bankruptcy Court," to the first page of your petition.

If you want to pay the filing fee in installments or through your plan, attach a filled-in application and order for payment in installments, plus any additional papers required by local court rules, and a money order or cashier's check for the administrative fee ($30). Instructions for paying in installments are in Section B, just below.

Step 8: Take or mail the original and copies of all forms to the correct bankruptcy court.

B. Paying in Installments

You must pay the $30 administrative fee in full when you file your petition. You can pay the $130 filing fee, however, in up to four installments over 120 days or propose to pay it through your Chapter 13 plan. (Bankruptcy Rule 1006(b)(1).)

You cannot apply for permission to pay in installments if you've paid an attorney or BPP to help you with your bankruptcy.

If you want to pay in installments, you must file a form called an Application to Pay Filing Fee in Installments when you file your petition. A blank copy of this form is in Appendix 3. The Application is easy to fill out. At the top, fill in the name of the court (this is on Form 1—Voluntary Petition), your name (and your spouse's name if you're filing jointly), and "13" in the blank following "Chapter." Leave the Case No. space blank. Then enter:

- the total filing fee you must pay, $130 (item 1)
- the amount you propose to pay when you file the petition, usually 25% of the total fee, or $32.50 (item 4, first blank)
- the number of additional installments you need, and
- the amount and date you propose for each installment payment. If you would like to make the payments through your Chapter 13 plan, cross a line through the words "on or before" and type in the blanks that follow "installments to be paid through plan."

You (and your spouse, if you're filing jointly) must sign and date the Application. If you use a BPP, have that person complete the second section. Leave the bottom section entitled "Order" blank for the judge to fill out. The judge will

either approve the application as submitted, or will modify it. You'll be informed of the judge's decision.

C. Emergency Filing

If you want to file for bankruptcy in a hurry to stop your creditors from bugging you, in most places you can accomplish that just by filing Form 1—Voluntary Petition and a mailing matrix. Some courts also require that you file a cover sheet and an Order Dismissing Chapter 13 Case, which will be processed if you don't file the rest of your papers within 15 days. If the bankruptcy court for your district requires either of those forms, you can get it from the court, a local bankruptcy attorney or bankruptcy petition preparer.

FILE THE REST OF YOUR PAPERS ON TIME

If you don't follow up by filing the additional documents—including your Chapter 13 repayment plan—within 15 days, your bankruptcy case will be dismissed and you may be fined $75 or $100. You can file again, if necessary, but you'll have to pay another filing fee. And if you file and dismiss several times, the court may rule that you are abusing the bankruptcy system and bar you from filing again for months, for years, or, in extreme cases, ever again.

For an emergency filing:

Step 1: Check with your court to find out exactly what forms must be submitted for an emergency filing.

Step 2: Fill in Form 1—Voluntary Petition. (See Ch. 6, *Completing the Bankruptcy Forms*, Section E.)

Step 3: On a mailing matrix (or whatever other form is required by your court), list all your creditors, as well as collection agencies, sheriffs, attorneys and others who are seeking to collect debts from you. (See Ch. 6, *Completing the Bankruptcy Forms*, Section H.)

Step 4: Fill in any other papers the court requires.

Step 5: File the originals (the copy you signed) and required number of copies, accompanied by your fee (or an application for payment of fee in installments) and a self-addressed envelope with the bankruptcy court. Keep copies of everything for your records.

Step 6: File all other required forms within 15 days. ∎

After You File Your Case

Once you have filed all of your Chapter 13 bankruptcy papers, including your repayment plan, the bankruptcy trustee and the court take over. They willexamine your papers and schedule court hearings. Your creditors also get into the act; it's time for them to file their claims, so they can get paid by the trustee once you start making plan payments. They may also object to your plan if they think they are getting shortchanged.

This chapter tells you how to move your bankruptcy case along and deal with any unexpected complications that arise. You will probably have to make two or three brief court appearances and do some negotiating with creditors.

⚠ EMERGENCY FILING REMINDER
If you have not filed all your bankruptcy papers, you must do so within 15 days of when you filed your petition. (Bankruptcy Rules 1007(c), 3015(b).) If you do not, the bankruptcy court will dismiss your case and probably fine you. (See Ch. 6, *Completing the Bankruptcy Forms.*)

A. The Automatic Stay

When you file for bankruptcy, something called the "automatic stay" goes into effect. The automatic stay prohibits virtually all creditors from taking any action directed at collecting the debts you owe them until the court says otherwise. In general, creditors cannot:

- take any collection activities, such as writing letters to you or calling you
- file a lawsuit or proceed with a pending lawsuit against you (with a few exceptions, discussed below)
- terminate utilities or public benefits, such as welfare or food stamps
- withhold money in their possession as a setoff for a debt (they can freeze other accounts in their possession, however)
- record liens against your property, or
- seize your property, such as the money in a bank account.

If a creditor tries to collect a debt in violation of the automatic stay, you can ask the bankruptcy court to hold the creditor in contempt of court and to fine the creditor. See a lawyer to help you make this request.

There are, however, some notable exceptions to the automatic stay. These proceedings are allowed to continue:

- Criminal proceedings. A criminal proceeding that can be broken down into a criminal component and a debt component will be divided, and only the criminal component will be allowed to continue. For example, if you were convicted of writing a bad check and have been sentenced to community service and ordered to pay a fine, your obligation to do community service will not be stopped by the automatic stay.
- A lawsuit that seeks to establish your paternity of a child or to establish, modify or collect child support or alimony.
- A tax audit, the issuance of a tax deficiency notice, a demand for a tax return, the issuance of a tax assessment and the demand for payment of such an assessment by the IRS. The automatic stay, however, does stop the IRS from recording a lien or seizing any of your property.

Creditors won't know to stop their collection efforts until they receive notice of your bankruptcy filing. The notice sent by the court may take several days or weeks to reach your creditors. If you want quicker results, send your own notice to bothersome creditors (and bill collectors, landlords or sheriffs). A sample letter is shown below. A fill-in-the-blanks copy is in Appendix 3.

How a Typical Chapter 13 Bankruptcy Proceeds

Step	When It Happens
1. You file for Chapter 13 bankruptcy.	
2. The automatic stay takes effect. It bars your creditors, once they learn of your filing, from taking any actions to collect what you owe.	When you file the bankruptcy petition.
3. The court appoints a trustee to oversee your case. You will receive a Notice of Appointment of Trustee from the court.	Within a few days after you file the bankruptcy petition.
4. The trustee sends you a Notice of Commencement of Case, which usually contains: • a summary of your Chapter 13 plan • the date of the meeting of creditors • the date of the confirmation hearing, and • the deadline by which creditors must file their claims.	Within a few days after you file your Chapter 13 plan.
5. You begin making payments under your repayment plan. (If your plan is never approved, the trustee will return your money, less administrative costs.)	Within 30 days after you file the bankruptcy petition.
6. You attend the meeting of the creditors, where the trustee and any creditors who show up can ask you about information in your papers. A creditor may raise objections to your plan with the hope of getting you to modify it before the confirmation hearing.	Within 40 days after you file the bankruptcy petition.
7. You file a modified plan, if you wish.	Anytime before the confirmation hearing.
8. Creditors file written objections to your plan, if they wish. The bankruptcy judge will rule on them at the confirmation hearing.	At least 25 days before the confirmation hearing.
9. You attend the confirmation hearing, where the court addresses any objections raised by creditors or the trustee and approves your repayment plan.	No set time. A few courts hold the hearing after the deadline for creditors to file claims has passed. Most courts hold the hearing right after the meeting of the creditors, which is before the deadline.
10. Creditors file their "proofs of claims," specifying how much they are owed.	Within 90 days after the meeting of the creditors.
11. You or the trustee file written objections to creditors' claims, if you have a reason to object.	As soon as possible after the creditors file their claims. You must notify your creditors at least 30 days in advance of the hearing on your objections.
12. The trustee sends you periodic statements, showing: • who has filed claims and for how much • how much money has been paid to each creditor • the balance due each creditor.	Commonly, twice a year.
13. The court grants your discharge. The court may schedule a brief final court appearance called a "discharge hearing." If there's no discharge hearing, you'll be mailed formal notice of your discharge.	36 to 60 months after you file if you complete your plan payments; sooner if you seek a hardship discharge.

NOTICE TO CREDITOR OF FILING FOR BANKRUPTCY

Lynn Adams
18 Orchard Park Blvd.
East Lansing, MI 48823

June 15, 19XX

Cottons Clothing Store
745 Main Street
Lansing, MI 48915

Dear Cottons Clothing:

On June 14, 19xx, I filed a voluntary petition under Chapter 13 of the U.S. Bankruptcy Code in the Bankruptcy Court for the Eastern District of Michigan. The case number is 123-456-7890. No attorney is representing me. Under 11 U.S.C. § 362(a), you may not:

- take any action against me or my property to collect any debt
- file or pursue any lawsuit against me
- place a lien on my real or personal property
- take any property to satisfy an already recorded lien
- repossess any property in my possession
- discontinue any service or benefit currently being provided to me, or
- take any action to evict me from where I live.

A violation of these prohibitions may be considered contempt of court and punished accordingly.

Very truly yours,

Lynn Adams

Lynn Adams

The court almost always lifts (removes) the stay at the end of the confirmation hearing, because your creditors are now bound by your plan.

B. Dealing With the Trustee

Within a few days after you file your bankruptcy petition, the bankruptcy court assigns a Chapter 13 trustee to oversee your case. You will receive a Notice of Appointment of Trustee from the court, giving the name, address and phone number of the trustee. It may also include a list of any financial documents the trustee wants copies of, such as bank statements, canceled checks and tax returns, and the date by which the trustee wants them.

Within a few days after the trustee is appointed, the trustee will send you a Notice of Commencement of Case. This notice usually contains:

- a summary of your Chapter 13 plan
- an explanation of the automatic stay
- the date, time and place of the meeting of creditors (see Section E, below)
- the date, time and place of the confirmation hearing (see Section H, below), and
- the date by which creditors must file their claims (see Section J, below).

SOME NOTICES ARE INCOMPLETE
Not all Notices of Commencement of Case include the date, time and place of the meeting of creditors. If yours does not, call the court clerk to find out.

Along with the notice, the trustee often includes a letter of introduction explaining how this trustee runs a Chapter 13 case. For example, many trustees require you to make your payments by cashier's check or money order, and don't accept personal checks or cash. The letter will probably remind you to make your first payment within 30 days of when you filed your petition.

Many Chapter 13 trustees play a fairly active role in the cases they administer. This is especially true in small suburban or rural judicial districts or districts with a lot of Chapter 13 bankruptcy cases. For example, a trustee may:

- give you financial advice and assistance, such as helping you create a realistic budget (the trustee cannot, however, give you legal advice)
- actively participate in modifying your plan at the meeting of the creditors, and
- participate at any hearing on the value of an item of secured property, possibly even hiring an appraiser.

For more information on the role of the Chapter 13 trustee, see Ch. 2, *An Overview of Chapter 13 Bankruptcy*, Section F.

1. Reporting Expenditures or Acquisitions to the Trustee

Once you file your bankruptcy papers, the property you owned before filing is under the supervision of the bankruptcy court. Don't throw out, give away, sell or otherwise dispose of any property unless and until the bankruptcy trustee says otherwise.

Despite the trustee's great interest in your finances, your financial relationship with the trustee is not as stifling as it may sound. In general, you still have complete control over money and property you acquire after filing—as long as you make the payments called for under your repayment plan, and you make all regular payments on your secured debts. If you don't make those payments, your creditors may object at the confirmation hearing or even file a motion to dismiss your case.

You can use income you earn after filing that's not going toward your plan payments to make day-to-day purchases such as groceries, personal effects and clothing. If you have any questions about using your post-filing income, ask the Chapter 13 bankruptcy trustee.

If you receive certain kinds of property (or become entitled to receive it), within 180 days after filing for bankruptcy, you must report it to the bankruptcy trustee. Here's the list:

- property you inherit or become entitled to inherit
- property from a marital settlement agreement or divorce decree, or
- death benefits or life insurance policy proceeds.

If any of this property is nonexempt, you might have to modify your plan to increase the amount your unsecured creditors receive, if they would no longer be receiving at least the value of your nonexempt property.

2. Providing the Trustee With Proof of Insurance

If you are behind on payments on a secured debt, such as a car loan, and you plan to make up the payments and get back on track during your Chapter 13 case, you may have to give the trustee proof that you have adequate insurance on the collateral. This requirement is meant to protect the creditor if the collateral is destroyed or damaged and your plan is not confirmed or you dismiss your case, and you want to give up the property.

C. Make Your First Payment

Within 30 days after you file your petition, you must make the first payment proposed in your Chapter 13 repayment plan. (11 U.S.C. § 1326.) This deadline usually comes up before the meeting of creditors, and always before your confirmation hearing. The reason you must make the payment so early is to establish that you can, in fact, make the payments.

It's crucial that you not miss this first deadline. So that you don't forget, count out 30 days from the date you filed your petition and mark the deadline on a calendar. It might be better, though, to make the payment a little earlier—for example, the day after you get paid, so you'll be sure to have the funds. If your wages are currently subject to a wage attachment, garnishment or voluntary payroll deduction, call the trustee and ask for help in getting those removed so that you have the money to make your Chapter 13 payments.

If you do not make your first payment on time, the bankruptcy court can convert your case to Chapter 7 bankruptcy, dismiss your case or deny confirmation of your plan. A few courts consider the failure to make the first payment evidence that the plan was not submitted in good faith and is an abuse of the Chapter 13 bankruptcy system. In that case, the court would lift the automatic stay and allow your creditors to continue their collection efforts. If the court felt you were egregiously abusing the system—for example, this is the fourth Chapter 13 bankruptcy case you've filed without making payments in any of them—the court would no doubt dismiss your case, and possibly fine you and bar you from ever filing for Chapter 13 bankruptcy again.

D. Keep Your Business Going

If you operate a business, by all means keep running it after you file your Chapter 13 papers. If your business has employees, don't forget to make all required payroll tax and withholding deposits with the IRS and your state taxing authority.

The trustee can require the following from you:

- an inventory of your business property, and
- a report on the recent operation of the business, including a statement of receipts and disbursements, if you didn't include one in your bankruptcy papers (you may have attached one to Schedule I—Current Income of Individual Debtor(s) or Form 7—Statement of Financial Affairs). (11 U.S.C. § 1304; Bankruptcy Rule 2015(c).)

The trustee may also direct you to send notification of your bankruptcy case to all entities who hold money or property that belongs to you. This includes financial institutions where you have accounts, landlords and utility companies who hold security deposits and insurance companies where you have business insurance with a cash surrender value. If the balance of the money or value of the property is high and your plan provides little or no payment to your unsecured creditors, the trustee might try to take this money or property for them.

E. The Meeting of Creditors

Your first court appearance is a fairly informal one; the bankruptcy judge isn't even present. The purpose of the creditors' meeting is to allow the trustee and your creditors to ask you about the information in your bankruptcy papers, including your repayment plan. The trustee will want to be sure that you can make the payments you've proposed in your plan.

You (and your spouse, if you are filing jointly) must attend. If you don't, you may be fined $100 or so by the judge. Even worse, your case may be dismissed. If you know in advance that you can't attend the creditors' meeting, call the trustee and try to reschedule it.

1. Preparing for the Meeting of the Creditors

Before the meeting, call the trustee. Explain that you're proceeding without a lawyer and ask what records you're required to bring. You'll need to bring at least the following documents:

- file-stamped copies of all the papers you've filed with the bankruptcy court
- copies of all documents that describe your debts and property, such as bills, deeds, contracts and licenses, and
- financial records, such as recent tax returns and check-books.

The night before the creditors' meeting, thoroughly review the papers you filed with the bankruptcy court. If you discover mistakes, make careful note of them. You'll probably have to correct your papers after the meeting, an easy process. (Instructions are in Section L, below.)

After reviewing your papers, go over the list of questions, below, the trustee is likely to ask you. Be sure you can answer them.

QUESTIONS YOU MAY BE ASKED AT THE CREDITORS' MEETING

- What are your full name and current address?
- Do you own or rent your home?
- Are you married?
- What is your spouse's name?
- When were you married?
- What is your (or your wife's) maiden name?
- Did you ever have another name?
- Did your spouse file with you?
- Is your spouse here today?
- Have you ever filed for bankruptcy before?
- If so, what kind of case (Chapter 7, Chapter 11, Chapter 12 or Chapter 13) and what was the outcome?
- Do you want to make any changes to your petition, schedules or repayment plan?
- Were you employed on the date you filed your petition?
- Are you still at that job?
- Has your income changed since you filed your petition?
- Do your Chapter 13 papers include your current income before and after deductions?
- Do your Chapter 13 papers include your current monthly budget (income and expenses)?
- Do you want to make any changes to your budget?
- Do your Chapter 13 papers include a list of:
  - all of your real property
  - all of your personal property
  - all of the property you claim as exempt
  - all of your bank accounts
  - all of your automobiles and other motor vehicles?
- Have you made any voluntary or involuntary transfers of real or personal property within the last year?
- Have you listed all of your creditors having priority?
- Have you listed all of your creditors holding security?
- Have you listed all of your creditors holding unsecured claims?
- Are any of these credit cards debts?
- Do you still have these credit cards?
- Specifically, how does your plan propose to pay your creditors?
- Have you paid the filing fee for your bankruptcy case?
- Did anyone help you prepare your bankruptcy papers? If so, who?

QUESTIONS YOU MAY BE ASKED AT THE CREDITORS' MEETING (CONTINUED)

Many bankruptcy trustees are lawyers who either practice bankruptcy law or belong to a law firm that does. The fact that trustees and non-lawyer bankruptcy petition preparers (BPPs) are often competitors leads some trustees to look for ways to harass local BPPs. One way they do this is to ferret out any instance of a BPP providing "legal advice," which is against the law.

If you used a BPP to help you with your bankruptcy papers, the trustee may ask you some questions about the help you received:

- Is the name of the BPP on this form the name of the person who prepared your petition?
- Did the BPP give you a copy of your bankruptcy papers?
- Are the signatures on the bankruptcy papers yours, or were your papers signed by someone else?
- Did you give the BPP the filing fees for your bankruptcy?
- How much did you pay the BPP?
- Have you included that charge on your papers? [If a BPP assisted you, you'll probably be required to file a "Statement by Debtor's Attorney of Fees Charged" or a "Statement by Debtor's Attorney of No Fees Charged." The BPP who helped you should fill it out for you and give it to you to submit.]

The information you provide about BPPs shouldn't affect your bankruptcy. If, however, your responses indicate that the BPP provided legal advice or charged you a fee considered too high by the court, the trustee may attempt to recapture the fee you paid the BPP. To help you prepare, ask the BPP whether the trustees in your area are likely to question you, and if so, what suggestions he has for your appearance at the creditors' meeting.

2. Getting to the Meeting of the Creditors

Most creditors' meetings take place in a room in or near the bankruptcy courthouse or federal courthouse. The date and time of the meeting are commonly stated on the Notice of Commencement of Case sent to you by the trustee; if they are not call the court clerk to find out. Give yourself at least an extra 30 minutes to find the right place, park, find the right building, go through security and find the right room.

When you get to the right room, look for the trustee. The trustee will probably be sitting at a table; lawyers may be milling around, waiting to ask questions. Ask the trustee if you have to "check in"—that is, give your name so the trustee knows you are present. Then just sit down and wait your turn.

TIGHT COURT SECURITY

On your way to any court hearing, you will probably spend some time getting through security. Like airports, these days federal courts have metal detectors, but set to an even higher sensitivity. If you set the detector off, you'll have to empty your pockets and take off any offending articles, such as a jacket or belt, and go through again. If you set it off again, the security guard may scan your body with a hand-held metal detector. In addition, items you're carrying—such as a purse, briefcase or knapsack—must go through an X-ray scanner. The security guard may confiscate objects such as pocket knives; you can reclaim them after your hearing.

3. What Happens at the Meeting of the Creditors

Most bankruptcy courts set aside one or two days a month to hold Chapter 13 bankruptcy creditors' meetings. This means that when you show up for your meeting, many other people who have filed for bankruptcy will be there, too. And commonly, everyone was told to come at the same time. That means that 50 cases may all be scheduled for 9:00 a.m.

To get a rough idea of when your name will be called, check the schedule that should posted outside the courtroom door. If your name is near the top of the list, you may not have too long to wait. If you're toward the bottom, you may be sitting there for quite some time. This time doesn't have to be wasted. A chance to observe other people at their meetings can be to your advantage; you'll quickly find out what to expect, where to stand, and maybe even what to say. And if you're nervous, watching other cases will probably help you calm down. If you're very nervous, you can visit the bankruptcy court a week or two before your own hearing and watch the proceedings. This should help relax you.

Your creditors' meeting, if it's typical, will last less than 15 minutes. When your name is called, you'll be asked to sit at a table near the front of the courtroom. The court clerk will swear you in and ask your name, address and other identifying information.

The trustee will briefly go over your forms with you, probably asking many of the questions listed above. Your answers should be both truthful and consistent with your bankruptcy papers. The trustee is likely to be most interested in the fairness of your plan and your ability to make the payments you have proposed.

When the trustee is finished, any creditors who showed up are given a chance to question you. Often, secured creditors come, especially if they have any objections to the plan—for example, that the interest rate you propose is too low, you are taking too long to pay your arrears or the value you assigned the collateral is wrong. An unsecured creditor who is receiving very little under your plan might show up too, if that creditor thinks you can cut your expenses and increase your disposable income. (See Section G, below, for a discussion on the types of objections creditors raise to repayment plans.)

At the end of the hearing, be ready to negotiate with the creditors. (See Ch. 7, *Writing Your Chapter 13 Bankruptcy Plan*, Section I, for information on negotiating with your creditors.) If you agree to make changes to accommodate their objections, you must submit a modified plan.

F. Modifying Your Plan Before the Confirmation Hearing

You have an absolute right to file modified plans with the bankruptcy court any time before the confirmation hearing, and most Chapter 13 debtors submit at least one. (11 U.S.C. § 1323(a).) All you do is file the new plan with the bankruptcy court clerk and give a copy to the trustee. The new plan replaces the old one.

Here are some common reasons to modify a plan:

- To correct errors—such as to add overlooked creditors or debts.
- To reflect financial changes—such as a new job, raise, inheritance or insurance settlement, reduction in income, or destruction of property secured by a debt.
- To reduce your proposed payments—for example, if you just lost your job or had your income reduced.
- To respond to creditors' objections or include terms you negotiated with a creditor at the end of the meeting of the creditors.
- To add debts you incurred after filing. In general, you should not incur debts after you file other than day-to-

day expenses. You can modify your plan, however, to add any debts that are necessary for you to keep following your plan (such as a medical bill) or unanticipated debts (such as a tax bill). (This is covered in Ch. 10, *After Your Plan is Approved*, Section C.)

G. Creditors' Objections to a Plan

It might seem odd to you that an unsecured creditor would object to your Chapter 13 plan. After all, in Chapter 13 bankruptcy, the creditor may get some money. By contrast, if you ignored the creditor or filed for Chapter 7 bankruptcy, the creditor probably wouldn't get anything.

The creditor isn't trying to derail your bankruptcy, but is trying to get you to modify your plan so that you can really make the payments under your plan. Because so many Chapter 13 debtors eventually dismiss their cases or convert them to Chapter 7 bankruptcy, your creditors have reason to doubt you. A creditor objects to a plan precisely because the creditor wants it to succeed.

A creditor who objects to your plan will probably attend the meeting of the creditors and try to get you to modify your plan before the confirmation hearing. The creditor will probably also file a formal paper, either a motion or an objection, with the bankruptcy court, asking the bankruptcy court to deny confirmation of or modify your plan. That way, in case you and the creditor can't reach an agreement informally, the judge will decide the issue. If the creditor doesn't file a motion or objection, the creditor can't raise the objection at the confirmation hearing. A copy of a Notice of Motion or Objection form is below.

Form 20A. Notice of Motion or Objection

UNITED STATES BANKRUPTCY COURT

_____ DISTRICT OF _____

In re _____ ,   Case No. _____

          (Name)   (If known)

                    Debtor

                                                          Chapter _____

NOTICE OF [MOTION TO   ] [OBJECTION TO   ]

_____ has filed papers with the court to [relief sought in motion or objection].

Your rights may be affected. You should read these papers carefully and discuss them with your attorney, if you have one in this bankruptcy case. (If you do not have an attorney, you may wish to consult one.)

If you do not want the court to [relief sought in motion or objection], or if you want the court to consider your views on the [motion] [objection], then on or before (date), you or your attorney must:

File with the court a written request for a hearing [_or, if the court requires a written response_, an answer, explaining your position] at:

[address of the bankruptcy clerk's office]

If you mail your [request] [response] to the court for filing, you must mail it early enough so the court will **receive** it on or before the date stated above.

You must also mail a copy to:

[movant's attorney's name and address]

[names and addresses of others to be served]

Attend the hearing scheduled to be held on (date) , (year) , at ___ a.m./p.m. in Courtroom _____, United States Bankruptcy Court, [address].

Other steps required to oppose a motion or objection under local rule or court order.

If you or your attorney do not take these steps, the court may decide that you do not oppose the relief sought in the motion or objection and may enter an order granting that relief.

Date: _____   Signature: _____

                                                      Name:_____

                                                      Address: _____

IF THE CREDITOR REQUESTS A DEPOSITION

It's rare, but a creditor who thinks you are hiding assets and could pay more into your plan might try to gather evidence about your financial situation through a formal legal process called "discovery." The discovery technique the creditor is most likely to use is a deposition—a proceeding in which you answer questions from the creditor's attorney orally, under oath, before a court reporter. If a creditor sends you a discovery request, the court will postpone the confirmation hearing to give the creditor time to conduct the discovery.

UNDERSTANDING DEPOSITIONS
For help in preparing for a deposition, see *Represent Yourself in Court,* by Paul Bergman & Sara J. Berman-Barrett (Nolo Press).

This section describes the four most common objections creditors raise to Chapter 13 plans.

1. The Plan Is Not Submitted in Good Faith

Probably the most common objection creditors raise is that a Chapter 13 plan was not proposed in good faith. (11 U.S.C. § 1325(a)(3).) The bankruptcy rules do not define good faith, but bankruptcy courts generally look to see that you have not proposed a plan that obviously will be impossible for you to meet. If you feel confident that you are filing your papers with the honest intention of getting back on your feet and can make the payments under the plan, you probably can overcome a "good faith" objection.

Occasionally, creditors make a good faith objection as a negotiating ploy. They want you to change your plan to satisfy them rather than argue the question of good faith before the bankruptcy court. If you think this is happening, you'll probably need the help of a lawyer to evaluate if any real good faith issues exist concerning your plan.

When creditors pursue good faith objections, most bankruptcy courts look at the following kinds of factors:

- **How often you have filed for bankruptcy.** Filing multiple bankruptcies (file, dismiss, file, dismiss and file again) in and of itself does not show bad faith. If within one year, however, you've filed and dismissed two or more other bankruptcy cases, the court may find lack of good faith if there are inconsistencies in your papers (except where actual changes occurred) or you cannot

show that your circumstances have changed since the previous dismissal. Changed circumstances include:
  - an increase in your income
  - a reduction of your debts
  - a new job that will permit use of an income deduction order
  - your spouse is now filing, too
  - the end of a condition that caused your previous dismissal, such as illness or unemployment.

Here's another example of lack of good faith. Let's say you received a Chapter 7 bankruptcy discharge, and then file for Chapter 13 less than six years later. In your Chapter 13 plan, you propose paying your unsecured creditors less than 100%. Your plan will not be confirmed because you are using Chapter 13 to circumvent Chapter 7's prohibition on filing a second case within six years of obtaining a discharge in a first case.

- **The accuracy of your bankruptcy papers and oral statements.** The court is likely to find a lack of good faith if you misrepresent your income, debts, expenses or assets, or you lie at the creditors' meeting or at a deposition. Creditors look for discrepancies by comparing your bankruptcy papers with credit applications and financial data you submitted to them. If there is any inaccuracy in your papers, be sure to point it out to the trustee at the creditors' meeting and amend your papers. (How to amend your papers is covered in Section L, below.)

- **Your motive for filing for Chapter 13 bankruptcy.** If you want to cure your mortgage default and get back on track with your house payments, pay off a tax debt or get some breathing room to pay off your creditors, you have nothing to worry about. If the court finds either of the following, however, it might also find bad faith:
  - You filed for bankruptcy for the sole purpose of rejecting a lease or contract, such as a timeshare or car lease.
  - You filed for bankruptcy to handle only one debt (other than mortgage arrears or back taxes). The court might especially find lack of good faith if you file for Chapter 13 only to pay a nondischargeable debt such as a student loan or criminal fine.

- **The length of the plan you've proposed.** If you will pay only a small percentage of your unsecured debts, some courts will find bad faith if your proposed plan is not for five years. An equal number of courts, however, allow small percentage plans that last only three years.

- **Your efforts to repay your debts.** If you will pay your unsecured creditors less than the full amount that you owe, you will have to show the court that you are stretching as much as you can. The court will want to see that you are living frugally and making extraordinary efforts to pay your unsecured creditors. You'll have few problems if you can show that you've eliminated payments on luxury items, depleted your investments, canceled your country club membership, decreased your religious contributions, brought down your living expenses and increased your hours at work.

- **The cause of your financial trouble.** Bankruptcy courts are reluctant to find bad faith if your financial problems are due to events beyond your control—for example, exceptional medical expenses or an accident, job loss, death or illness in the family.

2. The Plan Is Not Feasible

The second most likely objection is that your plan is not feasible—that is, you won't be able to make the payments or comply with the other terms of the plan. (11 U.S.C. § 1325(a)(6).)

To overcome a feasibility objection, your monthly income must exceed your monthly expenses by at least enough to allow you to make payments. In Ch. 4, *Calculating Your Disposable Income*, you totaled up your income and expenses. If a creditor raises this objection, bring to the confirmation hearing your worksheets and any other documents (such as pay stubs and monthly bills) you have showing your income and expenses.

Your creditors might also question your job stability, the likelihood that you'll incur extraordinary expenses and whether you have any outside sources of money. The court will likely deny confirmation on the ground that your plan isn't feasible if any of the following is true:

- Your business has been failing, but you've predicted a rebound and intend to use business income to make your plan payments.
- You propose making plan payments from the proceeds of the sale of certain property, but nothing points to the likelihood of a sale—for example, your house has been on the market for a long time and you've had no offers.
- Your plan includes a balloon payment, but you have not identified a source of money with which to make the payment.
- You owe back alimony or child support and have been held in contempt of court for failing to pay.
- You've been convicted of a crime, and you have not convinced the bankruptcy court that you will stay out of jail.

3. The Plan Fails the Best Interest of the Creditors Test

When you file for Chapter 13 bankruptcy, you must pay your unsecured creditors at least as much as they would have received if you had filed for Chapter 7 bankruptcy. (11 U.S.C. § 1325(a)(4).) (This is explained in Ch. 5, *Calculating the Value of Your Nonexempt Property*.) This is called the "best interest of the creditors" test.

If a creditor raises this objection, bring to the confirmation hearing your worksheets from Ch. 5 and any other documents you have showing the values of your nonexempt items of property, such as a recent appraisal or a publication showing the value of your automobile.

4. The Plan Unfairly Discriminates

In your plan, you must specify which unsecured creditors get paid in full and which get less. To do that, you can create classes of unsecured creditors, specifying how much (or what percentage) each class will receive, as long as you do not unfairly discriminate against any specific creditor. Ch. 7, *Writing Your Chapter 13 Bankruptcy Plan*, Section J, describes common classes of creditors and creditors' likely objections.

If a creditor objects to classes you've created, you can either fight it out in court at the confirmation hearing (which will require that you research how your bankruptcy court district has ruled in previous cases on the subject) or amend your plan to eliminate the class.

H. The Confirmation Hearing

A judge must approve your Chapter 13 plan for it to be valid. This is done at a confirmation hearing, where the judge addresses any objections raised by creditors or the trustee. You (and your spouse, if you are filing jointly) must attend. In a few courts, the judge schedules a confirmation hearing only if a creditor has filed a formal motion objecting to the plan. If the judge doesn't schedule a hearing, it means your plan is approved as filed.

Often, the court holds the confirmation meeting the same day as the meeting of the creditors, which is before the deadline has passed for creditors to file claims. (As discussed in Section J, below, a creditor must file with the court something called a "proof of claim" in order to get paid through your Chapter 13 plan.) In this situation, the court must approve or deny your plan without knowing exactly which creditors want to be paid through it. If creditors file claims after the court approves your plan, you may need to pay more into the plan than you expected. (See Ch. 10, *After Your Plan Is Approved*, Section A.)

1. Preparing for the Confirmation Hearing

A few days before the confirmation hearing, review your plan and the objections raised by your creditors or trustee. If you're confident that you can make the payments under your plan and that your plan is fair to your creditors, gather the documents that support your plan—such as pay stubs showing your income. You're ready to go.

If you have lingering feelings that the objections have some merit, you'll probably need to hit the law library. There, you can do a little legal research to see how bankruptcy appeals and federal appeals courts for your district have ruled in similar disputes. Ch. 12, *Help Beyond the Book*, suggests some excellent resources to help you do your bankruptcy research.

If you find cases that support your position, photocopy them and bring them to court. If you find material that supports the objection, be ready to modify your plan.

2. Getting to the Confirmation Hearing

The confirmation hearing is held in a bankruptcy courtroom. The tips in Section E, above, apply here.

3. What Happens at the Confirmation Hearing

Most bankruptcy districts set aside one or two days a month to hold Chapter 13 bankruptcy confirmation hearings—and in many courts, confirmation hearings are scheduled at the same time as other hearings, such as hearings on motions to dismiss, motions to convert to Chapter 7 and motions to establish the value of property. The courtroom will probably be filled with people who have all been told to come at the same time.

Watch the cases before yours so you know where to go when your name is called. If your case is called first, just ask the judge, clerk or trustee—whoever is calling the cases—where you should stand. The judge or court clerk will ask you to state your name.

Unlike a creditors' meeting, the confirmation hearing is run by the judge. Judges like to get easy cases in and out of their courtrooms as quickly as possible. This means that all uncontested matters will be heard first. Next will be cases where the outcome is fairly obvious—often motions to dismiss in cases where the plans were approved but the debtors have missed several payments. If yours is a case in which the trustee or a creditor has filed an objection, your confirmation hearing will probably be toward the end. Bring a big book with you.

The judge is most interested in your ability to make the payments under your plan, and will question you about that or about plan provisions that are unclear.

After these questions, the judge will ask you if the objections have been resolved. If they haven't been, the judge may ask the trustee or creditors to elaborate on their objections, ask you for any response and then make a ruling. If the judge still has a lot of cases to get through, the judge may reschedule the rest of your hearing to a less busy day.

If the judge agrees with an objection, you will probably be allowed to submit a modified plan. (See Section I, below.) But if it's obvious that Chapter 13 bankruptcy just isn't realistic for you—for example, you earn very little money to pay into a plan—the judge will order that your case be dismissed or converted to Chapter 7 bankruptcy.

4. Issuing an Income Deduction Order

If you have a regular job with regular income, the bankruptcy judge may order, at the confirmation hearing, that the monthly payments under your Chapter 13 plan be automatically deducted from your wages and sent to the bankruptcy court. (11 U.S.C. § 1325(c).) This is called an income deduction order. Income deduction orders work if you are regularly paid a salary or wages. They are almost impossible to issue, however, if you are:

- self-employed
- funding your plan with public benefits, such as Social Security—the Social Security Act prohibits the Social Security Administration from complying with an income deduction order, or
- funding your plan with pension benefits—many pension plans prohibit the administrator from paying proceeds to anyone other than the beneficiary (you), which means that the administrator will ignore the income deduction order.

In many districts, the bankruptcy court automatically issues an income deduction order at the confirmation hearing—and possibly even earlier. In some districts, the bankruptcy court leaves it up to the debtor whether or not to issue an order. And in a few districts, the court doesn't issue the order unless you miss a payment in your plan.

You may not like the idea of the order, but the court is likely to deny your plan for lack of feasibility if you refuse to comply with it. And you should realize that the order will probably make it easier for you to complete your plan. The success rate of Chapter 13 cases is higher for debtors with income deduction orders than for debtors who pay the trustee themselves.

One benefit of an income deduction order is that it usually forbids your employer from making other deductions from your paycheck. This means that all wage attachments, garnishments and voluntary payroll deductions will end (if they haven't already) when the order takes effect.

If the court does issue an income deduction order, you will have to find out from the court clerk or trustee who is responsible for preparing and giving your employer the order—the clerk, the trustee or you. (If it's you, see Ch. 6, *Completing the Bankruptcy Forms*, Section I.)) To avoid having someone from your job accidentally mention your bankruptcy when the income deduction order arrives, you could inform the payroll department that you've filed for Chapter 13 bankruptcy and to expect an income deduction order from the bankruptcy court.

Once the income deduction order takes effect, you will need to tell the trustee if you change jobs. You can just call, or write a letter if you'd prefer.

YOUR EMPLOYER CAN'T FIRE YOU FOR FILING FOR BANKRUPTCY

Don't be worried that your employer, who learns of your bankruptcy because of an income deduction order, will fire you because you filed for bankruptcy. Employers rarely care. If your employer does punish you for having filed for bankruptcy, let someone in charge know that under the Bankruptcy Act, all private and public employers are prohibited from terminating you or otherwise discriminating against you solely because you filed for bankruptcy. (11 U.S.C. §§ 525(a), 525(b).) (See Ch. 11, *Life After Bankruptcy*, Section C, for more on the laws against this kind of discrimination.)

---

5. The Judge's Order Confirming Your Plan

A court order granting confirmation of your repayment plan is binding on your creditors; they must accept the payments the trustee will make to them under the terms of your plan. This includes creditors who do not file claims by the deadline and creditors who objected to your plan. (11 U.S.C. § 1327(a).)

When the court approves your plan, you usually must file an Order Confirming Chapter 13 Plan with the bankruptcy court clerk and send notice that your plan was confirmed to all your creditors. If the judge doesn't say anything, ask the judge if you must prepare the order and send notice.

Below are a sample Order and sample Notice form. To complete your own, type up the samples—filling in the information requested in italics—using photocopies of the paper in Appendix 3 with the numbers on the left side (called pleading paper). Attach a copy of your confirmed plan to the Order, and then file the Order and Notice with the bankruptcy court clerk. After you've filed the papers, you must send a copy of the Notice to each of your creditors.

I. Modifying Your Plan After the Confirmation Hearing

If your plan isn't confirmed at the hearing, the court will usually give you a certain amount of time in which you can try again. If you don't submit a modified plan by the deadline (or if the court found bad faith or a lack of feasibility), the court will dismiss your case or convert it to a Chapter 7 bankruptcy case. In that situation, the trustee must return your payments to you, less the amount of administrative expenses. (11 U.S.C. § 1326(a)(1).)

If you want to submit a modified plan, call the trustee and ask for an appointment. Then, if you don't already know, find out from the trustee what it will take to get your plan confirmed. If you do know, ask the trustee if the ideas you have to modify your plan are likely to be approved by the judge.

In most cases, you'll need to do one or more of the following to get your modified plan confirmed:
- extend your plan (if it's under five years)
- speed up the time you pay off secured debt arrears
- change an interest rate on secured debt arrears
- increase the secured portion of a debt that is partially secured and partially unsecured
- create or eliminate a class of unsecured creditors, or
- increase the amount a particular class of creditors receives.

After you type up your modified plan, call the court and ask how many copies you need to submit when filing a modified Chapter 13 plan. (You may need to submit more than you did when you filed the original.) Next, call the trustee and ask who sends the modified plan to your creditors—you or the court. (If it's you, ask the trustee the procedure.)

1

2

3

[Your Name
Your Street Address
Your City, State, Zip
Your Phone Number]
In Propria Persona

4

5

6

7

8   UNITED STATES BANKRUPTCY COURT

9   _____*[name of district]*_____ DISTRICT OF _____*[your state]*_____

10   _____*[name of division, if any]*_____ DIVISION

11

12   In re:)
     [your name(s)]   )   Case No. ____*[copy from your Voluntary Petition]*____
)
13   )   Chapter 13
)
14   )   Order Confirming Chapter 13 Plan
)
15   _____ Debtor(s)   )

16

17   The Chapter 13 Plan confirmation came on for hearing on _*[date and time of hearing]*_ in the above-captioned court, the

18   Honorable ___*[name of judge]*___ presiding. ___*[your name(s)]*___, Debtor(s), appeared without counsel. ____*[name of trustee]*____

19   appeared as the Chapter 13 Trustee.

20   Upon recommendation of the Trustee, there being no opposition by any creditor, and good cause appearing therefore,

21   IT IS HEREBY ORDERED, ADJUDGED AND DECREED:

22   Debtor's Chapter 13 Plan, attached as Exhibit A, is confirmed.

23

24   Dated: _____   _____

25   U.S. Bankruptcy Judge

26

27

28

1 | *[Your Name*
   | *Your Street Address*
2 | *Your City, State, Zip*
   | *Your Phone Number]*
3 | In Propria Persona

4

5

6

7

8   UNITED STATES BANKRUPTCY COURT

9 _____ *[name of district]* _____ DISTRICT OF _____ *[your state]* _____

10   _____ *[name of division, if any]* ___ DIVISION

11

In re:)
[your name(s)]   )   Case No. ____ *[copy from your Voluntary Petition]* ____
)
)   Chapter 13
)
)   Notice of Entry of Order
)   Confirming Chapter 13 Plan
_____ Debtor(s) _____)

12
13
14
15
16

17

18   TO ALL INTERESTED PARTIES AND THEIR ATTORNEYS OF RECORD:

19   NOTICE IS HEREBY GIVEN pursuant to Bankruptcy Rule 3020(c) of the Order Confirming Chapter 13 Plan entered on _*[date judge*

20 *signed Order].*

21

22 Dated: _____   _____

23   Debtor in Propria Persona

24

25

26

27

28

After you file the modified plan, the court will schedule a new confirmation hearing. You'll get a notice with the date and time. It will be at least 25 days after you filed the modified plan; your creditors must be given at least 25 days to file any objections.

J. Creditors' Claims

After you file for bankruptcy, the trustee sends a notice of your bankruptcy filing to all the creditors you listed in your papers. In general, creditors who want to be paid must file a claim within 90 days after the meeting of creditors is *scheduled* to be held. If the meeting is rescheduled, the deadline is still 90 days from the originally-scheduled date. As explained in Section E, above, the deadline is usually after your confirmation hearing.

Sometimes, a creditor you want to pay through your Chapter 13 plan forgets to file a claim. You then may have to file it for the creditor within 30 days after the deadline the creditor missed. (Bankruptcy Rule 3004.) (Reasons you might want to file a claim for a creditor are explained, below.)

1. Filing a Proof of Claim

Most claims are filed on an official court form. Most bankruptcy courts will also accept an informal document or letter, as long as it shows the creditor intends to assert a claim.

A blank proof of claim form is in Appendix 3; a completed sample is shown below. You must attach to the form evidence of your debt, such as your mortgage agreement and any notice of default. Ask the trustee whether you should file it with the court clerk or directly with the trustee.

How the claim procedure works depends on whether the creditor is classified as secured, priority or unsecured.

Secured creditors. The bankruptcy code does not expressly require secured creditors to file claims to be paid, but few trustees will pay secured creditors unless there's a claim on file. (Even if a secured creditor doesn't file a claim, however, the creditor's lien stays on the property.)

If you want to make up missed payments on a secured debt in your Chapter 13 case and the creditor doesn't file a claim, you will have to file it on the creditor's behalf. For example, if you have missed three house payments, but the lender doesn't file a claim, the trustee won't pay your arrears through your plan. The lender would probably ask the court for permission to proceed with a foreclosure.

Priority creditors. Priority creditors must file a claim to be paid. If a government agency misses the 90-day deadline for a good reason, it can seek an extension (for an undefined but "reasonable" time). (Bankruptcy Rule 3002(c)(1).) The IRS is notoriously late at filing claims, but it is usually granted extensions.

Many lawyers might advise you to file a claim on behalf of the IRS for a tax debt that would be nondischargeable if you convert to Chapter 7 bankruptcy. This is an odd strategy, however, because you are assuming that your Chapter 13 case will fail and will convert to a Chapter 7 bankruptcy. Some Chapter 13 cases do succeed, and not all that fail convert to Chapter 7 bankruptcy. If your case succeeds, you will have paid a tax claim that otherwise would have been discharged.

Unsecured creditors. Unsecured creditors must file a claim to be paid. If an unsecured creditor does not, that creditor's debt will be discharged when you complete your plan, unless the debt is nondischargeable.

If you want to pay a nondischargeable unsecured debt through your Chapter 13 plan (to avoid having the debt remain after your case ends) and the creditor doesn't file a claim, you will have to file it on the creditor's behalf.

2. Objecting to a Creditor's Claim

Unless you submit to the court a written objection to a creditor's claim, the trustee will pay the claim. (In bankruptcy legalese, claims the trustee pays are called "allowed" claims.) Your objection can be as informal as a letter. You can file an objection at any time, but the sooner the better. The court will schedule a hearing at which the creditor must prove you owe the claim.

Possible reasons for objecting to a creditor's claim include:

- You owe less than the creditor claims you do.
- A secured creditor has overstated the value of the collateral.
- The creditor has characterized the debt as secured (meaning you'll have to pay it in full), and you think it's unsecured.
- The claim was filed late. Most courts disallow late claims. Some, however, allow late claims if the creditor shows "excusable neglect" or another good reason for the failure to file on time.

K. Asking the Court to Eliminate Liens

During your Chapter 13 case, you may be able to get the court to reduce or eliminate liens on your property. If you succeed, you'll still owe the debt, but it will be unsecured. You pay the creditor just what you are paying your other

FORM 10. PROOF OF CLAIM

		PROOF OF CLAIM
United States Bankruptcy Court ___XXXX___ District of Arizona, Tucson Division		

Name of Debtor Herchoo, Martin & Ellen	Case Number C139000417

NOTE: This form should not be used to make a claim for an administrative expense arising after the commencement of the case. A "request" for payment of an administrative expense may be filed pursuant to 11 U.S.C. § 503.

Name of Creditor (The person or other entity to whom the debtor owes money or property): Big Home Loan Bank	☐ Check box if you are aware that anyone else has filed a proof of claim relating to your claim. Attach copy of statement giving particulars.	
Name and address where notices should be sent: 232 Desert Way Tucson, AZ 85700 Attn: Ed Mist	☐ Check box if you have never received any notices from the bankruptcy court in this case. ☐ Check box if the address differs from the address on the envelope sent to you by the court.	
Telephone number: (602) 555-1830		This Space is for Court Use Only

Account or other number by which creditor identifies debtor: XX-1149-2081	Check here if this claim ☐ replaces ☐ amends a previously filed claim dated: _____

1. Basis for Claim
- ☒ Goods sold
- ☐ Services performed
- ☐ Money loaned
- ☐ Personal injury/wrongful death
- ☐ Taxes
- ☐ Other _____

- ☐ Retiree benefits as defined in 11 U.S.C. § 1114(a)
- ☐ Wages, salaries, and compensation (fill out below)
  - Your SS #: _____ _____ _____
  - Unpaid compensation for services performed
  - from _____ to _____
  - (date)   (date)

2. Date debt was incurred: 11/27/XX	**3. If court judgment, date obtained:**

4. Total Amount of Claim at Time Case Filed: $ 10,800 _____

If all or part of your claim is secured or entitled to priority, also complete Item 5 or 6 below.

☒ Check this box if claim includes interest or other charges in addition to the principal amount of the claim. Attach itemized statement of all interest or additional charges.

5. Secured Claim.

☒ Check this box if your claim is secured by collateral (including a right of setoff).

Brief Description of Collateral:
- ☒ Real Estate   ☐ Motor Vehicle
- ☐ Other _____

Value of Collateral: $ 275,000 _____

Amount of arrearage and other charges at time case filed included in secured claim, if any: $ 10,800 _____

6. Unsecured Priority Claim.

☐ Check this box if you have an unsecured priority claim
Amount entitled to priority $ _____
Specify the priority of the claim:

- ☐ Wages salaries, or commissions (up to $4,300),* earned within 90 days before filing of the bankruptcy petition or cessation of the debtor's business, whichever is earlier — 11 U.S.C. § 507(a)(3).
- ☐ Contributions to an employee benefit plan — 11 U.S.C. § 507(a)(4).
- ☐ Up to $1,950* of deposits toward purchase, lease, or rental of property or services for personal, family, or household use — 11 U.S.C. § 507(a)(6).
- ☐ Alimony, maintenance, or support owed to a spouse, former spouse, or child — 11 U.S.C. § 507(a)(7).
- ☐ Taxes or penalties owed to governmental units — 11 U.S.C. § 507(a)(8).
- ☐ Other — Specify applicable paragraph of 11 U.S.C. § 507(a)(____).

*Amounts are subject to adjustment on 4/1/98 and every 3 years thereafter with respect to cases commenced on or after the date of adjustment.

7. Credits: The amount of all payments on this claim has been credited and deducted for the purpose of making this proof of claim.

8. Supporting Documents: Attach copies of supporting documents, such as promissory notes, purchase orders, invoices, itemized statements of running accounts, contracts, court judgments, mortgages, security agreements, and evidence of perfection of lien. DO NOT SEND ORIGINAL DOCUMENTS. If the documents are not available, explain. If the documents are voluminous, attach a summary.

9. Date-Stamped Copy: To receive an acknowledgment of the filing of your claim, enclose a stamped, self-addressed envelope and copy of this proof of claim.

This Space is for Court Use Only

Date 7/8/XX	Sign and print the name and title, if any, of the creditor or other person authorized to file this claim (attach copy of power of attorney, if any): *Martin Herchoo*

Penalty for presenting fraudulent claim: Fine of up to $500,000 or imprisonment for up to 5 years, or both. 18 U.S.C. §§ 152 and 3571.

unsecured creditors and you keep the property. Even if you're paying your other unsecured creditors 100%, avoiding the lien is still worthwhile, because you get to keep your property with clear title.

1. Avoiding a Lien

Lien avoidance is a procedure by which you ask the bankruptcy court to "avoid" (eliminate or reduce) certain liens. If in your Chapter 13 repayment plan you proposed to pay nothing or very little on your unsecured debts, lien avoidance makes a lot of sense. As long as there's a lien, you have to pay it in full to keep your secured property.

Lien avoidance is available only in very limited circumstances. See Ch. 3, *Adding Up Your Secured and Unsecured Debts,* Section A, for a detailed discussion of when lien avoidance is possible.

You request lien avoidance by typing and filing a motion. It is quite simple and can be done without a lawyer. In most courts, you must file your motion with the court within 30 days after you file for bankruptcy. But some courts require it to be filed before the creditors' meeting. Check your local rules.

What goes in your motion papers depends on the kind of lien you're trying to get eliminated. Again, refer to Ch. 3, Section A, to determine whether or not lien avoidance is possible for you and if so, what kind of lien you want the court to avoid. Read Subsection a, below, if you're dealing with a nonpossessory nonpurchase money security interest, and Subsection b, below, if you want to avoid a judicial lien.

a. Nonpossessory, Nonpurchase Money-Security Interests

You will need to fill out one complete set of forms for each affected creditor—generally, each creditor holding a lien on that property. Sample forms are shown below. Some courts have their own forms; if yours does, use them and adapt these instructions to fit.

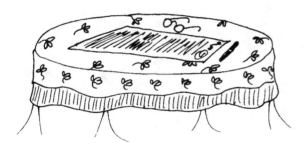

CHECKLIST OF FORMS FOR MOTION TO AVOID NONPOSSESSORY, NONPURCHASE-MONEY SECURITY INTEREST

- ☐ Motion to Avoid Nonpossessory, Nonpurchase Money Security Interest
- ☐ Order to Avoid Nonpossessory, Nonpurchase Money Security Interest
- ☐ Notice of Motion to Avoid Nonpossessory, Nonpurchase Money Security Interest
- ☐ Proof of Service by Mail

Step 1: If your court publishes local rules, refer to them for time limits, format of papers and other details of a motion proceeding.

Step 2: Make at least five copies of the blank, line-numbered legal paper in Appendix 3. Use those sheets to type your motion to avoid the lien. Type from line number 1 to line 13 as follows (see samples, below):

Line 1: Your name, and that of your spouse if you're filing jointly.

Line 1.5: Your address.

Line 2: Your city, state and zip code.

Line 2.5: Your phone number.

Line 3: "In Propria Persona."

Line 8: Center and type UNITED STATES BANKRUPTCY COURT, in capital letters.

Line 9: Center and type the name of the judicial district and state you are in. Copy this information from your bankruptcy petition.

Lines 11-15: Type as shown in the example.

Step 3: Make several photocopies of the page with the information you have typed so far. This will save you typing later, because you can use this same heading for all the forms you need to file your motion.

Step 4: Using one of the copies that you just made, start typing again at line 14, prepare a Motion to Avoid Nonpossessory, Nonpurchase-Money Security Interest, as shown in the example.

Step 5: Call the court clerk and give your name and case number. Say you'd like to file a motion to avoid a lien and need to find out when and where the judge will hear arguments on your motion. The clerk will give you a hearing date; ask for one at least 31 days in the future, because you must mail notice of your motion to the creditor at least 30 days before the hearing (unless local rules state differently). Write down the information.

MOTION TO AVOID NONPOSSESSORY, NONPURCHASE-MONEY SECURITY INTEREST

```
 1   [Your Name
 2   Your Street Address
 3   Your City, State, Zip
     Your Phone Number]
     In Propria Persona
 4
 5
 6
 7
 8
 9                           UNITED STATES BANKRUPTCY COURT
10
                    [Name of district]     DISTRICT OF        [your state]
11
                    [Name of division, if any]        DIVISION
12   In re:                                 Case No.  [Copy from your petition]
     [your name(s)]
13                                          Chapter 13
14
                                           AL   [Fill in when you file papers]
15   Debtor(s)
16
17          MOTION TO AVOID NONPOSSESSORY, NONPURCHASE-MONEY SECURITY INTEREST
18   1.  Debtors   [your name(s)]       , filed a voluntary petition for relief under Chapter 13 of Title 11 of the United States
19   Code on    [date you filed for bankruptcy]     .
20   2.  This court has jurisdiction over this motion, filed pursuant to 11 U.S.C. § 522(f), to avoid a nonpossessory nonpurchase-money
21   security interest held by   [name of lender]    on property held by the debtor.
22   3.  On or about   [date you incurred the debt]    debtors borrowed $  [amount of loan]    from   [name of
23   lender]   . As security for loan,  [name of lender]   insisted upon, and the debtors executed, a note and security agreement granting
24   to  [name of lender]    a security interest in and on the debtor's personal property, which consisted of  [items held as security as
25   listed in your loan agreement]   which are held primarily for the family and household use of the debtors and their dependents.
26   4.  All such possessions of debtors have been claimed as fully exempt in their bankruptcy case.
27   5.  The money borrowed from   [name of lender]    does not represent any part of the purchase money of any of the articles
28   covered in the security agreement executed by the debtors, and all of the articles so covered remain in the possession of the debtors.
```

```
 1   6.  The existence of   [name of lender] 's   lien on debtor's household and personal goods impairs exemptions to which the
 2   debtors would be entitled under 11 U.S.C. § 522(b).
 3          WHEREFORE, pursuant to 11 U.S.C. § 522(f), debtors request an order avoiding the security interest in their personal and household
 4   goods, and for such additional or alternative relief as many be just and proper.
 5
 6   Dated:  _____
 7                                   _____
 8   Dated:  _____     Debtor in Propria Persona
 9                                   _____
10                                        Debtor in Propria Persona
11
12
13
14
15
16
17
18
19
20
21
22
23
24
25
26
27
28
```

NOTICE OF MOTION TO AVOID NONPOSSESSORY, NONPURCHASE-MONEY SECURITY INTEREST & ORDER TO AVOID NONPOSSESSORY, NONPURCHASE-MONEY SECURITY INTEREST

Notice of Motion

[Your Name
Your Street Address
Your City, State, Zip
Your Phone Number]
In Propria Persona

UNITED STATES BANKRUPTCY COURT

_____ [name of district] DISTRICT OF _____ [your state]

_____ [name of division, if any] DIVISION

In re:
[your name(s)]

Case No. _____ [Copy from your petition]

Chapter 13

A___ [Fill in when you file papers]

Debtor(s)

NOTICE OF MOTION TO AVOID NONPOSSESSORY, NONPURCHASE-MONEY SECURITY INTEREST

Please take notice of motion is set for a hearing on: _____ [leave blank] , 19___ at _____ [leave blank] o'clock ___ m. at _____ [leave blank] , in courtroom _____ [leave blank] .

Order

[Your Name
Your Street Address
Your City, State, Zip
Your Phone Number]
In Propria Persona

UNITED STATES BANKRUPTCY COURT

_____ [name of district] DISTRICT OF _____ [your state]

_____ [name of division, if any] DIVISION

In re:
[your name(s)]

Case No. _____ [Copy from your petition]

Chapter 13

A___ [Fill in when you file papers]

Debtor(s)

ORDER TO AVOID NONPOSSESSORY, NONPURCHASE-MONEY SECURITY INTEREST

The motion of the above-named debtor(s) _____ [your name(s)] , to avoid the lien of the respondent, _____ [name of lender] is sustained.

The lien is a nonpossessory, nonpurchase-money lien that impairs the debtor's exemptions in the following property:

[list all items held as security as listed in your loan agreement]

Unless debtor's bankruptcy case is dismissed, the lien of the respondent is hereby extinguished and the lien shall not survive bankruptcy or affix to or remain enforceable against the aforementioned property of the debtor.

_____ [Name of lender] shall take all necessary steps to remove any record of the lien from the aforementioned property of the debtor.

Dated: _____

_____
U.S. Bankruptcy Judge

PROOF OF SERVICE BY MAIL

1 [Your Name
2 Your Street Address
3 Your City, State, Zip
   Your Phone Number]
   In Propria Persona

UNITED STATES BANKRUPTCY COURT

[name of district] DISTRICT OF [your state]

[name of division, if any] DIVISION

In re:
[your name(s)]   Case No. ___ [Copy from your petition]
                      Chapter 13
                      AL ___ [Fill in when you file papers]
Debtor(s)

PROOF OF SERVICE BY MAIL

I, [friend's name] , declare that : I am resident or employed in the County of [the county where friend lives or works] , State of [state where friend lives or works] . My residence/business address is [friend's address]

I am over the age of eighteen years and not a party to this case.

On [leave blank] 19__ I served the :

[list papers served]

on [lender or lienholder's name] , by placing true and correct copies thereof enclosed in a sealed envelope with postage thereon fully prepaid in the United States Mail at [city of post office where papers will be mailed] address as follows:

///

[address of affected lender or lienholder and trustee]

I declare under penalty of perjury that the foregoing is true and correct, and that this declaration was executed on.

Dated: ___ , 19__ at ___ (City and State)

_____ (Signature)

If the clerk won't give you the information over the phone, go to the bankruptcy court with a copy of your motion filled out. File that form and schedule the hearing. Write down the information about when and where your motion will be heard by the judge.

Step 6: Prepare a proposed Order to Avoid Nonpossessory, Nonpurchase-Money Security Interest. This is the document the judge signs to grant your request. (See sample.) Specify exactly what property the creditor has secured in the space indicated in the sample. You can get this information from the security agreement you signed. Make two extra copies, and take them with you to the hearing. The court's local rules may require you to file the proposed order with the rest of your motion papers.

Step 7: Prepare a Notice of Motion, putting the place, date and time of the hearing in the places indicated on the sample.

Step 8: Prepare at least two Proofs of Service by Mail (see sample), one for each affected creditor and one for the trustee. These forms state that a friend or relative of yours, who is at least 18 years old and not a party to the bankruptcy, mailed your papers to the creditor(s) or the trustee. Fill in the blanks as indicated. Have your friend sign and date the form at the end as shown on the sample.

Step 9: Make at least three extra copies of all forms.

Step 10: Keep the Proofs of Service. Have your friend mail one copy of the Motion, Notice of Motion, and proposed Order to each affected creditor and the trustee.

Step 11: File (in person or by mail) the original (signed) Notice of Motion, Motion (and proposed Order, if required in your area) and Proof of Service with the bankruptcy court. There is no fee.

Step 12: The trustee or creditors affected by your motion may submit a written response. In most areas they are not required to respond in writing and can simply show up in court to argue their side. In some courts, however, if the trustee or a creditor doesn't file a written response to your motion, it may be automatically granted. Consult your local rules.

Step 13: Attend the hearing. The hearing is usually very short, ten minutes or less. Because you filed the motion, you argue your side first. Explain briefly how your property falls within the acceptable categories of exempt property, that the lien is a nonpossessory nonpurchase-money security interest and that the lien impairs your exemption. (11

U.S.C. § 522(f)(2).) "Impairs your exemption" means that because of the lien, your ownership interest (title) in this item of exempt property has been reduced.

The trustee or creditor (or an attorney) responds. The judge either decides the matter and signs your proposed order, or takes it "under advisement" and mails you the order in a few days.

b. Judicial Lien

To eliminate a judicial lien, follow the steps in Subsection a, above, but use the Motion to Avoid Judicial Lien and Order to Avoid Judicial Lien forms. Samples are below.

If you are eliminating a judicial lien on your home, use the Motion to Avoid Judicial Lien (on Real Estate) and Order to Avoid Judicial Lien (on Real Estate) in this chapter as samples.

CHECKLIST OF FORMS FOR MOTION TO AVOID JUDICIAL LIEN

- ☐ Motion to Avoid Judicial Lien or Motion to Avoid Judicial Lien (on Real Estate)
- ☐ Notice of Motion to Avoid Judicial Lien
- ☐ Order to Avoid Judicial Lien
- ☐ Proof of Service (use form from Section I, above)

---

2. Challenging a Tax Lien

If your federal tax debt is secured, you may have a basis for challenging the lien. Quite often, the IRS makes mistakes when it records a notice of federal tax lien.

HELP FROM A LAWYER
You will need the help of a tax or bankruptcy attorney—preferably one who has experience in both areas—to challenge a tax lien.

Here are some possible grounds for asking the court to remove the lien:

- The notice of federal tax lien was never recorded, though the IRS claims it was.
- The notice of federal tax lien was recorded after the automatic stay took effect.
- The notice of federal tax lien was recorded in the wrong county—it must be recorded where you own real estate.

MOTION TO AVOID JUDICIAL LIEN

[Your Name
Your Street Address
Your City, State, Zip
Your Phone Number]
In Propria Persona

UNITED STATES BANKRUPTCY COURT

[name of district] DISTRICT OF _[your state]_

[name of division, if any] DIVISION

In re:
[your name(s)]

Case No. _[Copy from your petition]_

Chapter 13

A[_[Fill in when you file papers]_

Debtor(s)

MOTION TO AVOID JUDICIAL LIEN

1. Debtor(s) _[your name(s)]_ commenced this case on _[date you filed for bankruptcy]_ by filing a voluntary petition for relief under Chapter 13 of Title 11 of the United States Code.

2. This court has jurisdiction over this motion, filed pursuant to 11 U.S.C. § 522(f) to avoid and cancel a judicial lien held by _[name of judicial lienholder]_ on property held by the debtor.

3. On _[date judicial lien was recorded]_ creditors recorded a judicial lien against the following items of debtor's property: _[list all exempt property affected by lien]_

This judicial lien is entered of record as follows: _[date of the lien, amount and court case number]_

4. All such possessions of debtor(s) have been claimed as fully exempt in their bankruptcy case.

///
///

5. The existence of _[name of judicial lienholder's]_ lien on debtor's household and personal goods impairs exemptions to which the debtor(s) would be entitled under 11 U.S.C. § 522 (b).

WHEREFORE, debtor(s) request an order against _[name of judicial lienholder]_ avoiding and cancelling the judicial lien in the above-mentioned property, and for such additional or alternative relief as may be just and proper.

Dated: _____

Debtor in Propria Persona

Dated: _____

Debtor in Propria Persona

MOTION TO AVOID JUDICIAL LIEN (REAL ESTATE)

1   *[Your Name*

2   *Your Street Address*

3   *Your City, State, Zip*
   Your Phone Number]
   In Propria Persona

4

5

6

7

8   UNITED STATES BANKRUPTCY COURT

9   _[name of district]_   DISTRICT OF _____   _[your state]_

10   _[name of division, if any]_   DIVISION

11   In re:

12   _[your name(s)]_   Case No. _____ _[Copy from your petition]_

13   Chapter 13

14   AL _[Fill in when you file papers]_

15   Debtor(s)

16   MOTION TO AVOID JUDICIAL LIEN ON REAL ESTATE

17

18   1. Debtor(s) _[your name(s)]_ , commenced this case on _[date you filed for_

19   _bankruptcy]_ by filing a voluntary petition for relief under Chapter 13 of Title 11 of the United States Code.

20   2. This court has jurisdiction over this motion, filed pursuant to 11 U.S.C. § 522(f) to avoid and cancel a

21   judicial lien held by _[name of judicial lienholder]_ on real property used as the debtor's residence, under 28

22   U.S.C. § 1334.

23   3. On _[date judicial lien was recorded]_ , creditors recorded a judicial lien against debtor's residence

24   at _[your address, city, state, zip code]_ . This judicial lien is entered of record as follows:

25   _[list judicial lien including date of the lien, amount and court case number]_

26   4. The debtor's interest in the property referred to in the preceding paragraph and encumbered by the lien

27   has been claimed as fully exempt in their bankruptcy case.

28   5. The existence of _[name of judicial lienholder]_ 's lien on debtor's real property impairs exemptions

---

1   to which the debtor(s) would be entitled under 11 U.S.C. §522(b).

2   WHEREFORE, debtor(s) request an order against _[name of judicial lienholder]_ , avoiding and cancelling the

3   judicial lien in the above-mentioned property, and for such additional or alternative relief as may be just and proper.

4   Dated: _____

5   _____
                                       Debtor in Propria Persona

6   Dated: _____

7   _____
                                       Debtor in Propria Persona

8   _____
                                       Address

9

10

11

12

13

14

15

16

17

18

19

20

21

22

23

24

25

26

27

28

NOTICE OF MOTION TO AVOID JUDICIAL LIEN & ORDER TO AVOID JUDICIAL LIEN

[Order to Avoid Judicial Lien]

1 [*Your Name*]
2 *Your Street Address*
   Your City, State, Zip
   Your Phone Number]
3 In Propria Persona

8 UNITED STATES BANKRUPTCY COURT

9 _____ [*name of district*] _____ DISTRICT OF _____ [*your state*]

10 _____ [*name of division, if any*] _____ DIVISION

12 In re: Case No. ____ [*Copy from your petition*]
   [*your name(s)*]
13 Chapter 13
14
15 AL ____ [*Fill in when you file papers*]
   Debtor(s)

16 ORDER TO AVOID JUDICIAL LIEN

18 The motion of the above-named debtor(s), _____ [*your name(s)*] _____, to avoid the lien of the respondent,
19 _____ [*name of judicial lienholder*] _____ is sustained.
20 The lien is a judicial lien that impairs the exemption as follows:
21 _____ [*list all exempt property subject to the judicial lien*]
22 Unless debtor's bankruptcy case is dismissed, the lien of the respondent is hereby extinguished and the lien shall not survive
23 bankruptcy or affix to or remain enforceable against the aforementioned property of the debtor.
24 _____ [*Name of judicial lienholder*] _____ shall take all necessary steps to remove any record of the lien from the
25 aforementioned property of the debtor.

27 Dated: _____   _____ U.S. Bankruptcy Judge

[Notice of Motion to Avoid Judicial Lien]

1 [*Your Name*]
2 *Your Street Address*
   Your City, State, Zip
   Your Phone Number]
3 In Propria Persona

8 UNITED STATES BANKRUPTCY COURT

9 _____ [*name of district*] _____ DISTRICT OF _____ [*your state*]

10 _____ [*name of division, if any*] _____ DIVISION

12 In re: Case No. ____ [*Copy from your petition*]
   [*your name(s)*]
13 Chapter 13
14
15 AL ____ [*Fill in when you file papers*]
   Debtor(s)

16 NOTICE OF MOTION TO AVOID JUDICIAL LIEN

18 Please take notice of motion is set for a hearing on:
19 _____ [*leave blank*] _____, 19___ at _____ o'clock ____m. at
20 _____ [*leave blank*]
21 in courtroom _____ [*leave blank*]

- The notice of federal tax lien was recorded against the wrong assets, such as your child's house, not yours.

Even if the notice of federal tax lien was recorded correctly, you still may have a basis to fight it if:
- the lien expired—liens last only ten years, or
- the lien is based on an invalid tax assessment by the IRS.

L. Amending Your Bankruptcy Forms

You can amend the bankruptcy forms you have filed (except the plan) at any time before your final discharge. This means that if you made a mistake, you can correct it easily. Also, you must amend your papers if you receive certain property within 180 days after filing. (These are described in Section B, above.) All you do is file a corrected document, labeling it, for example, "Amended Schedule B."

IF THE JUDGE SAYS "NO"
Bankruptcy rules state clearly that you have a right to amend any time before your case is closed. (Bankruptcy Rule 1009.) But judges sometimes balk. For instance, some courts may not let you amend your exemption schedule after if it's too late for creditors to object to the exemptions you claimed. If you run into this problem, consult a bankruptcy attorney.

If your mistake means that notice of your bankruptcy filing must be sent to additional creditors (for instance, if you inadvertently left off a creditor who must be notified), you'll have to pay a fee of $20 to file the amendment. If your mistake doesn't require new notice (for example, you just add information about property you owned when you filed), you do not have to pay an additional filing fee. If you amend your schedules to add creditors before the meeting of creditors, you'll usually be required to provide the newly-listed creditors with notice of the meeting as well as with notice of your amendment.

If you become aware of debts or property that you should have included in your papers, amending your papers will avoid any suspicion that you're trying to conceal things from the trustee. If you fail to amend your papers in situation and someone else discovers your error, the judge may dismiss your bankruptcy petition or rule that one or more of your debts is nondischargeable.

1. Common Amendments

Here are some of the more common reasons for amendments and the forms that you may need to amend.

AMEND ALL RELEVANT FORMS
Even a simple change in one form may require changes in several other forms. Exactly what forms you'll have to change depends on your court's rules.

a. Add or Delete Exempt Property on Schedule C

If you want to add or delete property from your list of exemptions, you must file an amended Schedule C. You may also need to change:
- Schedule A, if the property is real estate and not listed there
- Schedule B, if the property is personal property and not listed there
- Schedule D, if the property is collateral for a secured debt and isn't already listed
- Form 7—The Statement of Financial Affairs, if any transactions regarding the property weren't described on that form as required
- the Mailing Matrix (if your court requires one), if the exempt item is tied to a particular creditor who isn't listed.

b. Add or Delete Property on Schedules A or B

If you forgot to list some of your property on your schedules or if you receive certain property within six months after filing (see Section B, above), you may need to file amendments to:
- Schedule A, if the property is real estate
- Schedule B, if the property is personal property
- Schedule C, if the property was claimed as exempt or you want to claim it as exempt
- Schedule D, if the property is collateral for a secured debt
- Form 7—The Statement of Financial Affairs, if any transactions regarding the property haven't been described as required by that form, or
- the Mailing Matrix (if your court requires one), if the item is tied to a particular creditor who isn't listed.

c. Correct Your List of Creditors

To correct your list of creditors, you may need to amend:
- Schedule C, if the debt is secured and you plan to claim the collateral as exempt
- Schedule D, if the debt is a secured debt
- Schedule E, if the debt is a priority debt
- Schedule F, if the debt is unsecured
- Form 7—The Statement of Financial Affairs, if any transactions regarding the property haven't been described as required by that form, or

• the Mailing Matrix (if your court uses it), which contains the names and addresses of all your creditors.

2. How to File an Amendment

To make an amendment, take these steps:

Step 1: Fill out the Amendment Cover Sheet in Appendix 3, if no local form is required. Otherwise, use the local form.

Step 2: Make copies of the blank forms you need to amend.

Step 3: Check your local court rules or ask the court clerk whether you must retype the whole form to make the correction, or if you can just type the new information on another blank form. If you can't find the answer, ask a local bankruptcy lawyer or bankruptcy petition preparer. If it's acceptable to just type the new information, precede the information you're typing with "ADD:," "CHANGE:" or "DELETE:" as appropriate. At the bottom of the form, type "AMENDED" in capital letters.

Step 4: If your amendment does not involve adding a creditor, go on to Step 5.

If the creditors' meeting hasn't yet been held, include with the amended papers you are preparing a copy of the Notice of the Meeting of Creditors you received from the court.

If the creditors' meeting has already been held, you must ask the court to schedule a second meeting of creditors and issue a new Notice of the Meeting of Creditors. You must send out the notice to the new creditor and to every creditor listed in Schedules D, E and F. Ask the court clerk whether it will notify the other creditors, or whether you must. If you must, you can include the Notice when you send the amended papers. (See Step 8, below.)

Step 5: Call or visit the court and ask what order it requires the papers in and how many copies it requires for amendments.

Step 6: Make the required number of copies, plus one copy for yourself, one for the trustee and one for any creditor affected by your amendment.

Step 7: Have a friend or relative mail, first class, a copy of your amended papers to the bankruptcy trustee and to any creditor affected by your amendment.

Step 8: Enter the name and complete address of every new creditor affected by your amendment on the Proof of Service by Mail (a copy is in Appendix 3). Also enter the name and address of the bankruptcy trustee. Then have the person who mailed the Amendments sign and date the Proof of Service.

Step 9: Mail or take the original Amendment and Proof of Service and copies to the bankruptcy court. Enclose or take a money order for the filing fee, if required. If you use the mail, enclose a self-addressed envelope so the clerk can return a file-stamped set of papers to you.

M. Filing a Change of Address

If you move while your bankruptcy case is still open, you must give the court, the trustee and your creditors your new address. Here's how to do it:

Step 1: Make one or two photocopies of the blank Notice of Change of Address and Proof of Service forms in Appendix 3.

Step 2: Fill in the Change of Address form.

Step 3: Make one photocopy for the trustee, one for your records and one for each creditor listed in Schedules D, E and F (or use the list of creditors on your Mailing Matrix, if you prepared one).

Step 4: Have a friend or relative mail a copy of the Notice of Change of Address to the trustee and to each creditor.

Step 5: Complete the Proof of Service by Mail form, listing the bankruptcy trustee and the names and addresses of all creditors the Notice was mailed to. Have the person who did the mailing sign it.

Step 6: File the original Notice of Change of Address and original Proof of Service with the bankruptcy court.

N. Dealing With Creditors' Motions

Most Chapter 13 cases progress fairly smoothly, and you'll probably be able to work out minor glitches as they arise. On rare occasions, however, a creditor throws a monkey wrench into the works and files a motion which, if successful, could mean the dismissal of your case.

Take heart in knowing even when a creditor raises these issues, few Chapter 13 trustees want to deal with them. Most Chapter 13 trustees handle thousands of cases a year. They do not want to get involved in drawn-out court battles unless the result is likely to have an impact on many other debtors in your district. So the trustee will encourage you and the creditor to settle the matter without a hearing. Some trustees even discourage creditors from filing a lot of motions (and creditors need to stay on the trustee's good side).

The bankruptcy rules state that you don't have to respond to a motion in writing unless a court orders otherwise. (Bankruptcy Rule 9014.) But some courts have done just this in their local rules, which means that unless you respond in writing, before the hearing on the motion, you lose automatically.

HELP FROM A LAWYER

You will need the help of a bankruptcy attorney if you want or need to file a response to a creditor's motion.

1. Objections to Your Eligibility for Chapter 13

A creditor might file a motion claiming that your debts exceed the Chapter 13 bankruptcy limits—$269,250 of unsecured debts and $807,750 of secured debts. (These limits are covered in detail in Ch. 1, *Should You File for Chapter 13 Bankruptcy?*, Section A.) A creditor may raise this kind of objection if your liability for a debt hasn't yet been determined, and the creditor is afraid you'll wipe it out in bankruptcy.

EXAMPLE: A few years ago, you and a partner started a business. It failed, you both lost a lot of money and your ex-partner blames you. He has been threatening to sue you for the money he claims you are responsible for him losing. During your business's lean times, you missed several house payments, didn't pay your personal income taxes and charged up your credit cards. You have filed for Chapter 13 bankruptcy, and your plan proposes to pay only 10% on your unsecured debts. Your ex-partner objects, claiming that you owe him at least $400,000, which exceeds the Chapter 13 limit for unsecured debts.

2. Motion for "Adequate Protection"

Any secured creditor will probably insist that you agree to protect the collateral against loss, damage or general depre-

ciation. This is called providing "adequate protection." You must do this in case you can't finish your Chapter 13 plan and later want to give the property back to the creditor. The protection you provide could be additional liens or proof of insurance. If you refuse to provide the creditor with sufficient protection, the creditor may file a motion with the court, asking the court to order you to protect the property. So you might as well comply and avoid a court fight that's a clear loser.

3. Motion for Relief From the Automatic Stay

When you file for bankruptcy, the automatic stay prohibits virtualné27all creditors from taking any action directed toward collecting the debts you owe them until the court says otherwise. (See Section A, above.)

In a Chapter 13 bankruptcy, the automatic stay bars your creditors from going after the property and wages you acquire after you file your petition and before your confirmation hearing. The court almost always lifts (removes) the stay at the end of the confirmation hearing, because your creditors are now bound by your plan. (The one exception to this is debts for which you have a codebter; see Section 4, below.) If the confirmation hearing is delayed, your creditors may ask that the stay be lifted early. The court is likely to grant such a motion in any of the following situations:

- You refuse to provide adequate protection to a secured creditor. (See Section 2, above.)
- Your filing is obviously in bad faith or your plan is totally unfeasible. (See Section G, above.)
- You are using the bankruptcy court to resolve a matter more appropriate for another court—for example, you file for bankruptcy the day before a lawsuit against you is set to begin.
- You have no equity in an item of secured property, and the creditor (who wants to repossess it) claims you don't need the item to carry out your Chapter 13 plan. You may be able to get around this if:
  - Your plan includes payments on the secured claim.
  - You can show that you do need the property to generate income—for example, if it's a car, you could argue that you need to drive to work, and there is no adequate alternative.
  - The property is your family residence. Many courts rule that the family home is always necessary. Some courts rule otherwise, however, if the creditor shows that comparable housing is available to you for less money. You would need to emphasize to the court your children's ties to their school, your proximity to your job and the cost of getting new housing and moving.

4. Motion for Relief From the Codebtor Stay

In Chapter 13 bankruptcy, the automatic stay applies to both you and any codebtors. So until the court lifts the stay on a debt for which you have a codebtor (which usually doesn't happen until the end of the case), the creditor is prohibited from seeking payment from your codebtor.

In any of the following situations, a creditor may ask the court to lift the automatic stay protecting a codebtor:

- Your codebtor, not you, used the property associated with the debt.

- Your plan does not propose to pay the claim in full. The creditor will want to pursue the codebtor for the balance.

- You are not paying interest on this debt. In Chapter 13 bankruptcy, you don't pay interest on unsecured claims. But some courts have ruled that a creditor is entitled to let interest accrue on a debt against the codebtor. These courts will probably lift the stay to let the creditor go after the codebtor for interest. ∎

After Your Plan Is Approved

Once the court has approved your repayment plan, you should be in for smooth sailing as long as you make your monthly payments. If an unforeseen problem arises, and you think you're going to have trouble making a payment, notify the trustee as quickly as you can. The trustee wants you to succeed and will help you over the rough spots.

A. Making Plan Payments

By the time your plan is confirmed, you will have made at least one plan payment, and probably more. The hardest part of Chapter 13 bankruptcy is making those payments.

1. Including Extra Money in Your Payments

You probably feel like you are stretching as far as you can to make your plan payments every month and still have enough to take care of your day-to-day needs. But sometimes it's a good idea to reach even a little deeper into your pocket and come up with a few extra dollars to add to each payment. Here's why.

Sometimes creditors file claims with the bankruptcy court after the judge approves your repayment plan at the confirmation hearing. Unless you regularly ask the trustee for a list of claims filed by creditors, you won't know who has filed claims.

Claims filed after your plan is confirmed can cause problems, for a number of reasons:

- If you forgot about a creditor (didn't list the creditor in your papers), but the creditor somehow hears about your bankruptcy and files a claim, the trustee will probably pay that creditor.
- If a creditor files a claim for more than the amount you think you owe, the trustee could end up paying out more than you had anticipated, especially if your plan pays each creditor a percentage of their claim, not a set dollar amount.
- If a creditor files a claim for payment of a secured debt (meaning you'll have to pay it in full) and you mistakenly thought it was unsecured, the trustee will

probably pay that creditor more than you planned. This is often the situation with Sears—someone charges items on a Sears card and assumes the debt is unsecured. Sears' paperwork states, however, that Sears takes a security interest in all items paid for using its card, so those debts are secured.

To avoid underpaying your creditors in your Chapter 13 plan, it's a good idea to include an extra few dollars ($5, $10, $25—whatever you can afford) in each payment. If you're paying the trustee directly, tell the trustee why you're adding a few dollars. If the court has issued an income deduction order, send the trustee a few extra dollars yourself each month.

If no creditor files a claim you hadn't anticipated, you will simply complete your plan early. On the other hand, if you don't add the money and creditors you hadn't thought of do file claims, you will probably still owe some money at the end of your Chapter 13 case. Either you will have to pay a lump sum to make up what you still owe or you will have to ask the court to extend your plan if it was less than five years.

To keep track of the new claims, you can monitor your case file at the bankruptcy court during the 90 days following the meeting of the creditors (the deadline for creditors to file proofs of claims). If you disagree with any of the claims filed, you will have to file a motion objecting to the claim. (See Ch. 9, *After You File Your Case*, Section J, for more information on objecting to a claim.)

2. If Your Income Increases

If the bankruptcy trustee thinks you've had an unanticipated increase in income that could be used to pay your creditors, the trustee might ask you to complete a financial questionnaire or submit copies of your tax return. Some trustees require this of Chapter 13 debtors once a year as a matter of course.

If your financial condition improves to the point that you could afford to pay more to your unsecured creditors (assuming they are not receiving 100% of what you owe), the trustee or an unsecured creditor may file a motion with the bankruptcy court. The motion will request that the court order you to increase each payment, pay a lump sum amount (especially if you've inherited valuable property or won the lottery) or extend your plan. (Section C, below, covers modifications in more detail.) The bankruptcy court will most likely grant the motion.

IF YOU GET A WINDFALL

If you win the lottery, get a substantial raise, receive an inheritance or if your house goes way up in value, you may be able to dismiss your case and pay off your debts outside of bankruptcy. But keep in mind that the interest and sometimes the penalties on your debts that stopped accruing while you were in bankruptcy can be added back when you dismiss your case. In addition, before assuming you can use the equity in your home, of course, apply for and obtain the loan. Don't dismiss your case and then apply for the loan. If you are rejected, you'll just have to refile your bankruptcy.

B. Selling Property

Certain property remains under the control of the bankruptcy court even after your plan is approved. (See Ch. 9, *After You File Your Case*, Section B.) If you want to sell any of this property, the court will have to approve the sale. And your unsecured creditors might object if after selling the property and paying off the liens, you'd pocket cash rather than use it to pay your unsecured creditors.

C. Modifying Your Plan When Problems Come Up

Chapter 13 bankruptcy isn't easy. You must live under a strict budget for at least three years and possibly as many as five. Problems are bound to arise. Fortunately, the Chapter 13 bankruptcy system has procedures built into it to handle the disruptions. Any time after your plan is confirmed, you, the trustee or an unsecured creditor who filed a claim can file a motion with the court, asking permission to modify the plan. (11 U.S.C. § 1329.)

This section discusses four common situations in which you might need to modify your plan. If you think you want to modify your plan, call the trustee and ask for help in filing your motion and scheduling your hearing before the judge. Your creditors will have to be sent notice of your motion at least 20 days before the hearing date. (Bankruptcy Rule 2002(a)(6).) Ask the trustee if you need to send the notice or if the trustee will do it.

The court hearing on modification of the plan is just like the original confirmation hearing. The rules and procedures are discussed in Ch. 9, *After You File Your* Case, Section H.

Your modified plan cannot last more than five years from the date your plan originally began.

1. You Miss a Payment

If the trustee doesn't receive a plan payment, expect a phone call. Sometimes, the problem will be easy to solve—the payment got lost in the mail, your employer forgot to send it (if there is an income deduction order) or you changed jobs and forgot to change the income deduction order.

If you missed the payment because you are struggling to make ends meet, resolving the problem may be more complicated. But don't lose heart. If the problem looks temporary, and you are several months or years into your plan, the trustee may suggest that you modify your plan to do any of the following:

- skip a few payments altogether, meaning your unsecured creditors would receive less than you originally proposed
- skip a few payments now and extend your plan to make them up, assuming your plan is less than five years
- make a lump sum payment to make up the payments you've missed, or
- increase several payments to cover the payments you missed.

If the problem looks likely to continue, or it happens very early in your Chapter 13 case, the trustee is less likely to support a modification of your plan. Instead, the trustee (or a creditor) is likely to file a motion to have your case dismissed or converted to a Chapter 7 case. (See Section E, below.)

If you file a motion to modify your plan because you've missed some payments, a creditor may ask that the modified plan contain what is called a "drop dead" clause. Such a clause provides that if you miss another payment, your case will case automatically convert to Chapter 7 bankruptcy or be dismissed by the court. Many courts include drop dead clauses in modified plans.

Your plan payment isn't the only payment you might miss. If the court approved your request to make direct payments to certain creditors (such as a mortgage lender) and you miss a payment, the creditor will run to the court. Most likely, the creditor will file a motion to have the automatic stay lifted, which would let the creditor go after any property you've acquired since filing for bankruptcy. Alternatively, the creditor may ask the court to dismiss your case or convert it to a Chapter 7 case. If it's early in your plan and you haven't missed any other payments, ask the court for permission to modify your plan to pay the new arrears immediately.

2. Your Disposable Income Goes Down

You wouldn't have filed for Chapter 13 bankruptcy if you hadn't had debt problems in your past—perhaps because of job losses or reduced work hours. Filing for bankruptcy doesn't make those kind of problems go away.

If your income goes down, you or your spouse suffer a serious illness, go on maternity leave or incur an extraordinary expense, call the trustee. The trustee is likely to suggest that you suspend payments for a month or two. You can make up the difference by modifying your plan to:

- make a lump sum payment when your income goes back up
- extend your plan, if it is less than five years, or
- decrease the amount or percentage that a certain class of creditor receives—for example, you might have

originally proposed to pay your general unsecured creditors 75% of what you owe but will now file a modified plan that calls for them to get only 45%.

Creditors rarely object to a short suspension in payments, and bankruptcy courts routinely grant those modifications. If you propose a longer-term suspension, however, your secured creditors may object, especially if the collateral is decreasing in value. You may have to continue your payments on secured debts and suspend only the unsecured portion for a while.

3. You Need to Replace Your Car

A lot can go wrong with a car during the three to five years you're paying into your Chapter 13 plan—especially if you bought a used car before you filed to minimize your expenses. Chapter 13 trustees often hear from debtors whose cars have died or are on their last legs. This situation raises several issues in a Chapter 13 bankruptcy case.

Taking out a new loan. Let's say your car dies, you need another one and you want to take out a loan to pay for it. You file a motion to modify your plan to include payments for the new loan. Will the court confirm the new plan? The court is likely to say "yes" if you *must* have the car to complete your plan—for example, you're a salesperson. If, however, the car is just a convenience, the payments will significantly increase your monthly expenses and you've had trouble making your plan payments, the court will probably say "no."

For most people, the need for a car isn't all or nothing. In that case, the court will probably allow you to take out the loan if the effect is to lower your bills (for example, you were still making payments on your previous car and the loan will reduce your payments) or to increase your income (for instance, it would take two hours each way to get to work by public transit and only 35 minutes by car, so with a car you can get paid for three more hours' work a day).

Giving back a wrecked car. Now let's assume that after your plan is confirmed, your car is wrecked or won't run. You want to give the car back to the lender and modify your plan to treat the balance due (called a deficiency) as an unsecured claim. At least four courts have allowed this. (*In re Rimmer*, 143 B.R. 871 (W.D. Tenn. 1992); *In re Rincon*, 133 B.R. 594 (N.D. Tex. 1991); *In re Jock*, 95 B.R. 75 (M.D. Tenn. 1989); *In re Stone*, 91 B.R. 423 (N.D. Ohio 1988).)

One court, however, ruled that a secured creditor cannot be reclassified into an unsecured creditor after a plan has been confirmed, and that the debtor still must pay the full balance owed the lender. (*In re Abercrombie*, 39 B.R. 178 (N.D. Ga. 1984).)

A court might look at how you got into the situation. If your negligence or recklessness caused the problem, the court may be more inclined to deny modification of your plan.

What happens to insurance proceeds. If your car was all paid off and damaged in an accident, you get any insurance money. The court will probably want you to use that money to get the new car you need. If your car wasn't paid off, the insurance money will go to pay off your lender. If the insurance proceeds exceed what you owe the lender under your plan, you get the difference. Remember, once the court determines the amount a secured creditor is entitled to get under the plan, that's all the creditor gets.

4. You Incur New Debt

If you fail to pay debts you incur after your plan is confirmed, you can amend your plan so these creditors are paid through your plan. You may have anticipated this by creating a class of postpetition creditors in your plan. If so, your plan should specify that these creditors receive 100% of what they are owed, plus interest. If you didn't create such a class, you'll have to handle postpetition debts as they arise.

No matter what your plan provides, your postpetition creditors will need to file a claim with the trustee in order to get paid through your plan.

a. Your Plan Includes a Class of Postpetition Creditors

If your plan includes 100% payment of your postpetition debts, your postpetition creditors are unlikely to object to being paid through the trustee.

If, however, the creditor disagrees with the terms of your plan or you miss a plan payment, the creditor might object. If this happens, you will have modify your plan to handle the creditor's objection. If the creditor is still not satisfied, the creditor might file a motion with the bankruptcy court asking the court to lift the automatic stay. If the court grants the motion, the creditor would be allowed to go after your postpetition property and income for payment.

> **EXAMPLE:** For the first year and one-half of your plan, you will be paying your priority tax debt and your mortgage arrears. Not until month 19 will the trustee pay your unsecured creditors, including a class of postpetition creditors. Three months into your plan, the court lets you incur a medical debt. The doctor objects to being paid through the plan because the first payment won't come for at least 16 months. You will probably have to amend your plan to pay your tax debt, mortgage arrears and the medical debt during the first several months of your plan.

b. Your Plan Does Not Include a Class of Postpetition Creditors

If your plan does not include a class of postpetition creditors, and you want to pay a new creditor through your plan, you will have to modify your plan. Sometimes, postpetition creditors themselves file a motion to be included in a modified Chapter 13 plan. The motion is likely to be granted.

If you don't modify your plan to include postpetition creditors to whom you default, the creditor may be able to take collection efforts against property you acquired after filing for bankruptcy.

D. Attempts to Revoke Your Confirmation

If a creditor or the trustee thinks you obtained your confirmation fraudulently—for example, because you used a false name, address or Social Security number—one of them may file something called an "adversary proceeding" asking the court to revoke your confirmation. (11 U.S.C. § 1330.) This is extremely rare. An adversary proceeding to revoke a confirmation must be filed within 180 days of the confirmation.

An adversary proceeding is much more formal than a motion. It creates an entirely new lawsuit, separate from your bankruptcy case, and proceeds like any other lawsuit. You will need a lawyer to help you.

The bankruptcy court won't revoke your confirmation because of fraud unless it finds that:

- you made a material (significant) false statement in your papers, in a deposition or in court
- you either knew the statement was false or made the statement with reckless disregard to its truth
- you intended to induce the court into relying on the statement, and
- the court did rely on the statement.

E. If You Cannot Complete Your Plan

Despite your best efforts to keep a handle on your finances and make your regular plan payments, you may come to a point where you realize that it's impossible for you to complete your plan. You are not alone—a significant percentage of Chapter 13 debtors eventually find themselves in this position. If it happens to you, you have three options: dismiss your case, convert it to a Chapter 7 bankruptcy or ask the court to grant you a hardship discharge.

1. Dismiss Your Case

Except if the bankruptcy court believes that you filed for bankruptcy in bad faith (see Ch. 9, Section G.1), you have the absolute right to dismiss your Chapter 13 bankruptcy case at any time, as long as it did not start out as a different type of case which you converted to Chapter 13 bankruptcy. You dismiss your case by filing a simple motion with the court. (The court may have a pre-printed dismissal form you can use; if it does not, ask the trustee for help.) There won't be any court hearing, and your motion will automatically be granted. A creditor or the trustee can also file a motion to have your case dismissed. Approximately 50% of all Chapter 13 bankruptcy cases filed are eventually dismissed.

If your case started as a different kind of bankruptcy and you converted to Chapter 13 bankruptcy, you have to ask the court for permission to dismiss it. The court may deny your request—and order you to convert to Chapter 7 bankruptcy—if it feels that you are abusing the bankruptcy system. Or, it may grant your request, but sanction (fine) you or issue an order barring you from filing for bankruptcy again for another year.

If your case is dismissed, there are several important consequences:

- You cannot refile for bankruptcy—Chapter 13, Chapter 7 or any other kind—within 180 days if you dismissed your bankruptcy case because a creditor filed a motion with the bankruptcy court asking for relief from the automatic stay.
- All liens on your property are reinstated.
- All money you have paid the trustee that has not yet been disbursed to your creditors will be returned to you, less the trustee's expenses.
- The automatic stay ends, meaning your creditors are free to go after you and your assets for payment.
- Interest (and in some cases penalties) that stopped accruing during your bankruptcy will be added on to your debts.

If you change your mind and decide you want your case to proceed, you can file a motion with the bankruptcy court within ten days of the dismissal asking that your case be reinstated. Unless you have a history of filing and dismissing, or you've had serious problems making the payments under this plan, the court will probably grant your motion.

2. Convert Your Case to Chapter 7 Bankruptcy

You have the absolute right to convert your Chapter 13 bankruptcy case to a Chapter 7 bankruptcy case at any time, as long as you haven't received a Chapter 7 discharge within the previous six years. (Chapter 7 bankruptcy is discussed in Ch. 1, *Should You File for Chapter 13 Bankruptcy?*, Section B.)

You convert your case by filing a simple motion with the court. (The court may have a pre-printed form you can use; if it does not, ask the trustee for help.) There won't be a court hearing, and your motion will automatically be granted. A creditor or the trustee can also file a motion to have your case converted. (11 U.S.C. § 1307.) Approximately 15% of all Chapter 13 bankruptcy cases convert to Chapter 7 bankruptcy.

If you want to convert your case, ask the trustee whether or not you must notify your creditors. When you convert your case, all money you have paid the trustee which has not yet been disbursed to your creditors will be returned to you, less the trustee's expenses.

In addition, usually the bankruptcy forms you filed for your Chapter 13 case become a part of your new case. (These are the forms in Ch. 6 of this book.) A few bankruptcy courts, however, require that you file an entire new set of schedules, even if nothing has changed. Within 30 days after you convert, you must file one additional bankruptcy form called the Statement of Intention. It tells the court what you plan to do with your secured debts. You will also have to attend a new meeting of creditors.

Because all debts you incurred after filing your Chapter 13 case can be discharged in your Chapter 7 case (if they are otherwise dischargeable), you must amend the appropriate forms:

- Schedule D (if you've incurred new secured debts)
- Schedule E (if you've incurred new unsecured priority debts)
- Schedule F (if you've incurred new unsecured nonpriority debts)
- Schedule G (if you entered into any new contracts or leases), and
- Schedule H (if you have new codebtors).
(11 U.S.C. § 348(d).)

If, in your Chapter 13 case, the court established a value for certain items of property or determined the amount of a secured claim, those values and amounts will apply in the converted case. (11 U.S.C. § 348(f)(1)(B).)

In general, property you have acquired since filing for Chapter 13 bankruptcy is not included in your Chapter 7 bankruptcy estate. This means that if you've acquired nonexempt property, you won't lose it in your Chapter 7 case. If, however, the court determines that your conversion to Chapter 7 bankruptcy is in bad faith, the court can order that the new property be included in your Chapter 7 bankruptcy estate. This is a new section of the Bankruptcy Code; no cases have determined what bad faith means in this context. (11 U.S.C. § 348(f)(2).)

RESOURCE FOR CHAPTER 7 BANKRUPTCY

How to File for Bankruptcy, by Stephen Elias, Albin Renauer & Robin Leonard (Nolo Press) contains detailed information on Chapter 7 bankruptcy. It includes the forms and instructions you will need to file the additional form and to amend the forms you've already filed.

3. Seek a Hardship Discharge

If you cannot complete your Chapter 13 repayment plan, you can file a motion with the bankruptcy court asking for a hardship discharge. (11 U.S.C. § 1328(b).) The court will grant your request only if three conditions are met:

1. Your failure to complete the payments under your plan is due to circumstances "for which you should not justly be held accountable." Your burden is to show the maximum possible misery and the worst of awfuls—that is, more than just a temporary job loss or temporary physical disability. Permanence of the condition is usually key; you may need to bring medical evidence to court.

2. Based on what you have already paid into the plan, your unsecured creditors have received at least the amount they would have received if you had filed for Chapter 7—that is, the value of your nonexempt property. (This is a hard condition to meet unless you have little or no nonexempt property.)

3. Modification of your plan is not practical. To meet this requirement, you do not have to file a motion for modification and lose it; you just have to show the bankruptcy court that you wouldn't be able to make payments under a modified plan.

If the court grants your motion for a hardship discharge, only your unsecured nonpriority dischargeable debts are discharged. You won't be eliminating arrears on your secured debts or any of the other debts listed below. (11 U.S.C. §§ 1322(b)(5), 523(a).)

DEBTS NOT INCLUDED IN A HARDSHIP DISCHARGE

Debts Generally Not Included in the Hardship Discharge:
- priority debts
- secured debts
- debts you didn't list in your bankruptcy papers
- recent student loans
- most federal, state and local taxes and any money borrowed or charged on a credit card to pay those taxes
- child support, alimony and debts in the nature of support
- fines imposed in a criminal-type proceeding
- debts resulting from intoxicated driving
- debts for dues or special assessments owed to a condominium or cooperative association
- debts you couldn't discharge in a previous bankruptcy that was dismissed due to fraud or misfeasance.

Debts Not Included If the Creditor Sucessfuly Objects in Court:
- debts incurred on the basis of fraudulent acts, including using a credit card when payment is impossible
- debts from willful or malicious injury to a person or property
- debts from embezzlement, larceny or breach of trust (fiduciary duty)
- debts arising from a marital settlement agreement or divorce decree.

If you have a debt that falls into the second category, your best approach is to do nothing and hope the creditor does the same. If the creditor does object, the court will examine the circumstances under which you incurred the debt to determine whether or not it can be legally eliminated. You should respond if you want the debt to be included in your hardship discharge. If the debt is large enough to justify the fees you'll have to pay, hire a bankruptcy attorney to handle it, or do some legal research yourself. See Ch. 12, *Help Beyond the Book.*

NONDISCHARGEABLE DEBTS
Extensive information on the nondischargeable debts listed above is contained in *How to File for Bankruptcy*, by Elias, Renauer and Leonard (Nolo Press).

F.   When You Complete Your Plan

It's quite an accomplishment and something to be proud of—to stick with a Chapter 13 plan to the end. After you have made all of your payments under your plan, the court grants a "full payment" discharge. (11 U.S.C. § 1328(a).) In most courts, the trustee simply files the discharge order on behalf of the court after determining that all payments have been made. In other courts, you must ask the trustee (by phone is fine) to file the discharge order.

1.   Debts Covered by the Discharge

Your Chapter 13 discharge wipes out the balance owed on all of your debts, as long as your plan contains some provision describing the debt and the debt does not fall into one of these categories:

- Long-term obligations for which last payment is still due—that is, it will be paid after you've made the final payment on your plan.
- Nondischargeable debts, described in Ch. 2, *An Overview of Chapter 13 Bankruptcy*, Section D.
- Debts you incurred after filing your Chapter 13 case, if the creditor was not paid or was only partially paid through the plan.

2.   The Discharge Hearing

After struggling for years to repay your debts, the long-awaited end of your bankruptcy case may be a little anti-climactic. The court may hold a brief hearing, called a discharge hearing, and require you to attend. At the hearing, the judge explains the effects of discharging your debts in bankruptcy and may lecture you about staying clear of debt.

Few courts, however, schedule a discharge hearing in Chapter 13 cases. Whether or not you must attend a discharge hearing, you'll receive a copy of your discharge order from the court within about four weeks after you complete your payments. If you don't, call the trustee. Make several photocopies of the order and keep them in a safe place. If it's necessary, send copies to creditors who attempt to collect their debt after your case is over or to credit bureaus that still list you as owing a discharged debt.

3.   Ending the Income Deduction Order

The trustee will probably remember to stop your income deduction order after you've made your last payment. If, however, the trustee forgets, you may need to call and remind him.

4.   Debtor Rehabilitation Program

A few Chapter 13 bankruptcy courts have created Debtor Rehabilitation/Credit Re-establishment programs. The purpose is to reward people who choose Chapter 13 bankruptcy instead of Chapter 7 bankruptcy and who succeed in completing their Chapter 13 cases. Currently, the most prominent programs are in the Southern District of Ohio, Western and Northern Districts of Texas, and Western District of New York.

If you have paid off a high percentage of your unsecured debts (often 75% or more), you may attend money management seminars and apply for credit from certain creditors. Creditors who participate in many of the programs include Sears, J.C. Penney, local banks (which grant Chapter 13 debtors personal loans and credit cards), and auto manufacturers' financing divisions, such as GMAC.

In the typical program, the court staff includes a person called a "credit liaison." This person will help you:

- acquire, review and correct your credit file—in particular, to get your credit file to show that you completed a Chapter 13 bankruptcy in which you paid back a high percentage of your debts
- set up a budget
- analyze your ability to repay new debts
- understand the different types of credit
- identify possible sources of credit and credit limits
- fill out credit applications
- obtain information to support your application, such as your Chapter 13 payment history and completed plan
- prepare for any in-person interview with a creditor (for a car loan, for example), and
- understand how creditors make their decisions about extending credit.

Ask the trustee whether your court has a rehabilitation program. If it doesn't, find out from the trustee if a nearby bankruptcy court does in which you might participate. If there's nothing nearby, you'll have to take your own steps to rebuild your credit. (See Ch. 11, *Life After Bankruptcy*, Section A.) ∎

CHAPTER 11

Life After Bankruptcy

Congratulations! After you receive your final discharge and your case is closed, you can get on with your life and enjoy the fresh start that bankruptcy offers. This chapter explains how you can start to rebuild your credit, and how to deal with any problems that come up.

A. Rebuilding Your Credit

A bankruptcy filing can legally remain on your credit record for ten years from the date you filed your papers, although most credit bureaus remove a Chapter 13 bankruptcy filing after seven years. (Major creditors, such as banks and department stores, have pressured bureaus to remove the notations after seven years as an incentive to debtors to choose Chapter 13 bankruptcy over Chapter 7 bankruptcy. Many creditors disregard bankruptcy after about five years.

In about two years, however, you can probably rebuild your credit to the point that you won't be turned down for a major credit card or loan. Most creditors look for steady employment and a history, since bankruptcy, of making and paying for purchases on credit.

RESOURCE FOR REBUILDING CREDIT
For more information on rebuilding your credit—including obtaining a copy of your credit file, requesting that the credit bureau correct mistakes, contacting creditors directly for help in cleaning up your credit and getting positive information into your credit file—see *Credit Repair*, by Robin Leonard (Nolo Press).

SHOULD YOU REBUILD YOUR CREDIT?

Habitual overspending can be just as hard to overcome as excessive gambling or drinking. If you think you may be a compulsive spender, one of the worst things you might do is rebuild your credit. Instead, you need to get a handle on your spending habits.

Debtors Anonymous, a 12-step support program similar to Alcoholics Anonymous, has programs nationwide. If a Debtors Anonymous group or a therapist recommends that you stay out of the credit system for a while, follow that advice. Even if you don't feel you're a compulsive spender, paying as you spend may still be the way to go.

To find a Debtors Anonymous meeting close by, call directory assistance or send a self-addressed stamped envelope to Debtors Anonymous, General Services Board, P.O. Box 400, New York, NY 10163-0400. Or call and leave a message at (212) 642-8220.

1. Create a Budget

The first step in rebuilding your credit is to create a budget. Making a budget will help you control impulses to overspend and help you start saving money—an essential part of rebuilding your credit.

Before you try to limit how much you spend, take some time to find out exactly how much money you spend now, using a Daily Expenses form like the one shown below. Make copies of the form, which is in Appendix 3, and fill one out for 30 days. Write down every cent you spend—50¢ for the paper, $2 for your morning coffee and muffin, $5 for lunch, $3 for the bridge or tunnel toll, and so on. If you omit any money spent, your picture of how much you spend, and your budget, will be inaccurate. If you're married or combine your finances with someone, make sure each person fills out the Daily Expense forms.

At the end of the 30 days, review your sheets. Are you surprised? Are you impulsively buying things, or do you tend to buy the same types of things consistently? If the latter, you'll have an easier time planning a budget than if your spending varies tremendously from day to day.

Think about the changes you need to make to put away a few dollars at the end of every week. Even if you think there's nothing to spare, try to set a small goal—even $5 a week. It will help. If you spend $2 each day on coffee and a muffin, that adds up to $10 per week and at least $40 per month. Eating breakfast at home might save you most of that amount. If you buy the newspaper at the corner store every day, consider subscribing. (A subscription doesn't involve extending credit; if you don't pay, they simply stop delivering.)

Once you understand your spending habits and identify what changes you need to make, you're ready to make a budget. At the top of a sheet of paper, write down your monthly net (after taxes and other mandatory deductions) income. At the left, list everything you spend money on in a month, any investments you plan to make (including into a savings or money market account), and any nondischargeable or other debts you make payments on. To the right of each item, write down the amount of money you spend, deposit or pay each month. Finally, total up the amount. If it exceeds your monthly income, make some changes (eliminate or reduce expenditures for non-necessities) and start over. Once your budget is final, stick to it.

AVOIDING FINANCIAL PROBLEMS

These nine rules, suggested by people who have been through bankruptcy, will help you stay out of financial hot water.

1. Create a realistic budget and stick to it.
2. Don't impulse buy. When you see something you hadn't planned to purchase, go home and think it over. It's unlikely you'll return to the store and buy it.
3. Avoid sales unless you are looking for something you absolutely need. Buying a $500 item on sale for $400 isn't a $100 savings if you didn't need the item in the first place—it's spending $400 unnecessarily.
4. Get medical insurance. You can't avoid medical emergencies, but living without medical insurance is an invitation to financial ruin.
5. Charge items only if you could pay for them now. Don't charge based on future income—sometimes that income doesn't materialize.
6. Avoid large house payments. Obligate yourself only for what you can now afford and increase your mortgage payments only as your income increases. Again, don't obligate yourself based on future income that you might not have.
7. Think long and hard before agreeing to cosign or guarantee a loan for someone. Your signature obligates you as if you were the primary borrower. You can't be sure that the other person will pay.
8. If possible, avoid joint obligations with people who have questionable spending habits. If you incur a joint debt, you're probably liable for it all if the other person defaults.
9. Avoid high-risk investments, such as speculative real estate, penny stocks and junk bonds. Invest conservatively in things such as certificates of deposit, money market funds and government bonds. And never invest more than you can afford to lose.

2. Keep Your Credit File Accurate

When you apply for credit, the creditor will contact a credit reporting agency (also called credit bureau) and request a copy of your credit file. The information in the file is primarily what a creditor uses to decide whether to grant or

DAILY EXPENSES

Date: 8/1

Item	Cost
coffee	1.20
paper	.35
lunch	6.16
toll	3.00
rent	650.00
Daily total	844.89

Date: 8/2

Item	Cost
coffee	2.75
paper	.35
toll	3.00
CD	17.58
Daily total	23.68

Date: 8/3

Item	Cost
coffee	1.20
paper	.35
lunch	3.00
toll	3.00
hardware store—light switches	17.11
dime store—sewing gadgets	19.06
Daily total	43.72

Date: 8/4

Item	Cost
Brunch	11.50
haircut	25.00
movie rental	2.99
Daily total	39.49

deny your credit request. In addition, some insurance companies, landlords and employers obtain credit reports when evaluating the potential insurance policy holder, tenant or employee.

So that creditors and other users of credit files see you in the best light, you want to keep incorrect and outdated information out of your credit file, and get current positive information into your file.

Start by obtaining a copy of your file from one of the "big three" credit reporting agencies:

- Experian, National Consumer Assistance Center, P.O. Box 949, Allen, TX 75002-0940; (800) 682-7654 or (800) 422-4879
- Equifax, P.O. Box 740241, Atlanta, GA 30374-0241; (404) 612-3321
- Trans Union, P.O. Box 390, Springfield, PA 19064; (610) 933-1200

You will need to send the agency your name and any previous names, addresses for the last two years, telephone number, year or date of birth, employer and Social Security number. If you're married, enclose the same information for your spouse.

You are entitled to a free copy of your report if you were denied credit because of an item in it, if you request your file within 60 days of being denied credit. You are also entitled to a free report if you are unemployed and applying for a job, receive welfare or believe your file contains errors due to fraud. Also, you are entitled to a free credit report if you live in Colorado, Georgia, Maryland, Massachusetts, New Jersey or Vermont. Expect to pay up to $8 for a copy of your file if you don't qualify for a free copy.

In addition to your credit history, your credit report will contain the sources of the information and the names of people who have received your file within the last year, or within the last two years if those people sought your file for employment reasons. (15 U.S.C. §§ 1681g(a)(3)(A), 1681g(a)(3)(B).)

You can dispute any item in your credit file. For example, if the file shows you owing $3,500 on your Visa bill and being 120 days late on payments, but the loan was discharged and you owe nothing, the item should be removed from your credit file or changed to show that is was discharged in bankruptcy.

Credit files can contain negative information for up to seven years, except for bankruptcy filings, which can stay for ten. As mentioned earlier, most credit bureaus report Chapter 13 bankruptcies for only seven years. You will want to challenge outdated, as well as incorrect or incomplete, information. The bureau must investigate

the accuracy of anything you challenge within 30 days. Then the bureau must either correct it, or if it can't verify the item, remove it.

If, after the investigation, the bureau keeps information in your file you still believe is wrong, you are entitled to write a statement of up to 100 words giving your version, to be included in your file. It's a good idea to include a statement tied to a particular item in your file. When the item eventually is removed from your file or corrected, the statement will be taken out. If you write a general "my life was a mess and I got into debt" statement, however, it will stay for a full seven years from the date you place it, even if the negative items come out sooner. An example of a statement is shown below.

SAMPLE 100-WORD STATEMENT TO CREDIT BUREAU

September 12, 19XX

Your records show that I am unemployed. That's incorrect. I am a self-employed cabinet maker and carpenter. I work out of my home and take orders from people who are referred to me through various sources. My work is known in the community and that's how I earn my living.

Denny Porter
Denny Porter

The agency must give the statement, or a summary of it, to anyone who's given your credit file. In addition, if you request it, the bureau must pass on a copy or summary of your statement to any person who received your report within the past year, or two years if it involved employment.

You also want to keep new negative information out of your file. To do this, remain current on your bills. What you owe, as well as how long it takes you to pay, are in that file.

Finally, modify public records to reflect what occurred in the bankruptcy, so wrong information won't appear in your credit file. For example, if a court case was pending against you at the time you filed for bankruptcy, and, as part of the bankruptcy, the potential judgment against you was discharged, be sure the court case is formally dismissed. You may need the help of an attorney. (See Ch. 12, *Help Beyond the Book.*)

AVOID CREDIT REPAIR AGENCIES

You've probably seen ads for companies that claim they can fix your credit, qualify you for a loan and get you a credit card. Stay clear of these companies—many of their practices are illegal. Some steal the credit files or Social Security numbers of people who have died or live in places like Guam or the U.S. Virgin Islands and replace your file with these other files. Others create new identities for debtors by applying to the IRS for a taxpayer I.D. number and telling debtors to use it in place of their Social Security number.

Even the legitimate companies can't do anything for you that you can't do yourself. If items in your credit file are correct, these companies cannot get them removed. If items are incorrect, they follow the same steps outlined above. About the only difference between using a legitimate credit repair agency and doing it yourself is saving the thousands of dollars those agencies charge.

3. Negotiate With Current Creditors

If you owe any debts that show up as past due on your credit file (perhaps the debt wasn't discharged in bankruptcy or was incurred after you filed), you can take steps to make them current. Contact the creditor and ask that the item be either removed in exchange for full or partial payment. On a revolving account (such as a department store), ask the creditor to "re-age" the account so that is shown as current. For help in negotiating with your creditors, consider contacting a local Consumer Credit Counseling Service office. (See Ch. 1, *Should You File for Chapter 13 Bankruptcy?*, Section C.)

4. Get a Secured Credit Card

Once you have your budget and some money saved, you can begin to get some positive information in your credit file. One way is to get a secured credit card. In a few years, banks and other large creditors will be more apt to grant you credit if, since your bankruptcy, you've made and paid for purchases on credit.

Some banks will give you a credit card and a line of credit if you deposit money into a savings account. In exchange, you are barred from removing the money from your account. If you don't pay your bill, the bank uses the money in your account to cover what you owe. Get such a card if you truly believe you'll control any impulses to overuse it.

A major drawback with these cards is that the interest rate often nears 22%. So use the card only to cash checks, buy inexpensive items you can pay for when the bill arrives, or guarantee a hotel reservation or car rental. Otherwise, you're going to pay a bundle in interest.

USE YOUR CREDIT CARDS

If you've hung onto a bank, department store or gasoline credit card through your bankruptcy case, judicious use of that card can help rebuild your credit. If you discharged the credit card debt, a creditor might agree to restore your credit privileges if you voluntarily pay the debt that was discharged. Call the lender's customer service department and ask.

AVOID LOOK-ALIKE CREDIT CARDS

Some lesser-known mail-order companies issue cards that look like credit cards, but allow you to make purchases only from their own catalogues. The items in the catalogue tend to be overpriced and of mediocre (if not poor) quality. And your use of the card isn't reported to credit bureaus, so you won't be rebuilding your credit.

5. Borrow From a Bank

Bank loans provide an excellent way to rebuild credit. A few banks offer something called a passbook savings loan, which is a lot like a secured credit card. You deposit a sum of money into a savings account, and in exchange the bank makes you a loan. You have no access to your savings account while your loan is outstanding. If you don't repay it, the bank will use the money in your savings account. The amount you can borrow depends on how much the bank requires you to deposit.

In most cases, though, you'll have to apply for a standard bank loan. You probably won't qualify unless you bring in a cosigner, offer some property as collateral or agree to a very high rate of interest.

Banks that offer passbook loans typically give you one to three years to repay the loan. But don't pay the loan back too soon—give it about six to nine months to appear on your credit file. Standard bank loans are paid back on a monthly schedule, usually for a year or two.

Before you take out any loan, be sure you understand the terms:

- **Interest rate.** The interest rate on the loan is usually between two and six percentage points over what the bank charges its customers with the best credit.
- **Prepayment penalties.** Usually, you can pay the loan back as soon as you want without incurring any prepayment penalties. Prepayment penalties are fees banks sometimes charge if you pay back a loan early and the bank doesn't collect as much interest from you as it had expected. The penalty is usually a small percentage of the loan amount.
- **Whether the bank reports the loan to a credit bureau.** This is key; the whole reason you take out the loan is to rebuild your credit. You may have to make several calls to find a bank that reports the loan.

6. Work With a Local Merchant

Another step to consider in rebuilding your credit is to approach a local merchant, such as a jewelry or furniture store, about purchasing an item on credit. Many local stores will work with you in setting up a payment schedule, but be prepared to put down a deposit of up to 30%, to pay a high rate of interest or to find someone to cosign the loan. This isn't an ideal way to rebuild your credit, but if all other lenders turn you down, it may be your only option.

B. Attempts to Collect Clearly Discharged Debts

If a debt was discharged in bankruptcy, the law prohibits creditors from filing a lawsuit, sending you collection letters, calling you, withholding credit or threatening to file or actually filing a criminal complaint against you. (11 U.S.C. § 524.) If a creditor tries to collect a debt that clearly was discharged in your bankruptcy, you should respond at once with a letter like the one shown below.

LETTER TO CREDITOR

> 1905 Fifth Road
> N. Miami Beach, FL 35466
>
> March 18, 19xx
>
> Bank of Miami
> 2700 Finances Highway
> Miami, FL 36678
>
> To Whom It May Concern:
>
> I've been contacted once by letter and once by phone by Rodney Moore of your bank. Mr. Moore claims that I owe $4,812 on Visa account number 1234 567 890 123.
>
> As you're well aware, this debt was discharged in bankruptcy (case number 111-999 in the Western District of Tennessee) on February 1, 19xx. Thus, your collection efforts violate federal law, 11 U.S.C. § 524. If they continue, I won't hesitate to pursue my legal rights, including bringing a lawsuit against you for harassment.
>
> Sincerely,
> *Dawn Schaffer*
> Dawn Schaffer

The court doesn't give you a list of debts that were discharged. But you can assume a debt was discharged if you listed it in your bankruptcy papers, the creditor didn't successfully object to its discharge and it isn't in one of the nondischargeable categories listed in Ch. 2, *An Overview of Chapter 13 Bankruptcy*, Section D. Also, if you live in a community property state and your spouse filed alone, your share of the community debts was discharged.

If the collection efforts don't immediately stop, you may want to hire a lawyer to write the creditor again—sometimes, a lawyer's letterhead gets results. If that doesn't work, you can sue the creditor for harassment. You can bring a lawsuit in state court or in the bankruptcy court. The bankruptcy court should be more familiar with the prohibitions against collection and more sympathetic to you.

If the creditor sues you over the debt, you'll want to raise the discharge as a defense and sue the creditor yourself to stop the illegal collection efforts. The court has the power to hold the creditor in contempt of court. The court may also fine the creditor for the humiliation, inconvenience and anguish caused you and order the creditor to pay your attorney's fees. For example, a bankruptcy court in North Carolina fined a creditor $900 for attempting to collect a discharged debt. (*In re Barbour*, 77 B.R. 530 (E.D.N.C. 1987).)

If the creditor sues you (almost certainly in state court), you or your attorney can file papers requesting that the case be transferred ("removed") to the bankruptcy court.

C. Post-Bankruptcy Discrimination

You may be afraid that after your bankruptcy, you'll have trouble getting or keeping a job or finding a place to live or will suffer other discrimination. Some employers and landlords *do* hold a bankruptcy filing against a person; many others don't care.

There are laws against discrimination by government and by private employers. Some employers or government agencies comply with these laws if they are brought to their attention; others have to be sued. If it ever comes to that, you'll have to weigh the cost, stress and time that a lawsuit takes against seeking a job or loan elsewhere.

1. Government Discrimination

All federal, state and local governmental units are prohibited from discriminating against you solely because you filed for bankruptcy. (11 U.S.C. § 525(a).) This includes denying, revoking, suspending or refusing to renew a license, permit, charter, franchise or other similar grant. Judges interpreting this law have ruled that the government cannot:

- deny you a job or fire you
- deny you or terminate your public benefits, even if you discharged a debt to the government for overpayment of public benefits
- deny you or evict you from public housing, even if you discharged a debt for public housing back rent
- deny you or refuse to renew your state liquor license
- exclude you from participating in a state home mortgage finance program
- withhold your college transcript
- deny you a driver's license
- deny you a contract, such as a contract for a construction project, or
- exclude you from participating in a government-guaranteed student loan program. (11 U.S.C. §525 (c)(1).)

In general, once any government-related debt has been discharged, all acts against you that arise out of that debt also must end. If, for example, you lost your driver's license because you didn't pay a court judgment that resulted from a car accident, once the debt is discharged, you must be granted a license. (If your license was also suspended because you didn't have state-required insurance, however, you may not get your license back until you meet the requirements set forth in your state's law.) If, however, the judgment wasn't discharged, you can still be denied your license until you pay up.

Keep in mind that only denials based solely on your bankruptcy are prohibited. You may be denied a loan, job or apartment for reasons unrelated to the bankruptcy (for example, because you earn too much to qualify for public housing), or for reasons related to your future creditworthiness (for example, because the government concludes you won't be able to repay a Small Business Administration loan).

2. Non-Government Discrimination

Private employers may not fire you or otherwise discriminate against you solely because you filed for bankruptcy. (11 U.S.C. § 525(b).) While the Bankruptcy Code expressly prohibits employers from firing you, it is unclear whether or not the act prohibits employers from not hiring you because you went through bankruptcy.

Other forms of discrimination in the private sector aren't illegal. If you seek to rent an apartment and the landlord does a credit check, sees your bankruptcy and refuses to rent to you, there's not much you can do other than try to show that you'll pay your rent and be a responsible tenant.

If you suffer illegal discrimination because of your bankruptcy, you can sue in state court or in the bankruptcy court. You'll probably need the assistance of an attorney.

D. Attempts to Revoke Your Discharge

In extremely rare instances, the trustee or a creditor can ask the bankruptcy court to revoke your discharge. The trustee or creditor must file a complaint within one year of your discharge.

Your discharge can be revoked only if it's proved that you obtained the discharge through fraud, which was discovered after your discharge. If your discharge is revoked, you'll owe your creditors as if you had not filed for bankruptcy. Any payment your creditors received from the trustee, however, will be credited against what you owe.

HELP FROM A LAWYER
If someone asks the bankruptcy court to revoke your discharge, consult a bankruptcy attorney right away. ■

Help Beyond the Book

Although this book covers routine Chapter 13 bankruptcy procedures in some detail, it doesn't come close to covering everything. That would require a 1,000-page treatise, most of which would be irrelevant for nearly all readers. That said, here are some suggestions if you need more information or advice than this book provides.

The major places to go for follow-up are:
- **Lawyers:** When you want information, advice or legal representation.
- **Bankruptcy Petition Preparers:** When you're ready to file for bankruptcy, but want help typing the forms.
- **The Law Library:** When you want more information on an issue raised in the course of your bankruptcy.

A. Bankruptcy Lawyers

Even if you want, for personal or financial reasons, to handle your Chapter 13 bankruptcy yourself, you may want at least limited help from a bankruptcy lawyer. Here are some of the things a bankruptcy lawyer can do for you:
- negotiate with your creditors
- speak for you in court
- coach you on how to prepare your papers
- coach you on appearing in court
- review your bankruptcy papers after you prepare them
- prepare your bankruptcy plan for you, or
- answer your legal questions as they arise.

1. How to Find a Bankruptcy Lawyer

Where there's a bankruptcy court, there are bankruptcy lawyers. They're listed in the Yellow Pages under attorneys and often advertise in newspapers. You should use an experienced bankruptcy lawyer, not a general practitioner.

There are several ways to find a bankruptcy lawyer suited to your job:
- **Personal Referrals:** This is your best approach. If you know someone who was pleased with the services of a lawyer, call that lawyer first. If that lawyer doesn't handle bankruptcies or can't take on your case, he or she may recommend someone else who's experienced, competent and available.
- **Bankruptcy Petition Preparers:** Reputable bankruptcy petition preparers commonly work closely with bankruptcy attorneys who are both competent and sympathetic to self-helpers. If there's a bankruptcy petition preparer in your area, ask for a recommendation.
- **Legal Aid:** Legal Aid offices are partially funded by the federal Legal Services Corporation and offer legal assistance in many areas; many offices do bankruptcies. To qualify for Legal Aid, you must be low income—that is, your household income cannot exceed 135 times the federal poverty level. To find a Legal Aid office, look in your local phone book.
- **Legal Clinic:** Many law schools sponsor legal clinics and provide free legal advice to consumers. Some legal clinics have the same income requirements as Legal Aid; others offer free services to low- to moderate-income people.
- **Group Legal Plans:** Some unions, employers and consumer action organizations offer group plans to their members or employees, who can obtain comprehensive legal assistance free or for low rates. If you're a member of such a plan, and the plan covers bankruptcies, check with it first for a lawyer.
- **Pre-paid Legal Insurance:** Pre-paid "legal insurance" plans offer some services for a low monthly fee and charge more for additional or different work. That means that participating lawyers may use the plan as a way to get clients, who are attracted by the low-cost basic services, and then sell them more expensive services.

If a plan offers extensive free advice, your initial membership fee may be worth the consultation you receive, even if you use it only once. You can always join a plan for a specific service and then not renew. For bankruptcy purposes, however, a plan won't be much help unless it offers the services of bankruptcy attorneys.

There's no guarantee that the lawyers available through these plans are of the best caliber; sometimes they aren't. As with any consumer transaction, check out the plan carefully before signing up. Ask about the plan's complaint system, whether you get to choose your lawyer and whether or not the lawyer will represent you in court.

• **Chain Law Firms:** Firms such as Hyatt Legal Services routinely offer bankruptcy services, although they tend to do more Chapter 7 bankruptcies than Chapter 13 cases. You can call and ask what the basic bankruptcy fee is, and probably get an initial consultation for about $50.

• **Lawyer Referral Panels:** Most county bar associations will give you the names of some bankruptcy attorneys who practice in your area. But bar associations usually provide only minimal screening for the attorneys listed, which means those who participate may not be the most experienced or competent. You may find a skilled attorney willing to work for a reasonable fee this way, but take the time to check out the credentials and experience of the person to whom you're referred.

LEGAL ADVICE OVER THE TELEPHONE

If you are seeking legal advice on a specific issue, you can consult Tele-Lawyer, a company that offers legal advice over the phone. You can talk to a lawyer who specializes in the subject area you're concerned about for $3 a minute. The average call lasts about 14 minutes and costs about $42.

If the lawyer can't answer a question, he or she will research it—for free—and get back to you. But most questions can be answered immediately because Tele-Lawyer provides its lawyers with a large database designed to help them answer common questions.

You can reach Tele-Lawyer at:

800-835-3529 (charge to Visa or MasterCard)
900-654-3000 (charge appears on your phone bill)
900-370-7000 (charge appears on your phone bill)
900-446-4529 (charge appears on your phone bill)

---

2.   What to Look For in a Lawyer

Once you have the names of a few bankruptcy lawyers, do a little screening before you commit yourself to hiring someone.

It's important that you be as comfortable as possible with any lawyer you hire. When making an appointment,

ask to talk directly to the lawyer. If you can't, this may give you a hint as to how accessible he or she is. Of course, if you're told that a paralegal will be handling the routine aspects of your case under the supervision of a lawyer, you may be satisfied with that arrangement.

If you do talk directly, ask some specific questions. Do you get clear, concise answers? If not, try someone else. If the lawyer says little except to suggest that he or she handle the problem (with a substantial fee, of course), watch out. You're talking with someone who doesn't know the answer and won't admit it (common), or someone who pulls rank on the basis of professional standing.

Finally, once you find a lawyer you like, make an hour-long appointment to discuss your situation fully. Your goal at the initial conference is to find out what the lawyer recommends and how much it will cost. Go home and think about the lawyer's suggestions. If they don't make complete sense or you have other reservations, call someone else.

⚠️ DON'T LET THE LAWYER TAKE OVER

Fight any urge you may have to surrender your will and be intimidated by a lawyer. You should be the one who decides what you feel comfortable doing about your legal and financial affairs. Don't hire a lawyer who wants you to be a passive client. Also, pay attention to how the lawyer responds to your considerable knowledge. By getting this book and learning about Chapter 13 bankruptcy, you're already better informed about the law than most clients (and some lawyers). Many lawyers are threatened when the client knows too much, or in some cases, anything.

3.   What Bankruptcy Attorneys Charge

Bankruptcy attorneys generally about $750 to $2,000 (plus the $160 filing and administrative fees) to handle an entire a Chapter 13 bankruptcy case. The lawyer's fee is usually paid through the Chapter 13 plan. This means you do not have to come up with a chunk of money to have a lawyer file a Chapter 13 bankruptcy for you. If you hire an attorney to perform a limited task, such as to represent you at court hearings, or to coach you on certain aspects of your case, expect to be charged somewhere between $150 and $250 an hour.

Fortunately, there are some limitations on what a bankruptcy attorney can charge. Because every penny you pay a bankruptcy lawyer is a penny not available to your creditors, the attorney must report the fee to the bankruptcy court. The court has the legal authority to call the attorney in to justify the fee. This rarely happens, because attorneys know what local bankruptcy judges will allow and set their fees accordingly.

Commonly, bankruptcy attorneys charge a basic fee for a routine case and then add set amounts for necessary additional procedures. For instance, the basic fee may be $1,000, but it will cost you $150 more to respond to a motion brought by a creditor and $250 more to file a motion to establish the fair market value of secured property.

B. Bankruptcy Petition Preparers

Even though you should be able to handle routine bankruptcy procedures yourself, you may want help with form preparation or basic, general information rather than specific advice on a course of action. In that case, you don't have to hire a lawyer. For this level of assistance, a bankruptcy petition preparer (BPP) can help you. BPPs are not lawyers, but they are familiar with the bankruptcy courts in your area. They can:

- type your forms
- help you over any rough spots you encounter when filling in the forms
- provide some basic information about local procedures and requirements, and
- help you prepare for negotiations with your creditors.

Generally, BPPs will type your bankruptcy papers for about $150 to $300. Many BPPs won't file the papers for you, though because the Bankruptcy Code prohibits them from taking the filing fee from you. (11 U.S.C. § 110(g)(1).) In this situation, you'll have to take the typed forms to the court for filing. Some BPPs will let you give them a cashier's check, made out to the court, to cover the filing fee. In this case, the BPP will also file your papers for you.

BPPs are very different from lawyers. They can't give legal advice or represent you in court—only lawyers are allowed to do those things. When you use a BPP, you remain responsible for the decision-making in your case. You must decide what information to put in the forms. You cannot, legally, pass this responsibility on to a BPP.

BPPs are springing up all over the country to help people who don't want or can't afford to hire a lawyer, but you're still more likely to find a BPP if you live on the west coast. A recommendation from someone who has used a particular BPP is the best way to find a reputable one in your area.

BPPs often advertise in classified sections of local newspapers and in the Yellow Pages. You may have to look hard to find BPPs, however, because the Bankruptcy Code bars them from using the term "legal" or any similar term in their advertisements or from advertising under any category that contains the word "legal" or a similar term. A local legal aid office may provide a reference, as will the occasional court clerk. And many BPPs have display ads in local throwaway papers like the Classified Flea Market or Giant Nickel.

WHAT LAWYERS SAY ABOUT BANKRUPTCY PETITION PREPARERS

In many parts of the country, bankruptcy attorneys are extremely unhappy with the competition from BPPs. Often, the attorneys charge that BPPs are practicing law without a license or that they're incompetent. Some BPPs probably are incompetent, just as some lawyers are. But the paperwork you'll get from a BPP is probably prepared just as competently as what you'd get from a bankruptcy lawyer's office; most routine bankruptcy work in a lawyer's office is done by non-lawyer personnel anyway. How to fill out bankruptcy forms isn't taught in law school and doesn't involve any skill that lawyers (as opposed to others) necessarily possess.

KNOW WHAT YOU'RE GETTING
A small percentage of BPPs can only be described as rip-off artists. They promise to prepare and file your bankruptcy case for you—but, in fact, complete and file only the bankruptcy petition. Filing this two-page document will get your case started, but you must file the remaining 12 forms and your repayment plan within 15 days or your case will be dismissed. These BPPs don't tell you that you must complete and file the other papers.

C. The Law Library

Often, you can handle a problem yourself if you're willing to do some research in a law library. The trick is in knowing what types of information you can find there. Sometimes, what you need to know isn't written down. For instance, if you want to know whether the local bankruptcy judge is strict or generous when you put together your monthly budget, you can't find out by going to the law library. You'll probably have to talk to a bankruptcy lawyer, a petition preparer or the trustee.

The library can help you, however, if your question involves a legal interpretation, such as how the judge is likely to rule if a creditor objects to your plan for a particular reason. You can find out how similar questions have been decided by bankruptcy courts and courts of appeal.

Here's what you can find in the average law library:

- books and articles by bankruptcy experts on almost every aspect of bankruptcy law and practice, including many of the local procedures peculiar to each court
- federal bankruptcy statutes (the Bankruptcy Code)
- federal bankruptcy rules, which govern bankruptcy court procedure
- published decisions of bankruptcy court judges and appellate courts that interpret the bankruptcy statutes and rules
- specific instructions for handling routine and non-routine bankruptcy procedures, and
- cross-reference tools to help you get from one statute, rule or case to another and to help you make sure the material you find is up to date.

Here, briefly, are the basic steps of researching bankruptcy questions.

1. Find a Law Library

To do legal research, you need to find a law library that's open to the public. Public law libraries are often found in county courthouses, public law schools and state capitals. If you can't find one, ask a public library reference librarian, court clerk or lawyer.

2. Use a Good Legal Research Resource

To find the answer to a legal question, or look up a statute or case, you need some guidance in basic legal research techniques. Any of the following resources that may be available in your law library will tell you how to do legal research:

- *Legal Research: How to Find and Understand the Law*, by Steve Elias and Susan Levinkind (Nolo Press)
- *Legal Research Made Easy: A Roadmap Through the Law Library Maze*, by Nolo Press and Robert Berring (Nolo Press/Legal Star Video)
- *How to Find the Law*, by Morris Cohen, Robert Berring and Kent Olson (West Publishing Co.)
- *The Legal Research Manual: A Game Plan for Legal Research and Analysis*, by Christopher and Jill Wren (A-R Editions)
- *Introduction to Legal Research: A Layperson's Guide to Finding the Law*, by Al Coco (Want Publishing Co.).

3. Use *Collier on Bankruptcy*

It's a good idea to get an overview of your subject before trying to find a precise answer to a precise question. The best way to do this is to find a general commentary on your subject by a bankruptcy expert. For example, if you want to find out whether a particular debt is nondischargeable, you should start by reading a general discussion about the type of debt you're dealing with.

The most complete source of this type of background information is a multi-volume treatise known as *Collier on Bankruptcy,* by Lawrence P. King, et al. (Matthew Bender). It's available in virtually all law libraries. *Collier* is both incredibly thorough and meticulously up-to-date; semiannual supplements, with all the latest developments, are located at the front of each volume. In addition to comments on every aspect of bankruptcy law, *Collier* contains the bankruptcy statutes, rules and exemption lists for every state.

Collier is organized according to the bankruptcy statutes. This means that the quickest way to find information in it is to know which section of the Bankruptcy Code relates to your question. If you don't know, start with the *Collier* subject matter index. Be warned, however, that the index can be difficult to use; it contains a lot of bankruptcy jargon you may be unfamiliar with.

4. Use Other Background Resources

For general discussions of bankruptcy issues, there are several other good places to start.

- *Consumer Bankruptcy Law and Practice.* This excellent all-around resource, published by the National Consumer Law Center, is updated every year. It contains a complete discussion of Chapter 13 bankruptcy procedures, the official bankruptcy forms and a marvelous bibliography. If your law library has this volume (or will order it), become familiar with it.
- *Chapter 13 Bankruptcy*, by Keith M. Lundin (Wiley Law). Judge Lundin is one of the nation's most respected Chapter 13 bankruptcy judges. (He sits in Nashville, Tennessee and was the Chapter 13 bankruptcy trustee before being appointed judge.) His three-volume treatise contains thorough information on every aspect of Chapter 13 bankruptcy. Although it is written for lawyers, laypeople will find it is easy to understand.
- *Chapter 13 Practice Guide*, by Keith M. Lundin (Wiley Law). Judge Lundin's second book contains the required, preferred or a sample Chapter 13 repayment plan for ever bankruptcy court in the nation. It also contains information on bankruptcy court procedures.

• Commerce Clearing House (CCH) *Bankruptcy Law Reporter* (BLR). In this looseleaf publication, you can find all three primary source materials relating to bankruptcy: statutes, rules and cases. BLR is multi-volume and looks scary to use. Don't be intimidated. Clear and complete instructions on using this extremely helpful resource are at the beginning of BLR Volume 1.

• Articles published in law journals—periodicals published by law schools, bar associations and law societies. Most law school and law society articles contain academic, not practical, material. You may, however, find some practical information in bar association journals. Look up Bankruptcy or Chapter 13 Bankruptcy in the *Index to Legal Periodicals*. You can find large collections of law journals in law school libraries and large public law libraries.

5. Find and Read Relevant Statutes

After consulting *Collier* or one of the other background resources, you may need to read a statute for yourself.

Statutes passed by Congress rule the bankruptcy courts, and your first step should be to figure out which statute governs the issue you're interested in. Sometimes you'll know this from the references (citations) in this book. For instance, the discussion of income deduction orders (Ch. 9, *After You File Your Case*) refers to 11 U.S.C. § 1325(c). The citation means Title 11 of the United States Code, Section 1325(c).

Federal statutes are collected in a multi-volume set of books known as the United States Code (U.S.C.) and

BANKRUPTCY CODE SECTIONS **(TITLE 11 OF THE UNITED STATES CODE)**	
§ 109	Who may file for which type of bankruptcy
§ 302	Who qualifies for filing joint cases
§ 341	Meeting of the creditors
§ 342	Giving notice of the meeting of the creditors
§ 343	Examination of the debtor at the meeting of the creditors
§ 348	Converting from one type of bankruptcy to another
§ 349	Dismissing a case
§ 350	Closing and reopening a case
§ 361	Providing adequate protection to a secured creditor
§ 362	The automatic stay
§ 365	Executory contracts and unexpired leases
§ 366	Continuing or reconnecting utility service
§ 501	Filing of proofs of claims
§ 502	Establishing the amount of a creditor's claim
§ 506	Determining secured claims and avoiding liens
§ 507	Claims having priority
§ 522	Exemptions
§ 523	Nondischargeable debts
§ 524	Reaffirmation of debts
§ 525	Prohibited post-bankruptcy discrimination
§ 541	Property of the estate (general)
§ 547	Preferences
§ 548	Fraudulent transfers
§ 553	Setoffs
§ 1301	Codebtor stay
§ 1304	Debtor engaged in business
§ 1305	Postpetition claims
§ 1306	Property of the estate (unique to Chapter 13)
§ 1307	Converting or dismissing a Chapter 13 case
§ 1322	Contents of the Chapter 13 plan
§ 1323	Modifying the plan before confirmation
§ 1325	Confirmation hearing
§ 1326	Making plan payments
§ 1327	Rights and obligations after confirmation
§ 1328	Discharge
§ 1329	Modifying the plan after confirmation

divided into 50 numbered titles. Title 11 contains the bankruptcy statutes.

If you need to research a question and don't know what statute to start with, there are two ways to find out. First, use the list above, which tells you what's covered by most of the bankruptcy statutes that might affect your case.

If the list doesn't help, two different publications of the United States Code contain not only the statutes, but also various types of clarifying information.

- *United States Code Annotated* (U.S.C.A., published by West Publishing Co.), and
- *United States Code Service* (U.S.C.S., published by Bancroft-Whitney/Lawyer's Coop).

The statutes are the same in both publications—for instance, you can find section 506 in Title 11 of either the *U.S.C.A.* or the *U.S.C.S.* The accompanying material, however, varies. Some libraries carry only one of these publications; larger libraries carry both.

To read a bankruptcy statute, find U.S.C.A. or U.S.C.S. in your law library. Find Title 11, turn to the section number and begin reading. After you read the statute in the hardcover portion of the book, turn to the very back of the book. There should be an insert pamphlet (called a pocket part) for the current year. Look to see if the statute is in the pocket part as well, to see whether it has been amended since the hardcover volume was published.

When you first read a bankruptcy statute you'll probably be totally confused, if not in tears. Relax. No one understands these statutes as they're written. You can go either to *Collier on Bankruptcy* and read its interpretation (remember, it's organized according to the bankruptcy statutes), or directly to court opinions that have interpreted the statute. You can locate these opinions in the case summaries that directly follow the statute in U.S.C.A. or U.S.C.S. (See Section 7, below.)

6. Read Procedural Rules

If you have a question about court procedures—for example, the time in which a creditor may withdraw a claim—then you'll need to look at the federal bankruptcy rules. They govern the procedural aspects of bankruptcy cases, such as time limits and the process of filing your papers. The rules cover other issues, too, which may seem like questions of substance, not procedure, such as paying the fee in installments. If you can't find your answer in the Bankruptcy Code, it may be in the rules.

You can find the bankruptcy rules in *Collier, Consumer Bankruptcy Law and Practice* and *Chapter 13 Practice Guide*.

7. Find and Read Relevant Cases

To understand bankruptcy statutes and rules, it's usually necessary to read a case (court decision) or two that has dealt with how the particular statute applies to situations like yours. There are two types of cases: those decided by a single bankruptcy judge and those decided by a court of appeal.

A bankruptcy judge who resolves a particular issue in a case may write a statement explaining the decision. If this statement, usually called a "memorandum opinion" or "findings of fact and conclusions of law," appears to be of interest to those who practice bankruptcy law, it will be published. If you want to persuade your bankruptcy judge of a particular point, it's to your advantage to find a supportive case which has been decided by another bankruptcy judge considering similar facts.

Several publications include bankruptcy cases; the one most commonly found in law libraries is the *Bankruptcy Reports* (West Publishing Co.), abbreviated as B.R. You can find summaries of cases published in the *Bankruptcy Reports* directly following each bankruptcy statute. For example, this case summary appears after 11 U.S.C. § 523, the bankruptcy statute that covers whether or not you can discharge your student loan in bankruptcy:

> "Refusal of college to provide copies of records to students as consequence of such students' failure to repay student loans obtained from such college, despite discharge of these loans in bankruptcy, was violation of 11 USCS § 523(a)(8) because college's refusal imposed hardship on debtors and denied debtors 'fresh start'... " *Lee v. Board of Higher Education*, 1 B.R. 781 (1979 S.D.N.Y.)

The case name is *Lee v. Board of Higher Education*. It was decided in 1979 by a bankruptcy court in the Southern District of New York. The case is published in the *Bankruptcy Reports* (B.R.). It's found in volume 1 at page 781.

If one of the parties to a bankruptcy dispute appeals the bankruptcy judge's ruling, the appeal is decided by a federal district court or a bankruptcy appellate panel. These decisions are published in the *Bankruptcy Reports* or the *Federal Reporter*, 2nd and 3rd Series (West Publishing Co.), abbreviated as F.2d and F.3d.

Once you find a relevant case or two, you can find similar cases by using cross-reference tools known as digests and *Shepards*. These are explained in *Legal Research: How to Find and Understand the Law*, by Steve Elias and Susan Levinkind (Nolo Press) and other legal research texts.

D. Online Legal Resources

Every day, a growing number of basic legal resources are available online through the Internet. The Internet is a worldwide network of computers that share rules for collecting and organizing data so that others can use the information easily. There are a number of different ways to use the Internet to search for material, but by far the most important and common tool for doing research on the Internet is the World Wide Web, or the Web. The Web provides links among documents and makes it easy to jump from one resource to another. Each resource is organized graphically like a book, allowing you to skip around by topic.

A wide variety of legal source materials is also available online through large commercial services such as America Online and Microsoft Network. These services have their own collections of resources and ways of organizing that information. These days, America Online, Microsoft Network and the other commercial services tend to include more information related to popular culture than legal and reference materials. But they also provide links to the Internet, including the Web.

The following resources can help you locate legal materials on the Web.

- *Law on the Net,* by James Evans (Nolo Press), provides basic instructions on how to understand and get into the extensive library of legal information available on the Internet.
- *Government on the Net,* by James Evans (Nolo Press), explains how to find government documents, including federal and state codes, available on the Internet.
- http://www.nolo.com, the Nolo Press online site, includes a vast amount of legal information for consumers. This includes sets of FAQs (frequently asked questions) on a wide variety of legal topics and articles on legal issues.

In addition, a wide variety of secondary sources intended for both lawyers and the general public have been posted on the Net by law schools and firms. If you are on the Web, for example, a good way to find these sources is to visit any of the following Web sites, each of which provides links to legal information by specific subject.

- **http://www.courttv.com**
  This is the site to Court TV's Law Center. You can find links to many federal and state laws.
- **http://www.law.cornell.edu/lii.table.html**
  This site is maintained by Cornell Law School. You can find the text of the U.S. Code and federal court decisions. You can also search for material by topic.
- **http://www.law.indiana.edu/law/v-lib/lawindex.html**
  This site is maintained by Indiana University's School of Law at Bloomington. You can search by organization, including the U.S. government, state governments and law journals, or by topic.

Specific bankruptcy information is available at a few sites, including:

- **http://www.agin.com/lawfind/**
  This site provides an extensive list of online bankruptcy-related materials, such as bankruptcy frequently asked questions (FAQs), important bankruptcy cases, United States Bankruptcy Code, federal bankruptcy rules, background on bankruptcy lawyers and links to other online bankruptcy sites.
- **http://nacba.com**
  This is the site for the National Association of Consumer Bankruptcy Attorneys. In addition to information about the organization and its activities, you can find the text of recent cases and legislative developments.

■

State and Federal Exemption Tables

Alabama A1/3	Montana A1/17
Alaska A1/3	Nebraska A1/17
Arizona A1/4	Nevada A1/18
Arkansas A1/4	New Hampshire A1/18
California—System 1 .... A1/5	New Jersey A1/19
California—System 2 .... A1/6	New Mexico A1/19
Colorado A1/6	New York A1/20
Connecticut A1/7	North Carolina A1/21
Delaware A1/7	North Dakota A1/21
District of Columbia A1/8	Ohio A1/22
Florida A1/8	Oklahoma A1/22
Georgia A1/9	Oregon A1/23
Hawaii A1/9	Pennsylvania A1/23
Idaho A1/10	Rhode Island A1/24
Illinois A1/10	South Carolina A1/24
Indiana A1/11	South Dakota A1/25
Iowa A1/11	Tennessee A1/25
Kansas A1/12	Texas A1/26
Kentucky A1/12	Utah A1/26
Louisiana A1/13	Vermont A1/27
Maine A1/13	Virginia A1/27
Maryland A1/14	Washington A1/28
Massachusetts A1/14	West Virginia A1/28
Michigan A1/15	Wisconsin A1/29
Minnesota A1/15	Wyoming A1/29
Mississippi A1/16	Federal Bankruptcy Exemptions A1/30
Missouri A1/16	Federal Non-Bankruptcy Exemptions A1/30

Alabama

Federal Bankruptcy Exemptions not available. All law references are to Alabama Code.

ASSET	EXEMPTION	LAW
homestead	Real property or mobile home to $5,000; property cannot exceed 160 acres (husband & wife may double)	6-10-2
	Must record homestead declaration before attempted sale of home	6-10-20
insurance	Annuity proceeds or avails to $250 per month	27-14-32
	Disability proceeds or avails to an average of $250 per month	27-14-31
	Fraternal benefit society benefits	27-34-27
	Life insurance proceeds or avails if beneficiary is insured's spouse or child	6-10-8
	Life insurance proceeds or avails if beneficiary is wife of insured	27-14-29
	Life insurance proceeds or avails if clause prohibits proceeds from being used to pay beneficiary's creditors	27-15-26
	Mutual aid association benefits	27-30-25
miscellaneous	Property of business partnership	10-8-72(b)(3)
pensions	Judges (only payments being received)	12-18-10(a), (b)
	Law enforcement officers	36-21-77
	State employees	36-27-28
	Teachers	16-25-23
personal property	Books	6-10-6
	Burial place	6-10-5
	Church pew	6-10-5
	Clothing needed	6-10-6
	Family portraits or pictures	6-10-6
public benefits	Aid to blind, aged, disabled, public assistance	38-4-8
	Coal miners' pneumoconiosis benefits	25-5-179
	Crime victims' compensation	15-23-15(e)
	Southeast Asian War POWs' benefits	31-7-2
	Unemployment compensation	25-4-140
	Workers' compensation	25-5-86(b)
tools of trade	Arms, uniforms, equipment that state military personnel are required to keep	31-2-78
wages	75% of earned but unpaid wages; bankruptcy judge may authorize more for low-income debtors	6-10-7
wild card	$3,000 of any personal property, except life insurance (*In re Morris*, 30 B.R. 392 (N.D. Ala. 1983))	6-10-6

Alaska

Alaska law states that only the items found in Alaska Statutes §§ 9.38.010, 9.38.015(a), 9.38.017, 9.38.020, 9.38.025 and 9.38.030 may be exempted in bankruptcy. In *In re McNutt*, 87 B.R. 84 (9th Cir. 1988), however, an Alaskan debtor used the federal bankruptcy exemptions. All law references are to Alaska Statutes.

ASSET	EXEMPTION	LAW
homestead	$54,000 (joint owners may each claim a portion, but total can't exceed $54,000)	9.38.010
insurance	Disability benefits	9.38.015(b), 9.38.030(e)(1), (5)
	Fraternal benefit society benefits	21.84.240
	Insurance proceeds for personal injury, to extent wages exempt (bankruptcy judge may authorize more—9.38.050(a))	9.38.030(e)(3)
	Insurance proceeds for wrongful death, to extent wages exempt	9.38.030(e)(3)
	Life insurance or annuity contract loan value to $10,000	9.38.017, 9.38.025
	Life insurance proceeds if beneficiary is insured's spouse or dependent, to extent wages exempt	9.38.030(e)(4)
	Medical, surgical or hospital benefits	9.38.015(a)(3)
miscellaneous	Alimony, to extent wages exempt	9.38.030(e)(2)
	Child support payments made by collection agency	9.38.015(b)
	Liquor licenses	9.38.015(a)(7)
	Permits for limited entry into Alaska Fisheries	9.38.015(a)(8)
	Property of business partnership	9.38.100(b)
pensions	Elected public officers (only benefits building up)	9.38.015(b)
	ERISA-qualified benefits deposited more than 120 days before filing bankruptcy	9.38.017
	Judicial employees (only benefits building up)	9.38.015(b)
	Public employees (only benefits building up)	9.38.015(b), 39.35.505
	Teachers (only benefits building up)	9.38.015(b)
	Other pensions, to extent wages exempt (only payments being received)	9.38.030(e)(5)
personal property	Books, musical instruments, clothing, family portraits, household goods & heirlooms to $3,000 total	9.38.020(a)
	Building materials	34.35.105
	Burial plot	9.38.015(a)(1)
	Health aids needed	9.38.015(a)(2)
	Jewelry to $1,000	9.38.020(b)
	Motor vehicle to $3,000; vehicle's market value can't exceed $20,000	9.38.020(e)
	Personal injury recoveries, to extent wages exempt	9.38.030(e)(3)
	Pets to $1,000	9.38.020(d)
	Proceeds for lost, damaged or destroyed exempt property	9.38.060
	Wrongful death recoveries, to extent wages exempt	9.38.030(e)(3)
public benefits	Adult assistance to elderly, blind, disabled	47.25.550
	Alaska longevity bonus	9.38.015(a)(5)
	Crime victims' compensation	9.38.015(a)(4)
	Federally exempt public benefits paid or due	9.38.015(a)(6)
	General relief assistance	47.25.210
	Public assistance	47.25.395
	45% of permanent fund dividends	43.23.065
	Tuition credits under an advance college tuition payment contract	9.38.015(a)(9)
	Unemployment compensation	9.38.015(b), 23.20.405
	Workers' compensation	23.30.160
tools of trade	Implements, books & tools of trade to $2,800	9.38.020(c)
wages	Weekly net earnings to $350; for sole wage earner in a household, $550; if you don't receive weekly, or semi-monthly pay, can claim $1,400 in cash or liquid assets paid any month; for sole wage earner in household, $2,200	9.38.030(a), (b), 9.38.050(b)
wild card	None	

Arizona

Federal Bankruptcy Exemptions not available. All law references are to Arizona Revised Statutes unless otherwise noted.

Note: Doubling is permitted for noted exemptions by Arizona Revised Statutes § 33-1121.01.

ASSET	EXEMPTION	LAW
homestead	Real property, an apartment or mobile home you occupy to $100,000; sale proceeds exempt 18 months after sale or until new home purchased, whichever occurs first (husband & wife may not double)	33-1101
	Must record homestead declaration before attempted sale of home	33-1102
insurance	Fraternal benefit society benefits	20-881
	Group life insurance policy or proceeds	20-1132
	Health, accident or disability benefits	33-1126(A)(4)
	Life insurance cash value to $1,000 per dependent ($25,000 total) (husband & wife may double)	33-1126(A)(6)
	Life insurance cash value to $2,000 per dependent ($25,000 total)	20-1131(D)
	Life insurance proceeds to $20,000 if beneficiary is spouse or child (husband & wife may double)	33-1126(A)(1)
miscellaneous	Allimony, child support needed for support	33-1126(A)(3)
	Minor child's earnings, unless debt is for child	33-1126(A)(2)
	Property of business partnership	29-225
pensions *also see wages*	Board of regents members	15-1628(I)
	ERISA-qualified benefits deposited more than 120 days before filing bankruptcy	33-1126(C)
	IRAs	*In re Herrscher,* 121 B.R. 29 (D. Ariz. 1990)
	Firefighters	9-968
	Police officers	9-931
	Public safety personnel	38-850(C)
	Rangers	41-955
	State employees	38-762
personal property *husband & wife may double all personal property exemptions*	2 beds & living room chair per person; 1 dresser, table, lamp, bedding per bed; kitchen table; dining room table & 4 chairs (1 more per person); living room carpet or rug; couch; 3 lamps; 3 coffee or end tables; pictures, paintings, drawings created by debtor; family portraits; refrigerator; stove; TV, radio or stereo;alarm clock; washer; dryer; vacuum cleaner to $4,000 total	33-1123
	Bank deposit to $150 in one account	33-1126(A)(8)
	Bible; bicycle; sewing machine; typewriter; burial plot; rifle, pistol or shotgun to $500 total	33-1125
	Books to $250; clothing to $500; wedding & engagement rings to $1,000; watch to $100; pets, horses, milk cows & poultry to $500; musical instruments to $250; prostheses, including wheelchair	33-1125
	Food & fuel to last 6 months	33-1124
	Motor vehicle to $1,500 ($4,000, if disabled)	33-1125(8)
	Prepaid rent or security deposit to $1,000 or 1½ times your rent, whichever is less, in lieu of homestead	33-1126(D)
	Proceeds for sold or damaged exempt property	33-1126(A)(5), (7)
public benefits	Unemployment compensation	23-783
	Welfare benefits	46-208
	Workers' compensation	23-1068
tools of trade	Arms, uniforms & accoutrements you're required to keep	33-1130(3)
	Farm machinery, utensils, seed, instruments of husbandry, feed, grain & animals to $2,500 total (husband & wife may double)	33-1130(2)
	Teaching aids of teacher	33-1127
	Tools, equipment, instruments & books (except vehicle driven to work) to $2,500	33-1130(1)
wages	Minimum 75% of earned but unpaid wages, pension payments; bankruptcy judge may authorize more for low-income debtors	33-1131
wild card	None	

Arkansas

Federal Bankruptcy Exemptions available. All law references are to Arkansas Code Annotated unless otherwise noted.

ASSET	EXEMPTION	LAW
homestead *choose option 1or 2, not both*	1. For head of family: real or personal property used as residence, to an unlimited value; property cannot exceed ¼ acre in city, town, village, or 80 acres elsewhere. If property is between ¼ -1 acre in city, town or village, or 80-160 acres elsewhere, to $2,500; no homestead may exceed 1 acre in city, town or village, or 160 acres elsewhere (husband & wife may not double, *In re Stevens,* 829 F.2d 693 (8th Cir. 1987))	Constitution 9-3, 9-4, 9-5; 16-66-210, 16-66-218(b)(3), (4)
	2. Real or personal property used as residence, to $800 if single; $1,250 if married	16-66-218(a)(1)
insurance	Annuity contract	23-79-134
	Disability benefits	23-79-133
	Fraternal benefit society benefits	23-74-403
	Group life insurance	23-79-132
	Life, health, accident or disability cash value or proceeds paid or due (limited to the $500 exemption provided by §§ 9-1 and 9-2 of the Arkansas Constitution, *In re Holt,* 97 B.R. 997 (W.D. Ark. 1988).)	16-66-209
	Life insurance proceeds if clause prohibits proceeds from being used to pay beneficiary's creditors	23-79-131
	Life insurance proceeds or avails if beneficiary isn't the insured	23-79-131
	Mutual assessment life or disability benefits to $1,000	23-72-114
	Stipulated insurance premiums	23-71-112
miscellaneous	Property of business partnership	4-42-502
pensions	Disabled firefighters	24-11-814
	Disabled police officers	24-11-417
	Firefighters	24-10-616
	IRA deposits to $20,000 if deposited over 1 year before filing for bankruptcy	16-66-218(b)(16)
	Police officers	24-10-616
	School employees	24-7-715
	State police officers	24-6-202, 24-6-205, 24-6-223
personal property	Burial plot to 5 acres, in lieu of homestead option 2	16-66-207, 16-66-218(a)(1)
	Clothing	Constitution 9-1, 9-2
	Motor vehicle to $1,200	16-66-218(a)(2)
	Wedding bands; any diamond can't exceed ½ carat	16-66-218(a)(3)
public benefits	Aid to blind, aged, disabled, public assistance	20-76-430
	Crime victims' compensation unless seeking to discharge debt for treatment of injury incurred during the crime	16-90-716(e)
	Unemployment compensation	11-10-109
	Workers' compensation	11-9-110
tools of trade	Implements, books & tools of trade to $750	16-66-218(a)(4)
wages	Earned but unpaid wages due for 60 days; in no event under $25 per week	16-66-208, 16-66-218(b)(6)
wild card	$500 of any personal property if married or head of family; else $200	Constitution 9-1, 9-2; 16-66-218(b)(1), (2)

California—System 1

Federal Bankruptcy Exemptions not available. California has two systems; you must select one or the other. All law references are to California Code of Civil Procedure unless otherwise noted.

ASSET	EXEMPTION	LAW
homestead	Real or personal property you occupy including mobile home, boat, stock cooperative, community apartment, planned development or condo to $50,000 if single & not disabled; $75,000 for families if no other member has a homestead (if only one spouse files, may exempt one-half of amount if home held as community property and all of amount if home held as tenants in common); $125,000 if 65 or older, or physically or mentally disabled; $125,000 if 55 or older, single & earn under $15,000 or married & earn under $20,000 & creditors seek to force the sale of your home; sale proceeds received exempt for 6 months after (husband & wife may not double)	704.710, 704.720, 704.730 *In re McFall,* 112 B.R. 336 (9th Cir. B.A.P. 1990)
	May file homestead declaration	704.920
insurance	Disability or health benefits	704.130
	Fidelity bonds	Labor 404
	Fraternal unemployment benefits	704.120
	Homeowners' insurance proceeds for 6 months after received, to homestead exemption amount	704.720(b)
	Life insurance proceeds if clause prohibits proceeds from being used to pay beneficiary's creditors	Ins. 10132, Ins. 10170, Ins. 10171
	Matured life insurance benefits needed for support	704.100(c)
	Unmatured life insurance policy loan value to $8,000 (husband & wife may double)	704.100(b)
miscellaneous	Business or professional licenses	695.060
	Inmates' trust funds to $1,000 (husband and wife may not double)	704.090
	Property of business partnership	Corp. 15025
pensions	County employees	Gov't 31452
	County firefighters	Gov't 32210
	County peace officers	Gov't 31913
	Private retirement benefits, including IRAs & Keoghs	704.115
	Public employees	Gov't 21201
	Public retirement benefits	704.110
personal property	Appliances, furnishings, clothing & food needed	704.020
	Bank deposits from Social Security Administration to $2,000 ($3,000 for husband and wife)	704.080
	Building materials to $2,000 to repair or improve home (husband and wife may not double)	704.030
	Burial plot	704.200
	Health aids	704.050
	Jewelry, heirlooms & art to $5,000 total (husband and wife may not double)	704.040
	Motor vehicles to $1,900, or $1,900 in auto insurance if vehicle(s) lost, damaged or destroyed (husband and wife may not double)	704.010
	Personal injury & wrongful death causes of action	704.140(a), 704.150(a)
	Personal injury & wrongful death recoveries needed for support; if receiving installments, at least 75%	704.140(b), (c), (d), 704.150(b), (c)

ASSET	EXEMPTION	LAW
public benefits	Aid to blind, aged, disabled, public assistance	704.170
	Financial aid to students	704.190
	Relocation benefits	704.180
	Unemployment benefits	704.120
	Union benefits due to labor dispute	704.120(b)(5)
	Workers' compensation	704.160
tools of trade	Tools, implements, materials, instruments, uniforms, books, furnishings, equipment, vessel, motor vehicle to $5,000 total; to $10,000 total if used by both spouses in same occupation (cannot claim motor vehicle under tools of trade exemption if claimed under motor vehicle exemption)	704.060
wages	Minimum 75% of wages	704.070
	Public employees vacation credits; if receiving installments, at least 75%	704.113
wild card	None	

California—System 2

Federal Bankruptcy Exemptions not available. All law references are to California Code of Civil Procedure unless otherwise noted.

Note: Married couples may not double any exemptions (*In re Talmadge,* 832 F.2d 1120 (9th Cir. 1987); *In re Baldwin,* 70 B.R. 612 (9th Cir. B.A.P. 1987))

ASSET	EXEMPTION	LAW
homestead	Real or personal property, including co-op, used as residence to $15,000; unused portion of homestead may be applied to any property	703.140 (b)(1)
insurance	Disability benefits	703.140 (b)(10)(C)
	Life insurance proceeds needed for support of family	703.140 (b)(11)(C)
	Unmatured life insurance contract accrued avails to $8,000	703.140 (b)(8)
	Unmatured life insurance policy other than credit	703.140 (b)(7)
miscellaneous	Alimony, child support needed for support	703.140 (b)(10)(D)
pensions	ERISA-qualified benefits needed for support	703.140 (b)(10)(E)
personal property	Animals, crops, appliances, furnishings, household goods, books, musical instruments & clothing to $400 per item	703.140 (b)(3)
	Burial plot to $15,000, in lieu of homestead	703.140 (b)(1)
	Health aids	703.140 (b)(9)
	Jewelry to $1,000	703.140 (b)(4)
	Motor vehicle to $2,400	703.140 (b)(2)
	Personal injury recoveries to $15,000 (not to include pain & suffering; pecuniary loss)	703.140 (b)(11)(D, E)
	Wrongful death recoveries needed for support	703.140 (b)(11)(B)
public benefits	Crime victims' compensation	703.140 (b)(11)(A)
	Public assistance	703.140 (b)(10)(A)
	Social Security	703.140 (b)(10)(A)
	Unemployment compensation	703.140 (b)(10)(A)
	Veterans' benefits	703.140 (b)(10)(B)
tools of trade	Implements, books & tools of trade to $1,500	703.140 (b)(6)
wages	None	
wild card	$800 of any property	703.140 (b)(5)
	Unused portion of homestead or burial exemption, of any property	703.140 (b)(5)

Colorado

Federal Bankruptcy Exemptions not available. All law references are to Colorado Revised Statutes.

ASSET	EXEMPTION	LAW
homestead	Real property, mobile home or manufactured home (mobile or manufactured home if loan incurred after 1/1/83) you occupy to $30,000; sale proceeds exempt 1 year after received.	38-41-201, 38-41-201.6, 38-41-203, 38-41-207
	Spouse or child of deceased owner may claim homestead exemption	38-41-204
	House trailer or coach used as residence to $3,500	13-54-102(1)(o)(I)
	Mobile home used as residence to $6,000	13-54-102(1)(o)(II)
insurance	Disability benefits to $200 per month; if receive lump sum, entire amount exempt	10-8-114
	Fraternal benefit society benefits	10-14-122
	Group life insurance policy or proceeds	10-7-205
	Homeowners' insurance proceeds for 1 year after received, to homestead exemption amount	38-41-209
	Life insurance avails to $5,000	13-54-102(1)(l)
	Life insurance proceeds if clause prohibits proceeds from being used to pay beneficiary's creditors	10-7-106
miscellaneous	Child support if recipient does not mix with other money or deposits into separate account for the benefit of the child	13-54-102.5
	Property of business partnership	7-60-125
pensions *also see wages*	ERISA-qualified benefits, including IRAs	13-54-102(1)(s)
	Firefighters	31-30-412, 31-30-518
	Police officers	31-30-313, 31-30-616
	Public employees	24-51-212
	Teachers	22-64-120
	Veterans	13-54-102(1)(h), 13-54-104
personal property	1 burial plot per person	13-54-102(1)(d)
	Clothing to $750	13-54-102(1)(a)
	Food & fuel to $300	13-54-102(1)(f)
	Health aids	13-54-102(1)(p)
	Household goods to $1,500	13-54-102(1)(e)
	Jewelry & articles of adornment to $500 total	13-54-102(1)(b)
	Motor vehicles used for work to $1,000; to $3,000 to get medical care, if elderly or disabled	13-54-102(j)(I), (II)
	Personal injury recoveries, unless debt related to injury	13-54-102(1)(n)
	Pictures & books to $750	13-54-102(1)(c)
	Proceeds for damaged exempt property	13-54-102(1)(m)
	Security deposit	13-54-102(1)(r)
public benefits	Aid to blind, aged, disabled, public assistance	26-2-131
	Crime victims' compensation	13-54-102(1)(q), 24-4.1-114
	Unemployment compensation	8-80-103
	Veterans' benefits for veteran, spouse or child if veteran served in war	13-54-102(1)(h)
	Workers' compensation	8-42-124
tools of trade	Horses, mules, wagons, carts, machinery, harness & tools of farmer to $2,000 total	13-54-102(1)(g)
	Library of professional to $1,500 or stock in trade, supplies, fixtures, machines, tools, maps, equipment & books to $1,500 total	13-54-102(1)(i), (k)
	Livestock & poultry of farmer to $3,000	13-54-102(1)(g)
wages	Minimum 75% of earned but unpaid wages, pension payments	13-54-104
wild card	None	

Connecticut

Federal Bankruptcy Exemptions available. All law references are to Connecticut General Statutes Annotated.

ASSET	EXEMPTION	LAW
homestead	Real property, including mobile or manufactured home, to $75,000	52-352b(t)
insurance	Disability benefits paid by association for its members	52-352b(p)
	Fraternal benefit society benefits	38a-637
	Health or disability benefits	52-352b(e)
	Life insurance proceeds if clause prohibits proceeds from being used to pay beneficiary's creditors	38a-454
	Life insurance proceeds or avails	38a-453
	Unmatured life insurance policy loan value to $4,000	52-352b(s)
miscellaneous	Alimony, to extent wages exempt	52-352b(n)
	Child support	52-352b(h)
	Farm partnership animals and livestock feed reasonably required to run farm where at least 50% of partners are members of same family	52-352d
	Property of business partnership	34-63
pensions	ERISA-qualified benefits, to extent wages exempt (only payments being received)	52-352b(m)
	Municipal employees	7-446
	Probate judges & employees	45-290
	State employees	5-171, 5-192w
	Teachers	10-183q
personal property	Appliances, food, clothing, furniture & bedding needed	52-352b(a)
	Burial plot	52-352b(c)
	Health aids needed	52-352b(f)
	Motor vehicle to $1,500	52-352b(j)
	Proceeds for damaged exempt property	52-352b(q)
	Residential utility & security deposits for 1 residence	52-352b(l)
	Wedding & engagement rings	52-352b(k)
public benefits	Aid to blind, aged, disabled, public assistance	52-352b(d)
	Crime victims' compensation	52-352b(o), 54-213
	Social Security	52-352b(g)
	Unemployment compensation	31-272(c), 52-352b(g)
	Veterans' benefits	52-352b(g)
	Vietnam veterans' death benefits	27-140i
	Wages from earnings incentive program	52-352b(d)
	Workers' compensation	52-352b(g)
tools of trade	Arms, military equipment, uniforms, musical instruments of military personnel	52-352b(i)
	Tools, books, instruments & farm animals needed	52-352b(b)
wages	Minimum 75% of earned but unpaid wages	52-361a(f)
wild card	$1,000 of any property	52-352b(r)

Delaware

Federal Bankruptcy Exemptions not available. All law references are to Delaware Code Annotated unless otherwise noted.

Note: A single person may exempt no more than $5,000 total in all exemptions; a husband & wife may exempt no more than $10,000 total (10-4914).

ASSET	EXEMPTION	LAW
homestead	None, however, property held as tenancy by the entirety may be exempt against debts owed by only one spouse	*In re Hovatter*, 25 B.R. 123 (D. Del. 1982)
insurance	Annuity contract proceeds to $350 per month	18-2728
	Fraternal benefit society benefits	18-6118
	Group life insurance policy or proceeds	18-2727
	Health or disability benefits	18-2726
	Life insurance proceeds if clause prohibits proceeds from being used to pay beneficiary's creditors	18-2729
	Life insurance proceeds or avails	18-2725
miscellaneous	Property of business partnership	6-1525
pensions	Kent County employees	9-4316
	Police officers	11-8803
	State employees	29-5503
	Volunteer firefighters	16-6653
personal property	Bible, books & family pictures	10-4902(a)
	Burial plot	10-4902(a)
	Church pew or any seat in public place of worship	10-4902(a)
	Clothing, includes jewelry	10-4902(a)
	Pianos and leased organs	10-4902(d)
	Sewing machines	10-4902(c)
public benefits	Aid to blind	31-2309
	Aid to aged, disabled, general assistance	31-513
	Unemployment compensation	19-3374
	Workers' compensation	19-2355
tools of trade	Tools, implements & fixtures to $75 in New Castle & Sussex Counties; to $50 in Kent County	10-4902(b)
wages	85% of earned but unpaid wages	10-4913
wild card	$500 of any personal property, except tools of trade, if head of family	10-4903

District of Columbia

Federal Bankruptcy Exemptions available. All law references are to District of Columbia Code unless otherwise noted.

ASSET	EXEMPTION	LAW
homestead	None, however, property held as tenancy by the entirety may be exempt against debts owed by only one spouse	*Estate of Wall*, 440 F.2d 215 (D.C. Cir. 1971)
insurance	Disability benefits	35-522
	Fraternal benefit society benefits	35-1211
	Group life insurance policy or proceeds	35-523
	Life insurance proceeds if clause prohibits proceeds from being used to pay beneficiary's creditors	35-525
	Life insurance proceeds or avails	35-521
	Other insurance proceeds to $200 per month, maximum 2 months, for head of family; else $60 per month	15-503
miscellaneous	Property of business partnership	41-124
pensions	Judges	11-1570(d)
also see wages	Public school teachers	31-1217, 31-1238
personal property	Beds, bedding, radios, cooking utensils, stoves, furniture, furnishings & sewing machines to $300 total	15-501(a)(2)
	Books to $400	15-501(a)(8)
	Clothing to $300	15-501(a)(1), 15-503(b)
	Cooperative association holdings to $50	29-1128
	Family pictures	15-501(a)(8)
	Food & fuel to last 3 months	15-501(a)(3), (4)
	Residential condominium deposit	45-1869
public benefits	Aid to blind, aged, disabled, general assistance	3-215.1
	Crime victims' compensation	3-407
	Unemployment compensation	46-119
	Workers' compensation	36-317
tools of trade	Library, furniture, tools of professional or artist to $300	15-501(a)(6)
	Mechanic's tools; tools of trade or business to $200	15-501(a)(5), 15-503(b)
	Motor vehicle, cart, wagon or dray, & horse or mule harness to $500	15-501(a)(7)
	Seal & documents of notary public	1-806
	Stock & materials to $200	15-501(a)(5)
wages	Minimum 75% of earned but unpaid wages, pension payments; bankruptcy judge may authorize more for low-income debtors 16-572	
	Non-wage (including pension) earnings for 60 days to $200 per month for head of family; else $60 per month 15-503	
wild card	None	

Florida

Federal Bankruptcy Exemptions not available. All law references are to Florida Statutes Annotated unless otherwise noted.

ASSET	EXEMPTION	LAW
homestead	Real or personal property including mobile or modular home to unlimited value; property cannot exceed ¹/₂ acre in municipality or 160 contiguous acres elsewhere; spouse or child of deceased owner may claim homestead exemption	222.01, 222.02, 222.03, 222.05, Constitution 10-4
	May file homestead declaration	222.01
	Property held as tenancy by the entirety may be exempt against debts owed by only one spouse	*In re Avins*, 19 B.R. 736 (S.D. Fla. 1982)
insurance	Annuity contract proceeds; does not include lottery winnings	222.14; *In re Pizzi*, 153 B.R. 357 (S.D. Fla. 1993)
	Death benefits payable to a specific beneficiary, not the deceased's estate	222.13
	Disability or illness benefits	222.18
	Fraternal benefit society benefits, if received before 10/1/96	632.619
	Life insurance cash surrender value	222.14
miscellaneous	Alimony, child support needed for support	222.201
	Damages to employees for injuries in hazardous occupations	769.05
	Pre-need funeral contract deposits	497.413(8)
	Property of business partnership	620.68
pensions	County officers, employees	122.15
also see wages	ERISA-qualified benefits	222.21(2)
	Firefighters	175.241
	Highway patrol officers	321.22
	Police officers	185.25
	State officers, employees	121.131
	Teachers	238.15
personal property	Any personal property to $1,000 (Husband & wife may double)	Constitution 10-4; *In re Hawkins*, 51 B.R. 348 (S.D. Fla. 1985)
	Health aids	222.25
	Motor vehicle to $1,000	222.25
public benefits	Crime victims' compensation unless seeking to discharge debt for treatment of injury incurred during the crime	960.14
	Hazardous occupation injury recoveries	769.05
	Public assistance	222.201
	Social Security	222.201
	Unemployment compensation	222.201, 443.051(2), (3)
	Veterans' benefits	222.201, 744.626
	Workers' compensation	440.22
tools of trade	None	
wages	100% of wages for heads of family up to $500 per week either unpaid or paid and deposited into bank account for up to 6 months	222.11
	Federal government employees pension payments needed for support & received 3 months prior	222.21
wild card	See personal property	

Georgia

Federal Bankruptcy Exemptions not available. All law references are to the Official Code of Georgia Annotated, not to the Georgia Code Annotated.

ASSET	EXEMPTION	LAW
homestead	Real or personal property, including co-op, used as residence to $5,000; unused portion of homestead may be applied to any property	44-13-100(a)(1)
insurance	Annuity & endowment contract benefits	33-28-7
	Disability or health benefits to $250 per month	33-29-15
	Fraternal benefit society benefits	33-15-20
	Group insurance	33-30-10
	Industrial life insurance if policy owned by someone you depended on, needed for support	33-26-5
	Life insurance proceeds if policy owned by someone you depended on, needed for support	44-13-100(a)(11)(C)
	Unmatured life insurance contract	44-13-100(a)(8)
	Unmatured life insurance dividends, interest, loan value or cash value to $2,000 if beneficiary is you or someone you depend on	44-13-100(a)(9)
miscellaneous	Alimony, child support needed for support	44-13-100(a)(2)(D)
pensions	Employees of non-profit corporations	44-13-100(a)(2.1)(B)
	ERISA-qualified benefits	18-4-22
	Public employees	44-13-100(a)(2.1)(A), 47-2-332
	Other pensions needed for support	18-4-22, 44-13-100(a)(2)(E), 44-13-100(a)(2.1)(C)
personal property	Animals, crops, clothing, appliances, books, furnishings, household goods, musical instruments to $200 per item, $3,500 total	44-13-100(a)(4)
	Burial plot, in lieu of homestead	44-13-100(a)(1)
	Health aids	44-13-100(a)(10)
	Jewelry to $500	44-13-100(a)(5)
	Lost future earnings needed for support	44-13-100(a)(11)(E)
	Motor vehicles to $1,000	44-13-100(a)(3)
	Personal injury recoveries to $7,500	44-13-100(a)(11)(C)
	Wrongful death recoveries needed for support	44-13-100(a)(11)(B)
public benefits	Aid to blind	49-4-58
	Aid to disabled	49-4-84
	Crime victims' compensation	44-13-100(a)(11)(A)
	Local public assistance	44-13-100(a)(2)(A)
	Old age assistance	49-4-35
	Social Security	44-13-100(a)(2)(A)
	Unemployment compensation	44-13-100(a)(2)(A)
	Veterans' benefits	44-13-100(a)(2)(B)
	Workers' compensation	34-9-84
tools of trade	Implements, books & tools of trade to $500	44-13-100(a)(7)
wages	Minimum 75% of earned but unpaid wages for private & federal workers; bankruptcy judge may authorize more for low-income debtors	18-4-20, 18-4-21
wild card	$400 of any property	44-13-100(a)(6)
	Unused portion of homestead exemption, of any property	44-13-100(a)(6)

Hawaii

Federal Bankruptcy Exemptions available. All law references are to Hawaii Revised Statutes unless otherwise noted.

ASSET	EXEMPTION	LAW
homestead	Head of family or over 65 to $30,000; all others to $20,000; property cannot exceed 1 acre. Sale proceeds exempt for 6 months after sale.	36-651-91, 36-651-92, 36-651-96
	Property held as tenancy by the entirety may be exempt against debts owed by only one spouse	*Security Pacific Bank v. Chang*, 818 F.Supp. 1343 (D. Ha. 1993)
insurance	Annuity contract or endowment policy proceeds if beneficiary is insured's spouse, child or parent	24-431:10-232(b)
	Disability benefits	24-431:10-231
	Fraternal benefit society benefits	24-432:2-403
	Group life insurance policy or proceeds	24-431:10-233
	Life or health insurance policy for spouse or child	24-431:10-234
	Life insurance proceeds if clause prohibits proceeds from being used to pay beneficiary's creditors	24-431:10-D:112
miscellaneous	Property of business partnership	23-425-125
pensions	ERISA-qualified benefits deposited over 3 years before filing bankruptcy	36-651-124
	Firefighters	7-88-169
	Police officers	7-88-169
	Public officers & employees	7-88-91, 36-653-3
personal property	Appliances & furnishings needed	36-651-121(1)
	Books	36-651-121(1)
	Burial plot to 250 square feet plus tombstones, monuments & fencing on site	36-651-121(4)
	Clothing	36-651-121(1)
	Housing down payments for home in state project	20-359-104
	Jewelry & articles of adornment to $1,000	36-651-121(1)
	Motor vehicle to wholesale value of $1,000	36-651-121(2)
	Proceeds for sold or damaged exempt property; sale proceeds exempt only 6 months	36-651-121(5)
public benefits	Public assistance paid by Dept. of Health Services for work done in home or workshop	20-346-33
	Unemployment compensation	21-383-163
	Unemployment work relief funds to $60 per month	36-653-4
	Workers' compensation	21-386-57
tools of trade	Tools, implements, books, instruments, uniforms, furnishings, fishing boat, nets, motor vehicle & other personal property needed for livelihood	36-651-121(3)
wages	Unpaid wages due for services of past 31 days; after 31 days, 95% of 1st $100, 90% of 2nd $100, 80% of rest	36-651-121(6), 36-652-1
	Prisoner's wages held by Dept. of Public Safety	20-353-22
wild card	None	

Idaho

Federal Bankruptcy Exemptions not available. All law references are to Idaho Code.

ASSET	EXEMPTION	LAW
homestead	Real property or mobile home to $50,000; sale proceeds exempt for 6 months	55-1003, 55-1113
	Must record homestead exemption for property that is not yet occupied	55-1004
insurance	Annuity contract proceeds to $350 per month	41-1836
	Death or disability benefits	11-604(1)(a), 41-1834
	Fraternal benefit society benefits	41-3218
	Group life insurance benefits	41-1835
	Homeowners' insurance proceeds to amount of homestead exemption	55-1008
	Life insurance proceeds if clause prohibits proceeds from being used to pay beneficiary's creditors	41-1930
	Life insurance proceeds or avails for beneficiary other than the insured	11-604(d), 41-1833
	Medical, surgical or hospital care benefits	11-603(5)
miscellaneous	Alimony, child support needed for support	11-604(1)(b)
	Liquor licenses	23-514
	Property of business partnership	53-325
pensions *also see wages*	ERISA-qualified benefits	55-1011
	Firefighters	72-1422
	Police officers	50-1517
	Public employees	59-1317
	Other pensions needed for support; payments can't be mixed with other money	11-604(1)(e)
personal property	Appliances, furnishings, books, clothing, pets, musical instruments, 1 firearm, family portraits & sentimental heirlooms to $500 per item, $4,000 total	11-605(1)
	Building materials	45-514
	Burial plot	11-603(1)
	Crops cultivated by debtor on maximum 50 acres, to $1,000; includes water rights of 160 inches	11-605(6)
	Health aids needed	11-603(2)
	Jewelry to $250	11-605(2)
	Motor vehicle to $1,500	11-605(3)
	Personal injury recoveries needed for support	11-604(1)(c)
	Proceeds for damaged exempt property for 3 months after proceeds received	11-606
	Wrongful death recoveries needed for support	11-604(1)(c)
public benefits	Aid to blind, aged, disabled	56-223
	Federal, state & local public assistance	11-603(4)
	General assistance	56-223
	Social Security	11-603(3)
	Unemployment compensation	11-603(6)
	Veterans' benefits	11-603(3)
	Workers' compensation	72-802
tools of trade	Arms, uniforms & accoutrements that peace officer, national guard or military personnel is required to keep	11-605(5)
	Implements, books & tools of trade to $1,000	11-605(3)
wages	Minimum 75% of earned but unpaid wages, pension payments; bankruptcy judge may authorize more for low-income debtors	11-207
wild card	None	

Illinois

Federal Bankruptcy Exemptions not available. All law references are to Illinois Annotated Statutes.

ASSET	EXEMPTION	LAW
homestead	Real or personal property including a farm, lot & buildings, condo, co-op or mobile home to $7,500; sale proceeds exempt 1 year from sale	735-5/12-901, 735-5/12-906
	Spouse or child of deceased owner may claim homestead exemption	735-5/12-902
	Husband & wife may double	*First National Bank v. Mohr,* 515 N.E. 2d 1356 (App. Ct. Ill. 1988)
insurance	Fraternal benefit society benefits	215-5/299.1a
	Health or disability benefits	735-5/12-1001(g)(3)
	Homeowners proceeds if home destroyed, to $7,500	735-5/12-907
	Life insurance, annuity proceeds or cash value if beneficiary is insured's child, parent, spouse or other dependent	215-5/238
	Life insurance policy if beneficiary is insured's spouse or child	735-5/12-1001(f)
	Life insurance proceeds if clause prohibits proceeds from being used to pay beneficiary's creditors	215-5/238
	Life insurance proceeds needed for support	735-5/12-1001(f), (g)(3)
miscellaneous	Alimony, child support needed for support	735-5/12-1001(g)(4)
	Property of business partnership	805-205/25
pensions	Civil service employees	40-5/11-223
	County employees	40-5/9-228
	Disabled firefighters; widows & children of firefighters	40-5/22-230
	ERISA-qualified benefits	735-5/12-1006
	Firefighters	40-5/4-135, 40-5/6-213
	General assembly members	40-5/2-154
	House of correction employees	40-5/19-117
	Judges	40-5/18-161
	Municipal employees	40-5/7-217(a), 40-5/8-244
	Park employees	40-5/12-190
	Police officers	40-5/3-144.1, 40-5/5-218
	Public employees	735-5/12-1006
	Public library employees	40-5/19-218
	Sanitation district employees	40-5/13-808
	State employees	40-5/14-147
	State university employees	40-5/15-185
	Teachers	40-5/16-190, 40-5/17-151
personal property	Bible, family pictures, schoolbooks & needed clothing	735-5/12-1001(a)
	Health aids	735-5/12-1001(e)
	Motor vehicle to $1,200	735-5/12-1001(c)
	Personal injury recoveries to $7,500	735-5/12-1001(g)(4)
	Proceeds of sold exempt property	735-5/12-1001
	Title certificate for boat over 12 feet long	652-45/3A-7
	Wrongful death recoveries needed for support	735-5/12-1001(h)(2)
public benefits	Aid to aged, blind, disabled, public assistance	305-5/11-3
	Crime victims' compensation	735-5/12-1001(h)(1)
	Restitution payments on account of WWII relocation of Aleuts and Japanese Americans	735-5/12-1001(12)(h)(5)
	Social Security	735-5/12-1001(g)(1)
	Unemployment compensation	735-5/12-1001(g) (1), (3)
	Veterans' benefits	735-5/12-1001(g)(2)
	Workers' compensation	820-305/21
	Workers' occupational disease compensation	820-310/21
tools of trade	Implements, books & tools of trade to $750	735-5/12-1001(d)
wages	Minimum 85% of earned but unpaid wages; bankruptcy judge may authorize more for low-income debtors	740-170/4
wild card	$2,000 of any personal property	735-5/12-1001(b)
	Includes wages	*In re Johnson,* 57 B.R. 635 (N.D. Ill. 1986)

Indiana

Federal Bankruptcy Exemptions not available. All law references are to Indiana Statutes Annotated.

ASSET	EXEMPTION	LAW
homestead	Real or personal property used as residence	
also see wild card	to $7,500 (homestead plus personal property	
	—except health aids—can't exceed $10,000,	
	34-28-1(c))	34-2-28-1(a)(1)
	Property held as tenancy by the entirety	
	may be exempt against debts incurred by	
	only one spouse	34-2-28-1(a)(5)
insurance	Fraternal benefit society benefits	27-11-6-3
	Group life insurance policy	27-1-12-29
	Life insurance policy, proceeds, cash value	
	or avails if beneficiary is insured's spouse	
	or dependent	27-1-12-14
	Life insurance proceeds if clause prohibits	
	proceeds to be used to pay beneficiary's	
	creditors	27-2-5-1
	Mutual life or accident proceeds	27-8-3-23
miscellaneous	Property of business partnership	23-4-1-25
pensions	Firefighters	36-8-7-22,
		36-8-8-17
	Police officers (only benefits building up)	10-1-2-9, 36-8-8-17
	Public employees	5-10.3-8-9
	Public or private retirement benefits	34-2-28-1(a)(6)
	Sheriffs (only benefits building up)	36-8-10-19
	State teachers	21-6.1-5-17
personal	Health aids	34-2-28-1(a)(4)
property	$100 of any intangible personal property,	
also see wild card	except money owed to you	34-2-28-1(a)(3)
public benefits	Crime victims' compensation unless seeking	
	to discharge debt for treatment of injury	
	incurred during the crime	12-18-6-36
	Unemployment compensation	22-4-33-3
	Workers' compensation	22-3-2-17
tools of trade	National guard uniforms, arms & equipment	10-2-6-3
wages	Minimum 75% of earned but unpaid wages;	
	bankruptcy judge may authorize more for	
	low-income debtors	24-4.5-5-105
wild card	$4,000 of any real estate or tangible	
	personal property	34-2-28-1(a)(2)

Iowa

Federal Bankruptcy Exemptions not available. All law references are to Iowa Code Annotated.

ASSET	EXEMPTION	LAW
homestead	Real property or an apartment to an unlimited	
	value; property cannot exceed ¹/₂ acre in town	499A.18, 561.2,
	or city, 40 acres elsewhere	561.16
	May record homestead declaration	561.4
insurance	Accident, disability, health, illness or life	
	proceeds or avails to $15,000, paid to	
	surviving spouse, child or other dependent	627.6(6)
	Employee group insurance policy or proceeds	509.12
	Life insurance proceeds to $10,000, acquired	
	within 2 years of filing for bankruptcy, paid to	
	spouse, child or other dependent	627.6(6)
	Life insurance proceeds if clause prohibits	
	proceeds from being used to pay	
	beneficiary's creditors	508.32
miscellaneous	Alimony, child support needed for support	627.6(8)(d)
	Liquor licenses	123.38
	Property of business partnership	544.25
pensions	Disabled firefighters, police officers (only	
	payments being received)	410.11
also see wages	Federal government pension	
	(only payments being received)	627.8
	Firefighters	411.13
	Peace officers	97A.12
	Police officers	411.13
	Public employees	97B.39
	Other pensions needed for support	
	(only payments being received)	627.6(8)(e)
personal	Appliances, furnishings & household goods	
property	to $2,000 total	627.6(5)
	Bibles, books, portraits, pictures & paintings	
	to $1,000 total	627.6(3)
	Burial plot to 1 acre	627.6(4)
	Clothing to $1,000 plus receptacles to	
	hold clothing	627.6(1)
	Health aids	627.6(7)
	Motor vehicle, musical instruments & tax	
	refund to $5,000 total, no more than $1,000	
	from tax refund	627.6(9)
	Rifle or musket; shotgun	627.6(2)
	Wedding or engagement rings	627.6(1)
public benefits	Adopted child assistance	627.19
	Local public assistance	627.6(8)(a)
	Social Security	627.6(8)(a)
	Unemployment compensation	627.6(8)(a)
	Veterans' benefits	627.6(8)(b)
	Workers' compensation	627.13
tools of trade	Farming equipment; includes livestock, feed	
	to $10,000 (can't include car, *In re Van*	
	Pelt, 83 B.R. 617 (S.D. Iowa 1987))	627.6(11)
	Non-farming equipment to $10,000 (can't	
	include car, *In re Van Pelt,* 83 B.R. 617	
	(S.D. Iowa 1987))	627.6(10)
wages	Minimum 75% of earned but unpaid wages,	
	pension payments; bankruptcy judge may	
	authorize more for low-income debtors	642.21
wild card	$100 of any personal property, including cash	627.6(13)

Kansas

Federal Bankruptcy Exemptions not available. All law references are to Kansas Statutes Annotated unless otherwise noted.

ASSET	EXEMPTION	LAW
homestead	Real property or mobile home you occupy or intend to occupy to unlimited value; property cannot exceed 1 acre in town or city, 160 acres on farm	60-2301, Constitution 15-9
insurance	Fraternal life insurance benefits	40-414(a)
	Life insurance forfeiture value if file for bankruptcy over 1 year after policy issued	40-414(b)
	Life insurance proceeds if clause prohibits proceeds from being used to pay beneficiary's creditors	40-414(a)
miscellaneous	Liquor licenses	41-326
	Property of business partnership	56-325
pensions	Elected & appointed officials in cities with populations between 120,000 & 200,000	13-14,102
	ERISA-qualified benefits	60-2308(b)
	Federal government pension needed for support & paid within 3 months of filing for bankruptcy (only payments being received)	60-2308(a)
	Firefighters	12-5005(e), 14-10a10
	Judges	20-2618
	Police officers	12-5005(e), 13-14a10
	Public employees	74-4923, 74-49,105
	State highway patrol officers	74-4978g
	State school employees	72-5526
personal property	Burial plot or crypt	60-2304(d)
	Clothing to last 1 year	60-2304(a)
	Food & fuel to last 1 year	60-2304(a)
	Funeral plan prepayments	16-310(d)
	Furnishings & household equipment	60-2304(a)
	Jewelry & articles of adornment to $1,000	60-2304(b)
	Motor vehicle to $20,000; if designed or equipped for disabled person, no limit	60-2304(c)
public benefits	Crime victims' compensation	74-7313(d)
	General assistance, social welfare	39-717
	Unemployment compensation	44-718(c)
	Workers' compensation	44-514
tools of trade	Books, documents, furniture, instruments, equipment, breeding stock, seed, grain & stock to $7,500 total	60-2304(e)
	National Guard uniforms, arms & equipment	48-245
wages	Minimum 75% of earned but unpaid wages; bankruptcy judge may authorize more for low-income debtors	60-2310
wild card	None	

Kentucky

Federal Bankruptcy Exemptions not available. All law references are to Kentucky Revised Statutes.

ASSET	EXEMPTION	LAW
homestead	Real or personal property used as residence to $5,000; sale proceeds exempt	427.060, 427.090
insurance	Annuity contract proceeds to $350 per month	304.14-330
	Cooperative life or casualty insurance benefits	427.110(1)
	Fraternal benefit society benefits	427.110(2)
	Group life insurance proceeds	304.14-320
	Health or disability benefits	304.14-310
	Life insurance policy if beneficiary is a married woman	304.14-340
	Life insurance proceeds if clause prohibits proceeds from being used to pay beneficiary's creditors	304.14-350
	Life insurance proceeds or cash value if beneficiary is someone other than insured	304.14-300
miscellaneous	Alimony, child support needed for support	427.150(1)
	Property of business partnership	362.270
pensions	Firefighters, police officers	67A.620, 95.878, 427.120, 427.125
	IRAs	In re Worthington, 28 B.R. 736 (W.D. Ky. 1983)
	State employees	61.690
	Teachers	161.700
	Urban county government employees	67A.350
	Other pensions	427.150(2)(e), (f)
personal property	Burial plot to $5,000, in lieu of homestead	427.060
	Clothing, jewelry, articles of adornment & furnishings to $3,000 total	427.010(1)
	Health aids	427.010(1)
	Lost earnings payments needed for support	427.150(2)(d)
	Medical expenses paid & reparation benefits received under motor vehicle reparation law	304.39-260
	Motor vehicle to $2,500	427.010(1)
	Personal injury recoveries to $7,500 (not to include pain & suffering or pecuniary loss)	427.150(2)(c)
	Wrongful death recoveries for person you depended on, needed for support	427.150(2)(b)
public benefits	Aid to blind, aged, disabled, public assistance	205.220
	Crime victims' compensation	427.150(2)(a)
	Unemployment compensation	341.470
	Workers' compensation	342.180
tools of trade	Library, office equipment, instruments & furnishings of minister, attorney, physician, surgeon, chiropractor, veterinarian or dentist to $1,000	427.040
	Motor vehicle of mechanic, mechanical or electrical equipment servicer, minister, attorney, physician, surgeon, chiropractor, veterinarian or dentist to $2,500	427.030
	Tools, equipment, livestock & poultry of farmer to $3,000	427.010(1)
	Tools of non-farmer to $300	427.030
wages	Minimum 75% of earned but unpaid wages; bankruptcy judge may authorize more for low-income debtors	427.010(2), (3)
wild card	$1,000 of any property	427.160

Louisiana

Federal Bankruptcy Exemptions not available. All law references are to Louisiana Revised Statutes Annotated unless otherwise noted.

ASSET	EXEMPTION	LAW
homestead	Property you occupy to $15,000; cannot exceed 160 acres on 1 tract, or on 2 or more tracts if there's a home on 1 tract and field, garden or pasture on others (husband & wife may not double)	20:1
	Spouse or child of deceased owner may claim homestead exemption; spouse given home in divorce gets homestead	
insurance	Fraternal benefit society benefits	22:558
	Group insurance policies or proceeds	22:649
	Health, accident or disability proceeds or avails	22:646
	Life insurance proceeds or avails; if policy issued within 9 months of filing, exempt only to $35,000	22:647
miscellaneous	Property of minor child	13:3881A(3), Civil 223
pensions	Gratuitous payments to employee or heirs whenever paid	20:33(2)
	ERISA-qualified benefits if contributions made over 1 year before filing for bankruptcy	13:3881D(1), 20:33(4)
personal property	Arms, military accoutrements, bedding, linens & bedroom furniture, chinaware, glassware, utensils, silverware (non-sterling), clothing, family portraits, musical instruments, heating & cooling equipment, living room & dining room furniture, poultry, fowl, 1 cow, household pets, pressing irons, sewing machine, refrigerator, freezer, stove, washer & dryer	13:3881A(4)
	Cemetery plot, monuments	8:313
	Engagement & wedding rings to $5,000	13:3881A(5)
public benefits	Aid to blind, aged, disabled, public assistance	46:111
	Crime victims' compensation	46:1811
	Unemployment compensation	23:1693
	Workers' compensation	23:1205
tools of trade	Tools, instruments, books, pickup truck (maximum 3 tons) or non-luxury auto & utility trailer, needed to work	13:3881A(2)
wages	Minimum 75% of earned but unpaid wages; bankruptcy judge may authorize more for low-income debtors	13:3881A(1)
wild card	None	

Maine

Federal Bankruptcy Exemptions not available. All law references are to Maine Revised Statutes Annotated.

ASSET	EXEMPTION	LAW
homestead	Real or personal property (including cooperative) used as residence to $12,500; if debtor over age 60 or physically or mentally disabled, $60,000 (joint debtors may double)	14-4422(1)
insurance	Annuity proceeds to $450 per month	24-A-2431
	Disability or health proceeds, benefits or avails	14-4422(13)A & C24-A-2429
	Fraternal benefit society benefits	24-A-4118
	Group health or life policy or proceeds	24-A-2430
	Life, endowment, annuity or accident policy, proceeds or avails	14-4422(14)C, 24-A-2428
	Life insurance policy, interest, loan value or accrued dividends for policy from person you depended on, to $4,000	14-4422(11)
	Unmatured life insurance policy, except credit insurance policy	14-4422(10)
miscellaneous	Alimony & child support needed for support	14-4422(13)D
	Property of business partnership	31-305
pensions	ERISA-qualified benefits	14-4422(13)E
	Judges	4-1203
	Legislators	3-703
	State employees	5-17054
personal property	Animals, crops, musical instruments, books, clothing, furnishings, household goods, appliances to $200 per item	14-4422(3)
	Balance due on repossessed goods; total amount financed can't exceed $2,000	9-A-5-103
	Burial plot in lieu of homestead exemption	14-4422(1)
	Cooking stove; furnaces & stoves for heat	14-4422(6)A & B
	Food to last 6 months	14-4422(7)A
	Fuel not to exceed 10 cords of wood, 5 tons of coal or 1,000 gallons of petroleum	14-4422(6)C
	Health aids	14-4422(12)
	Jewelry to $750; no limit for 1 wedding & 1 engagement ring	14-4422(4)
	Lost earnings payments needed for support	14-4422(14)E
	Military clothes, arms & equipment	37-B-262
	Motor vehicle to $2,500	14-4422(2)
	Personal injury recoveries to $12,500, not to include pain & suffering	14-4422(14)D
	Seeds, fertilizers & feed to raise & harvest food for 1 season	14-4422(7)B
	Tools & equipment to raise & harvest food	14-4422(7)C
	Wrongful death recoveries needed for support	14-4422(14)B
public benefits	Crime victims' compensation	14-4422(14)A
	Public assistance	22-3753
	Social Security	14-4422(13)A
	Unemployment compensation	14-4422(13)A & C
	Veterans' benefits	14-4422(13)B
	Workers' compensation	39-67
tools of trade *also see personal property*	Boat not exceeding 5 tons used in commercial fishing	14-4422(9)
	Books, materials & stock to $5,000	14-4422(5)
	1 of each type of farm implement needed to harvest & raise crops	14-4422(8)
wages	None	
wild card	Unused portion of homestead exemption to $6,000 of animals, crops, musical instruments, books, clothing, furnishings, household goods, appliances, tools of the trade and personal injury recoveries	14-4422(15)
	$400 of any property	14-4422(15)

Maryland

Federal Bankruptcy Exemptions not available. All law references are to Annotated Code of Maryland unless otherwise noted.

ASSET	EXEMPTION	LAW
homestead	None, however, property held as tenancy by the entirety may be exempt against debts owed by only one spouse	*In re Sefren,* 41 B.R. 747 (D. Md. 1984)
insurance	Disability or health benefits, including court awards, arbitrations & settlements	Courts & Jud. Proceedings 11-504(b)(2)
	Fraternal benefit society benefits	48A-328, Estates & Trusts 8-115
	Life insurance or annuity contract proceeds or avails if beneficiary is insured's dependent, child or spouse	48A-385, Estates & Trusts 8-115
	Medical benefits deducted from wages	Commercial 15-601.1
miscellaneous	Property of business partnership	Corporation 9-502
pensions	Deceased Baltimore police officers (only benefits building up)	73B-49
	ERISA-qualified benefits, except IRAs	Courts & Jud. Proceedings 11-504(h)
	State employees	73B-17, 73B-125
	State police	88B-60
	Teachers	73B-96, 73B-152
personal property	Appliances, furnishings, household goods, books, pets & clothing to $500 total	Courts & Jud. Proceedings 11-504(b)(4)
	Burial plot	23-164
	Health aids	Courts & Jud. Proceedings 11-504(b)(3)
	Lost future earnings recoveries	Courts & Jud. Proceedings 11-504(b)(2)
public benefits	Crime victims' compensation	26A-13
	General assistance	88A-73
	Unemployment compensation	Labor & Employment 8-106
	Workers' compensation	Labor & Employment 9-732
tools of trade	Clothing, books, tools, instruments & appliances to $2,500; can't include car (*In re Chapman,* 68 B.R. 745 (D. Md. 1986))	Courts & Jud. Proceedings 11-504(b)(1)
wages	Earned but unpaid wages, the greater of 75% or $145 per week; in Kent, Caroline, & Queen Anne's of Worcester Counties, the greater of 75% of actual wages or 30% of federal minimumwage	Commercial 15-601.1
wild card	$5,500 of any property	Courts & Jud. Proceedings 11-504(b)(5), (f)

Massachusetts

Federal Bankruptcy Exemptions available. All law references are to Massachusetts General Laws Annotated.

ASSET	EXEMPTION	LAW
homestead	Property you occupy or intend to occupy to $100,000; if over 65 or disabled, $200,000 (joint owners may not double)	188-1, 188-1A
	Must record homestead declaration before filing bankruptcy	188-2
	Spouse or child of deceased owner may claim homestead exemption	188-4
	Property held as tenancy by the entirety may be exempt against non-necessity debts	209-1
insurance	Disability benefits to $400 per week	175-110A
	Fraternal benefit society benefits	176-22
	Group annuity policy or proceeds	175-132C
	Group life insurance policy	175-135
	Life or endowment policy, proceeds or cash value	175-125
	Life insurance annuity contract which says it's exempt	175-125
	Life insurance policy if beneficiary is married woman	175-126
	Life insurance proceeds if clause prohibits proceeds from being used to pay beneficiary's creditors	175-119A
	Medical malpractice self-insurance	175F-15
miscellaneous	Property of business partnership	108A-25
pensions	ERISA-qualified benefits	235-34A, 246-28
	Private retirement benefits	32-41
also see wages	Public employees	32-19
	Savings bank employees	168-41, 168-44
personal property	Bank deposits to $125; food or cash for food to $300	235-34
	Beds, bedding & heating unit; clothing needed	235-34
	Bibles & books to $200 total; sewing machine to $200	235-34
	Burial plots, tombs & church pew	235-34
	Cash for fuel, heat, water or light to $75 per month	235-34
	Cash to $200 per month for rent, in lieu of homestead	235-34
	Cooperative association shares to $100	235-34
	2 cows, 12 sheep, 2 swine, 4 tons of hay	235-34
	Furniture to $3,000; motor vehicle to $750	235-34
	Moving expenses for eminent domain	79-6A
	Trust company, bank or credit union deposits to $500	246-28A
public benefits	Aid to aged, disabled	235-34
	Public assistance	118-10
	Unemployment compensation	151A-36
	Veterans' benefits	115-5
	Workers' compensation	152-47
tools of trade	Arms, accoutrements & uniforms you're required to keep	235-34
	Boats, fishing tackle & nets of fisherman to $500	235-34
	Materials you designed & procured to $500	235-34
	Tools, implements & fixtures to $500 total	235-34
wages	Earned but unpaid wages to $125 per week	246-28
wild card	None	

Michigan

Federal Bankruptcy Exemptions available. All law references are to Michigan Compiled Laws Annotated unless otherwise noted.

ASSET	EXEMPTION	LAW
homestead	Real property including condo to $3,500; property cannot exceed 1 lot in town, village,city, or 40 acres elsewhere	559.214, 600.6023(1)(h), (i), 600.6023(3), 600.6027
	Spouse or child of deceased owner may claim homestead exemption; property held as tenancy by the entirety may be exempt against debts owed by only one spouse	*SNB Bank & Trust v. Kensey*, 378 N.W. 2d 594 (Ct. App. Mich. 1985)
insurance	Disability, mutual life or health benefits	600.6023(1)(f)
	Fraternal benefit society benefits	500.8181
	Life, endowment or annuity proceeds if clause prohibits proceeds from being used to pay beneficiary's creditors	500.4054
miscellaneous	Property of business partnership	449.25
pensions	Firefighters, police officers	38.559(6)
	ERISA-qualified benefits	600.6023(1)(k)
	IRAs	600.6023(1)(l)
	Judges	38.826
	Legislators	38.1057
	Probate judges	38.927
	Public school employees	38.1346
	State employees	38.40
personal property	Appliances, utensils, books, furniture & household goods to $1,000 total	600.6023(1)(b)
	Building & loan association shares to $1,000 par value, in lieu of homestead	600.6023(1)(g)
	Burial plots, cemeteries; church pew, slip, seat	600.6023(1)(c)
	Clothing; family pictures	600.6023(1)(a)
	2 cows, 100 hens, 5 roosters, 10 sheep, 5 swine; hay & grain to last 6 months if you're a head of household	600.6023(1)(d)
	Food & fuel to last 6 months if you're a head of household	600.6023(1)(a)
public benefits	Crime victims' compensation	18.362
	Social welfare benefits	400.63
	Unemployment compensation	421.30
	Veterans' benefits for Korean War veterans	35.977
	Veterans' benefits for Vietnam veterans	35.1027
	Veterans' benefits for WWII veterans	35.926
	Workers' compensation	418.821
tools of trade	Arms & accoutrements you're required to keep	600.6023(1)(a)
	Tools, implements, materials, stock, apparatus, team, motor vehicle, horse & harness to $1,000 total	600.6023(1)(e)
wages	60% of earned but unpaid wages for head of household; else 40%; head of household may keep at least $15 per week plus $2 per week per non-spouse dependent; others may keep at least $10 per week	600.5311
wild card	None	

Minnesota

Federal Bankruptcy Exemptions available. All law references are to Minnesota Statutes Annotated.Note: Section 550.37(4)(a) requires that certain exemptions be adjusted for inflation on July 1 of even-numbered years. The below exemptions include all changes through July 1, 1994. For additional information, contact the Minnesota Department of Commerce at (612) 296-2297.

ASSET	EXEMPTION	LAW
homestead	Real property, mobile home or manufactured home to $200,000 or, if the homestead is used primarily for agricultural purposes, $500,000; cannot exceed ½ acre in city or 160 acres elsewhere	510.01, 510.02, 550.37 subd. 12
insurance	Accident or disability proceeds	550.39
	Fraternal benefit society benefits	64B.18
	Life insurance proceeds if beneficiary is spouse or child of insured to $32,000, plus $8,000 per dependent	550.37 subd. 10
	Police, fire or beneficiary association benefits	550.37 subd. 11
	Unmatured life insurance contract dividends, interest or loan value to $6,400 if insured is debtor or someone debtor depends on	550.37 subd. 23
miscellaneous	Earnings of minor child	550.37 subd. 15
	Property of business partnership	323.24
pensions	ERISA-qualified benefits needed for support, which do not exceed $48,000 in present value	550.37 subd. 24
	IRAs needed for support, which do not exceed $48,000 in present value	550.37 subd. 24
	Private retirement benefits (only benefits building up)	181B.16
	Public employees	353.15
	State employees	352.96
	State troopers	352B.071
personal property	Appliances, furniture, radio, phonographs & TV to $7,200 total	550.37 subd. 4(b)
	Bible, books & musical instruments	550.37 subd. 2
	Burial plot; church pew or seat	550.37 subd. 3
	Clothing (includes watch), food & utensils	550.37 subd. 4(a)
	Motor vehicle to $3,200 (up to $32,000 if vehicle has been modified for disability)	550.37 subd. 12(a)
	Personal injury recoveries	550.37 subd. 22
	Proceeds for damaged exempt property	550.37 subds. 9, 16
	Wrongful death recoveries	550.37 subd. 22
public benefits	Crime victims' compensation	611A.60
	Supplemental assistance, general assistance, supplemental security income	550.37 subd. 14
	Unemployment compensation	268.17 subd. 2
	Veterans' benefits	550.38
	Workers' compensation	176.175
tools of trade *total tools of trade (except teaching materials) can't exceed $13,000*	Farm machines, implements, livestock, farm produce & crops of farmers to $13,000 total	550.37 subd. 5
	Teaching materials (including books, chemical apparatus) of public school teacher	550.37 subd. 8
	Tools, implements, machines, instruments, furniture, stock in trade & library to $8,000 total	550.37 subd. 6
wages	Earned but unpaid wages, paid within 6 months of returning to work, if you received welfare in past	550.37 subd. 13
	Minimum 75% of earned but unpaid wages	571.922
	Wages deposited into bank accounts for 20 days after depositing	550.37 subd. 13
	Wages of released inmates paid within 6 months of release	550.37 subd. 14
wild card	None	

Note: Some courts have held "unlimited" exemptions (such as fraternal benefit society benefits, musical instruments, personal injury recoveries) unconstitutional under the Minnesota Constitution which allows debtors to exempt only a reasonable amount of property. See *In re Tveten*, 402 N.W. 2d 551 (Minn. 1987) and *In re Medill*, 119 B.R. 685, (D. Minn. 1990).

Mississippi

Federal Bankruptcy Exemptions not available. All law references are to Mississippi Code.

ASSET	EXEMPTION	LAW
homestead	Property you occupy unless over 60 & married or widowed, to $75,000; property cannot exceed 160 acres; sale proceeds exempt	85-3-1(b)(i), 85-3-21, 85-3-23
	May file homestead declaration	85-3-27, 85-3-31
insurance	Disability benefits	85-3-1(b)(ii)
	Fraternal benefit society benefits	83-29-39
	Homeowners' insurance proceeds to $75,000	85-3-23
	Life insurance proceeds if clause prohibits proceeds from being used to pay beneficiary's creditors	83-7-5
miscellaneous	Property of business partnership	79-12-49
pensions	ERISA-qualified benefits deposited over 1 year before filing bankruptcy	85-3-1(b)(iii)
	Firefighters	21-29-257
	Highway patrol officers	25-13-31
	IRAs deposited over 1 year before filing bankruptcy	85-3-1(b)(iii)
	Keoghs deposited over 1 year before filing bankruptcy	85-3-1(b)(iii)
	Private retirement benefits to extent tax-deferred	71-1-43
	Police officers	21-29-257
	Public employees retirement & disability benefits	25-11-129
	State employees	25-14-5
	Teachers	25-11-201(1)(d)
personal property	Tangible personal property of any kind to $10,000	85-3-1(a)
	Personal injury judgments to $10,000	85-3-17
	Proceeds for exempt property	85-3-1(b)(i)
public benefits	Assistance to aged	43-9-19
	Assistance to blind	43-3-71
	Assistance to disabled	43-29-15
	Crime victims' compensation	99-41-23
	Social Security	25-11-129
	Unemployment compensation	71-5-539
	Workers' compensation	71-3-43
tools of trade	See personal property	
wages	Earned but unpaid wages owed for 30 days; after 30 days, minimum 75% (bankruptcy judge may authorize more for low-income debtors)	85-3-4
wild card	See personal property	

Missouri

Federal Bankruptcy Exemptions not available. All law references are to Annotated Missouri Statutes unless otherwise noted.

ASSET	EXEMPTION	LAW
homestead	Real property to $8,000 or mobile home to $1,000 (joint owners may not double)	513.430(6), 513.475
	Property held as tenancy by the entirety may be exempt against debts owed by only one spouse	In re Anderson, 12 B.R. 483 (W.D. Mo. 1981)
insurance	Assessment or insurance premium proceeds	377.090
	Disability or illness benefits	513.430(10)(c)
	Fraternal benefit society benefits to $5,000, bought over 6 months before filing	513.430(8)
	Life insurance dividends, loan value or interest to $5,000, bought over 6 months before filing	513.430(8)
	Life insurance proceeds if policy owned by a woman & insures her husband	376.530
	Life insurance proceeds if policy owned by unmarried woman & insures her father or brother	376.550
	Stipulated insurance premiums	377.330
	Unmatured life insurance policy	513.430(7)
miscellaneous	Alimony, child support to $500 per month	513.430(10)(d)
	Property of business partnership	358.250
pensions	Employees of cities with 100,000 or more people	71.207
	ERISA-qualified benefits needed for support (only payments being received)	513.430(10)(e)
	Firefighters	87.090, 87.365, 87.485
	Highway & transportation employees	104.250
	Police department employees	86.190, 86.353, 86.493, 86.780
	Public officers & employees	70.695
	State employees	104.540
	Teachers	169.090
personal property	Appliances, household goods, furnishings, clothing, books, crops, animals & musical instruments to $1,000 total	513.430(1)
	Burial grounds to 1 acre or $100	214.190
	Health aids	513.430(9)
	Jewelry to $500	513.430(2)
	Motor vehicle to $1,000	513.430(5)
	Personal injury causes of action	In re Mitchell, 73 B.R. 93 (E.D. Mo. 1987)
	Wrongful death recoveries for person you depended on	513.430(11)
public benefits	Public assistance	513.430(10)(a)
	Social Security	513.430(10)(a)
	Unemployment compensation	288.380(10)(l), 513.430(10)(c)
	Veterans' benefits	513.430(10)b)
	Workers' compensation	287.260
tools of trade	Implements, books & tools of trade to $2,000	513.430(4)
wages	Minimum 75% of earned but unpaid wages (90% for head of family); bankruptcy judge may authorize more for low-income debtors	525.030
	Wages of servant or common laborer to $90	513.470
wild card	$1,250 of any property if head of family, else $400; head of family may claim additional $250 per child	513.430(3), 513.440

Montana

Federal Bankruptcy Exemptions not available. All law references are to Montana Code Annotated.

ASSET	EXEMPTION	LAW
homestead	Real property or mobile home you occupy to $60,000; sale, condemnation or insurance proceeds exempt 18 months	70-32-104, 70-32-201, 70-32-216
	Must record homestead declaration before filing for bankruptcy	70-32-105
insurance	Annuity contract proceeds to $350 per month	33-15-514
	Disability or illness proceeds, avails or benefits	25-13-608(1)(d), 33-15-513
	Fraternal benefit society benefits	33-7-522
	Group life insurance policy or proceeds	33-15-512
	Hail insurance benefits	80-2-245
	Life insurance proceeds if clause prohibits proceeds from being used to pay beneficiary's creditors	33-20-120
	Medical, surgical or hospital care benefits	25-13-608(1)(e)
	Unmatured life insurance contracts to $4,000	25-13-609(4)
miscellaneous	Alimony, child support	25-13-608(1)(f)
	Property of business partnership	35-10-502
pensions	ERISA-qualified benefits deposited over 1 year before filing bankruptcy in excess of 15% of debtor's yearly income	31-2-106
	Firefighters	19-11-612(1), 19-13-1004
	Game wardens	19-8-805(2)
	Highway patrol officers	19-6-705(2)
	Judges	19-5-704
	Police officers	19-9-1006, 19-10-504(1)
	Public employees	19-3-105(1)
	Sheriffs	19-7-705(2)
	Teachers	19-4-706(2)
	University system employees	19-21-212
personal property	Appliances, household furnishings, goods, animals with feed, crops, musical instruments, books, firearms, sporting goods, clothing & jewelry to $600 per item, $4,500 total	25-13-609(1)
	Burial plot	25-13-608(1)(g)
	Cooperative association shares to $500 value	35-15-404
	Health aids	25-13-608(1)(a)
	Motor vehicle to $1,200	25-13-609(2)
	Proceeds for damaged or lost exempt property for 6 months after received	25-13-610
public benefits	Aid to aged, disabled	53-2-607
	Crime victims' compensation	53-9-129
	Local public assistance	25-13-608(1)(b)
	Silicosis benefits	39-73-110
	Social Security	25-13-608(1)(b)
	Subsidized adoption payments	53-2-607
	Unemployment compensation	31-2-106(2), 39-51-3105
	Veterans' benefits	25-13-608(1)(c)
	Vocational rehabilitation to the blind	53-2-607
	Workers' compensation	39-71-743
tools of trade	Implements, books & tools of trade to $3,000	25-13-609(3)
	Uniforms, arms, accoutrements needed to carry out government functions	25-13-613(b)
wages	Minimum 75% of earned but unpaid wages; bankruptcy judge may authorize more for low-income debtors	25-13-614
wild card	None	

Nebraska

Federal Bankruptcy Exemptions not available. All law references are to Revised Statutes of Nebraska.

ASSET	EXEMPTION	LAW
homestead	$12,500; cannot exceed 2 lots in city or village, 160 acres elsewhere; sale proceeds exempt 6 months after sale	40-101, 40-111, 40-113
	May record homestead declaration	40-105
insurance	Fraternal benefit society benefits to $10,000 loan value unless beneficiary convicted of a crime related to the benefits	44-1089
	Life insurance or annuity contract proceeds to $10,000 loan value	44-371
miscellaneous	Property of business partnership	67-325
pensions *also see wages*	County employees	23-2322
	ERISA-qualified benefits needed for support	25-1563.01
	Military disability benefits to $2,000	25-1559
	School employees	79-1060, 79-1552
	State employees	84-1324
personal property	Burial plot	12-517
	Clothing needed	25-1556
	Crypts, lots, tombs, niches, vaults	12-605
	Food & fuel to last 6 months	25-1556
	Furniture & kitchen utensils to $1,500	25-1556
	Perpetual care funds	12-511
	Personal injury recoveries	25-1563.02
	Personal possessions	25-1556
public benefits	Aid to disabled, blind, aged, public assistance	68-1013
	Unemployment compensation	48-647
	Workers' compensation	48-149
tools of trade	Equipment or tools including a vehicle used in/or for commuting to principal place of business to $2,400	25-1556
	Husband & wife may double	*In re Keller*, 50 B.R. 23 (D. Neb. 1985)
wages	Minimum 85% of earned but unpaid wages or pension payments for head of family; 75% for all others; bankruptcy judge may authorize more for low-income debtors	25-1558
wild card	$2,500 of any personal property, except wages, in lieu of homestead	25-1552

Nevada

Federal Bankruptcy Exemptions not available. All law references are to Nevada Revised Statutes Annotated.

ASSET	EXEMPTION	LAW
homestead	Real property or mobile home to $125,000 (husband & wife may not double)	21.090(1)(m), 115.010
	Must record homestead declaration before filing for bankruptcy	115.020
insurance	Annuity contract proceeds to $350 per month	687B.290
	Fraternal benefit society benefits	695A.220
	Group life or health policy or proceeds	687B.280
	Health proceeds or avails	687B.270
	Life insurance policy or proceeds if annual premiums not over $1,000	21.090(1)(k)
	Life insurance proceeds if you're not the insured	687B.260
miscellaneous	Property of business partnership	87.250
pensions	ERISA-qualified benefits to $100,000	21.090(1)(q)
	Public employees	286.670
personal property	Appliances, household goods, furniture, home & yard equipment to $3,000 total	21.090(1)(b)
	Books to $1,500	21.090(1)(a)
	Burial plot purchase money held in trust	452.550
	Funeral service contract money held in trust	689.700
	Health aids	21.090(1)(p)
	Keepsakes & pictures	21.090(1)(a)
	Metal-bearing ores, geological specimens, art curiosities or paleontological remains; must be arranged, classified, catalogued & numbered in reference books	21.100
	Motor vehicle to $4,500; no limit if vehicle equipped to provide mobility for disabled person	21.090(1)(f), (o)
	One gun	21.090(1)(i)
public benefits	Aid to blind, aged, disabled, public assistance	422.291
	Industrial insurance (workers' compensation)	616.550
	Unemployment compensation	612.710
	Vocational rehabilitation benefits	615.270
tools of trade	Arms, uniforms & accoutrements you're required to keep	21.090(1)(j)
	Cabin or dwelling of miner or prospector; cars, implements & appliances for mining & mining claim you work to $4,500 total	21.090(1)(e)
	Farm trucks, stock, tools, equipment & seed to $4,500	21.090(1)(c)
	Library, equipment, supplies, tools & materials to $4,500	21.090(1)(d)
wages	Minimum 75% of earned but unpaid wages; bankruptcy judge may authorize more for low-income debtors	21.090(1)(g)
wild card	None	

New Hampshire

Federal Bankruptcy Exemptions available. All law references are to New Hampshire Revised Statutes Annotated.

ASSET	EXEMPTION	LAW
homestead	Real property or manufactured housing (and the land it's on if you own it) to $30,000	480:1
insurance	Firefighters' aid insurance	402:69
	Fraternal benefit society benefits	418:24
	Homeowners' insurance proceeds to $5,000	512:21(VIII)
miscellaneous	Child support	161-C-11
	Jury, witness fees	512:21(VI)
	Property of business partnership	304A:25
	Wages of minor child	512:21(III)
pensions	Federally created pension (only benefits building up)	512:21(IV)
	Firefighters	102:23
	Police officers	103:18
	Public employees	100A:26
personal property	Automobile to $4,000	511:2(XVI)
	Beds, bedsteads, bedding & cooking utensils needed	511:2(II)
	Bibles & books to $800	511:2(VIII)
	Burial plot, lot	511:2(XIV)
	Church pew	511:2(XV)
	Clothing needed	511:2(I)
	Cooking & heating stoves, refrigerator	511:2(IV)
	Cow, 6 sheep or fleece; 4 tons of hay	511:2(XI), (XII)
	Domestic fowl to $300	511:2(XIII)
	Food & fuel to $400	511:2(VI)
	Furniture to $3,500	511:2(III)
	Hog, pig or pork (if already slaughtered)	511:2(X)
	Jewelry to $500	511:2(XVII)
	Proceeds for lost or destroyed exempt property	512:21(VIII)
	Sewing machine	511:2(V)
public benefits	Aid to blind, aged, disabled, public assistance	167:25
	Unemployment compensation	282A:159
	Workers' compensation	281A:52
tools of trade	Tools of your occupation to $5,000	511:2(IX)
	Uniforms, arms & equipment of military member	511:2(VII)
	Yoke of oxen or horse needed for farming or teaming	511:2(XII)
wages	Earned but unpaid wages; judge decides amount exempt based on a percentage of the federal minimum wage	512:21(II)
	Earned but unpaid wages of spouse	512:21(III)
wild card	$1,000 of any property	511:2(XVIII)
	Unused portion of automobile, bibles & books, food & fuel, furniture, jewelry and tools of occupation exemptions to $7,000 in any property	511:2(XVIII)

New Jersey

Federal Bankruptcy Exemptions available. All law references are to New Jersey Statutes Annotated.

ASSET	EXEMPTION	LAW
homestead	None	
insurance	Annuity contract proceeds to $500 per month	17B:24-7
	Disability or death benefits for military member	38A:4-8
	Disability, death, medical or hospital benefits for civil defense workers	App. A:9-57.6
	Fraternal benefit society benefits	17:44A-19
	Group life or health policy or proceeds	17B:24-9
	Health or disability benefits	17:18-12, 17B:24-8
	Life insurance proceeds if clause prohibits proceeds from being used to pay beneficiary's creditors	17B:24-10
	Life insurance proceeds or avails if you're not the insured	17B:24-6b
miscellaneous	Property of business partnership	42:1-25
pensions	Alcohol beverage control officers	43:8A-20
	City boards of health employees	43:18-12
	Civil defense workers	App. A:9-57.6
	County employees	43:10-57, 43:10-105
	ERISA-qualified benefits	43:13-9
	Firefighters, police officers, traffic officers	43:16-7, 43:16A-17
	IRAs	In re Yuhas, No. 96-5146 (3rd Cir. 1/22/97)
	Judges	43:6A-41
	Municipal employees	43:13-44
	Prison employees	43:7-13
	Public employees	43:15A-53
	School district employees	18A:66-116
	State police	53:5A-45
	Street & water department employees	43:19-17
	Teachers	18A:66-51
	Trust containing personal property created pursuant to federal tax law unless conveyance into trust done fraudulently or debt is for child support or alimony	25:2-1
personal property	Goods & chattels, personal property & stock or interest in corporations to $1,000 total	2A:17-19
	Burial plots	8A:5-10
	Clothing	2A:17-19
	Furniture & household goods to $1,000	2A:26-4
public benefits	Crime victims' compensation	52:4B-30
	Old-age, permanent disability assistance	44:7-35
	Unemployment compensation	43:21-53
	Workers' compensation	34:15-29
tools of trade	None	
wages	90% of earned but unpaid wages if income under $7,500; if income over $7,500, judge decides amount that is exempt	2A:17-56
	Wages or allowances received by military personnel	38A:4-8
wild card	None	

New Mexico

Federal Bankruptcy Exemptions available. All law references are to New Mexico Statutes Annotated.

ASSET	EXEMPTION	LAW
homestead	Married, widowed or supporting another may claim real property to $30,000 (joint owners may double)	42-10-9
insurance	Benevolent association benefits to $5,000	42-10-4
	Fraternal benefit society benefits	59A-44-18
	Life, accident, health or annuity benefits, withdrawal or cash value, if beneficiary is a New Mexican citizen	42-10-3
miscellaneous	Ownership interest in unincorporated association	53-10-2
	Property of business partnership	54-1-25
pensions	Pension or retirement benefits	42-10-1, 42-10-2
	Public school employees	22-11-42A
personal property	Books, health equipment & furniture	42-10-1, 42-10-2
	Building materials	48-2-15
	Clothing	42-10-1, 42-10-2
	Cooperative association shares, minimum amount needed to be member	53-4-28
	Jewelry to $2,500	42-10-1, 42-10-2
	Materials, tools & machinery to dig, torpedo, drill, complete, operate or repair oil line, gas well or pipeline	70-4-12
	Motor vehicle to $4,000	42-10-1, 42-10-2
public benefits	Crime victims' compensation paid before 7/1/93	31-22-15
	General assistance	27-2-21
	Occupational disease disablement benefits	52-3-37
	Unemployment compensation	51-1-37
	Workers' compensation	52-1-52
tools of trade	$1,500	42-10-1, 42-10-2
wages	Minimum 75% of earned but unpaid wages; bankruptcy judge may authorize more for low-income debtors	35-12-7
wild card	$500 of any personal property	42-10-1
	$2,000 of any property, in lieu of homestead	42-10-10

New York

Federal Bankruptcy Exemptions not available. All law references are to Consolidated Laws of New York, Civil Practice Law & Rules, unless otherwise noted.

ASSET	EXEMPTION	LAW
homestead	Real property including co-op, condo or mobile home, to $10,000	5206(a)
	Husband & wife may double	*In re Pearl*, 723 F.2d 193 (2nd Cir. 1983)
insurance	Annuity contract benefits due or prospectively due the debtor, who paid for the contract; if purchased within 6 months prior & not tax-deferred, only $5,000	Insurance 3212(d), Debtor & Creditor 283(1)
	Disability or illness benefits to $400 per month	Insurance 3212(c)
	Life insurance proceeds left at death with the insurance company pursuant to agreement, if clause prohibits proceeds from being used to pay beneficiary's creditors	Estates, Powers & Trusts 7-1.5(a)(2)
	Life insurance proceeds and avails if the person effecting the policy is the spouse of the insured	Insurance 3212(b)(2)
miscellaneous	Alimony, child support needed for support	Debtor & Creditor 282(2)(d)
	Property of business partnership	Partnership 51
pensions	ERISA-qualified benefits needed for support	Debtor & Creditor 282(2)(e)
	IRAs	Debtor & Creditor 282(2)(e), 5205(c)
	Keoghs	Debtor & Creditor 282(2)(e), 5205(c)
	Public retirement benefits	Insurance 4607
	State employees	Retirement & Social Security 110
	Village police officers	Unconsolidated 5711-o
personal property	Bible; schoolbooks; books to $50; pictures; clothing; church pew or seat; stoves with fuel to last 60 days; sewing machine; domestic animal with food to last 60 days, to $450; food to last 60 days; furniture; refrigerator; TV; radio; wedding ring; watch to $35; crockery, cooking utensils and tableware needed, to $5,000 total (with farm machinery, etc.)	5205(1)-(6), Debtor & Creditor 283(1)
	Burial plot, without structure to 1/4 acre	5206(f)
	Cash, the lesser of either $2,500, or an amount, that, with annuity, totals $5,000; in lieu of homestead	Debtor & Creditor 283(2)
	Health aids, including animals with food	5205(h)
	Lost earnings recoveries needed for support	Debtor & Creditor 282(3)(iv)
	Motor vehicle to $2,400	Debtor & Creditor 282(1)
	Personal injury recoveries to $7,500 (not to include pain & suffering)	Debtor & Creditor 282(3)(iii)
	Security deposits to landlord, utility company	5205(g)
	Trust fund principal, 90% of income	5205(c), (d)
	Wrongful death recoveries for person you depended on, needed for support	Debtor & Creditor 282(3)(ii)

ASSET	EXEMPTION	LAW
public benefits	Aid to blind, aged, disabled	Debtor & Creditor 282(2)(c)
	Crime victims' compensation	Debtor & Creditor 282(3)(i)
	Home relief, local public assistance	Debtor & Creditor 282(2)(a)
	Social Security	Debtor & Creditor 282(2)(a)
	Unemployment compensation	Debtor & Creditor 282(2)(a)
	Veterans' benefits	Debtor & Creditor 282(2)(b)
	Workers' compensation	Debtor & Creditor 282(2)(c)
tools of trade	Farm machinery, team, food for 60 days, professional furniture, books & instruments to $600 total	5205(b)
	Uniforms, medal, equipments, emblem, horse, arms & sword of military member	5205(e)
wages	90% of earnings from milk sales to milk dealers	5205(f)
	90% of earned but unpaid wages received within 60 days prior (100% for a few militia members)	5205(d), (e)
wild card	None	

North Carolina

Federal Bankruptcy Exemptions not available. All law references are to General Statutes of North Carolina unless otherwise noted.

ASSET	EXEMPTION	LAW
homestead	Real or personal property, including co-op, used as residence to $10,000; up to $3,500 of unused portion of homestead may be applied to any property	1C-1601(a)(1), (2)
	Property held as tenancy by the entirety may be exempt against debts owed by only one spouse	*In re Crouch,* 33 B.R. 271 (E.D. N.C. 1983)
insurance	Employee group life policy or proceeds	58-58-165
	Fraternal benefit society benefits	58-24-85
miscellaneous	Property of business partnership	59-55
pensions	Firefighters & rescue squad workers	58-86-90
	Law enforcement officers	143-166.30(g)
	Legislators	120-4.29
	Municipal, city & county employees	128-31
	Teachers & state employees	135-9, 135-95
personal property	Animals, crops, musical instrument, books, clothing, appliances, household goods & furnishings to $3,500 total; may add $750 per dependent, up to $3,000 total additional	1C-1601(a)(4)
	Burial plot to $10,000, in lieu of homestead	1C-1601(a)(1)
	Health aids	1C-1601(a)(7)
	Motor vehicle to $1,500	1C-1601(a)(3)
	Personal injury recoveries for person you depended on	1C-1601(a)(8)
	Wrongful death recoveries for person you depended on	1C-1601(a)(8)
public benefits	Aid to blind	111-18
	Crime victims' compensation	15B-17
	Special adult assistance	108A-36
	Unemployment compensation	96-17
	Workers' compensation	97-21
tools of trade	Implements, books & tools of trade to $750	1C-1601(a)(5)
wages	Earned but unpaid wages received 60 days before filing for bankruptcy, needed for support	1-362
wild card	$3,500 less any amount claimed for homestead or burial exemption, of any property	1C-1601(a)(2)

North Dakota

Federal Bankruptcy Exemptions not available. All law references are to North Dakota Century Code.

ASSET	EXEMPTION	LAW
homestead	Real property, house trailer or mobile home to $80,000	28-22-02(10), 47-18-01
insurance	Fraternal benefit society benefits	26.1-15.1-18, 26.1-33-40
	Life insurance proceeds payable to deceased's estate, not to a specific beneficiary	26.1-33-40
	Life insurance surrender value to $100,000 per policy, if beneficiary is insured's relative & owned over 1 year before filing for bankruptcy; no limit if more needed for support; with ERISA-qualified benefits, IRAs and Keoghs exempt under 28-22-03.1 (except pensions for disabled veterans), total cannot exceed $200,000	28-22-03.1(3)
miscellaneous	Property of business partnership	45-08-02
pensions	Disabled veterans' benefits, except military retirement pay	28-22-03.1(4)(d)
	ERISA-qualified benefits to $100,000 per plan; no limit if more needed for support; with insurance exempt under 28-22-03.1, total cannot exceed $200,000	28-22-03.1(3)
	IRAs to $100,000 per plan; no limit if more needed for support; with insurance exempt under 28-22-03.1, total cannot exceed $200,000	28-22-03.1(3)
	Keoghs to $100,000 per plan; no limit if more needed for support; with insurance exempt under 28-22-03.1, total cannot exceed $200,000	28-22-03.1(3)
	Public employees	28-22-19(1)
personal property	1. All debtors may exempt:	
	Bible, books to $100 & pictures; clothing	28-22-02(1), (4), (5)
	Burial plots, church pew	28-22-02(2), (3)
	Cash to $7,500, in lieu of homestead	28-22-03.1(1)
	Crops or grain raised on debtor's tract to 160 acres (64.75 hectares) on 1 tract	28-22-02(8)
	Food & fuel to last 1 year	28-22-02(6)
	Motor vehicle to $1,200	28-22-03.1(2)
	Personal injury recoveries to $7,500 (not to include pain & suffering)	28-22-03.1(4)(b)
	Wrongful death recoveries to $7,500	28-22-03.1(4)(a)
	2. Head of household not claiming crops or grain may claim $5,000 of any personal property or:	28-22-03
	Books & musical instruments to $1,500	28-22-04(1)
	Furniture, including bedsteads & bedding, to $1,000	28-22-04(2)
	Library & tools of professional to $1,000	28-22-04(4)
	Livestock & farm implements to $4,500	28-22-04(3)
	Tools of mechanic & stock in trade to $1,000	28-22-04(4)
	3. Non-head of household not claiming crops or grain, may claim $2,500 of any personal property	28-22-05
public benefits	Crime victims' compensation	28-22-19(2)
	Public assistance	28-22-19(3)
	Social Security	28-22-03.1(4)(c)
	Unemployment compensation	52-06-30
	Vietnam veterans' adjustment compensation	37-25-07
	Workers' compensation	65-05-29
tools of trade	See personal property	
wages	Minimum 75% of earned but unpaid wages; bankruptcy judge may authorize more for low-income debtors	32-09.1-.03
wild card	See personal property	

Ohio

Federal Bankruptcy Exemptions not available. All law references are to Ohio Revised Code unless otherwise noted.

ASSET	EXEMPTION	LAW
homestead	Real or personal property used as residence to $5,000	2329.66(A)(1)(b)
	Property held as tenancy by the entirety may be exempt against debts owed by only one spouse	In re Thomas, 14 B.R. 423 (N.D. Ohio 1981)
insurance	Benevolent society benefits to $5,000	2329.63, 2329.66(A)(6)(a)
	Disability benefits to $600 per month	2329.66(A)(6)(e), 3923.19
	Fraternal benefit society benefits	2329.66(A)(6)(d), 3921.18
	Group life insurance policy or proceeds	2329.66(A)(6)(c), 3917.05
	Life, endowment or annuity contract avails for your spouse, child or dependent	2329.66(A)(6)(b), 3911.10
	Life insurance proceeds for a spouse	3911.12
	Life insurance proceeds if clause prohibits proceeds from being used to pay beneficiary's creditors	3911.14
miscellaneous	Alimony, child support needed for support	2329.66(A)(11)
	Property of business partnership	1775.24, 2329.66(A)(14)
pensions	ERISA-qualified benefits needed for support	2329.66(A)(10)(b)
	Firefighters, police officers	742.47
	Firefighters', police officers' death benefits	2329.66(A)(10)(a)
	IRAs needed for support	2329.66(A)(10)(c)
	Keoghs needed for support	2329.66(A)(10)(c)
	Public employees	145.56
	Public school employees	3307.71, 3309.66
	State highway patrol employees	5505.22
	Volunteer firefighters' dependents	146.13
personal property *Note: Jewelry must be counted toward the $1,500/$2,000 totals*	Animals, crops, books, musical instruments, appliances, household goods, furnishings, hunting & fishing equipment & firearms to $200 per item, $1,500 total ($2,000 if no homestead claimed)	2329.66(A)(4)(b), (d)
	Beds, bedding & clothing to $200 per item	2329.66(A)(3)
	Burial plot	517.09, 2329.66(A)(8)
	Cash, money due within 90 days, bank & security deposits & tax refund to $400 total (spouse without income can't exempt tax refund, In re Smith, 77 B.R. 633 (N.D. Ohio 1987))	2329.66(A)(4)(a)
	Cooking unit & refrigerator to $300 each	2329.66(A)(3)
	Health aids	2329.66(A)(7)
	Jewelry to $200 per item (1 item may be to $400)	239.66 (A)(4)(c),(d)
	Lost future earnings needed for support, received during 12 months before filing	2329.66(A)(12)(d)
	Motor vehicle to $1,000	2329.66(A)(2)(b)
	Personal injury recoveries to $5,000 (not to include pain & suffering), received during 12 months before filing	2329.66(A)(12)(c)
	Wrongful death recoveries for person debtor depended on, needed for support, received during 12 months before filing	2329.66(A)(12)(b)
public benefits	Crime victim's compensation, received during 12 months before filing	2329.66(A)(12)(a), 2743.66
	Disability assistance payments	2329.66(A)(9)(f), 5113.07
	Public assistance	2329.66(A)(9)(d), 5107.12
	Tuition credit	2329.66(A)(16)
	Unemployment compensation	2329.66(A)(9)(c), 4141.32
	Vocational rehabilitation benefits	2329.66(A)(9)(a), 3304.19
	Workers' compensation	2329.66(A)(9)(b), 4123.67
tools of trade	Implements, books & tools of trade to $750	2329.66(A)(5)
	Seal, official register of notary public	2329.66(A)(15), 147.04
wages	Minimum 75% of earned but unpaid wages due for 30 days; bankruptcy judge may authorize more for low-income debtors	2329.66(A)(13)
wild card	$400 of any property	2329.66(A)(17)

Oklahoma

Federal Bankruptcy Exemptions not available. All law references are to Oklahoma Statutes Annotated.

ASSET	EXEMPTION	LAW
homestead	Real property or manufactured home to unlimited value; property cannot exceed ¼ acre. If property exceeds ¼ acre, may claim $5,000 on 1 acre in city, town or village, or 160 acres elsewhere (need not occupy homestead to claim it exempt as long as you don't acquire another)	31-1(A)(1), 31-1(A)(2), 31-2
insurance	Assessment or mutual benefits	36-2410
	Fraternal benefit society benefits	36-2720
	Funeral benefits prepaid & placed in trust	36-6125
	Group life policy or proceeds	36-3632
	Limited stock insurance benefits	36-2510
miscellaneous	Alimony, child support	31-1(A)(19)
	Property of business partnership	54-225
pensions	County employees	19-959
	Disabled veterans	31-7
	ERISA-qualified benefits	31-1(A)(20)
	Firefighters	11-49-126
	Law enforcement employees	47-2-303.3
	Police officers	11-50-124
	Public employees	74-923
	Tax exempt benefits	60-328
	Teachers	70-17-109
personal property	Books, portraits, pictures & gun	31-1(A)(7), (14)
	2 bridles & 2 saddles	31-1(A)(12)
	Burial plots	31-1(A)(4), 8-7
	100 chickens, 10 hogs, 2 horses, 5 cows & calves under 6 months, 20 sheep; forage for livestock to last 1 year (cows must be able to produce milk for human consumption)	31-1(A)(10), (11), (15), (16)
	Clothing to $4,000	31-1(A)(8)
	Furniture, health aids, food to last 1 year	31-1(A)(3), (9), (17)
	Motor vehicle to $3,000	31-1(A)(13)
	Personal injury, wrongful death & workers' compensation recoveries to $50,000 total; cannot include punitive damages	31-1(A)(21); In re Luckinbill, 163 B.R. 856 (W.D. Okla. 1994)
public benefits	Crime victims' compensation	21-142.13
	Public assistance	56-173
	Social Security	56-173
	Unemployment compensation	40-2-303
	Workers' compensation (see personal property)	85-48
tools of trade	Husbandry implements to farm homestead, tools, books & apparatus to $5,000 total	31-1(A)(5), (6), 31-1(C)
wages	75% of wages earned in 90 days before filing bankruptcy; bankruptcy judge may allow more if you show hardship	12-1171.1, 31-1(A)(18)
wild card	None	

Oregon

Federal Bankruptcy Exemptions not available. All law references are to Oregon Revised Statutes.

ASSET	EXEMPTION	LAW
homestead	Real property, mobile home or houseboat you occupy or intend to occupy to $25,000 ($33,000 for joint owners); if you don't own land mobile home is on, to $23,000 ($30,000 for joint owners); property cannot exceed 1 block in town or city or 160 acres elsewhere; sale proceeds exempt 1 year from sale, if you intend to purchase another home	23.164, 23.240, 23.250
insurance	Annuity contract benefits to $500 per month	743.049
	Fraternal benefit society benefits	748.207
	Group life policy or proceeds not payable to insured	743.047
	Health or disability proceeds or avails	743.050
	Life insurance proceeds or cash value if you are not the insured	743.046
miscellaneous	Alimony, child support needed for support	23.160(1)(i)
	Liquor licenses	471.301(1)
	Property of business partnership	68.420
pensions	ERISA-qualified benefits	23.170
	Public officers, employees	237.201
	School district employees	239.261
personal property	Bank deposits to $7,500; cash for sold exempt property	23.166
	Books, pictures & musical instruments to $600 total (husband & wife may double)	23.160(1)(a)
	Burial plot	65.870
	Clothing, jewelry & other personal items to $1,800 total (husband & wife may double)	23.160(1)(b)
	Domestic animals, poultry with food to last 60 days to $1,000	23.160(1)(e)
	Food & fuel to last 60 days if debtor is householder	23.160(1)(f)
	Furniture, household items, utensils, radios & TVs to $3,000 total	23.160(1)(f)
	Health aids	23.160(1)(h)
	Lost earnings payments for debtor or someone debtor depended on, to extent needed (husband & wife may double)	23.160(1)(j)(C)
	Motor vehicle to $1,700 (husband & wife may double)	23.160(1)(d)
	Personal injury recoveries to $10,000, not to include pain & suffering (husband & wife may double)	23.160(1)(j)(B)
	Pistol; rifle or shotgun if owned by person over 16, to $1,000	23.200
public benefits	Aid to blind	412.115
	Aid to disabled	412.610
	Civil defense & disaster relief	401.405
	Crime victims' compensation (husband & wife may double)	23.160(1)(j)(A), 147.325
	General assistance	411.760
	Injured inmates' benefits	655.530
	Medical assistance	414.095
	Old-age assistance	413.130
	Unemployment compensation	657.855
	Vocational rehabilitation	344.580
	Workers' compensation	656.234
tools of trade	Tools, library, team with food to last 60 days, to $3,000 (husband & wife may double)	23.160(1)(c)
wages	Minimum of 75% of earned but unpaid wages; bankruptcy judge may authorize more for low-income debtors	23.185
	Wages withheld in state employee's bond savings accounts	292.070
wild card	$400 of any personal property, however, can't use to increase existing exemption	23.160(1)(k)
	Husband & wife may double	*In re Wilson,* 22 B.R. 146 (D. Or. 1982)

Pennsylvania

Federal Bankruptcy Exemptions available. All law references are to Pennsylvania Consolidated Statutes Annotated unless otherwise noted.

ASSET	EXEMPTION	LAW
homestead	None, however, property held as tenancy by the entirety may be exempt against debts owed by only one spouse	*Keystone Savings Ass'n v. Kitsock,* 633 A.2d 165 (Pa. Super. Ct. 1993)
insurance	Accident or disability benefits	42-8124(c)(7)
	Fraternal benefit society benefits	Annotated Statute 40-1141-403; 42-8124(c)(1), (8)
	Group life policy or proceeds	42-8124(c)(5)
	Insurance policy or annuity contract payments, where insured is the beneficiary, cash value or proceeds to $100 per month	42-8124(c)(3)
	Life insurance annuity policy, cash value or proceeds if beneficiary is insured's dependent, child or spouse	42-8124(c)(6)
	Life insurance proceeds if clause prohibits proceeds from being used to pay beneficiary's creditors	42-8214(c)(4)
	No-fault automobile insurance proceeds	42-8124(c)(9)
miscellaneous	Property of business partnership	15-8341
pensions	City employees	53-13445, 53-23572, 53-39383
	County employees	16-4716
	Municipal employees	53-881.115
	Police officers	53-764, 53-776, 53-23666
	Private retirement benefits if clause prohibits proceeds from being used to pay beneficiary's creditors, to extent tax-deferred; exemption limited to $15,000 per year deposited; no exemption for amount deposited within 1 year of filing	42-8124(b)
	Public school employees	24-8533
	State employees	71-5953
personal property	Bibles, schoolbooks & sewing machines	42-8124(a)(2), (3)
	Clothing	42-8124(a)(1)
	Tangible personal property at an international exhibit sponsored by U.S. government	42-8125
	Uniform & accoutrements	42-8124(a)(4)
public benefits	Crime victims' compensation	71-180-7.10
	Korean conflict veterans' benefits	51-20098
	Unemployment compensation	42-8124(a)(10), 43-863
	Veterans' benefits	51-20012
	Workers' compensation	42-8124(c)(2)
tools of trade	None	
wages	Earned but unpaid wages	42-8127
wild card	$300 of any property	42-8123

Rhode Island

Federal Bankruptcy Exemptions available. All law references are to General Laws of Rhode Island.

ASSET	EXEMPTION	LAW
homestead	None	
insurance	Accident or sickness proceeds, avails or benefits	27-18-24
	Fraternal benefit society benefits	27-25-18
	Life insurance proceeds if clause prohibits proceeds from being used to pay beneficiary's creditors	27-4-12
	Temporary disability insurance	28-41-32
miscellaneous	Earnings of a minor child	9-26-4(9)
	Property of business partnership	7-12-36
pensions	ERISA-qualified benefits	9-26-4(11)
	Firefighters	9-26-5
	IRAs	9-26-4(12)
	Police officers	9-26-5
	Private employees	28-17-4
	State & municipal employees	36-10-34
personal property	Beds, bedding, furniture & family stores of a housekeeper, to $1,000 total	9-26-4(3)
	Bibles & books to $300	9-26-4(4)
	Body of deceased person	9-26-3
	Burial plot	9-26-4(5)
	Clothing needed	9-26-4(1)
	Consumer cooperative association holdings to $50	7-8-25
	Debt secured by promissory note or bill of exchange	9-26-4(7)
public benefits	Aid to blind, aged, disabled, general assistance	40-6-14
	State disability benefits	28-41-32
	Unemployment compensation	28-44-58
	Veterans' disability or survivors' death benefits	30-7-9
	Workers' compensation	28-33-27
tools of trade	Library of professional in practice	9-26-4(2)
	Working tools to $500	9-26-4(2)
wages	Earned but unpaid wages to $50	9-26-4(8)(C)
	Earned but unpaid wages due military member on active duty	30-7-9
	Earned but unpaid wages due seaman	9-26-4(6)
	Earned but unpaid wages if received welfare during year before filing bankruptcy	9-26-4(8)(B)
	Wages of spouse	9-26-4(9)
	Wages paid by charitable organization to the poor	9-26-4(8)(A)
wild card	None	

South Carolina

Federal Bankruptcy Exemptions available. All law references are to Code of Laws of South Carolina.

ASSET	EXEMPTION	LAW
homestead	Real property, including co-op, to $5,000 (joint owners may double)	15-41-30(1)
insurance	Accident & disability benefits	38-63040(D)
	Benefits accruing under life insurance policy after death of insured, where proceeds left with insurance company pursuant to agreement; benefits not exempt from action to recover necessaries if parties so agree	38-63-50
	Disability or illness benefits	15-41-30(10)(C)
	Fraternal benefit society benefits	38-37-870
	Life insurance avails from policy for person you depended on to $4,000	15-41-30(8)
	Life insurance proceeds from policy for person you depended on, needed for support	15-41-30(11)(C)
	Proceeds & cash surrender value of life insurance payable to beneficiary other than insured's estate expressly intended to benefit spouse, children or dependents of insured unless purchased within 2 years of filing	38-63040(A)
	Proceeds of group life insurance	38-63040(C)
	Proceeds of life insurance or annuity contract	38-63040(B)
	Unmatured life insurance contract, except credit insurance policy	15-41-30(7)
miscellaneous	Alimony, child support	15-41-30(10)(D)
	Property of business partnership	33-41-720
pensions	ERISA-qualified benefits	15-41-30(10)(E)
	Firefighters	9-13-230
	General assembly members	9-9-180
	Judges, solicitors	9-8-190
	Police officers	9-11-270
	Public employees	9-1-1680
personal property	Animals, crops, appliances, books, clothing, household goods, furnishings, musical instruments to $2,500 total	15-41-30(3)
	Burial plot to $5,000, in lieu of homestead (joint owners may double)	15-41-30(1)
	Cash & other liquid assets to $1,000, in lieu of burial or homestead exemption	15-41-30(5)
	Health aids	15-41-30(9)
	Jewelry to $500	15-41-30(4)
	Motor vehicle to $1,200	15-41-30(2)
	Personal injury recoveries	15-41-30(11)(B)
	Wrongful death recoveries	15-41-30(11)(B)
public benefits	Crime victims' compensation	15-41-30(11)(A), 16-3-1300
	General relief, aid to aged, blind, disabled	43-5-190
	Local public assistance	15-41-30(10)(A)
	Social Security	15-41-30(10)(A)
	Unemployment compensation	15-41-30(10)(A)
	Veterans' benefits	15-41-30(10)(B)
	Workers' compensation	42-9-360
tools of trade	Implements, books & tools of trade to $750	15-41-30(6)
wages	None	
wild card	None	

South Dakota

Federal Bankruptcy Exemptions not available. All law references are to South Dakota Codified Laws.

ASSET	EXEMPTION	LAW
homestead	Real property (or mobile home larger than 240 square feet at its base and registered in state at least 6 months before filing for bankruptcy) to unlimited value; property cannot exceed 1 acre in town or 160 acres elsewhere; sale proceeds to $30,000 (unlimited if you're over age 70 or an unmarried widow or widower) exempt for 1 year after sale (can't exempt gold or silver mine, mill or smelter, 43-31-5)	43-31-1, 43-31-2, 43-31-3, 43-31-4
	Spouse or child of deceased owner may claim homestead exemption	43-31-13
	May file homestead declaration	43-31-6
insurance	Annuity contract proceeds to $250 per month	58-12-6, 58-12-8
	Endowment, life insurance policy, proceeds or cash value to $20,000 (husband & wife may not double, *In re James*, 31 B.R. 67 (D. S.D. 1983))	58-12-4
	Fraternal benefit society benefits	58-37-68
	Health benefits to $20,000	58-12-4
	Life insurance proceeds, held pursuant to agreement by insurer, if clause prohibits proceeds from being used to pay beneficiary's creditors	58-15-70
	Life insurance proceeds to $10,000, if beneficiary is surviving spouse or child	43-45-6
miscellaneous	Property of business partnership	48-4-14
pensions	City employees	9-16-47
	Public employees	3-12-115
personal property	1. All debtors may exempt bible, books to $200, pictures, burial plots, church pew, food & fuel to last 1 year & clothing	43-45-2
	2. Head of family may claim $4,000 of any personal property or:	43-45-4, 43-45-5
	Books & musical instruments to $200	43-45-5(1)
	2 cows, 5 swine, 25 sheep with lambs under 6 months; wool, cloth or yarn of sheep; food for all to last 1 year	43-45-5(3)
	Farming machinery, utensils, tackle for teams, harrow, 2 plows, sleigh, wagon to $1,250 total	43-45-5(3)
	Furniture, including bedsteads & bedding to $200	43-45-5(2)
	Library & tools of professional to $300	43-45-5(5)
	Tools of mechanic & stock in trade to $200	43-45-5(4)
	2 yoke of oxen, or span of horses or mules	43-45-5(3)
	3. Non-head of family may claim $2,000 of any personal property	43-45-4
public benefits	Public assistance	28-7-16
	Unemployment compensation	61-6-28
	Workers' compensation	62-4-42
tools of trade	See personal property	
wages	Earned wages owed 60 days before filing bankruptcy, needed for support of family	15-20-12
	Wages of prisoners in work programs	24-8-10
wild card	See personal property	

Tennessee

Federal Bankruptcy Exemptions not available. All law references are to Tennessee Code Annotated unless otherwise noted.

ASSET	EXEMPTION	LAW
homestead	$5,000; $7,500 for joint owners	26-2-301
	Life estate	26-2-302
	2-15 year lease	26-2-303
	Spouse or child of deceased owner may claim homestead exemption	26-2-301
	Property held as tenancy by the entirety may be exempt against debts owed by only one spouse	*In re Arango*, 136 B.R. 740, aff'd, 992 F.2d 611 (6th Cir. 1993)
insurance	Accident, health or disability benefits for resident & citizen of Tennessee	26-2-110
	Disability or illness benefits	26-2-111(1)(C)
	Fraternal benefit society benefits	56-25-1403
	Homeowners' insurance proceeds to $5,000	26-2-304
miscellaneous	Alimony owed for 30 days before filing for bankruptcy	26-2-111(1)(E)
	Property of business partnership	61-1-124
pensions	ERISA-qualified benefits	26-2-111(1)(D)
	Public employees	8-36-111
	State & local government employees	26-2-104
	Teachers	49-5-909
personal property	Bible, schoolbooks, pictures, portraits, clothing & storage containers	26-2-103
	Burial plot to 1 acre	26-2-305, 46-2-102
	Health aids	26-2-111(5)
	Lost earnings payments for you or person you depended on	26-2-111(3)
	Personal injury recoveries to $7,500 (not to include pain & suffering); wrongful death recoveries to $10,000 (you can't exempt more than $15,000 total for personal injury, wrongful death & crime victims' compensation)	26-2-111(2)(B), 26-2-111(2)(C)
public benefits	Aid to blind	71-4-117
	Aid to disabled	71-4-1112
	Crime victims' compensation to $5,000 (see personal property)	26-2-111(2)(A), 29-13-111
	Local public assistance	26-2-111(1)(A)
	Old-age assistance	71-2-216
	Social Security	26-2-111(1)(A)
	Unemployment compensation	26-2-111(1)(A)
	Veterans' benefits	26-2-111(1)(B)
	Workers' compensation	50-6-223
tools of trade	Implements, books & tools of trade to $1,900	26-2-111(4)
wages	Minimum 75% of earned but unpaid wages, plus $2.50 per week per child; bankruptcy judge may authorize more for low-income debtors	26-2-106, 26-2-107
wild card	$4,000 of any personal property	26-2-102

Texas

Federal Bankruptcy Exemptions available. All law references are to Texas Revised Civil Statutes Annotated unless otherwise noted.

ASSET	EXEMPTION	LAW
homestead	Unlimited; property cannot exceed 1 acre in town, village, city or 100 acres (200 for families) elsewhere; sale proceeds exempt for 6 months after sale (need not occupy if not acquire another home, Property 41.003)	Property 41.001, 41.002
	Must file homestead declaration	Property 41.005
insurance	Church benefit plan benefits	1407a-6
	Fraternal benefit society benefits	Insurance 10.28
	Life, health, accident or annuity benefits or monies, including policy proceeds and cash values to be paid or rendered to beneficiary or insured	Insurance 21.22
	Life insurance present value if beneficiary is debtor or debtor's dependent (see note under personal property)	Property 42.002(a)(12)
	Retired public school employees group insurance	Insurance 3.50-4(11)(a)
	Texas employee uniform group insurance	Insurance 3.50-2(10)(a)
	Texas state college or university employee benefits	Insurance 3.50-3(9)(a)
miscellaneous	Property of business partnership	6132b-25
pensions	County & district employees	Government 811.005
	ERISA-qualified government or church benefits, including Keoghs and IRAs	Property 42.0021
	Firefighters	6243e(5), 6243e.1(12), 6243e.2(12)
	IRAs to extent tax-deferred	Property 42.0021
	Judges	Government 811.005
	Keoghs to extent tax-deferred	Property 42.0021
	Law enforcement officers' survivors	6228f(8)
	Municipal employees	6243g, Government 811.005
	Police officers	6243d-1(17), 6243j(20), 6243g-1(23B)
	Retirement benefits to extent tax-deferred	Property 42.0021
	State employees	Government 811.005
	Teachers	Government 811.005
personal property *total includes tools of trade, unpaid commissions, life insurance cash value*	Athletic and sporting equipment, including bicycles; 2 firearms; home furnishings, including family heirlooms; food; clothing; jewelry (not to exceed 25% of total exemption); 1 two-, three- or four-wheeled motor vehicle per member of family or single adult who holds a driver's license (or who operates vehicle for someone else who does not have a license); 2 horses, mules or donkeys and a saddle, blanket and bridle for each; 12 head of cattle; 60 head of other types of livestock; 120 fowl; and pets to $30,000 total ($60,000 for head of family)	Property 42.001, 42.002
	Burial plots	Property 41.001
	Health aids	Property 42.001(b)(2)
public benefits	Crime victims' compensation	8309-1(7)(f)
	Medical assistance	Hum. Res. 32.036
	Public assistance	Hum. Res. 31.040
	Unemployment compensation	5221b-13
	Workers' compensation	8308-4.07
tools of trade *see note under personal property*	Farming or ranching vehicles and implements	Property 42.002(a)(3)
	Tools, equipment (includes boat & motor vehicles) & books	Property 42.002(a)(4)
wages	Earned but unpaid wages	Property 42.001(b)(1)
	Unpaid commissions to 75% (see note under personal property)	Property 42.001(d)
wild card	None	

Utah

Federal Bankruptcy Exemptions not available. All law references are to Utah Code.

ASSET	EXEMPTION	LAW
homestead	Real property, mobile home or water rights to $10,000 (joint owners may double)	78-23-3
	Must file homestead declaration before attempted sale of home	78-23-4
insurance	Disability, illness, medical or hospital benefits	78-23-5(1)(c), (d)
	Fraternal benefit society benefits	31A-9-603
	Life insurance policy cash surrender value to $1,500	78-23-7
	Life insurance proceeds if beneficiary is insured's spouse or dependent, as needed for support	78-73-6(2)
miscellaneous	Alimony needed for support	78-23-5(1)(k), 78-23-6(1)
	Child support	78-23-5(1)(f), (k)
	Property of business partnership	48-1-22
pensions	ERISA-qualified benefits	78-23-5(1)(j)
	Public employees	49-1-609
	Other pensions needed for support	78-23-6(3)
personal property	Animals, books & musical instruments to $500 total	78-23-8(1)(b)
	Artwork depicting, or done by, family member	78-23-5(1)(h)
	Bed, bedding, carpets, washer & dryer	78-23-5(1)(g)
	Burial plot	78-23-5(1)(a)
	Clothing (cannot claim furs or jewelry)	78-23-5(1)(g)
	Dining & kitchen tables & chairs to $500	78-23-8(1)(a)
	Food to last 3 months	78-23-5(1)(g)
	Health aids needed	78-23-5(1)(b)
	Heirloom to $500	78-23-8(1)(c)
	Motor vehicle to $2,500	78-23-8(2)
	Personal injury recoveries for you or person you depended on	78-23-5(1)(i)
	Proceeds for damaged exempt property	78-23-9
	Refrigerator, freezer, microwave, stove & sewing machine	78-23-5(1)(g)
	Sofas, chairs & related furnishings to $500	78-23-8(1)(a)
	Wrongful death recoveries for person you depended on	78-23-5(1)(i)
public benefits	Crime victims' compensation	63-63-21
	General assistance	55-15-32
	Occupational disease disability benefits	35-2-35
	Unemployment compensation	35-4-18
	Veterans' benefits	78-23-5(1)(e)
	Workers' compensation	35-1-80
tools of trade	Implements, books & tools of trade to $3,500	78-23-8(2)
	Military property of National Guard member	39-1-47
	Motor vehicle to $2,500	78-23-8(3)
wages	Minimum 75% of earned but unpaid wages; bankruptcy judge may authorize more for low-income debtors	70C-7-103
wild card	None	

Vermont

Federal Bankruptcy Exemptions available. All law references are to Vermont Statutes Annotated unless otherwise noted.

ASSET	EXEMPTION	LAW
homestead	Real property or mobile home to $75,000; may also claim rents, issues, profits & out-buildings	27-101
	Spouse of deceased owner may claim homestead exemption	27-105
	Property held as tenancy by the entirety may be exempt against debts owed by only one spouse	In re McQueen, 21 B.R. 736 (D. Ver. 1982)
insurance	Annuity contract benefits to $350 per month	8-3709
	Disability benefits that supplement life insurance or annuity contract	8-3707
	Disability or illness benefits needed for support	12-2740(19)(C)
	Fraternal benefit society benefits	8-4478
	Group life or health benefits	8-3708
	Health benefits to $200 per month	8-4086
	Life insurance proceeds if beneficiary is not the insured	8-3706
	Life insurance proceeds for person you depended on	12-2740(19)(H)
	Life insurance proceeds if clause prohibits proceeds from being used to pay beneficiary's creditors	8-3705
	Unmatured life insurance contract other than credit	12-2740(18)
miscellaneous	Alimony, child support needed for support	12-2740(19)(D)
	Property of business partnership	11-1282
pensions	Municipal employees	24-5066
	Self-directed accounts (IRAs, Keoghs) to $10,000	12-2740(16)
	State employees	3-476
	Teachers	16-1946
	Other pensions	12-2740(19)(J)
personal property	Appliances, furnishings, goods, clothing, books, crops, animals, musical instruments to $2,500 total	12-2740(5)
	Cow, 2 goats, 10 sheep, 10 chickens; 3 swarms of bees & their honey; feed to last 1 winter; 10 cords of firewood, 5 tons of coal or 500 gallons of oil; 500 gallons of bottled gas; growing crops to $5,000; 2 harnesses, 2 halters, 2 chains, plow & ox yoke; yoke of oxen or steers & 2 horses	12-2740(6), 12-2740(9)-(14)
	Jewelry to $500; wedding ring unlimited	12-2740(3), (4)
	Motor vehicles to $2,500; bank deposits to $700	12-2740(1), (15)
	Personal injury recoveries for person you depended on	12-2740(19)(F)
	Stove, heating unit, refrigerator, freezer, water heater & sewing machines; lost future earnings for you or person you depended on; health aids	12-2740(8), 12-2740(17), 12-2740(19)(I)
	Wrongful death recoveries for person you depended on	12-2740(19)(G)
public benefits	Aid to blind, aged, disabled, general assistance	33-124
	Crime victims' compensation needed for support	12-2740(19)(E)
	Social Security needed for support	12-2740(19)(A)
	Unemployment compensation	21-1367
	Veterans' benefits needed for support	12-2740(19)(B)
	Workers' compensation	21-681
tools of trade	Books & tools of trade to $5,000	12-2740(2)
wages	Minimum 75% of earned but unpaid wages; bankruptcy judge may authorize more for low-income debtors	12-3170
	Wages, if received welfare during 2 months before filing	12-3170
wild card	$7,000 less any amount of appliances, et al, growing crops, jewelry, motor vehicle & tools of trade, of any property	12-2740(7)
	$400 of any property	12-2740(7)

Virginia

Federal Bankruptcy Exemptions not available. All law references are to Code of Virginia unless otherwise noted.

ASSET	EXEMPTION	LAW
homestead	$5,000 plus $500 per dependent; may also claim rents & profits; sale proceeds exempt to $5,000 (husband & wife may double, Cheeseman v. Nachman, 656 F.2d 60 (4th Cir. 1981)); unused portion of homestead may be applied to any personal property	34-4,34-18,34-20
	May include mobile home	In re Goad, 161 B.R. 161 (W.D. Va. 1993)
	Must file homestead declaration before filing for bankruptcy	34-6
	Property held as tenancy by the entirety may be exempt against debts owed by only one spouse	In re Harris, 155 B.R. 948 (E.D. Va. 1993)
insurance	Accident or sickness benefits	38.2-3549
	Burial society benefits	38.2-4021
	Cooperative life insurance benefits	38.2-3811
	Fraternal benefit society benefits	38.2-4118
	Group life or accident insurance for government officials	51.1-510
	Group life insurance policy or proceeds	38.2-3339
	Industrial sick benefits	38.2-3549
miscellaneous	Property of business partnership	50-25
pensions	City, town & county employees	51.1-802
	ERISA-qualified benefits to $17,500 per year	34-34
also see wages	Judges	51.1-102
	State employees	51.1-102
personal property	Bible	34-26(1)
	Burial plot	34-26(3)
	Clothing to $1,000	34-26(4)
you must be a householder to exempt any personal property	Family portraits and heirlooms to $5,000 total	34-26(2)
	Health aids	34-26(6)
	Household furnishings to $5,000	34-26(4)(a)
	Motor vehicle to $2,000	34-26(8)
	Personal injury causes of action	34-28.1
	Personal injury recoveries	34-28.1
	Pets	34-26(5)
	Wedding and engagement rings	34-26(1)(a)
public benefits	Aid to blind, aged, disabled, general relief	63.1-88
	Crime victims' compensation unless seeking to discharge debt for treatment of injury incurred during crime	19.2-368.12
	Unemployment compensation	60.2-600
	Workers' compensation	65.2-531
tools of trade	Horses, mules (pair) with gear, wagon or cart, tractor to $3,000, plows (2), drag, harvest cradle, pitchfork, rake, iron wedges (2), fertilizer to $1,000 of farmer (you must be a householder)	34-27
	Tools, books and instruments of trade, including motor vehicles, to $10,000, needed in your occupation or education (you must be a householder)	34-26
	Uniforms, arms, equipment of military member	44-96
wages	Minimum 75% of earned but unpaid wages, pension payments; bankruptcy judge may authorize more for low-income debtors	34-29
wild card	Unused portion of homestead, of any personal property	34-13
	$2,000 of any property for disabled veterans (you must be a householder)	34-4.1

Washington

Federal Bankruptcy Exemptions available. All law references are to Revised Code of Washington Annotated.

ASSET	EXEMPTION	LAW
homestead	Real property or mobile home to $30,000 (no limit if seeking to discharge debt based on failure to pay a state income tax assessed on retirement benefits received while a resident of Washington, 6.15.030)	6.13.010, 6.13.030
	Must record homestead declaration before sale of home if property unimproved or home unoccupied	6.15.040
insurance	Annuity contract proceeds to $250 per month	48.18.430
	Disability proceeds, avails or benefits	48.18.400
	Fire insurance proceeds for destroyed exemption	6.15.030
	Fraternal benefit society benefits	48.36A.180
	Group life insurance policy or proceeds	48.18.420
	Life insurance proceeds or avails if beneficiary is not the insured	48.18.410
miscellaneous	Property of business partnership	25.04.250
pensions	City employees	41.28.200
	ERISA-qualified benefits	6.15.020
	IRAs	6.15.020
	Public employees	41.40.380
	State patrol officers	43.43.310
	Volunteer firefighters	41.24.240
personal property	Appliances, furniture, household goods, home & yard equipment to $2,700 total (no limit on any property located within Washington if seeking to discharge debt based on failure to pay a state income tax assessed on retirement benefits received while a resident of Washington, 6.15.025)	6.15.010(3)(a)
	Books to $1,500	6.15.010(2)
	Burial plots sold by nonprofit cemetery association	68.20.120
	Clothing, no more than $1,000 in furs, jewelry, ornaments	6.15.010(1)
	Food & fuel for comfortable maintenance	6.15.010(3)(a)
	Keepsakes & pictures	6.15.010(2)
	Two motor vehicles to $2,500 total	6.15.010(3)(c)
public benefits	Child welfare	74.13.070
	Crime victims' compensation	7.68.070, 51.32.040
	General assistance	74.04.280
	Industrial insurance (workers' compensation)	51.32.040
	Old-age assistance	74.08.210
	Unemployment compensation	50.40.020
tools of trade	Farm trucks, stock, tools, seed, equipment & supplies of farmer to $5,000 total	6.15.010(4)(a)
	Library, office furniture, office equipment & supplies of physician, surgeon, attorney, clergy or other professional to $5,000 total	6.15.010(4)(b)
	Tools & materials used in another's trade to $5,000	6.15.010(4)(c)
wages	Minimum 75% of earned but unpaid wages; bankruptcy judge may authorize more for low-income debtors	6.27.150
wild card	$1,000 of any personal property (no more than $100 in cash, bank deposits, bonds, stocks & securities)	6.15.010(3)(b)

West Virginia

Federal Bankruptcy Exemptions not available. All law references are to West Virginia Code.

ASSET	EXEMPTION	LAW
homestead	Real or personal property used as residence to $15,000; unused portion of homestead may be applied to any property	38-10-4(a)
insurance	Fraternal benefit society benefits	33-23-21
	Group life insurance policy or proceeds	33-6-28
	Health or disability benefits	38-10-4(j)(3)
	Life insurance payments from policy for person you depended on, needed for support	38-10-4(k)(3)
	Unmatured life insurance contract, except credit insurance policy	38-10-4(g)
	Unmatured life insurance contract's accrued dividend, interest or loan value to $8,000, if debtor owns contract & insured is either debtor or a person on whom debtor is dependent	38-10-4(h)
miscellaneous	Alimony, child support needed for support	38-10-4(j)(4)
	Property of business partnership	47-8A-25
pensions	ERISA-qualified benefits needed for support	38-10-4(j)(5)
	Public employees	5-10-46
	Teachers	18-7A-30
personal property	Animals, crops, clothing, appliances, books, household goods, furnishings, musical instruments to $400 per item, $8,000 total	38-10-4(c)
	Burial plot to $15,000, in lieu of homestead	38-10-4(a)
	Health aids	38-10-4(i)
	Jewelry to $1,000	38-10-4(d)
	Lost earnings payments needed for support	38-10-4(k)(5)
	Motor vehicle to $2,400	38-10-4(b)
	Personal injury recoveries to $15,000 (not to include pain & suffering)	38-10-4(k)(4)
	Wrongful death recoveries needed for support, for person you depended on	38-10-4(k)(2)
public benefits	Aid to blind, aged, disabled, general assistance	9-5-1
	Crime victims' compensation	14-2A-24, 38-10-4(k)(1)
	Social Security	38-10-4(j)(1)
	Unemployment compensation	38-10-4(j)(1)
	Veterans' benefits	38-10-4(j)(2)
	Workers' compensation	23-4-18
tools of trade	Implements, books & tools of trade to $1,500	38-10-4(f)
wages	80% of earned but unpaid wages; bankruptcy judge may authorize more for low-income debtors	38-5A-3
wild card	$800 of any property	38-10-4(e)
	Unused portion of homestead or burial exemption, of any property	38-10-4(e)

Wisconsin

Federal Bankruptcy Exemptions available. All law references are to Wisconsin Statutes Annotated.

ASSET	EXEMPTION	LAW
homestead	Property you occupy or intend to occupy to $40,000; sale proceeds exempt for 2 years from sale if you plan to obtain another home (husband and wife may not double)	815.20
insurance	Federal disability insurance	815.18(3)(ds)
	Fire proceeds for destroyed exempt property for 2 years from receiving	815.18(3)(e)
	Fraternal benefit society benefits	614.96
	Life insurance policy or proceeds to $5,000, if beneficiary is a married woman	766.09
	Life insurance proceeds held in trust by insurer, if clause prohibits proceeds from being used to pay beneficiary's creditors	632.42
	Life insurance proceeds if beneficiary was dependent of insured, needed for support	815.18(3)(i)(a)
	Unmatured life insurance contract, except credit insurance contract, owned by debtor & insuring debtor, dependent of debtor or someone debtor is dependent on	815.18(3)(f)
	Unmatured life insurance contract's accrued dividends, interest or loan value (to $4,000 total in all contracts), if debtor owns contract & insured is debtor, dependent of debtor or someone debtor is dependent on	815.18(3)(f)
miscellaneous	Alimony, child support needed for support	815.18(3)(c)
	Property of business partnership	178.21
pensions	Certain municipal employees	66.81
	Firefighters, police officers who worked in city with population over 100,000	815.18(3)(ef)
	Military pensions	815.18(3)(n)
	Private or public retirement benefits	815.18(3)(j)
	Public employees	40.08(1)
personal property	Burial provisions	815.18(3)(a)
	Deposit accounts to $1,000	815.18(3)(k)
	Household goods and furnishings, clothing, keepsakes, jewelry, appliances, books, musical instruments, firearms, sporting goods, animals and other tangible property held for personal, family or household use to $5,000 total	815.18(3)(d)
	Lost future earnings recoveries, needed for support	815.18(3)(i)(d)
	Motor vehicles to $1,200	815.18(3)(g)
	Personal injury recoveries to $25,000	815.18(3)(i)(c)
	Tenant's lease or stock interest in housing co-op, to homestead amount	182.004(6)
	Wages used to purchase savings bonds	20.921(1)(e)
	Wrongful death recoveries, needed for support	815.18(3)(i)(b)
public benefits	Crime victims' compensation	949.07
	Social services payments	49.41
	Unemployment compensation	108.13
	Veterans' benefits	45.35(8)(b)
	Workers' compensation	102.27
tools of trade	Equipment, inventory, farm products, books and tools of trade to $7,500 total	815.18(3)(b)
wages	75% of earned but unpaid wages; bankruptcy judge may authorize more for low-income debtors	815.18(3)(h)
wild card	None	

Wyoming

Federal Bankruptcy Exemptions not available. All law references are to Wyoming Statutes Annotated unless otherwise noted.

ASSET	EXEMPTION	LAW
homestead	Real property you occupy to $10,000 or house trailer you occupy to $6,000 (joint owners may double)	1-20-101, 1-20-102, 1-20-104
	Spouse or child of deceased owner may claim homestead exemption	1-20-103
	Property held as tenancy by the entirety may be exempt against debts owed by only one spouse	*In re Anselmi*, 52 B.R. 479 (D. Wy. 1985)
insurance	Annuity contract proceeds to $350 per month	26-15-132
	Disability benefits if clause prohibits proceeds from being used to pay beneficiary's creditors	26-15-130
	Fraternal benefit society benefits	26-29-218
	Group life or disability policy or proceeds	26-15-131
	Life insurance proceeds held by insurer, if clause prohibits proceeds from being used to pay beneficiary's creditors	26-15-133
miscellaneous	Liquor licenses & malt beverage permits	12-4-604
pensions	Criminal investigators, highway officers	9-3-620
	Firefighters, police officers (only payments being received)	15-5-209
	Game & fish wardens	9-3-620
	Private or public retirement funds and accounts	1-20-110
	Public employees	9-3-426
personal property	Bedding, furniture, household articles & food to $2,000 per person in the home	1-20-106(a)(iii)
	Bible, schoolbooks & pictures	1-20-106(a)(i)
	Burial plot	1-20-106(a)(ii), 35-8-104
	Clothing & wedding rings needed, up to $1,000	1-20-105
	Funeral contracts, pre-paid	26-32-102
	Motor vehicle to $2,400	1-20-106(a)(iv)
public benefits	Crime victims' compensation	1-40-113
	General assistance	42-2-113
	Unemployment compensation	27-3-319
	Workers' compensation	27-14-702
tools of trade	Library & implements of professional to $2,000 or tools, motor vehicle, implements, team & stock in trade to $2,000	1-20-106(b)
wages	Earnings of National Guard members	19-2-501
	Minimum 75% of earned but unpaid wages	1-15-511
	Wages of inmates on work release	7-16-308
wild card	None	

Federal Bankruptcy Exemptions

Married couples may double all exemptions. All references are to 11 U.S.C. § 522. These exemptions were last adjusted in 1994. On April 1, 1998, and at every three-year interval ending on April 1 thereafter, these amounts shall be adjusted to reflect changes in the Consumer Price Index.

Debtors in the following states may select the Federal Bankruptcy Exemptions:

Arkansas	Massachusetts	New Mexico	Texas
Connecticut	Michigan	Pennsylvania	Vermont
District of Columbia	Minnesota	Rhode Island	Washington
Hawaii	New Jersey	South Carolina	Wisconsin

ASSET	EXEMPTION	SUBSECTION
homestead	Real property, including co-op or mobile home, to $16,150; unused portion of homestead to $8,075 may be applied to any property	(d)(1)
insurance	Disability, illness or unemployment benefits	(d)(10)(C)
	Life insurance payments for person you depended on, needed for support	(d)(11)(C)
	Life insurance policy with loan value, in accrued dividends or interest, to $8,625	(d)(8)
	Unmatured life insurance contract, except credit insurance policy	(d)(7)
miscellaneous	Alimony, child support needed for support	(d)(10)(D)
pensions	ERISA-qualified benefits needed for support; may include IRAs	(d)(10)(E); *Carmichael v. Osherow*, [100 F.3d 375 (5th Cir. 1996)]
personal property	Animals, crops, clothing, appliances, books, furnishings, household goods, musical instruments to $425 per item, $8,625 total	(d)(3)
	Health aids	(d)(9)
	Jewelry to $1,075	(d)(4)
	Lost earnings payments	(d)(11)(E)
	Motor vehicle to $2,575	(d)(2)
	Personal injury recoveries to $16,150 (not to include pain & suffering or pecuniary loss)	(d)(11)(D)
	Wrongful death recoveries for person you depended on	(d)(11)(B)
public benefits	Crime victims' compensation	(d)(11)(A)
	Public assistance	(d)(10)(A)
	Social Security	(d)(10)(A)
	Unemployment compensation	(d)(10)(A)
	Veterans' benefits	(d)(10)(A)
tools of trade	Implements, books & tools of trade to $1,625	(d)(6)
wages	None	
wild card	$850 of any property	(d)(5)
	Unused portion homestead exemption to $8,075, low-income debtors	(d)(5)

Federal Non-Bankruptcy Exemptions

These exemptions are available only if you select your state exemptions; they cannot be claimed if you claim the federal bankruptcy exemptions. All law references are to the United States Code.

ASSET	EXEMPTION	LAW
retirement benefits	CIA employees	50 § 403
	Civil service employees	5 § 8346
	Foreign service employees	22 § 4060
	Military honor roll pensions	38 § 562
	Military service employees	10 § 1440
	Railroad workers	45 § 231m
	Social Security	42 § 407
	Veterans' benefits	38 § 3101
	Veterans' medal of honor benefits	38 § 562
survivor's benefits	Judges, U.S. court directors, judicial center directors, supreme court chief justice administrators	28 § 376
	Lighthouse workers	33 § 775
	Military service	10 § 1450
death & disability benefits	Government employees	5 § 8130
	Longshoremen & harbor workers	33 § 916
	War risk hazard death or injury compensation	42 § 1717
miscellaneous	Klamath Indians tribe benefits for Indians residing in Oregon	25 § 543, 25 § 545
	Military deposits in savings accounts while on permanent duty outside U.S.	10 § 1035
	Military group life insurance	38 § 770(g)
	Railroad workers' unemployment insurance	45 § 352(e)
	Seamen's clothing	46 § 11110
	Seamen's wages (while on a voyage) pursuant to a written contract	46 § 11111
	75% of earned but unpaid wages; bankruptcy judge may authorize more for low-income debtors	15 § 1673

Addresses of Bankruptcy Courts

Alabama   112th & Noble Streets, 122 U.S. Courthouse, **Anniston**, AL 36201, 205-236-6421

1800 5th Ave. North, Room 120, **Birmingham**, AL 35203, 205-731-0850

P.O. Box 1289, 222 Federal Courthouse, **Decatur**, AL 35602, 205-353-2817

201 St. Louis Street, **Mobile**, AL 36602, 334-441-5391

P.O. Box 1248, Suite 127, One Court Square, **Montgomery**, AL 36102, 334-223-7622

1118 Greensboro Ave., **Tuscaloosa**, AL 35401, 205-752-0426

Alaska   605 W. 4th Ave., Suite 138, **Anchorage**, AK 99501, 907-271-2655

Arizona   2929 N. Central Ave., 9th Floor, **Phoenix**, AZ 85012, 602-640-5800

110 South Church Ave., Suite 8112, **Tucson**, AZ 85701, 602-620-7500

325 West 19th St., **Yuma**, AZ 85364, 520-783-2288

Arkansas   P.O. Drawer 2381, 600 W. Capitol Ave., **Little Rock**, AR 72203, 501-324-6357

California   5301 U.S. Courthouse, 1130 O St., **Fresno**, CA 93721, 209-487-5217

255 E. Temple, **Los Angeles**, CA 90012, 213-894-6046

P.O. Box 5276, 1130 - 12th St., **Modesto**, CA 95352, 209-521-5160

P.O. Box 2070, **Oakland**, CA 94604 (mail) or 1300 Clay St., Suite 300, **Oakland**, CA 94612 (person), 510-879-3600

8308 U.S. Courthouse, 650 Capitol Mall, **Sacramento**, CA 95814, 916-498-5525

222 E. Carrillo St., Room 101, **Santa Barbara**, CA 93101, 805-897-3880

699 N. Arrowhead Ave, Room 105, **San Bernardino**, CA 92401, 909-383-5742

325 West F Street, **San Diego**, CA 92101, 619-557-5536

P.O. Box 7341, **San Francisco**, CA 94120 (mail) or 235 Pine Street, **San Francisco**, CA 94104 (person), 415-705-3200

280 South First St., Room 3035, **San Jose**, CA 95113, 408-535-5118

506 Federal Building, 34 Civic Center Plaza, **Santa Ana**, CA 92701, 714-836-2993

99 South E St., **Santa Rosa**, CA 95404, 707-525-8520

Colorado   U.S. Customs House, 721 19th St., **Denver**, CO 80202, 303-844-4045

Connecticut   U.S. Courthouse, 915 Lafayette Blvd., **Bridgeport**, CT 06604, 203-579-5808

712 U.S. Courthouse, 450 Main St., **Hartford**, CT 06103, 203-240-3675

Delaware   824 Market, **Wilmington**, DE 19801, 302-573-6174

District of Columbia	U.S. Courthouse, Room 4400, 3rd & Constitution Aves., NW, **Washington**, DC 20001, 202-273-0042
Florida	299 E. Broward Blvd., Room 206B, **Ft. Lauderdale**, FL 33301, 305-356-7224
	P.O. Box 559, U.S. Post Office & Courthouse, **Jacksonville**, FL 32201 (mail) or 311 W. Monroe St., **Jacksonville**, FL 32202 (person), 904-232-2852
	51 SW First Ave., **Miami**, FL 33130, 305-536-4320
	135 W. Central Ave., Room 950, **Orlando**, FL 32801, 407-648-6364
	220 W. Garden St., Room 700, **Pensacola**, FL 32501, 904-435-8475
	227 N. Bronough St., Room 3120, **Tallahassee**, FL 32301, 904-942-8933
	4921 Memorial Highway, Room 200, **Tampa**, FL 33634, 813-243-5041
	701 Clematis St., Room 335, **West Palm Beach**, FL 33401, 407-655-6774
Georgia	1340 R.B. Russell Building, 75 Spring St. SW, **Atlanta**, GA 30303, 404-331-6886
	827 Telfaire St., P.O. Box 1487, **Augusta**, GA 30901, 706-724-2421
	P.O. Box 2147, 901 Front Ave., One Arsenal Place, Room 310, **Columbus**, GA 31902, 706-649-7837
	Federal Building, 126 Washington St., Room 201, **Gainsville**, GA 30501, 404-536-0556
	P.O. Box 1957, Old Federal Building, **Macon**, GA 31202, 912-752-3506
	P.O. Box 2328, **Newnan**, GA 30264, 404-251-5583
	P.O. Box 5231, **Rome**, GA 30161, 706-291-5639
	P.O. Box 8347, 212 U.S. Courthouse, **Savannah**, GA 31412, 912-652-4100
Hawaii	First Hawaiian Tower, 1132 Bishop St., Suite 250L, **Honolulu**, HI 96813, 808-522-8100
Idaho	550 W. Fort St., Box 042 Federal Building, **Boise**, ID 83724, 208-334-1074
Illinois	301 W. Main St., **Benton**, IL 62812, 618-435-2200
	U.S. Courthouse, 219 S. Dearborn St., Room 614, **Chicago**, IL 60604, 312-435-5587
	P.O. Box 657, 301 Federal Building, Room 127, 201 N. Vermilion St., **Danville**, IL 61834, 217-431-4817
	P.O. Box 309, 750 Missouri Ave., 1st Floor, **East St. Louis**, IL 62202, 618-482-9400
	156 Federal Building, 100 NE Monroe St., **Peoria**, IL 61602, 309-671-7035
	211 S. Court St., **Rockford**, IL 61101, 815-987-4352
	P.O. Box 2438, 226 U.S. Courthouse, 600 E. Monroe St., **Springfield**, IL 62705, 217-492-4551
Indiana	101 NW Martin Luther King Blvd., **Evansville**, IN 47708, 812-465-6440
	1188 Federal Building, 1300 S. Harrison St., **Ft. Wayne**, IN 46802, 219-420-5100
	221 Federal Building, 610 Connecticut St., **Gary**, IN 46402, 219-881-3335
	123 U.S. Courthouse, 46 E. Ohio St., **Indianapolis**, IN 46204, 317-226-6821
	102 Federal Building, **New Albany**, IN 47150, 812-948-5254
	224 U.S. Courthouse, 204 S. Main St., **South Bend**, IN 46601-2196, 219-236-8247
	203 Post Office Building, 30 N. 7th St., **Terre Haute**, IN 47808, 812-238-1550

Iowa	P.O. Box 74890, **Cedar Rapids**, IA 52407 (mail) or 800 The Center, 425 2nd St., S.E., **Cedar Rapids**, IA 52401 (person), 319-362-9696
	P.O. Box 9264, **Des Moines**, IA 50309 (mail) or 318 U.S. Courthouse, **Des Moines**, IA 50306 (person), 515-284-6230
	U.S. Courthouse, 320 6th St., **Sioux City**, IA 51101, 712-252-3757
Kansas	500 State Ave., **Kansas City**, KS 66101, 913-551-6732
	240 U.S. Courthouse, 444 SE Quincy St., **Topeka**, KS 66683, 913-295-2750
	167 U.S. Couthouse, 401 N. Market St., **Wichita**, KS 67202, 316-269-6486
Kentucky	P.O. Box 1111, 200 Merrill Lynch Plaza, **Lexington**, KY 40588, 606-233-2608
	546 G. Snyder Courthouse and Customs House, 601 W. Broadway, **Louisville**, KY 40202, 502-582-6136
Louisiana	P.O. Box 111, **Alexandria**, LA 71309 (mail) or 300 Jackson St., **Alexandria**, LA 71301, 318-473-7366
	412 N. 4th St., Room 301, **Baton Rouge**, LA 70802, 504-389-0211
	Hale Boggs Federal Building, 501 Magazine St., Suite 701, **New Orleans**, LA 70130, 504-589-6506
	205 Federal Building, Corner of Union & Vine, **Opelousas**, LA 70570, 318-942-2161
	300 Fannin St., **Shreveport**, LA 71101, 318-676-4267
Maine	P.O. Box 1109, 331 U.S. Courthouse, 202 Harlow St., **Bangor**, ME 04401, 207-945-0348
	U.S. Courthouse, 537 Congress, **Portland**, ME 04101, 207-780-3482
Maryland	U.S. Courthouse, 101 W. Lombard St., Room 919, **Baltimore**, MD 21201, 410-962-2688
	6500 Cherry Wood Lane, **Greenbelt**, MD 20770, 301-344-8018
Massachusetts	T.P. O'Neill Federal Office Building, 10 Causeway St., Room 1101, **Boston**, MA 02222, 617-565-6051
	Edwards Building, 10 Mechanic St., **Worcester**, MA 01608, 508-793-0542
Michigan	111 First St., **Bay City**, MI 48707, 517-894-8850
	U.S. Courthouse, 231 W. Lafayette, Room 1060, **Detroit**, MI 48226, 313-226-6395
	226 W. Second St., **Flint**, MI 48502, 810-235-3220
	P.O. Box 3310, 299 Federal Building, 110 Michigan St. NW, **Grand Rapids**, MI 49503, 616-456-2693
	P.O. Box 909, 314 Post Office Bldg., **Marquette**, MI 49855, 906-226-2117
Minnesota	416 U.S. Courthouse, 515 W. 1st St., **Duluth**, MN 55802, 218-720-5253
	205 U.S. Courthouse, 118 S. Mills St., **Fergus Falls**, MN 56537, 218-739-4671
	600 Towle Building, 330 Second Ave. South, **Minneapolis**, MN 55401, 612-348-1855
	200 U.S. Courthouse, 316 N. Robert St., **St. Paul**, MN 55101, 612-290-3184
Mississippi	Biloxi Federal Building, 725 Washington Loop, Room 117, **Biloxi**, MS 39533, 601-432-5542
	P.O. Drawer 2448, **Jackson**, MS 39225, 601-965-5301

Missouri	U.S. Courthouse, 811 Grand Ave., Room 913, **Kansas City**, MO 64106, 816-426-3321
	1 Metropolitan Square, 211 N. Broadway, 7th Floor, **St. Louis**, MO 63102, 314-425-4222
Montana	273 Federal Building, 400 N. Main St., P.O. Box 689, **Butte**, MT 59701, 406-782-3354
Nebraska	P.O. Box 428 Downtown Sta., 215 N. 17th St., New Federal Building, **Omaha**, NB 68101, 402-221-4687
	460 Federal Building, 100 Centennial Mall N., **Lincoln**, NB 68508, 402-437-5100
Nevada	300 Las Vegas Blvd. South, **Las Vegas**, NV 89101, 702-388-6257
	4005 Federal Building & Courthouse, 300 Booth St., **Reno**, NV 89509, 702-784-5559
New Hampshire	275 Chestnut St., Room 404, **Manchester**, NH 03101, 603-666-7532
New Jersey	15 N. 7th St., **Camden**, NJ 08102, 609-757-5023
	50 Walnut St., **Newark**, NJ 07102, 201-645-4764
	U.S. Post Office & Courthouse, 402 E. State St., **Trenton**, NJ 08608, 609-989-2198
New Mexico	421 Gold Ave. SW, 3rd Floor, **Albuquerque**, NM 87102, 505-766-8473
New York	327 James T. Foley Courthouse, 445 Broadway, **Albany**, NY 12201, 518-431-0188
	75 Clinton St., **Brooklyn**, NY 11201, 718-330-2188
	310 U.S. Courthouse, 68 Court St., **Buffalo**, NY 14202, 716-551-4130
	601 Veterans Hwy., **Hauppauge**, NY 11788, 516-361-8038
	1 Bowling Green, **New York**, NY 10004, 212-668-2870
	P.O. Box 1000, **Poughkeepsie**, NY 12602, 914-452-4200
	100 State St., Room 2120, **Rochester**, NY 14614, 716-263-3148
	Alexander Pirnie Federal Building, Room 230, **Utica**, NY 13501, 315-793-8101
	1635 Privado Rd., **Westbury**, NY 11590, 516-832-8801
	300 Quarropas St., 5th Floor, **White Plains**, NY 10601, 914-390-4061
North Carolina	401 W. Trade St., **Charlotte**, NC 28202, 704-344-6103
	P.O. Box 26100, 202 S. Elm St., **Greensboro**, NC 27420, 919-333-5647
	P.O. Box 1441, **Raleigh**, NC 27602, 919-856-4752
	P.O. Drawer 2807, 1760 Parkwood Blvd., **Wilson**, NC 27894, 919-237-0248
North Dakota	P.O. Box 1110, 655 1st Ave., **Fargo**, ND 58107, 701-239-5120
Ohio	455 Federal Building, 2 S. Main St., **Akron**, OH 44308, 216-375-5840
	U.S. Bankruptcy Court, 201 Cleveland Ave. SW, **Canton**, OH 44702, 216-489-4426
	Atruim Two, Suite 800, 221 E. 4th St., **Cincinnati**, OH 45202, 513-684-2572
	U.S. Courthouse, 127 Public Square, **Cleveland**, OH 44114, 216-522-4373
	970 N. High St., **Columbus**, OH 43215, 614-469-6638
	120 W. 3rd St., **Dayton**, OH 45402, 513-225-2516
	411 U.S. Courthouse, 1716 Spielbusch Ave., **Toledo**, OH 43624, 419-259-6440
	9 West Front, **Youngstown**, OH 44501, 216-746-7027

Oklahoma	Post Office-Courthouse , 215 D. A. McGee Ave., **Oklahoma City**, OK 73102, 405-231-5642
	P.O. Box 1347, U.S. Post Office & Federal Building, **Okmulgee**, OK 74447, 918-756-9248
	224 S. Boulder Ave., **Tulsa**, OK 74103, 918-581-7645
Oregon	P.O. Box 1335, **Eugene**, OR 97440 (mail) or 404 Federal Building, 211 E. 7th St., **Eugene**, OR 97401 (person), 503-465-6448
	1001 SW 5th Ave., 9th Floor, **Portland**, OR 97204, 503-326-2231
Pennsylvania	717 State Street, Suite 501, **Erie**, PA 16501, 814-453-7580
	P.O. Box 908, Federal Building, 3rd & Walnut Sts., **Harrisburg**, PA 17108, 717-980-2800
	3726 U.S. Courthouse, 601 Market St., **Philadelphia**, PA 19106, 215-597-0926
	1602 Federal Building, 1000 Liberty Ave., **Pittsburgh**, PA 15222, 412-644-2700
	400 Washington St., The Madison, Room 350, **Reading**, PA 19601, 215-320-5255
	217 Federal Building, 197 S. Main St., **Wilkes-Barre**, PA 18701, 717-826-6450
Rhode Island	380 Westminster Mall, Federal Center, **Providence**, RI 02903, 401-528-4477
South Carolina	P.O. Box 1448, 1100 Laurel St., **Columbia**, SC 29202, 803-765-5436
South Dakota	203 Federal Building, 225 S. Pierre St., **Pierre**, SD 57501, 605-224-6013
	104 Federal Building & U.S. Courthouse, 400 S. Phillips Ave., P.O. Box 5060, **Sioux Falls**, SD 57117, 605-330-4541
Tennessee	31 E. 11th St., **Chattanooga**, TN 37401, 615-752-5163
	P.O. Box 1527, **Jackson**, TN 38302, 901-424-9751
	200 Jefferson Ave., Room 413, **Memphis**, TN 38103, 901-544-3202
	207 Customs House, 701 Broadway, **Nashville**, TN 37203, 615-736-5590
Texas	624 S. Polk St., **Amarillo**, TX 79101, 806-376-2302
	816 Congress, First City Centre, Room 1420, **Austin**, TX 78701, 512-482-5237
	300 Willow St., Suite 100, **Beaumont**, TX 77701, 409-839-2617
	615 Leopard St., Suite 113, **Corpus Christi**, TX 78476, 512-888-3484
	14-A-7 U.S. Courthouse, 1100 Commerce St., **Dallas**, TX 75242, 214-767-0814
	111 E. Broadway, Room L100, **Del Rio**, TX 78840, 512-775-2021
	8515 Lockheed Dr., **El Paso**, TX 79925, 915-779-7362
	501 W. 10th St., Room 310, **Fort Worth**, TX 76102, 817-334-3802
	Federal Building, 515 Rusk Ave., 4th Floor, **Houston**, TX 77002, 713-250-5115
	102 Federal Building, 1205 Texas Ave., **Lubbock**, TX 79401, 806-743-7336
	USPO Annex, Room P-163, 100 F Wall St., 200 Wall St., **Midland**, TX 79701, 915-683-1650
	First Interstate Bank Bldg., 660 North Central Expressway,Suite 300B, **Plano**, TX 75074, 214-423-6605
	P.O. Box 1439, Old Post Office Building, **San Antonio**, TX 78295 (mail) or 615 E. Houston St., Room 139, **San Antonio**, TX 78205, 512-229-5187
	200 E. Ferguson St., 2nd Floor, **Tyler**, TX 75702, 903-592-0904
	St. Charles Place, Suite 20, 600 Austin Ave., **Waco**, TX 76701, 817-754-1481

Utah	350 S. Main St., **Salt Lake City**, UT 84101, 801-524-6565
Vermont	P.O. Box 6648, 67 Merchants Row, **Rutland**, VT 05702, 802-747-7629
Virginia	408 Dominion Bank Building, 206 N. Washington St., Room 401, **Alexandria**, VA 22314, 703-557-1716
	P.O. Box 586, 320 Federal Building, **Harrisonburg**, VA 22801, 703-434-6747
	P.O. Box 442, 226 Federal Building, 1100 Main St., **Lynchburg**, VA 24505, 804-845-8880
	222 U.S. Post Office Building 101, 25th Floor, **Newport News**, VA 23612, 804-595-9805
	480 Courthouse, 600 Gramby St., Room 480, **Norfolk**, VA 23510, 804-441-6651
	U.S. Courthouse, Annex Building, **Richmond**, VA 23206, 804-771-2878
	P.O. Box 2390, 200 Old Federal Building, 210 Church Ave., **Roanoke**, VA 24011, 703-857-2391
Washington	315 Park Place Building, 1200 6th Ave., Room 315, **Seattle**, WA 98101, 206-553-7545
	P.O. Box 2164, **Spokane**, WA 92210 (mail) or 904 W. Riverside Ave., Room 321, **Spokane**, WA 99201 (person), 509-353-2404
	1717 Pacific Ave., Room 2100, **Tacoma**, WA 98402, 206-593-6310
West Virginia	P.O. Box 3924, 500 Quarrier St., Room 2201, **Charleston**, WV 25339, 304-347-5114
	P.O. Box 70, 12th & Chapline St., **Wheeling**, WV 26003, 304-233-1655
Wisconsin	P.O. Box 5009, 500 S. Barstow Commons, **Eau Claire**, WI 54702, 715-839-2980
	P.O. Box 548, Room 340, **Madison**, WI 53701 (mail) or 120 N. Henry, Madison, WI 53703 (person), 608-264-5178
	126 U.S. Courthouse, 517 E. Wisconsin Ave., **Milwaukee**, WI 53202, 414-297-3293
Wyoming	111 S. Wolcott St., Room 101, **Casper**, WY 82601, 307-261-5444
	P.O. Box 1107, New Post Office & Courthouse, 2120 Capitol Ave., **Cheyenne**, WY 82003, 307-772-2191

Form	Chapter
Worksheet 1: How Much Will You Have to Repay?	2
Worksheet 2: Secured Debts With Voluntary Security Interests	3
Worksheet 3: Secured Debts Created Without Your Consent	3
Worksheet 4: Unsecured Debts	3
Worksheet 5: Your Total Monthly Income	4
Worksheet 6: Your Total Monthly Expenses	4
Worksheet 7: Your Disposable Income	4
Worksheet 8: Your Exempt and Nonexempt Property	5
Letter to Bankruptcy Court	6
Form 1, Voluntary Petition	6
Form 6, Schedule A—Real Property	6
Form 6, Schedule B—Personal Property	6
Form 6, Schedule C—Property Claimed as Exempt	6
Form 6, Schedule D—Creditors Holding Secured Claims	6
Form 6, Schedule E—Creditors Holding Unsecured Priority Claims	6
Form 6, Schedule F—Creditors Holding Unsecured Nonpriority Claims	6
Form 6, Schedule G—Executory Contracts and Unexpired Leases	6
Form 6, Schedule H—Codebtors	6
Form 6, Schedule I—Current Income of Individual Debtor(s)	6
Form 6, Schedule J—Current Expenditures of Individual Debtor(s)	6
Form 6, Summary of Schedules	6
Form 6, Declaration Concerning Debtor's Schedules	6
Form 7, Statement of Financial Affairs	6
Mailing Matrix	6
Chapter 13 plans	7
Form 3, Application to Pay Filing Fee in Installments	8
Notice to Creditor of Filing for Bankruptcy	9
Form 10, Proof of Claim	9
Amendment Cover Sheet	9
Notice of Change of Address	9
Proof of Service	9
Pleading Paper	9
Daily Expense Form	11

WORKSHEET 1: HOW MUCH WILL YOU HAVE TO REPAY?

1. Total value of your nonexempt property, plus any increase
   for priority debts or to pay back a higher percentage $ _____

2. Amount overdue to mortgage lender; add interest unless
   loan was obtained after October 20, 1994 $ _____

3. Amount overdue to other secured creditors,
   or the value of the collateral lender, plus interest $ _____

4. Compensation on payments on unsecured debts $ _____

5. Trustee's fee $ _____

   Minimum Amount You Will Pay Into Your Plan $ _____

WORKSHEET 2: SECURED DEBTS WITH VOLUNTARY SECURITY INTERESTS

1 Description of debt/ name of creditor	2 Total outstanding balance	3 Regular monthly payment	4 Total amount of arrears	5 Present value of collateral
Mortgages and home equity loans				
Motor vehicle loans				
Personal loans				
Department store charges with security agreements				
Other				

Total $ _____

WORKSHEET 3: SECURED DEBTS CREATED WITHOUT YOUR CONSENT

1 Description of debt/ name of creditor	2 Amount of debt	3 Property affected by lien	4 Present value of property

Judicial liens

_____

_____

_____

_____

_____

Statutory liens

_____

_____

_____

_____

_____

Tax liens

_____

_____

_____

_____

_____

Total $ _____

WORKSHEET 4: UNSECURED DEBTS

1 Description of debt/ name of creditor	2 Total outstanding balance	3 Regular monthly payment	4 Total amount of arrears
Student loans			
Unsecured consolidation loans			
Unsecured personal loans			
Medical (doctors', dentists' and hospital) bills			
Lawyers' and accountants' bills			
Credit and charge cards			
Department store and gasoline credit cards			

WORKSHEET 4: UNSECURED DEBTS (CONTINUED)

1 Description of debt/ name of creditor	2 Total outstanding balance	3 Regular monthly payment	4 Total amount of arrears
Alimony or child support arrears			
Back rent			
Unpaid utility bills (gas, electric, water, phone, cable, garbage)			
Tax debts (no lien recorded or undersecured portion)			
Other			

Total $ _____

If your unsecured debts add up to
more than $250,000 you cannot
file for Chapter 13 bankruptcy.

WORKSHEET 5: YOUR TOTAL MONTHLY INCOME

1 Source of Income		2 Amount of each payment	3 Period covered by each payment	4 Amount per month
A. Wages or Salary				
Job 1:	Gross pay, including overtime:	$ _____	_____	
_____	Subtract:			
	Federal taxes	_____		
	State taxes	_____		
	Social Security (FICA)	_____		
	Union dues	_____		
	Insurance payments	_____		
	Child support wage withholding	_____		
	Other mandatory deductions (specify):			
	_____	_____		
	Subtotal	$ _____		_____
Job 2:	Gross pay, including overtime:	$ _____	_____	
_____	Subtract:			
	Federal taxes	_____		
	State taxes	_____		
	Social Security (FICA)	_____		
	Union dues	_____		
	Insurance payments	_____		
	Child support wage withholding	_____		
	Other mandatory deductions (specify):			
	_____	_____		
	Subtotal	$ _____		_____
Job 3:	Gross pay, including overtime:	$ _____	_____	
_____	Subtract:			
	Federal taxes	_____		
	State taxes	_____		
	Social Security (FICA)	_____		
	Union dues	_____		
	Insurance payments	_____		
	Child support wage withholding	_____		
	Other mandatory deductions (specify):			
	_____	_____		
	Subtotal	$ _____		_____

WORKSHEET 5: YOUR TOTAL MONTHLY INCOME (CONTINUED)

1 Source of Income		2 Amount of each payment	3 Period covered by each payment	4 Amount per month
B. Self-Employment Income				
Job 1:	Pay	$ _____	_____	
_____	Subtract:			
	Federal taxes	_____		
	State taxes	_____		
	Self-employment taxes	_____		
	Other mandatory deductions (specify):			
	_____	_____		
	Subtotal	$ _____		_____
Job 2:	Pay	$ _____	_____	
_____	Subtract:			
	Federal taxes	_____		
	State taxes	_____		
	Self-employment taxes	_____		
	Other mandatory deductions (specify):			
	_____	_____		
	Subtotal	$ _____		_____
C. Other Sources				
Bonuses _____		_____	_____	_____
Dividends and interest _____		_____	_____	_____
Rent, lease or license income _____		_____	_____	_____
Royalties _____		_____	_____	_____
Note or trust income _____		_____	_____	_____
Alimony or child support you receive _____		_____	_____	_____
Pension or retirement income _____		_____	_____	_____
Social Security _____		_____	_____	_____
Other public assistance _____		_____	_____	_____
Other (specify): _____		_____	_____	_____
	Total monthly income			$ _____

WORKSHEET 6: YOUR TOTAL MONTHLY EXPENSES

1 Expenses	2 Amount per month
A. Your residence	
Rent or mortgage	_____
Second mortgage or home equity loan	_____
Homeowners' association fee	_____
Property taxes	_____
Homeowners' or renters' insurance	_____
Maintenance and upkeep	_____
B. Utilities	
Telephone	_____
Gas, heating fuel, electricity	_____
Water and sewer	_____
Garbage	_____
Cable	_____
C. Food	
At home	_____
Restaurants	_____
D. Personal effects	
Toiletries	_____
Drug store items	_____
Personal grooming (haircuts)	_____
Other	_____
E. Clothing	
Purchases	_____
Laundry/dry cleaning	_____
F. Medical	
Medical or health insurance	_____
Dental insurance	_____
Deductibles and copayments	_____
Doctor	_____
Dentist	_____
Eye doctor	_____
Medicines/prescriptions	_____
Hospital	_____
Therapist	_____
G. Transportation	
Car payment	_____
Gasoline	_____
Tolls and parking	_____
Auto insurance	_____

1 Expenses	2 Amount per month
Maintenance	_____
Registration	_____
H. Dependents	
Child care	_____
Allowances	_____
Clothes	_____
Tuition	_____
School books	_____
I. Your or your spouse's education	
(Do not include student loan payment)	
Tuition	_____
Books and fees	_____
J. Miscellaneous personal expenses	
Entertainment	_____
Recreation/hobbies	_____
Newspapers and magazines	_____
Books	_____
Gifts	_____
Memberships	_____
Pet supplies/veterinarian	_____
K. Charitable contributions	_____
L. Insurance	
(Do not include health, home or motor vehicle insurance)	
Disability	_____
Life	_____
Other	_____
M. Support payments	
Alimony, maintenance or spousal support	_____
Child support	_____
Support of other dependents not living at home	_____
N. Regular business expenses	_____
O. Other	
(Do not include back income taxes or unsecured	_____
installment debts, such as student loan,	_____
personal loan or credit card accounts.	_____
These debts will be paid through your plan.)	_____
Total monthly expenses	$ _____

WORKSHEET 7: YOUR DISPOSABLE INCOME

1. **Total Monthly Income** (from Worksheet 5) $ _____

2. subtract **Total Monthly Expenses** (from Worksheet 6)   –   _____

3. **Total Monthly Disposable Income** $ _____

Total Amount Proposed to Pay Unsecured Creditors

typical Chapter 13 repayment plan   x   36 months = $ _____

extended Chapter 13 repayment plan   x   60 months = $ _____

WORKSHEET 8: YOUR EXEMPT AND NONEXEMPT PROPERTY

1 Your property	2 Value of property (actual dollar or garage sale value)	3 Your ownership share (%, $)	4 Amount of liens	5 Amount of your equity	6 Exempt? If not, enter non-exempt amount
1. Real estate					
2. Cash on hand (state source, such as wages, public benefits, etc.)					
3. Deposits of money (state source, such as wages, public benefits, etc.)					
4. Security deposits					
5. Household goods, supplies and furnishings					
6. Books, pictures, art objects; stamp, coin and other collections					

WORKSHEET 8: YOUR EXEMPT AND NONEXEMPT PROPERTY (CONTINUED)

1 Your property	2 Value of property (actual dollar or garage sale value)	3 Your ownership share (%, $)	4 Amount of liens	5 Amount of your equity	6 Exempt? If not, enter non- exempt amount
7. Apparel					
8. Jewelry					
9. Firearms, sports equipment and other hobby equipment					
10. Interests in insurance policies					
11. Annuities					
12. Pension or profit-sharing plans (do not include ERISA-qualified pensions; see Chapter 5, Section A.3)					
13. Stocks and interests in incorporated and unincorporated companies					

WORKSHEET 8: YOUR EXEMPT AND NONEXEMPT PROPERTY (CONTINUED)

1 Your property	2 Value of property (actual dollar or garage sale value)	3 Your ownership share (%, $)	4 Amount of liens	5 Amount of your equity	6 Exempt? If not, enter non- exempt amount
14. Interests in partnerships					
_____	_____	_____	_____	_____	_____
_____	_____	_____	_____	_____	_____
_____	_____	_____	_____	_____	_____
15. Government and corporate bonds and other investment instruments					
_____	_____	_____	_____	_____	_____
_____	_____	_____	_____	_____	_____
_____	_____	_____	_____	_____	_____
_____	_____	_____	_____	_____	_____
_____	_____	_____	_____	_____	_____
_____	_____	_____	_____	_____	_____
16. Accounts receivable					
_____	_____	_____	_____	_____	_____
_____	_____	_____	_____	_____	_____
_____	_____	_____	_____	_____	_____
17. Family support					
_____	_____	_____	_____	_____	_____
_____	_____	_____	_____	_____	_____
_____	_____	_____	_____	_____	_____
18. Other debts owed you where the amount owed is known and definite					
_____	_____	_____	_____	_____	_____
_____	_____	_____	_____	_____	_____
_____	_____	_____	_____	_____	_____
_____	_____	_____	_____	_____	_____
19. Powers exercisable for your benefit other than those listed under real estate					
_____	_____	_____	_____	_____	_____
_____	_____	_____	_____	_____	_____
20. Interests due to another person's death					
_____	_____	_____	_____	_____	_____
_____	_____	_____	_____	_____	_____

WORKSHEET 8: YOUR EXEMPT AND NONEXEMPT PROPERTY (CONTINUED)

1 Your property	2 Value of property (actual dollar or garage sale value)	3 Your ownership share (%, $)	4 Amount of liens	5 Amount of your equity	6 Exempt? If not, enter non- exempt amount
21. All other contingent claims and claims where the amount owed you is not known					
22. Patents, copyrights and other intellectual property					
23. Licenses, franchises and other general intangibles					
24. Automobiles and other vehicles					
25. Boats, motors and accessories					
26. Aircraft and accessories					
27. Office equipment, furnishings and supplies					
28. Machinery, fixtures, equipment and supplies used in business					

WORKSHEET 8: YOUR EXEMPT AND NONEXEMPT PROPERTY (CONTINUED)

1 Your property	2 Value of property (actual dollar or garage sale value)	3 Your ownership share (%, $)	4 Amount of liens	5 Amount of your equity	6 Exempt? If not, enter non- exempt amount
29. Business inventory					
30. Livestock, poultry and other animals					
31. Crops					
32. Farming equipment and implements					
33. Farm supplies, chemicals and feed					
34. Other personal property					

Subtotal _____

Wild Card Exemption − _____

Total Value of Nonexempt Property _____

This is the minimum amount you will have to pay your
unsecured creditors through your Chapter 13 plan.

United States Bankruptcy Court
TO THE COURT CLERK:

Please send me the following materials or information:

- A copy of all local forms published by this court for filing a Chapter 13 bankruptcy, such as:
  - ☐ Chapter 13 bankruptcy cover sheet
  - ☐ Chapter 13 plan
  - ☐ worksheet showing the Chapter 13 plan calculation
  - ☐ summary of the Chapter 13 plan
  - ☐ separate creditor mailing list (matrix)
  - ☐ income deduction order and information on when to submit it
  - ☐ business report for debtor engaged in business
  - ☐ proof of claim (in case I must file claim on behalf of a creditor).
- Copies of all local rules applicable in a Chapter 13 case—rules for the judicial district, this bankruptcy court and any applicable division.
- A copy of the court's calendar.
- The number of copies or sets of all forms I must file.
- The order in which forms should be submitted.

I have additional questions:

1. Is the filing fee still $130? Is the administrative fee still $30?
2. Can I make my plan payments with a personal check? If not, can I use cash or am I limited to cashier's checks and money orders?
3. Is there more than one division for this bankruptcy court? If so, in which division should I file?
4. Must I submit a mailing matrix?
5. Must I submit an income deduction order?
6. Should I two-hole punch my papers or is that done by the court?

I've enclosed a self-addressed envelope for your reply. Thank you.

Sincerely,

FORM 1. VOLUNTARY PETITION

United States Bankruptcy Court _____ District of _____	**Voluntary Petition**

Name of Debtor (if individual, enter Last, First, Middle):	Name of Joint Debtor (Spouse) (Last, First, Middle):
All Other Names used by the Debtor in the last 6 years (include married, maiden, and trade names):	All Other Names used by the Joint Debtor in the last 6 years (include married, maiden, and trade names):
Soc. Sec./Tax I.D. No. (if more than one, state all):	Soc. Sec./Tax I.D. No. (if more than one, state all):
Street Address of Debtor (No. & Street, City, State & Zip Code):	Street Address of Joint Debtor (No. & Street, City, State & Zip Code):
County of Residence or of the Principal Place of Business:	County of Residence or of the Principal Place of Business:
Mailing Address of Debtor (if different from street address):	Mailing Address of Joint Debtor (if different from street address):

Location of Principal Assets of Business Debtor (if different from street address above):

Information Regarding the Debtor (Check the Applicable Boxes)

Venue (Check any applicable box)

☐ Debtor has been domiciled or has had a residence, principal place of business, or principal assets in this District for 180 days immediately preceding the date of this petition or for a longer part of such 180 days than in any other District.

☐ There is a bankruptcy case concerning debtor's affiliate, general partner, or partnership pending in this District.

Type of Debtor (Check all boxes that apply)	**Chapter or Section of Bankruptcy Code Under Which the Petition is Filed** (Check one box)
☐ Individual(s) ☐ Railroad ☐ Corporation ☐ Stockbroker ☐ Partnership ☐ Commodity Broker ☐ Other _____	☐ Chapter 7 ☐ Chapter 11 ☐ Chapter 13 ☐ Chapter 9 ☐ Chapter 12 ☐ Sec. 304 – Case ancillary to foreign proceeding

Nature of Debts (Check one box)	**Filing Fee** (Check one box)
☐ Consumer/Non-Business ☐ Business **Chapter 11 Small Business** (Check all boxes that apply) ☐ Debtor is a small business as defined in 11 U.S.C. § 101 ☐ Debtor is and elects to be considered a small business under 11 U.S.C. §1121(e) (Optional)	☐ Full Filing Fee attached ☐ Filing Fee to be paid in installments. (Applicable to individuals only.) Must attach signed application for the court's consideration certifying that the debtor is unable to pay fee except in installments. Rule 1006(b). See Official Form No. 3.

Statistical/Administrative Information (Estimates only)	This Space for Court Use Only
☐ Debtor estimates that funds will be available for distribution to unsecured creditors. ☐ Debtor estimates that, after any exempt property is excluded and administrative expenses paid, there will be no funds available for distribution to unsecured creditors.	

Estimated Number of Creditors	1-15	16-49	50-99	100-199	200-999	1000-over
	☐	☐	☐	☐	☐	☐

Estimated Assets							
$0 to $50,000	$50,001 to $100,000	$100,001 to $500,000	$500,001 to $1 million	$1,000,001 to $10 million	$10,000,001 to $50 million	$50,000,001 to $100 million	More than $100 million
☐	☐	☐	☐	☐	☐	☐	☐

Estimated Debts							
$0 to $50,000	$50,001 to $100,000	$100,001 to $500,000	$500,001 to $1 million	$1,000,001 to $10 million	$10,000,001 to $50 million	$50,000,001 to $100 million	More than $100 million
☐	☐	☐	☐	☐	☐	☐	☐

Voluntary Petition
(This page must be completed and filed in every case.)

Name of Debtor(s):

Form 1, Page 2

Prior Bankruptcy Case Filed Within Last 6 Years (If more than one, attach additional sheet)		
Location Where Filed:	Case Number:	Date Filed:

Pending Bankruptcy Case Filed by any Spouse, Partner or Affiliate of this Debtor (If more than one, attach additional sheet)		
Name of Debtor:	Case Number:	Date Filed:
District:	Relationship:	Judge:

Signatures

Signature(s) of Debtor(s) (Individual/Joint)

I declare under penalty of perjury that the information provided in this petition is true and correct.

[If petitioner is an individual whose debts are primarily consumer debts and has chosen to file under chapter 7] I am aware that I may proceed under chapter 7, 11, 12 or 13 of title 11, United States Code, understand the relief available under each such chapter, and choose to proceed under chapter 7.

I request relief in accordance with the chapter of title 11, United States Code, specified in this petition.

X _____
Signature of Debtor

X _____
Signature of Joint Debtor

_____
Telephone Number (If not represented by attorney)

_____
Date

Signature of Debtor (Corporation/Partnership)

I declare under penalty of perjury that the information provided in this petition is true and correct and that I have been authorized to file this petition on behalf of the debtor.

The debtor requests relief in accordance with the chapter of title 11, United States Code, specified in this petition.

X _____
Signature of Authorized Individual

_____
Printed Name of Authorized Individual

_____
Title of Authorized Individual

_____
Date

Signature of Attorney

X _____
Signature of Attorney for Debtor(s)

_____
Printed Name of Attorney for Debtor(s)

_____
Firm Name

_____
Address

_____

_____
Telephone Number

_____
Date

Signature of Non-Attorney Petition Preparer

I certify that I am a bankruptcy petition preparer as defined in 11 U.S.C. § 110, that I prepared this document for compensation, and that I have provided the debtor with a copy of this document.

_____
Printed Name of Bankruptcy Petition Preparer

_____
Social Security Number

_____
Address

_____

Names and Social Security numbers of all other individuals who prepared or assisted in preparing this document:

Exhibit A

(To be completed if debtor is required to file periodic reports (e.g., forms 10K and 10Q) with the Securities and Exchange Commission pursuant to Section 13 or 15(d) of the Securities Exchange Act of 1934 and is requesting relief under chapter 11.)

☐ Exhibit A is attached and made a part of this petition.

If more than one person prepared this document, attach additional sheets conforming to the appropriate official form for each person.

Exhibit B

(To be completed if debtor is an individual whose debts are primarily consumer debts.)

I, the attorney for the petitioner named in the foregoing petition, declare that I have informed the petitioner that [he or she] may proceed under chapter 7, 11, 12, or 13 of title 11, United States Code, and have explained the relief available under each such chapter.

X _____
Signature of Attorney for Debtor(s)   Date

X _____
Signature of Bankruptcy Petition Preparer

_____
Date

A bankruptcy petition preparer's failure to comply with the provisions of title 11 and the Federal Rules of Bankruptcy Procedure may result in fines or imprisonment or both. 11 U.S.C. § 110; 18 U.S.C. § 156.

In re _____ ,   Case No. _____
                        Debtor   (If known)

SCHEDULE A—REAL PROPERTY

Except as directed below, list all real property in which the debtor has any legal, equitable, or future interest, including all property owned as a co-tenant, community property, or in which the debtor has a life estate. Include any property in which the debtor holds rights and powers exercisable for the debtor's own benefit. If the debtor is married, state whether husband, wife, or both own the property by placing an "H," "W," "J," or "C" in the column labeled "Husband, Wife, Joint, or Community." If the debtor holds no interest in real property, write "None" under "Description and Location of Property."

Do not include interests in executory contracts and unexpired leases on this schedule. List them in Schedule G—Executory Contracts and Unexpired Leases.

If an entity claims to have a lien or hold a secured interest in any property, state the amount of the secured claim. See Schedule D. If no entity claims to hold a secured interest in the property, write "None" in the column labeled "Amount of Secured Claim."

If the debtor is an individual or if a joint petition is filed, state the amount of any exception claimed in the property only in Schedule C—Property Claimed as Exempt.

DESCRIPTION AND LOCATION OF PROPERTY	NATURE OF DEBTOR'S INTEREST IN PROPERTY	HUSBAND, WIFE, JOINT, OR COMMUNITY	CURRENT MARKET VALUE OF DEBTOR'S INTEREST IN PROPERTY WITHOUT DEDUCTING ANY SECURED CLAIM OR EXEMPTION	AMOUNT OF SECURED CLAIM

Total ➡ $ _____

(Report also on Summary of Schedules.)

In re _____, Case No._____
                    Debtor   (If known)

SCHEDULE B—PERSONAL PROPERTY

Except as directed below, list all personal property of the debtor of whatever kind. If the debtor has no property in one or more of the categories, place an "X" in the appropriate position in the column labeled "None." If additional space is needed in any category, attach a separate sheet properly identified with the case name, case number, and the number of the category. If the debtor is married, state whether husband, wife, or both own the property by placing an "H," "W," "J," or "C" in the column labeled "Husband, Wife, Joint, or Community." If the debtor is an individual or a joint petition is filed, state the amount of any exemptions claimed only in Schedule C—Property Claimed as Exempt.

Do not include interests in executory contracts and unexpired leases on this schedule. List them in Schedule G—Executory Contracts and Unexpired Leases.

If the property is being held for the debtor by someone else, state that person's name and address under "Description and Location of Property."

TYPE OF PROPERTY	NONE	DESCRIPTION AND LOCATION OF PROPERTY	HUSBAND, WIFE, JOINT, OR COMMUNITY	CURRENT MARKET VALUE OF DEBTOR'S INTEREST IN PROPERTY, WITHOUT DEDUCTING ANY SECURED CLAIM OR EXEMPTION
1. Cash on hand.				
2. Checking, savings or other financial accounts, certificates of deposit, or shares in banks, savings and loan, thrift, building and loan, and homestead associations, or credit unions, brokerage houses, or cooperatives.				
3. Security deposits with public utilities, telephone companies, landlords, and others.				
4. Household goods and furnishings, including audio, video, and computer equipment.				

In re _____,   Case No._____
                    Debtor   (If known)

SCHEDULE B—PERSONAL PROPERTY
(Continuation Sheet)

TYPE OF PROPERTY	NONE	DESCRIPTION AND LOCATION OF PROPERTY	HUSBAND, WIFE, JOINT, OR COMMUNITY	CURRENT MARKET VALUE OF DEBTOR'S INTEREST IN PROPERTY, WITHOUT DEDUCTING ANY SECURED CLAIM OR EXEMPTION
5. Books, pictures and other art objects, antiques, stamp, coin, record, tape, compact disc, and other collections or collectibles.				
6. Wearing apparel.				
7. Furs and jewelry.				
8. Firearms and sports, photo-graphic, and other hobby equipment.				
9. Interests in insurance policies. Name insurance company of each policy and itemize surrender or refund value of each.				
10. Annuities. Itemize and name each issuer.				
11. Interests in IRA, ERISA, Keogh, or other pension or profit sharing plans. Itemize.				
12. Stock and interests in incor-porated and unincorporated businesses. Itemize.				
13. Interests in partnerships or joint ventures. Itemize.				

In re _____, Case No._____
  Debtor   (If known)

SCHEDULE B—PERSONAL PROPERTY
(Continuation Sheet)

TYPE OF PROPERTY	NONE	DESCRIPTION AND LOCATION OF PROPERTY	HUSBAND, WIFE, JOINT, OR COMMUNITY	CURRENT MARKET VALUE OF DEBTOR'S INTEREST IN PROPERTY, WITHOUT DEDUCTING ANY SECURED CLAIM OR EXEMPTION
14. Government and corporate bonds and other negotiable and non-negotiable instruments.				
15. Accounts receivable.				
16. Alimony, maintenance, support, and property settlements to which the debtor is or may be entitled. Give particulars.				
17. Other liquidated debts owing debtor including tax refunds. Give particulars.				
18. Equitable or future interest, life estates, and rights or powers exercisable for the benefit of the debtor other than those listed in Schedule of Real Property.				
19. Contingent and noncontingent interests in estate of a decedent, death benefit plan, life insurance policy, or trust.				
20. Other contingent and unliquidated claims of every nature, including tax refunds, counter claims of the debtor, and rights to setoff claims. Give estimated value of each.				
21. Patents, copyrights, and other intellectual property. Give particulars.				
22. Licenses, franchises, and other general intangibles. Give particulars.				

In re _____,   Case No._____
              Debtor   (If known)

SCHEDULE B—PERSONAL PROPERTY
(Continuation Sheet)

TYPE OF PROPERTY	NONE	DESCRIPTION AND LOCATION OF PROPERTY	HUSBAND, WIFE, JOINT, OR COMMUNITY	CURRENT MARKET VALUE OF DEBTOR'S INTEREST IN PROPERTY, WITHOUT DEDUCTING ANY SECURED CLAIM OR EXEMPTION
23. Automobiles, trucks, trailers, and other vehicles and accessories.				
24. Boats, motors, and accessories.				
25. Aircraft and accessories.				
26. Office equipment, furnishings, and supplies.				
27. Machinery, fixtures, equipment, and supplies used in business.				
28. Inventory.				
29. Animals.				
30. Crops—growing or harvested. Give particulars.				
31. Farming equipment and implements.				
32. Farm supplies, chemicals, and feed.				
33. Other personal property of any kind not already listed, such as season tickets. Itemize.				
			Total ➡	$

_____ continuation sheets attached

(Include amounts from any continuation sheets attached. Report total also on Summary of Schedules.)

In re _____,   Case No._____
                    Debtor   (If known)

SCHEDULE C—PROPERTY CLAIMED AS EXEMPT

Debtor elects the exemptions to which debtor is entitled under:

(Check one box)

☐ 11 U.S.C. § 522(b)(1):   Exemptions provided in 11 U.S.C. § 522(d). **Note: These exemptions are available only in certain states.**

☐ 11 U.S.C. § 522(b)(2):   Exemptions available under applicable nonbankruptcy federal laws, state or local law where the debtor's domicile has been located for the 180 days immediately preceding the filing of the petition, or for a longer portion of the 180-day period than in any other place, and the debtor's interest as a tenant by the entirety or joint tenant to the extent the interest is exempt from process under applicable nonbankruptcy law.

DESCRIPTION OF PROPERTY	SPECIFY LAW PROVIDING EACH EXEMPTION	VALUE OF CLAIMED EXEMPTION	CURRENT MARKET VALUE OF PROPERTY WITHOUT DEDUCTING EXEMPTIONS

In re _____,   Case No._____
              Debtor   (If known)

SCHEDULE D—CREDITORS HOLDING SECURED CLAIMS

State the name, mailing address, including zip code, and account number, if any, of all entities holding claims secured by property of the debtor as of the date of filing of the petition. List creditors holding all types of secured interest such as judgment liens, garnishments, statutory liens, mortgages, deeds of trust, and other security interests. List creditors in alphabetical order to the extent practicable. If all secured creditors will not fit on this page, use the continuation sheet provided.

If any entity other than a spouse in a joint case may be jointly liable on a claim, place an "X" in the column labeled "Codebtor," include the entity on the appropriate schedule of creditors, and complete Schedule H—Codebtors. If a joint petition is filed, state whether husband, wife, both of them, or the marital community may be liable on each claim by placing an "H," "W," "J," or "C" in the column labeled "Husband, Wife, Joint, or Community."

If the claim is contingent, place an "X" in the column labeled "Contingent." If the claim is unliquidated, place an "X" in the column labeled "Unliquidated." If the claim is disputed, place an "X" in the column labeled "Disputed." (You may need to place an "X" in more than one of these three columns.)

Report the total of all claims listed on this schedule in the box labeled "Total" on the last sheet of the completed schedule. Report this total also on the Summary of Schedules.

☐   Check this box if debtor has no creditors holding secured claims to report on this Schedule D.

CREDITOR'S NAME AND MAILING ADDRESS INCLUDING ZIP CODE	CODEBTOR	HUSBAND, WIFE, JOINT, OR COMMUNITY	DATE CLAIM WAS INCURRED, NATURE OF LIEN, AND DESCRIPTION AND MARKET VALUE OF PROPERTY SUBJECT TO LIEN	CONTINGENT	UNLIQUIDATED	DISPUTED	AMOUNT OF CLAIM WITHOUT DEDUCTING VALUE OF COLLATERAL	UNSECURED PORTION, IF ANY
ACCOUNT NO.								
			VALUE $					
ACCOUNT NO.								
			VALUE $					
ACCOUNT NO.								
			VALUE $					
ACCOUNT NO.								
			VALUE $					

_____ continuation sheets attached

                                                Subtotal ➡ $_____
                                       (Total of this page)

                                                     Total ➡ $_____
                                       (Use only on last page)

                                 (Report total also on Summary of Schedules)

In re _____ ,   Case No._____
                    Debtor   (If known)

SCHEDULE D—CREDITORS HOLDING SECURED CLAIMS
(Continuation Sheet)

CREDITOR'S NAME AND MAILING ADDRESS INCLUDING ZIP CODE	CODEBTOR	HUSBAND, WIFE, JOINT, OR COMMUNITY	DATE CLAIM WAS INCURRED, NATURE OF LIEN, AND DESCRIPTION AND MARKET VALUE OF PROPERTY SUBJECT TO LIEN	CONTINGENT	UNLIQUIDATED	DISPUTED	AMOUNT OF CLAIM WITHOUT DEDUCTING VALUE OF COLLATERAL	UNSECURED PORTION, IF ANY
ACCOUNT NO.								
			VALUE $					
ACCOUNT NO.								
			VALUE $					
ACCOUNT NO.								
			VALUE $					
ACCOUNT NO.								
			VALUE $					
ACCOUNT NO.								
			VALUE $					
ACCOUNT NO.								
			VALUE $					

Subtotal ➡ $
(Total of this page)

Total ➡ $
(Use only on last page)

Sheet no. _____ of _____ continuation sheets attached to
Schedule of Creditors Holding Secured Claims

(Report total also on Summary of Schedules)

In re _____,   Case No._____
                          Debtor   (If known)

SCHEDULE E—CREDITORS HOLDING UNSECURED PRIORITY CLAIMS

A complete list of claims entitled to priority, listed separately by type of priority, is to be set forth on the sheets provided. Only holders of unsecured claims entitled to priority should be listed in this schedule. In the boxes provided on the attached sheets, state the name and mailing address, including zip code, and account number, if any, of all entities holding priority claims against the debtor or the property of the debtor, as of the date of the filing of the petition.

If any entity other than a spouse in a joint case may be jointly liable on a claim, place an "X" in the column labeled "Codebtor," include the entity on the appropriate schedule of creditors, and complete Schedule H—Codebtors. If a joint petition is filed, state whether husband, wife, both of them, or the marital community may be liable on each claim by placing an "H," "W," "J," or "C" in the column labeled "Husband, Wife, Joint, or Community."

If the claim is contingent, place an "X" in the column labeled "Contingent." If the claim is unliquidated, place an "X" in the column labeled "Unliquidated." If the claim is disputed, place an "X" in the column labeled "Disputed." (You may need to place an "X" in more than one of these three columns.)

Report the total of all claims listed on each sheet in the box labeled "Subtotal" on each sheet. Report the total of all claims listed on this Schedule E in the box labeled "Total" on the last sheet of the completed schedule. Repeat this total also on the Summary of Schedules.

☐ **Check this box if debtor has no creditors holding unsecured priority claims to report on this Schedule E.**

TYPES OF PRIORITY CLAIMS (Check the appropriate box(es) below if claims in that category are listed on the attached sheets)

☐ **Extensions of credit in an involuntary case**

Claims arising in the ordinary course of the debtor's business or financial affairs after the commencement of the case but before the earlier of the appointment of a trustee or the order for relief. 11 U.S.C. § 507(a)(2).

☐ **Wages, salaries, and commissions**

Wages, salaries, and commissions, including vacation, severance, and sick leave pay owing to employees and commissions owing to qualifying independent sales representatives up to $4,300* per person, earned within 90 days immediately preceding the filing of the original petition, or the cessation of business, whichever occurred first, to the extent provided in 11 U.S.C. § 507(a)(3).

☐ **Contributions to employee benefit plans**

Money owed to employee benefit plans for services rendered within 180 days immediately preceding the filing of the original petition, or the cessation of business, whichever occurred first, to the extent provided in 11 U.S.C. § 507(a)(4).

☐ **Certain farmers and fishermen**

Claims of certain farmers and fishermen, up to a maximum of $4,300* per farmer or fisherman, against the debtor, as provided in 11 U.S.C. § 507(a)(5).

☐ **Deposits by individuals**

Claims of individuals up to a maximum of $1,950* for deposits for the purchase, lease, or rental of property or services for personal, family, or household use, that were not delivered or provided. 11 U.S.C. § 507(a)(6).

☐ **Alimony, Maintenance, or Support**

Claims of a spouse, former spouse, or child of the debtor for alimony, maintenance, or support, to the extent provided in 11 U.S.C. § 507(a)(7).

☐ **Taxes and Certain Other Debts Owed to Governmental Units**

Taxes, customs, duties, and penalties owing to federal, state, and local governmental units as set forth in 11 U.S.C. § 507(a)(8).

☐ **Commitments to Maintain the Capital of an Insured Depository Institution**

Claims based on commitments to the FDIC, RTC, Director of the Office of Thrift Supervision, Comptroller of the Currency, or Board of Governors of the Federal Reserve system, or their predecessors or successors, to maintain the capital of an insured depository institution. 11 U.S.C. § 507 (a)(9).

* Amounts are subject to adjustment on April 1, 1998, and every three years thereafter with respect to cases commenced on or after the date of adjustment.

_____ continuation sheets attached

In re _____,   Case No. _____
                    Debtor   (If known)

SCHEDULE E—CREDITORS HOLDING UNSECURED PRIORITY CLAIMS
(Continuation Sheet)

TYPE OF PRIORITY _____

CREDITOR'S NAME AND MAILING ADDRESS INCLUDING ZIP CODE	CODEBTOR	HUSBAND, WIFE, JOINT, OR COMMUNITY	DATE CLAIM WAS INCURRED AND CONSIDERATION FOR CLAIM	CONTINGENT	UNLIQUIDATED	DISPUTED	TOTAL AMOUNT OF CLAIM	AMOUNT ENTITLED TO PRIORITY
ACCOUNT NO.								
ACCOUNT NO.								
ACCOUNT NO.								
ACCOUNT NO.								
ACCOUNT NO.								

Subtotal ➡ $
(Total of this page)

Total ➡ $
(Use only on last page)

Sheet no. _____ of _____ sheets attached to
Schedule of Creditors Holding Unsecured Priority Claims

(Report total also on Summary of Schedules)

In re _____,   Case No._____
                  Debtor   (If known)

SCHEDULE F—CREDITORS HOLDING UNSECURED NONPRIORITY CLAIMS

State the name, mailing address, including zip code, and account number, if any, of all entities holding unsecured claims without priority against the debtor or the property of the debtor as of the date of filing of the petition. Do not include claims listed in Schedules D and E. If all creditors will not fit on this page, use the continuation sheet provided.

If any entity other than a spouse in a joint case may be jointly liable on a claim, place an "X" in the column labeled "Codebtor," include the entity on the appropriate schedule of creditors, and complete Schedule H—Codebtors. If a joint petition is filed, state whether husband, wife, both of them, or the marital community may be liable on each claim by placing an "H," "W," "J," or "C" in the column labeled "Husband, Wife, Joint, or Community."

If the claim is contingent, place an "X" in the column labeled "Contingent." If the claim is unliquidated, place an "X" in the column labeled "Unliquidated." If the claim is disputed, place an "X" in the column labeled "Disputed." (You may need to place an "X" in more than one of these three columns.)

Report the total of all claims listed on this schedule in the box labeled "Total" on the last sheet of the completed schedule. Report this total also on the Summary of Schedules.

☐ Check this box if debtor has no creditors holding unsecured nonpriority claims to report on this Schedule F.

CREDITOR'S NAME AND MAILING ADDRESS INCLUDING ZIP CODE	CODEBTOR	HUSBAND, WIFE, JOINT, OR COMMUNITY	DATE CLAIM WAS INCURRED AND CONSIDERATION FOR CLAIM. IF CLAIM IS SUBJECT TO SETOFF, SO STATE	CONTINGENT	UNLIQUIDATED	DISPUTED	AMOUNT OF CLAIM
ACCOUNT NO.							
ACCOUNT NO.							
ACCOUNT NO.							
ACCOUNT NO.							

_____ continuation sheets attached

Subtotal ➡ (Total of this page) $

Total ➡ (Use only on last page) $

(Report total also on Summary of Schedules)

In re _____, Case No._____
                    Debtor   (If known)

SCHEDULE F—CREDITORS HOLDING UNSECURED NONPRIORITY CLAIMS
(Continuation Sheet)

CREDITOR'S NAME AND MAILING ADDRESS INCLUDING ZIP CODE	CODEBTOR	HUSBAND, WIFE, JOINT, OR COMUNITY	DATE CLAIM WAS INCURRED AND CONSIDERATION FOR CLAIM. IF CLAIM IS SUBJECT TO SETOFF, SO STATE	CONTINGENT	UNLIQUIDATED	DISPUTED	AMOUNT OF CLAIM
ACCOUNT NO.							
ACCOUNT NO.							
ACCOUNT NO.							
ACCOUNT NO.							
ACCOUNT NO.							

Subtotal ➡ $ _____
(Total of this page)

Total ➡ $ _____
(Use only on last page)

Sheet no. _____ of _____ continuation sheets attached to
Schedule of Creditors Holding Unsecured Nonpriorty Claims

(Report total also on Summary of Schedules)

In re _____,   Case No._____
               Debtor   (If known)

SCHEDULE G—EXECUTORY CONTRACTS AND UNEXPIRED LEASES

Describe all executory contracts of any nature and all unexpired leases of real personal property. Include any timeshare interests.

State nature of debtor's interest in contract, i.e., "Purchaser," "Agent," etc. State whether debtor is the lessor or lessee of a lease.

Provide the names and complete mailing addresses of all other parties to each lease or contract described.

NOTE: A party listed on this schedule will not receive notice of the filing of this case unless the party is also scheduled in the appropriate schedule of creditors.

☐ Check this box if debtor has no executory contracts or unexpired leases.

NAME AND MAILING ADDRESS, INCLUDING ZIP CODE, OF OTHER PARTIES TO LEASE OR CONTRACT	DESCRIPTION OF CONTRACT OR LEASE AND NATURE OF DEBTOR'S INTEREST. STATE WHETHER LEASE IS FOR NONRESIDENTIAL REAL PROPERTY. STATE CONTRACT NUMBER OF ANY GOVERNMENT CONTRACT

In re _____,   Case No._____
Debtor   (If known)

SCHEDULE H—CODEBTORS

    Provide the information requested concerning any person or entity, other than a spouse in a joint case, that is also liable on any debts listed by debtor in the schedules of creditors. Include all guarantors and co-signers. In community property states, a married debtor not filing a joint case should report the name and address of the nondebtor spouse on this schedule. Include all names used by the nondebtor spouse during the six years immediately preceding the commencement of this case.

    ☐ Check this box if debtor has no codebtors.

NAME AND ADDRESS OF CODEBTOR	NAME AND ADDRESS OF CREDITOR

In re _____, Case No._____
                    Debtor   (If known)

SCHEDULE I—CURRENT INCOME OF INDIVIDUAL DEBTOR(S)

The column labled "Spouse" must be completed in all cases filed by joint debtors and by a married debtor in a Chapter 12 or 13 case whether or not a joint petition is filed, unless the spouses are separated and a joint petition is not filed.

DEBTOR'S MARITAL STATUS:	DEPENDENTS OF DEBTOR AND SPOUSE		
	NAMES	AGE	RELATIONSHIP

Employment:	DEBTOR	SPOUSE
Occupation		
Name of Employer		
How long employed		
Address of Employer		

INCOME: (Estimate of average monthly income)	DEBTOR	SPOUSE
Current monthly gross wages, salary, and commissions (pro rate if not paid monthly)	$ _____	$ _____
Estimated monthly overtime	$ _____	$ _____
SUBTOTAL	$ _____	$ _____
LESS PAYROLL DEDUCTIONS		
a. Payroll taxes and Social Security	$ _____	$ _____
b. Insurance	$ _____	$ _____
c. Union dues	$ _____	$ _____
d. Other (Specify: _____)	$ _____	$ _____
SUBTOTAL OF PAYROLL DEDUCTIONS	$ _____	$ _____
TOTAL NET MONTHLY TAKE HOME PAY	$ _____	$ _____
Regular income from operation of business or profession or farm (attach detailed statement)	$ _____	$ _____
Income from real property	$ _____	$ _____
Interest and dividends	$ _____	$ _____
Alimony, maintenance or support payments payable to the debtor for the debtor's use or that of dependents listed above	$ _____	$ _____
Social Security or other government assistance (Specify:_____)	$ _____	$ _____
Pension or retirement income	$ _____	$ _____
Other monthly income (Specify:_____)	$ _____	$ _____
_____	$ _____	$ _____
TOTAL MONTHLY INCOME	$ _____	$ _____

TOTAL COMBINED MONTHLY INCOME $ _____   (Report also on Summary of Schedules)

Describe any increase or decrease of more than 10% in any of the above categories anticipated to occur within the year following the filing of this document:

In re _____ ,   Case No._____
                                    Debtor   (If known)

SCHEDULE J—CURRENT EXPENDITURES OF INDIVIDUAL DEBTOR(S)

Complete this schedule by estimating the average monthly expenses of the debtor and the debtor's family. Pro rate any payments made bi-weekly, quarterly, semi-annually, or annually to show monthly rate.

☐ Check this box if a joint petition is filed and debtor's spouse maintains a separate household. Complete a separate schedule of expenditures labeled "Spouse."

Rent or home mortgage payment (include lot rented for mobile home)	$ _____
Are real estate taxes included? Yes _____ No _____	
Is property insurance included? Yes _____ No _____	
Utilities: Electricity and heating fuel	$ _____
Water and sewer	$ _____
Telephone	$ _____
Other _____	$ _____
Home maintenance (repairs and upkeep)	$ _____
Food	$ _____
Clothing	$ _____
Laundry and dry cleaning	$ _____
Medical and dental expenses	$ _____
Transportation (not including car payments)	$ _____
Recreation, clubs and entertainment, newspapers, magazines, etc.	$ _____
Charitable contributions	$ _____
Insurance (not deducted from wages or included in home mortgage payments)	
Homeowner's or renter's	$ _____
Life	$ _____
Health	$ _____
Auto	$ _____
Other _____	$ _____
Taxes (not deducted from wages or included in home mortgage payments)	
(Specify: _____)	$ _____
Installment payments: (In Chapter 12 and 13 cases, do not list payments to be included in the plan)	
Auto	$ _____
Other _____	$ _____
Other _____	$ _____
Alimony, maintenance, and support paid to others	$ _____
Payments for support of additional dependents not living at your home	$ _____
Regular expenses from operation of business, profession, or farm (attach detailed statement)	$ _____
Other _____	$ _____
TOTAL MONTHLY EXPENSES (Report also on Summary of Schedules)	$ _____

[FOR CHAPTER 12 AND CHAPTER 13 DEBTORS ONLY]
Provide the information requested below, including whether plan payments are to be made bi-weekly, monthly, annually, or at some other regular interval.

A. Total projected monthly income	$ _____
B. Total projected monthly expenses	$ _____
C. Excess income (A minus B)	$ _____
D. Total amount to be paid into plan each _____	$ _____
(interval)	

United States Bankruptcy Court

_____ District of _____

In re _____ ,   Case No._____
                     Debtor   (If known)

SUMMARY OF SCHEDULES

Indicate as to each schedule whether that schedule is attached and state the number of pages in each. Report the totals from Schedules A, B, D, E, F, I and J in the boxes provided. Add the amounts from Schedules A and B to determine the total amount of the debtor's assets. Add the amounts from Schedules D, E and F to determine the total amount of the debtor's liabilities.

NAME OF SCHEDULE		ATTACHED (YES/NO)	NUMBER OF SHEETS	AMOUNTS SCHEDULED		
				ASSETS	LIABILITIES	OTHER
A	Real Property			$		
B	Personal Property			$		
C	Property Claimed as Exempt					
D	Creditors Holding Secured Claims				$	
E	Creditors Holding Unsecured Priority Claims				$	
F	Creditors Holding Unsecured Nonpriority Claims				$	
G	Executory Contracts and Unexpired Leases					
H	Codebtors					
I	Current Income of Individual Debtor(s)					$
J	Current Expenditures of Individual Debtor(s)					$

Total Number of Sheets of All Schedules ➡

Total Assets ➡ $

Total Liabilities ➡ $

In re _____,   Case No._____
                    Debtor   (If known)

DECLARATION CONCERNING DEBTOR'S SCHEDULES

DECLARATION UNDER PENALTY OF PERJURY BY INDIVIDUAL DEBTOR

I declare under penalty of perjury that I have read the foregoing summary and schedules consisting of _____
sheets, and that they are true and correct to the best of my knowledge, information, and belief.   (Total shown on summary page plus 1)

Date_____   Signature_____
                                                                                                    Debtor

Date_____   Signature_____
                                                                                        (Joint Debtor, if any)

                                                        [If joint case, both spouses must sign.]

CERTIFICATION AND SIGNATURE OF NON-ATTORNEY BANKRUPTCY PETITION PREPARER (See 11 U.S.C. § 110)

I certify that I am a bankruptcy petition preparer as defined in 11 U.S.C. § 110, that I prepared this document for compensation, and that I have provided the debtor with a copy of this document.

_____   _____
Printed or Typed Name of Bankruptcy Petition Preparer   Social Security No.

_____
Address

Names and Social Security numbers of all other individuals who prepared or assisted in preparing this document:

If more than one person prepared this document, attach additional signed sheets conforming to the appropriate Official Form for each person.

X_____   _____
Signature of Bankruptcy Petition Preparer   Date

A bankruptcy petition preparer's failure to comply with the provisions of Title 11 and the Federal Rules of Bankruptcy Procedure may result in fine or imprisonment or both. 11 U.S.C. § 110; 18 U.S.C. § 156.

DECLARATION UNDER PENALTY OF PERJURY ON BEHALF OF CORPORATION OR PARTNERSHIP

I, the _____ [the president or other officer or an authorized agent of the corporation or a member or an authorized agent of the partnership] of the _____ [corporation or partnership] named as debtor in this case, declare under penalty of perjury that I have read the foregoing summary and schedules, consisting of _____ sheets, and that they are true and correct to the best of my knowledge, information, and belief.
(Total shown on summary page plus 1)

Date_____   Signature_____

                                                        _____
                                                        [Print or type name of individual signing on behalf of debtor]

[An individual signing on behalf of a partnership or corporation must indicate position or relationship to debtor.]

Penalty for making a false statement or concealing property: Fine of up to $500,000, imprisonment for up to 5 years, or both. 18 U.S.C. §§ 152 and 3571.

FORM 7. STATEMENT OF FINANCIAL AFFAIRS

UNITED STATES BANKRUPTCY COURT
_____ DISTRICT OF _____

In re: _____ ,   Case No. _____
                              (Name)   (If known)
                              Debtor

STATEMENT OF FINANCIAL AFFAIRS

This statement is to be completed by every debtor. Spouses filing a joint petition may file a single statement on which the information for both spouses is combined. If the case is filed under Chapter 12 or Chapter 13, a married debtor must furnish information for both spouses whether or not a joint petition is filed, unless the spouses are separated and a joint petition is not filed. An individual debtor engaged in business as a sole proprietor, partner, family farmer, or self-employed professional, should provide the information requested on this statement concerning all such activities as well as the individual's personal affairs.

Questions 1–15 are to be completed by all debtors. Debtors that are or have been in business, as defined below, also must complete Questions 16–21. **Each question must be answered. If the answer to any question is "None," or the question is not applicable, mark the box labeled "None."** If additional space is needed for the answer to any question, use and attach a separate sheet properly identified with the case name, case number (if known), and the number of the question.

DEFINITIONS

"In business." A debtor is "in business" for the purpose of this form if the debtor is a corporation or partnership. An individual debtor is "in business" for the purpose of this form if the debtor is or has been, within the two years immediately preceding the filing of this bankruptcy case, any of the following: an officer, director, managing executive, or person in control of a corporation; a partner, other than a limited partner, of a partnership; a sole proprietor or self-employed.

"Insider." The term "insider" includes but is not limited to: relatives of the debtor; general partners of the debtor and their relatives; corporations of which the debtor is an officer, director, or person in control; officers, directors, and any person in control of a corporate debtor and their relatives; affiliates of the debtor and insiders of such affiliates; any managing agent of the debtor. 11 U.S.C. § 101(30).

---

1. **Income from employment or operation of business**

None
☐   State the gross amount of income the debtor has received from employment, trade, or profession, or from operation of the debtor's business from the beginning of this calendar year to the date this case was commenced. State also the gross amounts received during the **two years** immediately preceding this calendar year. (A debtor that maintains, or has maintained, financial records on the basis of a fiscal rather than a calendar year may report fiscal year income. Identify the beginning and ending dates of the debtor's fiscal year.) If a joint petition is filed, state income for each spouse separately. (Married debtors filing under Chapter 12 or Chapter 13 must state income of both spouses whether or not a joint petition is filed, unless the spouses are separated and a joint petition is not filed.)

    AMOUNT   SOURCE (If more than one)

2. **Income other than from employment or operation of business**

None State the amount of income received by the debtor other than from employment, trade, profession, or operation of the debtor's business
☐ during the **two years** immediately preceding the commencement of this case. Give particulars. If a joint petition is filed, state income for each spouse separately. (Married debtors filing under Chapter 12 or Chapter 13 must state income for each spouse whether or not a joint petition is filed, unless the spouses are separated and a joint petition is not filed.)

AMOUNT	SOURCE

3. **Payments to creditors**

None a. List all payments on loans, installment purchases of goods or services, and other debts, aggregating more than $600 to any creditor, made
☐ within **90 days** immediately preceding the commencement of this case. (Married debtors filing under Chapter 12 or Chapter 13 must include payments by either or both spouses whether or not a joint petition is filed, unless the spouses are separated and a joint petition is not filed.)

NAME AND ADDRESS OF CREDITOR	DATES OF PAYMENTS	AMOUNT PAID	AMOUNT STILL OWING

None b. List all payments made within **one year** immediately preceding the commencement of this case, to or for the benefit of, creditors who
☐ are or were insiders. (Married debtors filing under Chapter 12 or Chapter 13 must include payments by either or both spouses whether or not a joint petition is filed, unless the spouses are separated and a joint petition is not filed.)

NAME AND ADDRESS OF CREDITOR; RELATIONSHIP TO DEBTOR	DATES OF PAYMENTS	AMOUNT PAID	AMOUNT STILL OWING

4. **Suits, executions, garnishments and attachments**

None a. List all suits to which the debtor is or was a party within **one year** immediately preceding the filing of this bankruptcy case. (Married
☐ debtors filing under Chapter 12 or Chapter 13 must include information concerning either or both spouses whether or not a joint petition is filed, unless the spouses are separated and a joint petition is not filed.)

CAPTION OF SUIT AND CASE NUMBER	NATURE OF PROCEEDING	COURT AND LOCATION	STATUS OR DISPOSITION

None b. Describe all property that has been attached, garnished or seized under any legal or equitable process within **one year** immediately preceding the commencement of this case. (Married debtors filing under Chapter 12 or Chapter 13 must include information concerning property of either or both spouses whether or not a joint petition is filed, unless the spouses are separated and a joint petition is not filed.)

NAME AND ADDRESS OF PERSON FOR WHOSE BENEFIT PROPERTY WAS SEIZED	DATE OF SEIZURE	DESCRIPTION AND VALUE OF PROPERTY

5. Repossessions, foreclosures and returns

None   List all property that has been repossessed by a creditor, sold at a foreclosure sale, transferred through a deed in lieu of foreclosure or returned to the seller within **one year** immediately preceding the commencement of this case. (Married debtors filing under Chapter 12 or Chapter 13 must include information concerning property of either or both spouses whether or not a joint petition is filed, unless the spouses are separated and a joint petition is not filed.)

NAME AND ADDRESS OF CREDITOR OR SELLER	DATE OF REPOSSESSION, FORECLOSURE SALE, TRANSFER OR RETURN	DESCRIPTION AND VALUE OF PROPERTY

6. Assignments and receiverships

None a. Describe any assignment of property for the benefit of creditors made within **120 days** immediately preceding the commencement of this case. (Married debtors filing under Chapter 12 or Chapter 13 must include any assignment by either or both spouses whether or not a joint petition is filed, unless the spouses are separated and a joint petition is not filed.)

NAME AND ADDRESS OF ASSIGNEE	DATE OF ASSIGNMENT	TERMS OF ASSIGNMENT OR SETTLEMENT

None b. List all property which has been in the hands of a custodian, receiver, or court-appointed official within **one year** immediately preceding
☐ the commencement of this case. (Married debtors filing under Chapter 12 or Chapter 13 must include information concerning property
of either or both spouses whether or not a joint petition is filed, unless the spouses are separated and a joint petition is not filed.)

NAME AND ADDRESS OF CUSTODIAN	NAME AND LOCATION OF COURT; CASE TITLE & NUMBER	DATE OF ORDER	DESCRIPTION AND VALUE OF PROPERTY

7. Gifts

None List all gifts or charitable contributions made within **one year** immediately preceding the commencement of this case except ordinary
☐ and usual gifts to family members aggregating less than $200 in value per individual family member and charitable contributions aggregating
less than $100 per recipient. (Married debtors filing under Chapter 12 or Chapter 13 must include gifts or contributions by either or both
spouses whether or not a joint petition is filed, unless the spouses are separated and a joint petition is not filed.)

NAME AND ADDRESS OF PERSON OR ORGANIZATION	RELATIONSHIP TO DEBTOR, IF ANY	DATE OF GIFT	DESCRIPTION AND VALUE OF GIFT

8. Losses

None List all losses from fire, theft, other casualty or gambling within **one year** immediately preceding the commencement of this case **or since**
☐ **the commencement of this case.** (Married debtors filing under Chapter 12 or Chapter 13 must include losses by either or both spouses
whether or not a joint petition is filed, unless the spouses are separated and a joint petition is not filed.)

DESCRIPTION AND VALUE OF PROPERTY	DESCRIPTION OF CIRCUMSTANCES AND, IF LOSS WAS COVERED IN WHOLE OR IN PART BY INSURANCE, GIVE PARTICULARS	DATE OF LOSS

9. Payments related to debt counseling or bankruptcy

None
☐

List all payments made or property transferred by or on behalf of the debtor to any person, including attorneys, for consultation concerning debt consolidation, relief under the bankruptcy law or preparation of a petition in bankruptcy within **one year** immediately preceding the commencement of this case.

NAME AND ADDRESS OF PAYEE	DATE OF PAYMENT; NAME OF PAYOR IF OTHER THAN DEBTOR	AMOUNT OF MONEY OR DESCRIPTION AND VALUE OF PROPERTY

10. Other transfers

None
☐

a. List all other property, other than property transferred in the ordinary course of the business or financial affairs of the debtor, transferred either absolutely or as security within **one year** immediately preceding the commencement of this case. (Married debtors filing under Chapter 12 or Chapter 13 must include transfers by either or both spouses whether or not a joint petition is filed, unless the spouses are separated and a joint petition is not filed.)

NAME AND ADDRESS OF TRANSFEREE; RELATIONSHIP TO DEBTOR	DATE	DESCRIBE PROPERTY TRANSFERRED AND VALUE RECEIVED

11. Closed financial accounts

None
☐

List all financial accounts and instruments held in the name of the debtor or for the benefit of the debtor which were closed, sold, or otherwise transferred within **one year** immediately preceding the commencement of this case. Include checking, savings, or other financial accounts, certificates of deposit, or other instruments; shares and share accounts held in banks, credit unions, pension funds, cooperatives, associations, brokerage houses and other financial institutions. (Married debtors filing under Chapter 12 or Chapter 13 must include information concerning accounts or instruments held by or for either or both spouses whether or not a joint petition is filed, unless the spouses are separated and a joint petition is not filed.)

NAME AND ADDRESS OF INSTITUTION	TYPE AND NUMBER OF ACCOUNT AND AMOUNT OF FINAL BALANCE	AMOUNT AND DATE OF SALE OR CLOSING

12. Safe deposit boxes

None   List each safe deposit or other box or depository in which the debtor has or had securities, cash, or other valuables within **one year** immediately preceding the commencement of this case. (Married debtors filing under Chapter 12 or Chapter 13 must include boxes or depositories of either or both spouses whether or not a joint petition is filed, unless the spouses are separated and a joint petition is not filed.)

NAME AND ADDRESS OF BANK OR OTHER DEPOSITORY	NAMES AND ADDRESSES OF THOSE WITH ACCESS TO BOX OR DEPOSITORY	DESCRIPTION OF CONTENTS	DATE OF TRANSFER OR SURRENDER, IF ANY

13. Setoffs

None   List all setoffs made by any creditor, including a bank, against a debt or deposit of the debtor within **90 days** preceding the commencement of this case. (Married debtors filing under Chapter 12 or Chapter 13 must include information concerning either or both spouses whether or not a joint petition is filed, unless the spouses are separated and a joint petition is not filed.)

NAME AND ADDRESS OF CREDITOR	DATE OF SETOFF	AMOUNT OF SETOFF

14. Property held for another person

None   List all property owned by another person that the debtor holds or controls.

NAME AND ADDRESS OF OWNER	DESCRIPTION AND VALUE OF PROPERTY	LOCATION OF PROPERTY

15. Prior address of debtor

None   If the debtor has moved within the **two years** immediately preceding the commencement of this case, list all premises which the debtor occupied during that period and vacated prior to the commencement of this case. If a joint petition is filed, report also any separate address of either spouse.

ADDRESS	NAME USED	DATES OF OCCUPANCY

The following questions are to be completed by every debtor that is a corporation or partnership and by any individual debtor who is or has been, within the **two years** immediately preceding the commencement of this case, any of the following: an officer, director, managing executive, or owner of more than 5 percent of the voting securities of a corporation; a partner, other than a limited partner, of a partnership; a sole proprietor or otherwise self-employed.

*(An individual or joint debtor should complete this portion of the statement **only** if the debtor is or has been in business, as defined above, within the two years immediately preceding the commencement of this case.)*

16. Nature, location and name of business

None a. If the debtor is an individual, list the names and addresses of all businesses in which the debtor was an officer, director, partner, or managing executive of a corporation, partnership, sole proprietorship, or was a self-employed professional within the **two years** immediately preceding the commencement of this case, or in which the debtor owned 5 percent or more of the voting or equity securities, within the **two years** immediately preceding the commencement of this case.

b. If the debtor is a partnership, list the names and addresses of all businesses in which the debtor was a partner or owned 5 percent or more of the voting securities, within the **two years** immediately preceding the commencement of this case.

c. If the debtor is a corporation, list the names and addresses of all businesses in which the debtor was a partner or owned 5 percent or more of the voting securities, within the **two years** immediately preceding the commencement of this case.

NAME	ADDRESS	NATURE OF BUSINESS	BEGINNING AND ENDING DATES OF OPERATION

17. Books, records and financial statements

None a. List all bookkeepers and accountants who within the **six years** immediately preceding the filing of this bankruptcy case kept or supervised the keeping of books of account and records of the debtor.

NAME AND ADDRESS	DATES SERVICES RENDERED

None b. List all firms or individuals who within the **two years** immediately preceding the filing of this bankruptcy case have audited the books of account and records, or prepared a financial statement of the debtor.

NAME AND ADDRESS	DATES SERVICES RENDERED

None c. List all firms or individuals who at the time of the commencement of this case were in possession of the books of account and records of the debtor. If any of the books of account and records are not available, explain.

NAME   ADDRESS

None d. List all financial institutions, creditors and other parties, including mercantile and trade agencies, to whom a financial statement was issued within the **two years** immediately preceding the commencement of this case by the debtor.

NAME AND ADDRESS   DATE ISSUED

18. Inventories

None a. List the dates of the last two inventories taken of your property, the name of the person who supervised the taking of each inventory, and the dollar amount and basis of each inventory.

| | | DOLLAR AMOUNT OF INVENTORY |
| DATE OF INVENTORY | INVENTORY SUPERVISOR | (Specify cost, market or other basis) |

None b. List the name and address of the person having possession of the records of each of the two inventories reported in a., above.

| | NAME AND ADDRESSES OF |
| DATE OF INVENTORY | CUSTODIAN OF INVENTORY RECORDS |

19. Current partners, officers, directors and shareholders

None a. If the debtor is a partnership, list the nature and percentage of partnership interest of each member of the partnership.

| NAME AND ADDRESS | NATURE OF INTEREST | PERCENTAGE OF INTEREST |

None b. If the debtor is a corporation, list all officers and directors of the corporation, and each stockholder who directly or indirectly owns, controls, or holds 5 percent or more of the voting securities of the corporation.

NAME AND ADDRESS	TITLE	NATURE AND PERCENTAGE OF STOCK OWNERSHIP

20. Former partners, officers, directors and shareholders

None a. If the debtor is a partnership, list each member who withdrew from the partnership within **one year** immediately preceding the commencement of this case.

NAME	ADDRESS	DATE OF WITHDRAWAL

None b. If the debtor is a corporation, list all officers or directors whose relationship with the corporation terminated within **one year** immediately preceding the commencement of this case.

NAME AND ADDRESS	TITLE	DATE OF TERMINATION

21. Withdrawals from a partnership or distributions by a corporation

None If the debtor is a partnership or corporation, list all withdrawals or distributions credited or given to an insider, including compensation in any form, bonuses, loans, stock redemptions, options exercised and any other perquisite during **one year** immediately preceding the commencement of this case

NAME AND ADDRESS OF RECIPIENT; RELATIONSHIP TO DEBTOR	DATE AND PURPOSE OF WITHDRAWAL	AMOUNT OF MONEY OR DESCRIPTION AND VALUE OF PROPERTY

[If completed by an individual or individual and spouse]

I declare under penalty of perjury that I have read the answers contained in the foregoing statement of financial affairs and any attachments thereto and that they are true and correct.

Date _____ Signature of Debtor_____

Date _____ Signature of Joint Debtor (if any) _____

CERTIFICATION AND SIGNATURE OF NON-ATTORNEY BANKRUPTCY PETITION PREPARER (See 11 U.S.C. § 110)

I certify that I am a bankruptcy petition preparer as defined in 11 U.S.C. § 110, that I prepared this document for compensation, and that I have provided the debtor with a copy of this document.

_____   _____
Printed or Typed Name of Bankruptcy Petition Preparer   Social Security No.

_____

_____
Address

Names and Social Security numbers of all other individuals who prepared or assisted in preparing this document:

If more than one person prepared this document, attach additional signed sheets conforming to the appropriate Official Form for each person.

X_____   _____
Signature of Bankruptcy Petition Preparer   Date

A bankruptcy petition preparer's failure to comply with the provisions of title 11 and the Federal Rules of Bankruptcy Procedure may result in fine or imprisonment or both. 11 U.S.C. § 110; 18 U.S.C. § 156.

[If completed by or on behalf of a partnership or corporation]

I declare under penalty of perjury that I have read the answers contained in the foregoing statement of financial affairs and any attachments thereto and that they are true and correct to the best of my knowledge, information and belief.

Date _____ Signature _____

_____
Print Name and Title

[An individual signing on behalf of a partnership or corporation must indicate position or relationship to debtor.]

_____ *continuation sheets attached*

Penalty for presenting fraudulent claim: Fine of up to $500,000 or imprisonment for up to 5 years, or both. 18 U.S.C. §§ 152 and 3571.

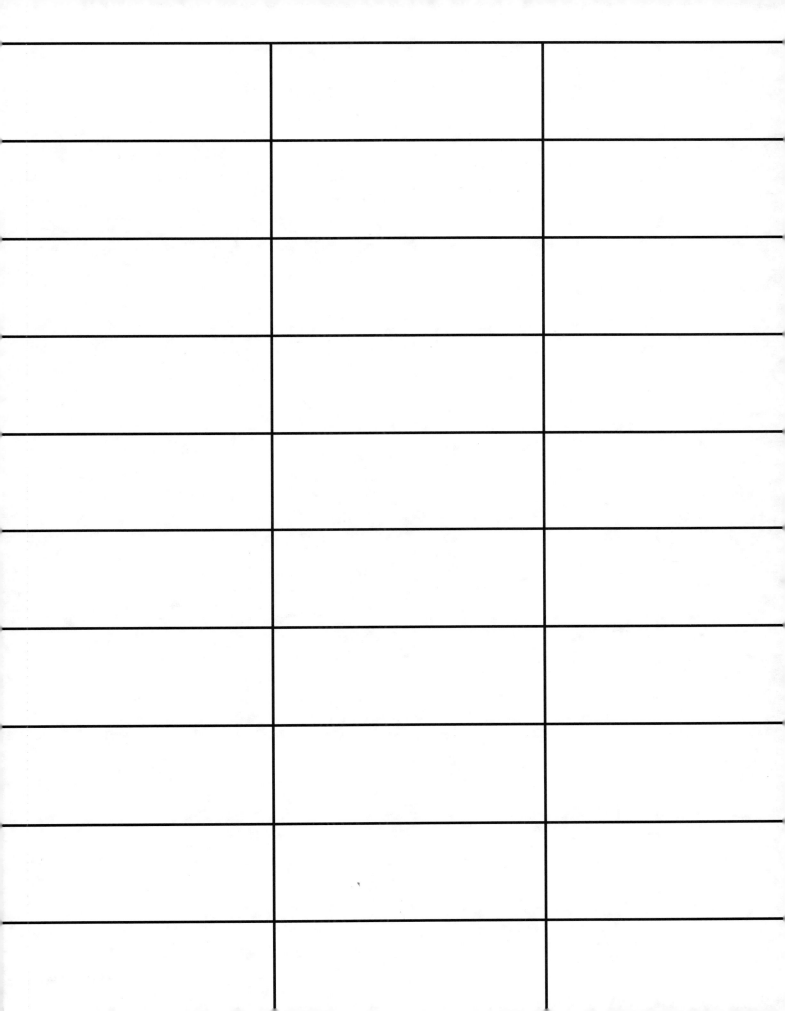

CHAPTER 13 PLAN

In Re: _____

Dated: _____

Debtor
In a joint case,
debtor means debtors in this plan.

Case No. _____

1. PAYMENTS BY DEBTOR —

    a. As of this date of this plan, the debtor has paid the trustee $ _____ .

    b. After the date of this plan, the debtor will pay the trustee $ _____ per _____ for _____ months, beginning within 30 days after the filing of this plan for a total of $ _____ .

    c. The debtor will also pay the trustee _____
    _____

    d. The debtor will pay the trustee a total of $ _____ [line 1(a) + line 1(b) + line 1(c)].

2. PAYMENTS BY TRUSTEE — The trustee will make payments only to creditors for which proofs of claim have been filed, make payments monthly as available, and collect the trustee's percentage fee of 10% for a total of $ _____ [line 1 (d) x .10] or such lesser percentage as may be fixed by the Attorney General. For purposes of this plan, month one (1) is the month following the month in which the debtor makes the debtor's first payment. Unless ordered otherwise, the trustee will not make any payments until the plan is confirmed. Payments will accumulate and be paid following confirmation.

3. PRIORITY CLAIMS — The trustee shall pay in full all claims entitled to priority under § 507, including the following. The trustee will pay the amounts actually allowed.

Creditor	Estimated Claim	Monthly Payment	Beginning in Month #	Number of Payments	TOTAL PAYMENTS
a. Attorney Fees	$_____	$_____	_____	_____	$_____
b. Internal Revenue Service	$_____	$_____	_____	_____	$_____
c. State Dept. of Revenue	$_____	$_____	_____	_____	$_____
d. _____	$_____	$_____	_____	_____	$_____
e. TOTAL					$_____

4. LONG-TERM SECURED CLAIMS NOT IN DEFAULT — The following creditor have secured claims. Payments are current and the debtor will continue to make all payments which come due after the date the petition was filed directly to the creditors. The creditors will retain their liens.

    a. _____

    b. _____

5. HOME MORTGAGES IN DEFAULT [§ 1322 (b)(5)] — The trustee will cure defaults (plus interest at the rate of 8 per cent per annum) on claims secured only by a security interest in real property that is the debtor's principal residence as follows. The debtor will maintain the regular payments which come due after the date the petition was filed. The creditors will retain their liens. The amounts of default are estimates only. The trustee will pay the actual amounts of default.

Creditor	Amount of Default	Monthly Payment	Beginning in Month #	Number of Payments	TOTAL PAYMENTS
a. _____	$_____	$_____	$_____	$_____	$_____
b. _____	$_____	$_____	$_____	$_____	$_____
c. _____	$_____	$_____	$_____	$_____	$_____
d. TOTAL					$_____

6. OTHER LONG-TERM SECURED CLAIMS IN DEFAULT [§ 1322 (b)(5)] — The trustee will cure defaults (plus interest at the rate of 8 per cent per annum) on other claims as follows and the debtor will maintain the regular payments which come due after the date the petition was filed. The creditors will retain their liens. The amounts of default are estimates only. The trustee will pay the actual amounts of default.

Creditor	Amount of Default	Monthly Payment	Beginning in Month #	Number of Payments	TOTAL PAYMENTS
a. _____	$ _____	$ _____	_____	_____	$ _____
b. _____	$ _____	$ _____	_____	_____	$ _____
c. _____	$ _____	$ _____	_____	_____	$ _____
d. TOTAL					$ _____

7. OTHER SECURED CLAIMS [§ 1325 (a)(5)] — The trustee will make payments to the following secured creditors having a value as of confirmation equal to the allowed amount of the creditor's secured claim using a discount rate of 8 percent. The creditor's allowed secured claim shall be the creditor's allowed claim or the value of the creditor's interest in the debtor's property, whichever is less. The creditors shall retain their liens. NOTE: NOTWITHSTANDING A CREDITOR'S PROOF OF CLAIM FILED BEFORE OR AFTER CONFIRMATION, THE AMOUNT LISTED IN THIS PARAGRAPH AS A CREDITOR'S SECURED CLAIM BINDS THE CREDITOR PURSUANT TO 11 U.S.C. § 1327 AND CONFIRMATION OF THE PLAN WILL BE CONSIDERED A DETERMINATION OF THE CREDITOR'S ALLOWED SECURED CLAIM UNDER 11 U.S.C. § 506 (a).

Creditor	Claim Amount	Secured Claim	Monthly Payment	Beginning in Month #	Number of Payments	TOTAL PAYMENTS
a. _____	$ _____	$ _____	$ _____	_____	_____	$ _____
b. _____	$ _____	$ _____	$ _____	_____	_____	$ _____
c. _____	$ _____	$ _____	$ _____	_____	_____	$ _____
d. TOTAL						$ _____

8. SEPARATE CLASS OF UNSECURED CREDITORS — In addition to the class of unsecured creditors specified in ¶ 9, there shall be a separate class of nonpriority unsecured creditors described as follows: _____

   a. The debtor estimates that the total claims in this class are $ _____ .

   b. The trustee will pay this class $ _____ .

9. TIMELY FILED UNSECURED CREDITORS — The trustee will pay holders of nonpriority unsecured claims for which proofs of claim were timely filed the balance of all payments received by the trustee and not paid under ¶ 2, 3, 5, 6, 7 and 8 their pro rata share of approximately $_____ [line 1(d) minus lines 2, 3(e), 5(d), 6(d), 7(d) and 8 (b)].

   a. The debtor estimates that the total unsecured claims held by creditors listed in ¶ 7 are $_____

   b. The debtor estimates that the debtor's total unsecured claims (excluding those in ¶ 7 and ¶ 8) are $_____ .

   c. Total estimated unsecured claims are $_____ [line 9(a) + line 9(b)].

10. TARDILY-FILED UNSECURED CREDITORS — All money paid by the debtor to the trustee under ¶ 1, but not distributed by the trustee under ¶ 2, 3, 5, 6, 7, 8 or 9 shall be paid to holders of nonpriority unsecured claims for which proofs of claim were tardily filed.

11. OTHER PROVISIONS —

12. SUMMARY PAYMENTS —

Trustee's Fee [Line 2] .... $ _____

Priority Claims [Line 3(e)] .... $ _____

Home Mortgage Defaults [Line 5(d)] .... $ _____

Long-Term Debt Defaults [Line 6(d)] .... $ _____

Other Secured Claims [Line 7(d)] .... $ _____

Separate Class [Line 8(b)] .... $ _____

Unsecured Creditors[Line 9(c)] .... $ _____

TOTAL [must equal Line 1(d)] .... $ _____

Signed: _____   Signed: _____
               DEBTOR   DEBTOR (if joint case)

(ATTORNEY NAME:) _____

(ADDRESS:) _____

(CITY) _____ (STATE:) _____

(ZIP:) _____

(PHONE NUMBER:) (____) _____

(BAR NUMBER:) _____

DEBTORS: _____   CASE NO.: _____

DEBTORS PRELIMINARY CHAPTER 13 PLAN

DATE OF PLAN _____   FIRST PAYMENT DUE TO TRUSTEE _____

INCOME $ _____   TRUSTEE PAYMENTS $ _____ FOR ____ MONTHS   PLAN BASE AMOUNT $ _____

EXPENSES $ _____ $ _____ FOR ____ MONTHS   UNSECURED % _____

SURPLUS $ _____ $ _____ FOR ____ MONTHS

ADMINISTRATIVE   NOTICING FEES: # _____ + 3 X 3 X .79 = $ _____

                   ATTORNEY FEES: TOTAL _____ THRU PLAN _____

HOME MORTGAGE   Regular payments beginning _____ to be paid direct. Arrearages to be paid by Trustee as follows:

	ARREARS	THRU	%	TERM	PAYMENT
1ST LIEN _____	$ _____	_____	_____	_____	$ _____
2ND LIEN _____	$ _____	_____	_____	_____	$ _____

SECURED CREDITORS	COLLATERAL	CLAIM	VALUE	%	TERM	PAYMENT
1. _____	_____	$ _____	$ _____	_____	_____	$ _____
2. _____	_____	$ _____	$ _____	_____	_____	$ _____
3. _____	_____	$ _____	$ _____	_____	_____	$ _____
4. _____	_____	$ _____	$ _____	_____	_____	$ _____
5. _____	_____	$ _____	$ _____	_____	_____	$ _____

ANY DEFICIENCY WILL AUTOMATICALLY BE "SPLIT" AND INCLUDED IN UNSECURED.

PRIORITY CREDITORS	TYPE	DISPUTED AMOUNT	CLAIM	TERM	PAYMENT
1. _____	_____	$ _____	$ _____	_____	$ _____
2. _____	_____	$ _____	$ _____	_____	$ _____

SPECIAL CLASS	BASIS	AMOUNT	TERM	PAYMENT
1. _____	_____	$ _____	_____	$ _____
2. _____	_____	$ _____	_____	$ _____

UNSECURED CREDITORS	CLAIM	CREDITORS	CLAIM	CREDITORS	CLAIM
1. _____	$ _____	6. _____	$ _____	11. _____	$ _____
2. _____	$ _____	7. _____	$ _____	12. _____	$ _____
3. _____	$ _____	8. _____	$ _____	13. _____	$ _____
4. _____	$ _____	9. _____	$ _____	14. _____	$ _____
5. _____	$ _____	10. _____	$ _____	15. _____	$ _____

TOTAL UNSECURED AND DEFICIENCIES $ _____

__ CHECK HERE IF ADDITIONAL INFORMATION APPEARS ON REVERSE SIDE (EXECUTORY CONTRACTS? MISCELLANEOUS?)

CERTIFICATE OF SERVICE

I certify that a copy of the above and foregoing "Debtor's Preliminary Chapter 13 Plan" and an "Authorization for Pre-Confirmation Disbursement" was by me on this _____ day _____ of 19____ served on the trustee and all creditors listed on the original matrix and any amended matrix filed in this case by United States First Class mail.

_____

Attorney for Debtor or Pro Se Debtor

SPECIAL PROVISIONS:
(Balloon, proceeds of sale;
recovery on lawsuit, etc.

_____

_____

_____

_____

ADDITIONAL CREDITORS:

HOME MORTGAGE:

	ARREARS	THRU	%	TERM	PAYMENT
3RD LIEN _____	$ _____	_____	____	_____	$ _____
4TH LIEN _____	$ _____	_____	____	_____	$ _____

SECURED CREDITORS	COLLATERAL	CLAIM	VALUE	%	TERM	PAYMENT
6. _____	_____	$ _____	$ _____	____	_____	$ _____
7. _____	_____	$ _____	$ _____	____	_____	$ _____
8. _____	_____	$ _____	$ _____	____	_____	$ _____
9. _____	_____	$ _____	$ _____	____	_____	$ _____
10. _____	_____	$ _____	$ _____	____	_____	$ _____

PRIORITY CREDITORS	DISPUTED AMOUNT	CLAIM	TERM	PAYMENT
3. _____	$ _____	$ _____	_____	$ _____
4. _____	$ _____	$ _____	_____	$ _____

SPECIAL CLASS	BASIS	AMOUNT	TERM	PAYMENT
3. _____	_____	$ _____	_____	$ _____
4. _____	_____	$ _____	_____	$ _____

UNSECURED CREDITORS	CLAIM	CREDITORS	CLAIM	CREDITORS	CLAIM
_____	$ _____	_____	$ _____	_____	$ _____
_____	$ _____	_____	$ _____	_____	$ _____
_____	$ _____	_____	$ _____	_____	$ _____
_____	$ _____	_____	$ _____	_____	$ _____
_____	$ _____	_____	$ _____	_____	$ _____

DEBTOR(S) _____   CASE NO. _____

CHAPTER 13 PLAN OR SUMMARY

I. The projected disposable income of the debtor(s) is submitted to the supervision and control of the Trustee and the Debtor(s) shall pay to the Trustee the sum of:

$ _____   ☐ Weekly   ☐ Bi-weekly   ☐ Semi-monthly   ☐ Monthly

☐ Direct Payment   ☐ Payroll Deduction on Wages of: ☐ Debtor   ☐ Spouse

Length of plan is approximately _____ months, and total debt to be paid through plan is approximately

$_____.

II. From the payments so received the Trustee shall make disbursements as follows:

A. <u>PRIORITY</u> payments described in 11 USC §507 in full in deferred cash payments.

B. The holder of each allowed <u>SECURED</u> claim shall retain the lien securing such claim until a discharge is granted and such claim shall be paid in full with interest at a rate of _____% per annum in deferred cash payments as follows:

1. Mortgage Debts:

Name of Mortgage company	Home-stead Yes/No	Total amount of debt	Arrears to be paid by Trustee	Months included in arrearage amount	Post-petition –OR– payments to begin Month/Year* (Direct to creditor)	Amount of regular mortgage to be paid by Trustee

2. Other Secured Debts:

Name of creditor	Total amount of debt	Debtor's value	Description collateral	If Applicable** Interest factor	If Applicable** Debtor's Fixed Payments

C. The Debtor(s) will make direct payments as follows:

Name of creditor	Total of debt	Description of collateral	Reason for direct payment

D. Special provisions. Explanation:

_____

_____

_____

_____

☐ This is an original plan.

☐ This is an amended plan replacing plan dated _____.

☐ This plan proposes to pay unsecured creditors _____ %.

☐ Insurance on vehicle: ☐ Proof of Insurance attached, OR:

                                  ☐ Insurance through Trustee requested

Dated: _____   _____
                                          Signature of Debtor

Dated: _____   _____
                                          Signature of Debtor

FORM 3. APPLICATION TO PAY FILING FEE IN INSTALLMENTS

UNITED STATES BANKRUPTCY COURT

_____ DISTRICT OF _____

In re _____,   Case No._____

Debtor   (If known)

                                                            Chapter _____

APPLICATION TO PAY FILING FEE IN INSTALLMENTS

1.   In accordance with Fed. R. Bankr. P. 1006, I apply for permission to pay the Filing Fee amounting to $_____ in installments.

2.   I certify that I am unable to pay the Filing Fee except in installments.

3.   I further certify that I have not paid any money or transferred any property to an attorney for services in connection with this case and that I will neither make any payment nor transfer any property for services in connection with this case until the filing fee is paid in full.

4.   I propose the following terms for the payment of the Filing Fee*

        $ _____   Check one   ☐   With the filing of the petition, or
                                                          ☐   On or before _____

        $ _____   on or before _____

        $ _____   on or before _____

        $ _____   on or before _____

*   The number of installments proposed shall not exceed four (4), and the final installment shall be payable not later than 120 days after filing the petition. For cause shown, the court may extend the time of any installment, provided the last installment is paid not later than 180 days after filing the petition. Fed. R. Bankr. P. 1006(b)(2).

5.   I understand that if I fail to pay any installment when due my bankruptcy case may be dismissed and I may not receive a discharge of my debts.

_____   _____
Signature of Attorney   Date   Signature of Debtor   Date
                                                                    (In a joint case, both spouses must sign.)

_____   _____
Name of Attorney   Signature of Joint Debtor (if any)   Date

CERTIFICATION AND SIGNATURE OF NON-ATTORNEY BANKRUPTCY PETITION PREPARER (See 11 U.S.C. § 110)

I certify that I am a bankruptcy petition preparer as defined in 11 U.S.C. § 110, that I prepared this document for compensation, and that I have provided the debtor with a copy of this document. I also certify that I will not accept money or any other property from the debtor before the filing fee is paid in full.

_____   _____
Printed or Typed Name of Bankruptcy Petition Preparer   Social Security No.

_____

Address

Names and Social Security numbers of all other individuals who prepared or assisted in preparing this document:

If more than one person prepared this document, attach additional signed sheets conforming to the appropriate Official Form for each person.

X_____   _____
Signature of Bankruptcy Petition Preparer   Date

A bankruptcy petition preparer's failure to comply with the provisions of title 11 and the Federal Rules of Bankruptcy Procedure may result in fine or imprisonment or both. 11 U.S.C. § 110; 18 U.S.C. § 156.

ORDER APPROVING PAYMENT OF FILING FEE IN INSTALLMENTS

IT IS ORDERED that the debtor(s) pay the filing fee in installments on the terms proposed in the foregoing application.

IT IS FURTHER ORDERED that until the filing fee is paid in full the debtor shall not pay any money for services in connection with this case, and the debtor shall not relinquish any property as payment for services in connection with this case.

BY THE COURT

Date: _____   _____

To Whom It May Concern:

On _____, I filed a voluntary petition under Chapter 13 of the U.S. Bankruptcy Code in the Bankruptcy Court for the _____.

The case number is _____. No attorney is representing me. Under 11 U.S.C. § 362(a), you may not:

- take any action against me or my property to collect any debt
- file or pursue any lawsuit against me
- place a lien on my real or personal property
- take any property to satisfy an already recorded lien
- repossess any property in my possession
- discontinue any service or benefit currently being provided to me, or
- take any action to evict me from where I live.

A violation of these prohibitions may be considered contempt of court and punished accordingly.

Very truly yours,

FORM 10. PROOF OF CLAIM

UNITED STATES BANKRUPTCY COURT _____ DISTRICT OF _____		**PROOF OF CLAIM**
Name of Debtor	Case Number	

NOTE: This form should not be used to make a claim for an administrative expense arising after the commencement of the case. A "request" for payment of an administrative expense may be filed pursuant to 11 U.S.C. § 503.

Name of Creditor (The person or other entity to whom the debtor owes money or property):	☐ Check box if you are aware that anyone else has filed a proof of claim relating to your claim. Attach copy of statement giving particulars.	
Name and address where notices should be sent:	☐ Check box if you have never received any notices from the bankruptcy court in this case.	
	☐ Check box if the address differs from the address on the envelope sent to you by the court.	
Telephone number:		THIS SPACE IS FOR COURT USE ONLY
Account or other number by which creditor identifies debtor:	Check here if this claim ☐ replaces a previously filed claim dated: _____ ☐ amends	

1. Basis for Claim
- ☐ Goods sold
- ☐ Services performed
- ☐ Money loaned
- ☐ Personal injury/wrongful death
- ☐ Taxes
- ☐ Other _____

- ☐ Retiree benefits as defined in 11 U.S.C. § 1114(a)
- ☐ Wages, salaries, and compensation (fill out below)

Your SS #: _____ _____ _____

Unpaid compensation for services performed

from _____ to _____
      (date)   (date)

2. Date debt was incurred:

3. If court judgment, date obtained:

4. Total Amount of Claim at Time Case Filed: $_____

If all or part of your claim is secured or entitled to priority, also complete Item 5 or 6 below.

☐ Check this box if claim includes interest or other charges in addition to the principal amount of the claim. Attach itemized statement of all interest or additional charges.

5. Secured Claim.
- ☐ Check this box if your claim is secured by collateral (including a right of setoff).

Brief Description of Collateral:
- ☐ Real Estate   ☐ Motor Vehicle
- ☐ Other _____

Value of Collateral: $_____

Amount of arrearage and other charges <u>at time case filed</u> included in secured claim, if any: $_____

6. Unsecured Priority Claim.
- ☐ Check this box if you have an unsecured priority claim

Amount entitled to priority $_____

Specify the priority of the claim:
- ☐ Wages, salaries, or commissions (up to $4,300),* earned within 90 days before filing of the bankruptcy petition or cessation of the debtor's business, whichever is earlier — 11 U.S.C. § 507(a)(3).
- ☐ Contributions to an employee benefit plan — 11 U.S.C. § 507(a)(4).
- ☐ Up to $1,950* of deposits toward purchase, lease, or rental of property or services for personal, family, or household use — 11 U.S.C. § 507(a)(6).
- ☐ Alimony, maintenance, or support owed to a spouse, former spouse, or child — 11 U.S.C. § 507(a)(7).
- ☐ Taxes or penalties owed to governmental units — 11 U.S.C. § 507(a)(8).
- ☐ Other — Specify applicable paragraph of 11 U.S.C. § 507(a)(____).

*Amounts are subject to adjustment on 4/1/98 and every 3 years thereafter with respect to cases commenced on or after the date of adjustment.

	THIS SPACE IS FOR COURT USE ONLY
7. Credits: The amount of all payments on this claim has been credited and deducted for the purpose of making this proof of claim. **8. Supporting Documents:** *Attach copies of supporting documents,* such as promissory notes, purchase orders, invoices, itemized statements of running accounts, contracts, court judgments, mortgages, security agreements, and evidence of perfection of lien. DO NOT SEND ORIGINAL DOCUMENTS. If the documents are not available, explain. If the documents are voluminous, attach a summary. **9. Date-Stamped Copy:** To receive an acknowledgment of the filing of your claim, enclose a stamped, self-addressed envelope and copy of this proof of claim.	
Date Sign and print the name and title, if any, of the creditor or other person authorized to file this claim (attach copy of power of attorney, if any):	

Penalty for presenting fraudulent claim: Fine of up to $500,000 or imprisonment for up to 5 years, or both. 18 U.S.C. §§ 152 and 3571.

Your Name, Address & Phone Number:

In Pro Per

UNITED STATES BANKRUPTCY COURT FOR THE _____

DISTRICT OF _____

In re _____)
)   Case No. _____
)
)
)   AMENDMENT COVER SHEET
                      Debtor(s)   )
_____

Presented herewith are the original and one copy of the following:

☐ Voluntary Petition (Note: Spouse may not be added or deleted subsequent to initial filing.)

☐ Schedule A—Real Property

☐ Schedule B—Personal Property

☐ Schedule C—Property Claimed as Exempt

☐ Schedule D—Creditors Holding Secured Claims

☐ Schedule E—Creditors Holding Unsecured Priority Claims

☐ Schedule F—Creditors Holding Unsecured Nonpriority Claims

☐ Schedule G—Executory Contracts and Unexpired Leases

☐ Schedule H—Codebtors

☐ Schedule I—Current Income of Individual Debtor(s)

☐ Schedule J—Current Expenditures of Individual Debtor(s)

☐ Summary of Schedules

☐ Statement of Financial Affairs

☐ I have enclosed $20 fee because I am adding new creditors or changing addresses after original Meeting of Creditors Notice has been sent.

_____   _____
Signature of Debtor   Signature of Debtor's Spouse

I (we) _____ and _____,

_____, the debtor(s) in this case, declare under penalty of perjury that the information set forth

in the amendment attached hereto consisting of _____ pages is true and correct to the best of my (our) information and belief.

Dated: _____, 19_____

_____   _____
Signature of Debtor   Signature of Debtor's Spouse

Your Name, Address & Phone Number:

In Pro Per

UNITED STATES BANKRUPTCY COURT FOR THE _____

DISTRICT OF _____

In re   )
)   Case No. _____
)
)   NOTICE OF CHANGE OF ADDRESS
                              Debtor(s)   )
_____

Social Security Number (H): _____

Social Security Number (W): _____

MY (OUR) FORMER MAILING ADDRESS AND PHONE NUMBER WAS:

Name: _____

Street: _____

City: _____

State/Zip: _____

Phone: (____) _____

PLEASE BE ADVISED THAT AS OF_____, 19_____, MY (OUR) NEW
MAILING ADDRESS AND PHONE NUMBER IS:

Name: _____

Street: _____

City: _____

State/Zip: _____

Phone: (____) _____

_____
Signature of Debtor

_____
Signature of Debtor's Spouse

Your Name, Address & Phone Number:

In Pro Per

UNITED STATES BANKRUPTCY COURT FOR THE _____

DISTRICT OF _____

In re)
) Case No. _____
)
)
Debtor(s))

PROOF OF SERVICE BY MAIL

I, _____, declare that:

I am over the age of 18 years and not a party to the within bankruptcy. I reside in or am employed in the County of _____

_____. My residence/business address is _____

_____.

On _____, I served the within _____

_____ by placing a true and correct copy of it in a sealed envelope with first-class postage fully prepaid, in

the United States mail at _____, addressed as follows:

I declare under penalty of perjury that the foregoing is true and correct. Executed on _____, 19_____ at

_____.

_____
Signature

DAILY EXPENSES

Date:

Item	Cost

Date:

Item	Cost

Date:

Item	Cost

Date:

Item	Cost

Index

A

Accountants' bills, as unsecured debt, 3/8
Accounts receivable, and bankruptcy estate, 5/2
Address change, filing, 9/26
"Adequate protection" of collateral, 7/9, 9/27
Administrative claims, and order of payment, 7/3, 7/4
Administrative fees. *See* Fees
Adversary proceedings, 10/4
Alimony
    as dischargeable debt, 2/3
    expenses, 4/8
    and funding repayment plan, 4/2
    as nondischargeable debt, 2/3-4, 7/14
    and order of payment, 7/3
    as unsecured debt, 3/8
Allowed claims, 9/15
Amendments to bankruptcy forms, 9/25-26, 10/5
    cover sheet, 9/26, Appendix 3
Antiques, valuation, 5/12
Application to Pay Filing Fee in Installments. *See* Form 3
Arm's-length creditors, 6/40
Assignments, 6/40-41
Attorneys. *See* Lawyers and other professional help
Automatic stay, 6/1, 8/1, 9/1, 9/3, 9/27
    and codebtors, 9/28

B

Back taxes. *See* Taxes
"Bad faith," 10/6. *See also* Good faith
Balloon mortgage payments, 7/6-7
Bank loans, and credit rebuilding, 11/5-6
Bankruptcy. *See specific type of bankruptcy* (Chapter 7; Chapter 13, *etc.*)
Bankruptcy Code (Title 11), Intro/3, 12/5-6
Bankruptcy courts, 2/5-6, 6/1-3
    addresses, Appendix 2
    security, 9/6
Bankruptcy estate, 5/1-3
Bankruptcy forms. *See* Forms
Bankruptcy law
    changes in, Intro/3
    geographical variations, 2/2
    See also Bankruptcy Code
Bankruptcy lawyers. *See* Lawyers and other professional help
Bankruptcy papers/petitions. *See* Forms

Bankruptcy payments, 2/1, 2/2-3, 10/1-4
    first, after filing bankruptcy petition, 9/4
    missed, 10/2-3
Bankruptcy petition preparers (BPPs), 8/2, 9/6, 12/3
Bankruptcy Reform Act of 1994, 3/7
Bankruptcy repayment plans. *See* Chapter 13 bankruptcy repayment plans
Bankruptcy Rules, 6/4
Bankruptcy trustees. *See* Trustees
Base plans, for repaying creditors, 7/12-13
Beneficial ownership, 6/10
"Best interests of the creditors" test, and bankruptcy plan, 9/10
Bill collector/creditor harassment, 1/5
Bonds, valuation, 5/12
Bonuses, and funding repayment plan, 4/5
BPPs (bankruptcy petition preparers), 8/2, 9/6, 12/3
Budgeting, 11/1-2
Business debtors, defined, 6/41
Businesses, Intro/1, 9/4
    income, and funding repayment plan, 4/2

C

California exemption system, 5/13
Cars. *See* Motor vehicles
Case numbers, 6/40
Cases and case law, 12/6
Cash advances, as unsecured debt, 3/7
CCCS (Consumer Credit Counseling Services), 1/5
Change of address, filing, 9/26
Chapter 7 bankruptcy, Intro/1
    and "Chapter 20" bankruptcy, 7/11
    compared to Chapter 13 bankruptcy, 1/2-4, 5/1
    conversion from Chapter 13 bankruptcy, 2/1, 9/14, 10/5-6
    conversion to Chapter 13 bankruptcy, 1/6, 2/1, 7/11
Chapter 11 bankruptcy, Intro/1, 1/1, 1/5-6
Chapter 12 bankruptcy, Intro/1, 1/2, 1/6
Chapter 13 bankruptcy, Intro/1-2, 2/1-6, 9/2
    alternatives, 1/4-6
    checklists, 2/2, 6/3, 7/2, 8/1
    compared to Chapter 7 bankruptcy, 1/2-4, 5/1
    conversion from Chapter 7 bankruptcy, 1/6, 2/1, 7/11
    conversion to Chapter 7 bankruptcy, 2/1, 9/14, 10/5-6
    and debts, 3/1-10
    dismissal, 2/1, 8/2, 9/11, 10/5
    eligibility, 1/1-2, 1/6, 9/27

fees. *See* Fees

forms. *See* Forms

geographic variations in law, 2/2

and income, 4/1-9

legal help, Intro /2-3, 12/1-3

multiple filings, 8/2, 9/9

overview, 2/1-6, 9/2

payments, 2/1, 2/2-3, 9/4, 10/1-4

post-bankruptcy experiences, 11/1-7

process and procedures, 2/1-2, 9/2

and property, 5/1-15

refiling, 2/1

trustees. *See* Trustees

Chapter 13 bankruptcy repayment plans, 2/1, 2/2-3, 7/1-21

     checklist, 7/2

     completion, 10/7

     and creditors, 7/2, 7/3, 7/14, 9/7, 9/9-10

     forms, 2/1, 7/1-2, 7/15-21, Appendix 3

     hardship discharge, 2/1, 2/4, 10/6

     inability to complete, 10/4-7

     income to fund, 4/2, 4/5

     modifications, 2/1, 9/7, 9/12, 9/15, 10/2-4

     and mortgage, 7/5-8

     objections to, 9/7, 9/9-10

     payment schedule, 7/3

     rejection, 4/5

     samples, 7/15-21, Appendix 3

     and taxes, 7/4-5

     time limits, 2/1, 2/2, 7/2-3

"Chapter 20" bankruptcy, 7/11

Charge card bills, as unsecured debt, 3/7. *See also* Credit cards and credit card bills

Charitable expenses, 4/8

Child support, 2/3-4

     expenses, 4/8

     and funding repayment plan, 4/2

     liens, 6/22

     as nondischargeable debt, 7/14

     and order of payment, 7/3, 7/4

     as unsecured debt, 3/8

Children, expenses, 4/8

Church dues, as unsecured debt, 3/8

Claims

     by creditors, 9/15, 10/1-2

     secured, 6/10, 6/20-23

Clothing expenses, 4/6

Codebtors, 3/2, 6/20, 6/32, 7/13, 9/28

Codebtors Schedule. *See* Schedule H

Collateral, 3/1, 3/6-7, 7/7-9

     and "adequate protection," 7/9, 9/27

     insurance on, 9/4

     for mortgage loan, 7/7-8

     surrender, 7/5-6, 7/8-9

     valuation, 7/9

     See also Secured debts

Collection agencies, and harassment, 1/5

Collections and collectibles, valuation, 5/12

Collier on Bankruptcy, 12/4

Commissions, and funding repayment plan, 4/2

Commodity brokers, 1/1

Community property, 5/3, 6/10

Confirmation, attempts to revoke, 10/4

Confirmation hearings, 2/5, 9/10-12

Consumer Credit Counseling Services (CCCS), 1/5

Contingent claims, 6/22

Continuation pages, 6/5

Contracts, 7/15

     denial of, 11/7

     executory, 6/30

Copies of bankruptcy forms, 6/3, 6/4, 8/1

Cost of Living Schedules, 4/6

Courts. *See* Bankruptcy courts

Credit

     counselors, 1/5

     files, 11/2, 11/4

     liaisons, 10/7

     rebuilding, 11/1-6

     re-establishment programs, 10/7

     repair agencies, 11/5

     reporting agencies, 11/2, 11/4

Credit cards and credit card debts, 6/20, 11/5

     as unsecured debt, 3/7

Creditors

     arm's length, 6/40

     claims, 9/15, 10/1-2

     correcting list, 9/25-26

     discrimination against, 9/10

     insider, 6/40

     meeting, 2/5, 9/4-7, 9/26

     motions, 9/26-28

     negotiations with, 1/5, 7/10, 11/5

     objections to bankruptcy plan, 9/7, 9/9-10

     order of payment, 7/2, 7/3

     overlooked, 6/29, 10/1-2

     and payment plans, 7/2, 7/3, 7/14, 9/7, 9/9-10

     payments directly to, 7/15

     postpetition, 10/4

     preferred, 6/40

     priority, 6/23, 7/4, 9/15

     secured, 6/22, 9/15

     unsecured, 7/12-15, 9/15

     See also Schedules D, E, and F

Creditors Holding ... Claims Schedules. *See* Schedules D, E, and F

Creditors' meeting, 2/5, 9/4-7, 9/26

Criminal fines. *See* Fines and penalties

Criminal proceedings, and automatic stay, 9/1

Curing the default, 7/6-7, 7/10-11

Current Expenditures/Income of Individual Debtor(s) Schedules. *See* Schedules I and J

D

Daily Expenses form, 11/1-2, 11/3, Appendix 3
    sample, 11/3, Appendix 3
Debtor Rehabilitation/Credit Re-establishment programs, 10/7
Debtors Anonymous, 11/1
Debts, 1/2
    and alternatives to bankruptcy, 1/4-6
    dischargeable, 7/13-14
    discharged, 11/6-7. *See also* Hardship discharge
    disputed, 3/2
    and hardship discharge, 2/1, 2/4, 10/6
    incurred after repayment plan confirmation, 10/4
    limits, 1/2
    marital, 2/3
    nondischargeable, 2/3-4, 7/3, 7/14
    order in which paid, 7/2, 7/3
    and rehabilitation programs, 10/7
    secured. *See* Secured debts
    statute of limitations, 1/4
    undersecured, 3/4, 3/6
    unsecured. *See* Unsecured debts
    worksheets, 3/3, 3/5, 3/9, Appendix 3
Declaration Concerning Debtor's Schedules, 6/36, 6/39, Appendix 3
    amendments, 9/25-26
    filing, 8/1-2
    instructions, 6/4-5, 6/36
    sample, 6/39, Appendix 3
Deeds of trust. *See* Mortgages
Deficiency balance, 7/5-6, 7/8
Dependents, expenses, 4/8
Depositions, 9/9
Disability payments, and funding repayment plan, 4/5
Discharge hearings, 2/6, 10/7
Discharge order, 10/7, 11/7
Dischargeable debts, 7/13-14
Discharged debts, attempts to collect, 11/6-7
Discovery technique, 9/9
Discrimination
    against creditors, in bankruptcy plan, 9/10
    and filing for bankruptcy, 9/12
    post-bankruptcy, 11/7
Dismissal of bankruptcy case, 2/1, 8/2, 9/11, 10/5
Disposable income, 1/1, 2/2-3, 4/9
    calculating, 4/1-9
    defined, 2/2, 4/1, 4/5, 4/9
    reduction in, and repayment plan, 10/3
    worksheet, 4/9, Appendix 3
Disputed claims, 6/22

Disputed debts, 3/2
Dividends
    and bankruptcy estate, 5/2
    and funding repayment plan, 4/5
Divorce, and judicial liens, 3/7
Divorce decree property, 9/4
Do nothing approach to debt problems, 1/4
Doubling, 5/13, 6/17
Driver's licenses, denial of, 11/7
Drunken driving fees, as nondischargeable debt, 2/4, 7/14

E

Easement holders, 6/10
Educational expenses, 4/8
Educational loans. *See* Student loans
Eligibility for Chapter 13 bankruptcy, 1/1-2, 1/6, 9/27
Emergency filings, 6/1, 8/1, 8/2, 9/1
Employee Retirement Income Security Act (ERISA), 4/5, 5/2, 5/14
Equity. *See* Home equity
ERISA (Employee Retirement Income Security Act), 4/5, 5/2, 5/14
Excise taxes, 7/5
Executory contracts, 6/30, 7/15
Executory Contracts and Unexpired Leases Schedule. *See* Schedule G
Exempt property, 1/2, 3/6, 5/13-15
Exempt Property Schedule. *See* Schedule C
Exemptions
    California rules, 5/13
    limits, on property, 5/13
    overview, 5/13
    systems, federal and state, 5/13-15, Appendix 1
Expenses and expenditures, 4/5-8
    "reasonable," 4/5, 4/6, 4/8
    worksheets, 4/7, Appendix 3
    See also Schedule J
Extensions granted to priority creditors, 9/15

F

Fair Debt Collections Practices Act, 1/5
Family farming bankruptcy. *See* Chapter 12 bankruptcy
Feasibility objection to bankruptcy plan, 9/10
Federal bankruptcy courts. *See* Bankruptcy courts
Federal bankruptcy exemption systems, 5/13-14, Appendix 1
Federal non-bankruptcy exemption systems, 5/13-14, Appendix 1
Federal taxes. *See* Taxes
Fee simple ownership, 6/9-10
Fees
    amending forms, 9/25
    bankruptcy petition preparers, 9/6, 12/3
    Chapter 7 bankruptcy, 1/2, 1/6
    Chapter 11 bankruptcy, 1/5-6
    Chapter 13 bankruptcy, filing and administrative, 1/6, 2/1, 6/2, 7/3, 7/4, 8/2

legal, Intro/3, 12/2-3
and order of payment, 7/4
trustees, 7/3-4
Filing bankruptcy forms, 8/1-2
emergency, 6/1, 8/1, 8/2, 9/1
multiple, 8/2, 9/9
See also specific forms and schedules
Fines and penalties, as nondischargeable debt, 2/4
Firing from job, and bankruptcy, 9/12, 11/7
Fixed percentage plans for repaying creditors, 7/12-13
Food expenses, 4/6
Foreclosures, 7/5, 7/6
Form 1 (Voluntary Petition), 6/5-9, Appendix 3
filing, 8/1-2
instructions, 6/5-6, 6/9
sample, 6/7-8, Appendix 3
Form 3 (Application to Pay Filing Fee in Installments), 6/3, 8/2, Appendix 3
instructions, 8/2
sample, Appendix 3
Form 6 (schedules, summary, and declaration), 6/9-39, Appendix 3
amendments, 9/25-26
filing, 8/1-2
instructions, 6/4-5
samples, Appendix 3
See also specific schedules
Form 7 (Statement of Financial Affairs), 6/40-52, Appendix 3
amendments, 9/25-26
filing, 8/1-2
instructions, 6/4-5, 6/40-41, 6/52
sample, 6/42-51, Appendix 3
Form 10 (Proof of Claim), 9/10, 9/15, 9/16, Appendix 3
filing, 9/15
sample, 9/16, Appendix 3
Form 20A (Notice of Motion or Objection), 9/7, 9/8
sample, 9/8
Forms, 6/1-54, 7/1-21, 8/1-2, Appendix 3
amendments, 9/25-27, 10/5
checklists, 6/3, 7/2, 8/1
completing, 6/4-5
continuation pages, 6/5
and conversion to Chapter 7 bankruptcy, 10/5-6
copies, 6/3, 6/4, 8/1
filing, 8/1-2
samples, Appendix 3
See also specific forms and schedules
Fraud, and revocation of confirmation, 10/4
Friends and relatives, and financial support
and funding repayment plan, 4/2, 4/5
as unsecured debt, 3/8
Full payment discharge, 10/7
Future interest, 6/10

G

Gifts, 5/2-3, 6/41
Good faith objection to bankruptcy plan, 2/1, 9/9-10
Government benefits, and funding repayment plan, 4/5
Grace period in repayment, 2/1
"Greater than" plans, for repaying creditors, 7/13

H

Harassment by bill collectors/creditors, 1/5
Hardship discharge, 2/1, 10/6
of student loans, 2/4
HEAL (Health Education Assistance Loans), 2/4
Health club dues, as unsecured debt, 3/8
Hearings, 2/5-6, 7/9-10, 9/10-12, 10/2, 10/7
Home equity, 5/12-13, 5/14
loans, 3/1
Homestead exemptions, 3/7, 5/13-14
Honesty, importance of, 6/4-5, 6/12
Housing expenses, 4/6

I

Icons used in book, Intro/3
"Impairs the exemption," defined, 9/21
Income, 4/1-9
disposable, 1/1, 2/2-3, 4/9, 10/3
increases in , 10/2
irregular, 4/2, 4/5
monthly, 4/1-5
"stable and regular" concept, 1/1
worksheets, 4/3-4, 4/9, Appendix 3
See also Schedule I
Income Deduction Order, 4/5, 6/52-54, 9/11-12
ending, 10/7
instructions, 6/52
sample, 6/53-54, Appendix 3
Income taxes. *See* Taxes
Inherited property, and bankruptcy estate, 5/2, 9/4
Injury compensation, and bankruptcy estate, 5/2
Insider creditors, 6/40
Installment payments, of fees, 8/2. *See also* Form 3
Insurance policies and proceeds
and bankruptcy estate, 5/2, 9/4
on collateral, 9/4
expenses, 4/8
proof of, 9/4
and repayment plan, 10/4
valuation, 5/12
Interest
and funding repayment plan, 4/5
on mortgage arrears, 7/7
on secured debts, 7/10, 7/14-15

on taxes, 7/4
Internal Revenue Service (IRS), 7/4-5
    and Chapter 7 bankruptcy, 1/4
    See also Tax liens; Taxes
Internet. *See* Web sites
Intoxicated driving fees, as nondischargeable debt, 2/4, 7/14

J

Jail, 1/4
Jewelry, valuation, 5/12
Joint debts, 3/2 . *See also* Codebtors
Judgment liens. *See* Judicial liens
"Judgment proof" concept, 1/4
Judicial districts and divisions, 6/1
Judicial liens, 3/4, 3/7, 6/22, 9/21

L

Law libraries, 12/3-6
Lawsuits, and debt liability, 3/8
Lawyers and other professional help, Intro/2-3, 12/1-3
    bills, as unsecured debt, 3/8
    and Chapter 11 bankruptcy, 1/6
    fees, Intro/3, 7/4, 12/2-3
Leases, 6/9, 7/15
    income from, and funding repayment plan, 4/2
    unexpired, 6/30
Legal paper (pleading paper), 6/52, 9/11, Appendix 3
    sample, Appendix 3
Legal research, 12/3-7
    online resources, 12/7
Letter(s)
    to bankruptcy court, sample, 6/2, Appendix 3
    to creditor, sample, 11/6
Libraries, legal, 12/3-6
License receipts, and funding repayment plan, 4/2
Lienholders, 6/10
Liens, 3/1-7, 5/12-13, 6/22
    avoidance (elimination), 3/6-7, 7/8, 7/11, 9/15, 9/17-25
    defined, 3/1
    types, 3/4, 6/22
    valuation, 6/10
Life estate, 6/10
Liquidation bankruptcy, Intro/1. *See also* Chapter 7 bankruptcy
Liquor licenses, denial of, 11/7
Living expenses, 4/5-8
Loans
    bank, 11/5-6
    home equity, 3/1
    personal, 3/2, 3/8
    student, 2/4, 3/8, 7/14, 11/7
Local court rules and forms, 6/2-3
Local merchants, and rebuilding credit, 11/6

M

Mailing Matrix, 6/52, Appendix 3
    amendments, 9/25-26
    filing, 8/1-2
    instructions, 6/4-5, 6/52
    sample, Appendix 3
Marital debts, 2/3
Marital settlement agreement property, 9/4
Marital status, defined, 6/32
Market value of property, defined, 5/11-12
Married couples
    as codebtors, 6/32
    and community property, 5/3, 6/10
    and doubling, 5/13, 6/17
    filing together, 2/4-5
    and property, 5/3, 5/11
Mechanic's/materialman's liens, 6/22
Medical expenses, 4/6, 4/8
    as unsecured debt, 3/8
Meeting of creditors. *See* Creditors' meeting
Merchants, local, and rebuilding credit, 11/6
Missed payments, 10/2-3
Modification of bankruptcy plan
    and confirmation hearing, 9/7, 9/12, 9/15
    and payment problems, 2/1, 10/2-4
Modification of mortgage, 7/7-8
Monthly expenses/income. *See* Expenses and expenditures; Income
Mortgages, 3/1, 7/5-8
    and balloon payments, 7/6-7
    default, and order of payment, 7/3
    expenses, 4/6
    second, 3/1
Motion for "adequate protection," 9/27
Motion for relief from automatic stay, 9/27
Motion for relief from codebtor stay, 9/28
Motion objecting to eligibility for bankruptcy, 9/27
Motion to Avoid Judicial Lien, 9/21, 9/22
Motion to Avoid Judicial Lien (on Real Estate), 9/21, 9/23
Motion to Avoid Nonpossessory, Nonpurchase Money Security Interest, 9/17, 9/18, 9/21
Motion to convert to Chapter 7 bankruptcy, 10/5
Motion to convert to Chapter 13 bankruptcy, 1/6
Motion to dismiss bankruptcy case, 10/5
Motion to reinstate bankruptcy case, 10/5
Motion to request lien avoidance, 3/6, 9/17-21
Motions (document), defined, 1/6
    of creditors, 9/26-28
Motor vehicles
    expenses, 4/8
    loans, 3/1
    replacement, and repayment plan, 10/3-4
    valuation, 5/11
Multiple bankruptcy filings, 8/2, 9/9

N

National Bankruptcy Review Commission (NBRC), Intro/3

Negotiations with creditors, 1/5, 7/10, 11/5

Nolo Press

    forms, 6/4

    Web site, Intro/3

Nonconsensual liens, 3/1, 3/4-6, 3/7

Nondischargeable debts, 2/3-4, 7/3, 7/14

Nonexempt property, 1/2, 2/2, 5/1-15

    valuation, 5/11-15

Nonpossessory nonpurchase money security interests, 3/6, 6/22, 9/17-19, 9/21

Nonpurchase money security interests, 3/6, 6/22, 9/17-19, 9/21

Note income, and funding repayment plan, 4/2

Notice of Appointment of Trustee, 9/3

Notice of Change of Address, 9/26, Appendix 3

    sample, Appendix 3

Notice of Commencement of Case, 9/3

Notice of Entry of Order Confirming Chapter 13 Plan, 9/12, 9/14

    sample, 9/14

Notice of Federal Tax Lien, 3/4

Notice of Motion or Objection. *See* Form 20A

Notice of Motion to Avoid Judicial Lien, sample, 9/24

Notice of Motion to Avoid Nonpossessory, Nonpurchase Money Security Interest, 9/19, 9/21

    sample, 9/19

Notice to Creditor of Filing for Bankruptcy, 9/1, 9/3, 9/26, Appendix 3

    sample, 9/3, Appendix 3

O

Online legal resources, 12/7

Order Confirming Chapter 13 Plan, 9/12, 9/13

    sample, 9/13

Order Dismissing Chapter 13 Case, 8/2

Order to Avoid Judicial Lien, 9/21, 9/24

    sample, 9/24

Order to Avoid Judicial Lien (on Real Estate), 9/21

Order to Avoid Nonpossessory, Nonpurchase Money Security Interest, 9/19, 9/21

    sample, 9/19

Ownership of property, 5/1-3, 6/9-10

P

Papers, bankruptcy. *See* Forms

Parental Loans for Students (PLUS), 2/4

Payment plans. *See* Chapter 13 bankruptcy repayment plans

Payments to creditors. *See* Bankruptcy payments

Payroll taxes, 7/5

Penalties and fines, as nondischargeable debt, 2/4

Pensions and pension benefits

    and bankruptcy estate, 5/2, 5/14

    and funding repayment plan, 4/5

    and income deduction order, 9/11

Per capita plans for repaying creditors, 7/13

Perjury, 6/4-5, 6/36. *See also* Honesty

Personal effects expenses, 4/6

Personal expenses, 4/8

Personal loans, 3/2

    as unsecured debt, 3/8

Personal Property Schedule. *See* Schedule B

Petitions, bankruptcy. *See* Forms

Pleading paper (blank legal paper), 6/52, 9/11, Appendix 3

    sample, Appendix 3

PLUS (Parental Loans for Students), 2/4

Possessory nonpurchase-money security interests, 6/22

Post-bankruptcy experiences, 9/12, 11/1-7

Postpetition creditors, 10/4

Postpetition debts, 7/14

Power of appointment, 6/10

Priority creditors, 6/23, 7/4, 9/15

Priority debts, 2/2, 7/3, 7/4

Pro rata plans for repaying creditors, 7/13

Pro tanto plans for repaying creditors, 7/12

Procedural rules, 12/6

Proof of claim, 9/10, 9/15, 9/16

Proof of Claim Form. *See* Form 10

Proof of Service by Mail, 9/20, 9/21, 9/26, Appendix 3

    sample, 9/20, Appendix 3

Property, 5/1-15

    acquired after filing for bankruptcy, 9/4, 10/6

    exempt, 1/2, 3/6, 5/13-15

    nonexempt, 1/2, 2/2, 5/1-15

    ownership, 5/1-3, 6/9-10

    sale, 4/5, 7/11, 10/2

    surrender, 7/5-6, 7/8-9

    taxes, 7/5. *See also* Taxes

    valuation, 5/11-15, 7/9-10

    worksheet, 5/8-10, Appendix 3

Property Claimed as Exempt Schedule. *See* Schedule C

Property Schedules. *See* Schedules A, B, and C

Public benefits

    denial of, 11/7

    and Income Deduction Order, 9/11

Public utilities. *See* Utility bills

Purchase-money security interests, 6/22

Q

Questions commonly asked at creditors' meeting, 9/5-6

R

Real estate

    valuation, 5/11

    See also Liens; Mortgages

Real Property Schedule. *See* Schedule A

Receiverships, 6/40-41

Redemption rights, 7/6

Refiling for bankruptcy, 2/1

Relief from stay hearing, 2/6

Rental expenses, 4/6

    unpaid, as unsecured debt, 3/8

Rental income

    and bankruptcy estate, 5/2

    and funding repayment plan, 4/2

Reorganization bankruptcy, Intro/1. *See also specific reorganization bankruptcy* (Chapter 11, 12, or 13)

Repayment plans. *See* Chapter 13 bankruptcy repayment plans

Restitution to victim, as nondischargeable debt, 2/4, 7/14

Retirement benefits, and funding repayment plan, 4/5

Royalties

    and bankruptcy estate, 5/2

    and funding repayment plan, 4/2

S

Salaries. *See* Wages and salaries

Sale of property, and funding repayment plan, 4/5

Sales commissions, and funding repayment plan, 4/2

Schedule A (Real Property), 6/9-11, Appendix 3

    amendments, 9/25-26

    filing, 8/1-2

    instructions, 6/4-5, 6/9-10

    sample, 6/11, Appendix 3

Schedule B (Personal Property), 6/12-17, Appendix 3

    amendments, 9/25-26

    filing, 8/1-2

    instructions, 6/4-5, 6/12, 6/17

    sample, 6/13-16, Appendix 3

Schedule C (Property Claimed as Exempt), 6/17-19, Appendix 3

    amendments, 9/25-26

    filing, 8/1-2

    instructions, 6/4-5, 6/17

    sample, 6/18-19, Appendix 3

Schedule D (Creditors Holding Secured Claims), 6/20-23, Appendix 3

    amendments, 9/25-26

    filing, 8/1-2

    instructions, 6/4-5, 6/20, 6/22-23

    sample, 6/21, Appendix 3

Schedule E (Creditors Holding Unsecured Priority Claims), 6/23-26, Appendix 3

    amendments, 9/25-26

    filing, 8/1-2

    instructions, 6/4-5, 6/23, 6/26

    sample, 6/24-25, Appendix 3

Schedule F (Creditors Holding Unsecured Nonpriority Claims), 6/26-29, Appendix 3

    amendments, 9/25-26

    filing, 8/1-2

    instructions, 6/4-5, 6/26, 6/29

    sample, 6/27-28, Appendix 3

Schedule G (Executory Contracts and Unexpired Leases), 6/30-31, Appendix 3

    amendments, 9/25-26

    filing, 8/1-2

    instructions, 6/4-5, 6/30

    sample, 6/31, Appendix 3

Schedule H (Codebtors), 6/32, 6/33, Appendix 3

    amendments, 9/25-26

    filing, 8/1-2

    instructions, 6/4-5, 6/32

    sample, 6/33, Appendix 3

Schedule I (Current Income of Individual Debtor(s)), 6/32, 6/34, 6/35, Appendix 3

    amendments, 9/25-26

    filing, 8/1-2

    instructions, 6/4-5, 6/32, 6/34

    sample, 6/35, Appendix 3

Schedule J (Current Expenditures of Individual Debtor(s)), 6/34, 6/36, 6/37, Appendix 3

    amendments, 9/25-26

    filing, 8/1-2

    instructions, 6/4-5, 6/34, 6/36

    sample, 6/37, Appendix 3

Sears, debts to, 3/1, 10/1

Seasonal work, and funding repayment plan, 4/2

Second mortgages, 3/1

Secured claims, 6/10, 6/20-23

Secured credit cards, 11/5

Secured creditors, 6/20, 9/15

Secured debts, 1/2, 3/1-7, 7/2, 7/8-11

    defaults, and order of payment, 7/3

    defined, 1/1, 3/1, 7/8

    interest rates, 7/10

    repayment plan, 7/8-11

    worksheets, 3/3, 3/5, Appendix 3

Security interests, 3/1-4, 3/6-7

Social Security benefits

    and funding repayment plan, 4/5

    and Income Deduction Order, 9/11

Sole proprietors, 1/1

Spousal support. *See* Alimony

Spouses. *See* Marital property; Married couples; *etc.*

State bankruptcy exemption systems, 5/13-14, Appendix 1

State taxes. *See* Taxes

Statement by Debtor's Attorney of Fees Charged, 9/6

Statement by Debtor's Attorney of No Fees Charged, 9/6

Statement of Financial Affairs. *See* Form 7

Statement of Intention, 10/5

Statement to credit bureau, sample, 11/4

Statute of limitations, 1/4

Statutes, legal, 12/5-6

Statutory liens, 3/4

Stay. *See* Automatic stay
Stockbrokers, 1/1
Stocks and stock dividends
    and bankruptcy estate, 5/2
    valuation, 5/12
Store charges, 3/1
Strike funds, and funding repayment plan, 4/5
Student loans
    consolidated, 2/4
    denial of, 11/7
    as dischargeable debt, 2/4
    as nondischargeable debt, 2/4, 7/14
    as unsecured debt, 3/8
Summary of Schedules, 6/36, 6/38, Appendix 3
    amendments, 9/25-26
    filing, 8/1-2
    instructions, 6/4-5, 6/36
    sample, 6/38, Appendix 3
Synagogue dues, as unsecured debt, 3/8

T

Tax liens, 3/4, 6/22, 9/21, 9/25
Taxes, 7/4-5, 9/15
    and Chapter 7 bankruptcy, 1/4
    penalties and interest, 7/4
    refunds, and bankruptcy estate, 5/2
Tear-out forms, Appendix 3
Tele-Lawyer, 12/2
Termination pay, and bankruptcy estate, 5/2
Timeshares, 6/9
Title 11 (Bankruptcy Code), Intro/3,12/5-6
Tools of trade or profession, 3/7
Transportation expenses, 4/8
Trucks. *See* Motor vehicles
Trust income, and funding repayment plan, 4/2
Trustees, Intro/1, 2/1, 2/5, 9/3-4
    and completion of repayment plan, 10/7
    and creditors' meeting, 9/4-7
    and creditors' motions, 9/27
    and dismissal of bankruptcy case, 10/5
    fees, 2/2, 2/5, 7/3-4
    and help with forms, 6/5
    and modifying repayment plan, 10/2-4

U

Undersecured debt, 3/4
Undue hardship
    and debts, 2/1
    and student loans, 2/4
Unemployment benefits, and funding repayment plan, 4/5
Unexpired leases, 6/30, 7/15
Unexpired Leases Schedule. *See* Schedule G
Union dues, as unsecured debt, 3/8
United States Code Title 11 (Bankruptcy Code), Intro/3, 12/5-6
Unliquidated claims, 6/22
Unsecured creditors, 7/12-15, 9/15
    classifying, 7/13-14
    and order of payment, 7/4
Unsecured debts, 1/2, 2/2, 3/7-10, 7/2, 7/12-15
    changing to secured, 3/8
    defined, 1/2, 3/7
    and repayment plan, 7/12-15
    worksheet, 3/9-10, Appendix 3
Utility bills, 4/6
    as unsecured debt, 3/8

V

Vacation pay, and bankruptcy estate, 5/2
Valuation hearings, 2/5, 7/10
Value of property, 5/11-15, 7/9-10
Vehicles. *See* Motor vehicles
Voluntary Petition. *See* Form 1

W

Wages and salaries
    and bankruptcy estate, 5/2
    garnishment, 9/4, 9/12
    and Income Deduction Order, 9/11-12
    owed, and order of payment, 7/4
Web sites, 12/7
    Kelley Blue Book, 5/11
    Nolo Press, Intro/3
Wild card exemptions, 5/15, 6/17
Workers' compensation benefits, and funding repayment plan, 4/5
Worksheets
    debts, 3/3, 3/5, 3/9-10, Appendix 3
    expenses, 4/7, Appendix 3
    income, disposable, 4/9, Appendix 3
    income, monthly, 4/3-4, Appendix 3
    property, 5/4-8, Appendix 3
    repayment amount, 2/3, Appendix 3

CATALOG

		PRICE	CODE

BUSINESS

	PRICE	CODE
The California Nonprofit Corporation Handbook	$29.95	NON
The California Professional Corporation Handbook	$34.95	PROF
The Employer's Legal Handbook	$29.95	EMPL
▣ Form Your Own Limited Liability Company (Book w/Disk—PC)	$34.95	LIAB
▣ Hiring Independent Contractors: The Employer's Legal Guide, (Book w/Disk—PC)	$29.95	HICI
▣ How to Form a CA Nonprofit Corp.—w/Corp. Records Binder & PC Disk	$49.95	CNP
▣ How to Form a Nonprofit Corp., Book w/Disk (PC)—National Edition	$39.95	NNP
▣ How to Form Your Own Calif. Corp.—w/Corp. Records Binder & Disk—PC	$39.95	CACI
▣ How to Form Your Own California Corporation (Book w/Disk—PC)	$34.95	CCOR
▣ How to Form Your Own Florida Corporation, (Book w/Disk—PC)	$39.95	FLCO
▣ How to Form Your Own New York Corporation, (Book w/Disk—PC)	$39.95	NYCO
▣ How to Form Your Own Texas Corporation, (Book w/Disk—PC)	$39.95	TCOR
How to Mediate Your Dispute	$18.95	MEDI
How to Write a Business Plan	$21.95	SBS
The Independent Paralegal's Handbook	$29.95	PARA
Legal Guide for Starting & Running a Small Business, Vol. 1	$24.95	RUNS
▣ Legal Guide for Starting & Running a Small Business, Vol. 2: Legal Forms	$29.95	RUNS2
Marketing Without Advertising	$19.00	MWAD
▣ The Partnership Book: How to Write a Partnership Agreement, (Book w/Disk—PC)	$34.95	PART
Sexual Harassment on the Job	$18.95	HARS
Starting and Running a Successful Newsletter or Magazine	$24.95	MAG
Take Charge of Your Workers' Compensation Claim (California Edition)	$29.95	WORK
Tax Savvy for Small Business	$28.95	SAVVY
Trademark: Legal Care for Your Business and Product Name	$29.95	TRD
Wage Slave No More: Law & Taxes for the Self-Employed	$24.95	WAGE
Your Rights in the Workplace	$21.95	YRW

CONSUMER

	PRICE	CODE
Fed Up With the Legal System: What's Wrong & How to Fix It	$9.95	LEG
How to Win Your Personal Injury Claim	$24.95	PICL
Nolo's Everyday Law Book	$21.95	EVL
Nolo's Pocket Guide to California Law	$11.95	CLAW
Trouble-Free Travel...And What to Do When Things Go Wrong	$14.95	TRAV

ESTATE PLANNING & PROBATE

	PRICE	CODE
8 Ways to Avoid Probate (Quick & Legal Series)	$15.95	PRO8
How to Probate an Estate (California Edition)	$34.95	PAE
Make Your Own Living Trust	$24.95	LITR
Nolo's Law Form Kit: Wills	$14.95	KWL
▣ Nolo's Will Book, (Book w/Disk—PC)	$29.95	SWIL
Plan Your Estate	$24.95	NEST
The Quick and Legal Will Book	$15.95	QUIC

FAMILY MATTERS

	PRICE	CODE
Child Custody: Building Parenting Agreements that Work	$24.95	CUST
Divorce & Money: How to Make the Best Financial Decisions During Divorce	$26.95	DIMO
Do Your Own Divorce in Oregon	$19.95	ODIV
Get a Life: You Don't Need a Million to Retire Well	$18.95	LIFE
The Guardianship Book (California Edition)	$24.95	GB
How to Adopt Your Stepchild in California	$22.95	ADOP
How to Change Child Support in California (Quick & Legal Series)	$19.95	CHLD
A Legal Guide for Lesbian and Gay Couples	$24.95	LG
The Living Together Kit	$24.95	LTK
Nolo's Pocket Guide to Family Law	$14.95	FLD

GOING TO COURT

	PRICE	CODE
Collect Your Court Judgment (California Edition)	$24.95	JUDG
The Criminal Law Handbook: Know Your Rights, Survive the System	$24.95	KYR
How to Seal Your Juvenile & Criminal Records (California Edition)	$24.95	CRIM
How to Sue For Up to 25,000...and Win!	$29.95	MUNI
Everybody's Guide to Small Claims Court in California	$18.95	CSCC
Everybody's Guide to Small Claims Court (National Edition)	$18.95	NSCC
Fight Your Ticket ... and Win! (California Edition)	$19.95	FYT
How to Change Your Name in California	$29.95	NAME

▣ Book with disk   ⦿ Book with CD-ROM

CALL 800-992-6656 OR USE THE ORDER FORM IN THE BACK OF THE BOOK

			PRICE	CODE
	Mad at Your Lawyer		$21.95	MAD
	Represent Yourself in Court: How to Prepare & Try a Winning Case		$29.95	RYC

HOMEOWNERS, LANDLORDS & TENANTS

	The Deeds Book (California Edition)		$16.95	DEED
	Dog Law		$14.95	DOG
	Every Landlord's Legal Guide (National Edition, Book w/Disk—PC)		$34.95	ELLI
	Every Tenant's Legal Guide		$24.95	EVTEN
	For Sale by Owner in California		$24.95	FSBO
	How to Buy a House in California		$24.95	BHCA
	The Landlord's Law Book, Vol. 1: Rights & Responsibilities (California Edition)		$34.95	LBRT
	The Landlord's Law Book, Vol. 2: Evictions (California Edition)		$34.95	LBEV
	Leases & Rental Agreements (Quick & Legal Series)		$18.95	LEAR
	Neighbor Law: Fences, Trees, Boundaries & Noise		$17.95	NEI
	Stop Foreclosure Now in California		$29.95	CLOS
	Tenants' Rights (California Edition)		$19.95	CTEN

IMMIGRATION

	How to Get a Green Card: Legal Ways to Stay in the U.S.A.		$24.95	GRN
	U.S. Immigration Made Easy		$39.95	IMEZ

MONEY MATTERS

	101 Law Forms for Personal Use: (Quick and Legal Series, Book w/disk—PC)		$24.95	101LAW
	Chapter 13 Bankruptcy: Repay Your Debts		$29.95	CH13
	Credit Repair (Quick & Legal Series)		$15.95	CREP
	The Financial Power of Attorney Workbook (Book w/disk—PC)		$24.95	FINPOA
	How to File for Bankruptcy		$26.95	HFB
	Money Troubles: Legal Strategies to Cope With Your Debts		$19.95	MT
	Nolo's Law Form Kit: Personal Bankruptcy		$14.95	KBNK
	Stand Up to the IRS		$24.95	SIRS
	Take Control of Your Student Loans		$19.95	SLOAN

PATENTS AND COPYRIGHTS

	The Copyright Handbook: How to Protect and Use Written Works (Book w/disk—PC) ...		$29.95	COHA
	Copyright Your Software		$39.95	CYS
	The Inventor's Notebook		$19.95	INOT
	License Your Invention (Book w/Disk—PC)		$39.95	LICE
	The Patent Drawing Book		$29.95	DRAW
	Patent, Copyright & Trademark		$24.95	PCTM
	Patent It Yourself		$44.95	PAT
	Software Development: A Legal Guide (Book with CD-ROM)		$44.95	SFT

RESEARCH & REFERENCE

	Government on the Net, (Book w/CD-ROM—Windows/Macintosh)		$39.95	GONE
	Law on the Net, (Book w/CD-ROM—Windows/Macintosh)		$39.95	LAWN
	Legal Research: How to Find & Understand the Law		$21.95	LRES
	Legal Research Made Easy (Video)		$89.95	LRME

SENIORS

	Beat the Nursing Home Trap		$18.95	ELD
	The Conservatorship Book (California Edition)		$29.95	CNSV
	Social Security, Medicare & Pensions		$19.95	SOA

SOFTWARE
Call or check our website for special discounts on Software!

	California Incorporator 2.0—DOS		$79.95	INCI
	Living Trust Maker CD—Windows/Macintosh		$79.95	LTM2
	Small Business Legal Pro 3 CD—Windows/Macintosh CD-ROM		$79.95	SBCD3
	Nolo's Partnership Maker 1.0—DOS		$79.95	PAGI1
	Personal RecordKeeper 4.0 CD—Windows/Macintosh		$49.95	RKM4
	Patent It Yourself CD—Windows		$229.95	PYP12
	WillMaker 6.0—Windows/Macintosh CD-ROM		$69.95	WD6

SPECIAL UPGRADE OFFER —Get 25% off the latest edition of your Nolo book

It's important to have the most current legal information. Because laws and legal procedures change often, we update our books regularly. To help keep you up-to-date we are extending this special upgrade offer. Cut out and mail the title portion of the cover of your old Nolo book and we'll give you 25% off the retail price of the NEW EDITION of that book when you purchase directly from us. For more information call us at 1-800-992-6656. This offer is to individuals only.

⬛ Book with disk ⬤ Book with CD-ROM

ORDER FORM

Code	Quantity	Title	Unit price	Total

Subtotal	
California residents add Sales Tax	
Basic Shipping ($6.50)	
UPS RUSH delivery $8.00–any size order*	
TOTAL	

Name

Address

(UPS to street address, Priority Mail to P.O. boxes)

* Delivered in 3 business days from receipt of order.
S.F. Bay Area use regular shipping.

FOR FASTER SERVICE, USE YOUR CREDIT CARD AND OUR TOLL-FREE NUMBERS

Order 24 hours a day	1-800-992-6656
Fax your order	1-800-645-0895
Online	www.nolo.com

METHOD OF PAYMENT

☐ Check enclosed
☐ VISA   ☐ MasterCard   ☐ Discover Card   ☐ American Express

Account #   Expiration Date

Authorizing Signature

Daytime Phone

PRICES SUBJECT TO CHANGE.

VISIT OUR OUTLET STORES!

You'll find our complete line of books and software, all at a discount.

BERKELEY
950 Parker Street
Berkeley, CA 94710
1-510-704-2248

SAN JOSE
111 N. Market Street, #115
San Jose, CA 95113
1-408-271-7240

VISIT US ONLINE!

on the Internet
www.nolo.com

N O L O   P R E S S   9 5 0   P A R K E R   S T . ,   B E R K E L E Y ,   C A   9 4 7 1 0

more from
NOLO PRESS

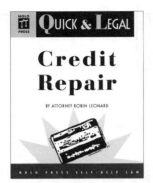

Credit Repair

Quick and Legal Series

by Attorney Robin Leonard

No matter how bad your credit is, it can always be improved and this book shows you how. Includes worksheets and sample letters to creditors.

"Credit Repair offers the concrete answers you need to regain financial stability."
—PERSONAL FINANCE

CREP/ $15.95

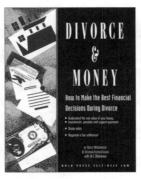

Divorce and Money

by Attorney Violet Woodhouse & Victoria F. Collins, with M.C. Blakeman

If you're going through a divorce, you know that you're facing an overwhelming number of financial decisions. This book tells you, clearly and in plain English, everything you need to know to get through a divorce without going broke.

DIMO/ $26.95

Stand Up to the IRS

by Attorney Robin Leonard

Tax attorney Fred Daily reveals secrets the IRS doesn't want you to know and arms you with all the infomation you need to survive an audit with the minimum amount of damage, appeal an audit decision, represent yourself in Tax Court, file delinquent tax returns and deal with IRS collectors. The book also covers concerns of small business people and shows how to get help from the IRS ombudsman.

CH13/$29.95

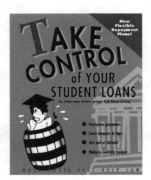

Take Control of Your Student Loans

by Attorneys Robin Leonard & Shae Irving

If you feel overwhelmed by student loan debt, there are simple and effective ways to get back on your feet, and this book lays them all out. It clearly explains all of your repayment options and tells you how to avoid or get out of default, how to handle collection efforts by the government and much more. Includes sample letters and forms.

SLOAN/ $19.95

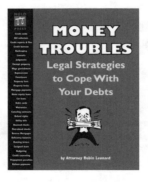

Money Troubles

by Attorney Robin Leonard

An indispensable guide to negotiating with creditors, challenging wage attachments, forcing bill collectors to stop their badgering and rebuilding your credit. Also covers credit reports and credit bureaus, student loan collections, selecting and using credit cards and protecting property when being sued or filing for bankruptcy.

MT/ $19.95

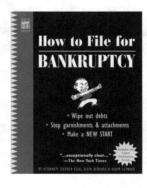

How to File for Bankruptcy

By Attorneys Stephen Elias, Albin Renauer & Robin Leonard

Every year, more than a million people file for bankruptcy. A clear and complete overview of Chapter 7 bankruptcy, *How to File for Bankruptcy* helps you decide if Chapter 7 is right for you. It provides all the background information you need and all the forms necessary to file, with step-by-step instructions to fill them out.

"...exceptionally clear."
—THE NEW YORK TIMES

HFB/$26.95

CALL 800-992-6656 OR USE THE ORDER FORM IN THIS BOOK

With our quarterly magazine, the **NOLO** *News*, you'll

- **Learn** about important legal changes that affect you
- **Find out first** about new Nolo products
- **Keep current** with practical articles on everyday law
- **Get answers** to your legal questions in *Ask Auntie Nolo's* advice column
- **Save money** with special Subscriber Only discounts
- **Tickle your funny bone** with our famous *Lawyer Joke* column.

It only takes a minute to reserve your free 1-year subscription or to extend your **NOLO** *News* subscription.

 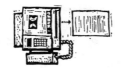

CALL	FAX	E-MAIL	OR MAIL US THIS REGISTRATION CARD
1-800-992-6656	**1-800-645-0895**	**NOLOSUB@NOLOPRESS.com**	

 *U.S. ADDRESSES ONLY. ONE YEAR INTERNATIONAL SUBSCRIPTIONS: CANADA & MEXICO $10.00; ALL OTHER FOREIGN ADDRESSES $20.00.

fold here

NOLO PRESS

REGISTRATION CARD

NAME _____ DATE _____

ADDRESS _____

CITY _____ STATE _____ ZIP _____

PHONE _____ E-MAIL _____

WHERE DID YOU HEAR ABOUT THIS PRODUCT? _____

WHERE DID YOU PURCHASE THIS PRODUCT? _____

DID YOU CONSULT A LAWYER? (PLEASE CIRCLE ONE)   YES   NO   NOT APPLICABLE _____

DID YOU FIND THIS BOOK HELPFUL?   (VERY)   5   4   3   2   1   (NOT AT ALL) _____

COMMENTS _____
_____
_____
_____

WAS IT EASY TO USE?   (VERY EASY)   5   4   3   2   1   (VERY DIFFICULT) _____

DO YOU OWN A COMPUTER? IF SO, WHICH FORMAT? (PLEASE CIRCLE ONE)   WINDOWS   DOS   MAC

❑ If you do not wish to receive mailings from these companies, please check this box.

❑ You can quote me in future Nolo Press promotional materials. Daytime phone number _____.   CH13 3.2

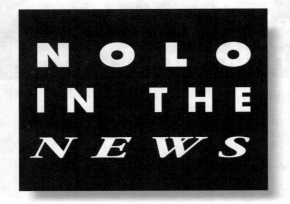
NOLO IN THE NEWS

"**N**olo helps lay people perform legal tasks without the aid—or fees—of lawyers."

—**USA TODAY**

Nolo books are ..."written in plain language, free of legal mumbo jumbo, and spiced with witty personal observations."

—**ASSOCIATED PRESS**

"...Nolo publications...guide people simply through the how, when, where and why of law."

—**WASHINGTON POST**

"Increasingly, people who are not lawyers are performing tasks usually regarded as legal work... And consumers, using books like Nolo's, do routine legal work themselves."

—**NEW YORK TIMES**

"...All of [Nolo's] books are easy-to-understand, are updated regularly, provide pull-out forms...and are often quite moving in their sense of compassion for the struggles of the lay reader."

—**SAN FRANCISCO CHRONICLE**

fold here

- -

Place
stamp here

NOLO PRESS
950 Parker Street
Berkeley, CA 94710-9867

Attn: | CH13 3.2 |